Colección Támesis

SERIE A: MONOGRAFÍAS, 220

A COMPANION TO MAGICAL REALISM

This new *Companion to Magical Realism* provides an assessment of the world-wide impact of a movement which was incubated in Germany, flourished in Latin America and then spread to the rest of the world. It provides a set of up-to-date assessments of the work of writers traditionally associated with magical realism such as Gabriel García Márquez (in particular his recently published memoirs), Alejo Carpentier, Miguel Ángel Asturias, Juan Rulfo, Isabel Allende, Laura Esquivel and Salman Rushdie, as well as bringing into the fold new authors such as W.B. Yeats, Seamus Heaney, José Saramago, Dorit Rabinyan, Ovid, María Luisa Bombal, Ibrahim al-Kawnī, Mayra Montero, Nakagami Kenji, José Eustasio Rivera and Elias Khoury, discussed for the first time in the context of magical realism. Written in a jargon-free style, and with all quotations translated into English, this book offers a refreshing new interdisciplinary slant on magical realism as an international literary phenomenon emerging from the trauma of colonial dispossession. The companion also has a Guide to Further Reading.

STEPHEN M. HART is Professor of Hispanic Studies, University College London and Doctor Honoris Causa of the Universidad Nacional Mayor de San Marcos, Lima, Peru.

WEN-CHIN OUYANG lectures in Arabic Literature and Comparative Literature at the School of Oriental and African Studies, London.

A COMPANION TO
MAGICAL REALISM

Edited by

Stephen M. Hart
and
Wen-chin Ouyang

TAMESIS

First published 2005 by Tamesis, Woodbridge

ISBN 1 85566 120 9

Tamesis is an imprint of Boydell & Brewer Ltd
PO Box 9, Woodbridge, Suffolk IP12 3DF, UK
and of Boydell & Brewer Inc.
668 Mt Hope Avenue, Rochester, NY 14620, USA
website: www.boydellandbrewer.com

A CIP catalogue record for this book is available
from the British Library

Library of Congress Cataloging-in-Publication Data

A companion to magical realism / edited by Stephen M. Hart and Wen-chin Ouyang.
   p. cm. – (Colección Támesis. Serie A, Monografías ; 220)
Summary: " A refreshing new interdisciplinary slant on magical realism as an international liter-
ary phenomenon emerging from the trauma of colonial dispossession"-Provided by publisher.
Includes bibliographical references and index.
ISBN 1–85566–120–9 (hardback : alk. paper)
1. Spanish American fiction – 20th century – History and criticism. 2. Fiction – 20th century –
History and criticism. 3. Magic realism (Literature) I. Hart, Stephen M. II. Ouyang, Wen-chin.
PQ7082.N7C625 2005
863'.60915–22

2005005295

This publication is printed on acid-free paper

Printed in Great Britain by
Antony Rowe Ltd., Chippenham, Wiltshire

CONTENTS

ACKNOWLEDGEMENTS

This book grew out of a three-year project on 'Genre Ideologies and Narrative Transformation' (2001–2004) funded by the AHRC and run under the auspices of the AHRC Centre for Asian and African Studies SOAS-UCL. A number of the essays in this book were originally read at the conference on magical realism at SOAS on 7–9 November 2002. We take this opportunity to acknowledge the support of the Arts and Humanities Research Board in funding the conference, and allowing a genuinely interdisciplinary space to be born. We would also like to thank the SOAS-UCL AHRC Centre for hosting the conference and providing all the necessary administrative support. We have been fortunate in the two research assistants assigned to the project. Stephanie Jones played an instrumental role in conceptualizing the project during its initial stages. Her intellectual rigor, insight and foresight, and organizational skills have been indispensable to us. Anna Guttman joined the project recently to take part in preparing the manuscript for publication. She practically edited the volume. Her astuteness, attention to detail and tireless efforts made meeting the publisher's deadline less painful. We would like to record our gratitude to Dr Helena Forsäs-Scott, Department of Scandinavian Studies at UCL, for helping us to identify Von Dardel's painting. A special thanks also for Ellie Ferguson, the Editor at Tamesis, whose efficiency and faith in the project allowed it all to happen. We are, above all, grateful to all the contributors, without whose contributions this book would not have been born. The editors are grateful to the New Left Review for permission to re-print Efraín Kristal's essay, 'Lessons from the Golden Age', in this volume. The jacket illustration, Nils Von Dardel's *Columbi Ägg* (1924), originally appeared in Franz Roh, *Nach Expressionismus: Magischer Realismus* (Leipzig: Klinkhardt & Bierman, 1925).

INTRODUCTION

Globalization of Magical Realism:
New Politics of Aesthetics

Stephen M. Hart and Wen-chin Ouyang

Magical Realism: Style and Substance

Stephen M. Hart

From a term used in 1925 by a German art critic, Franz Roh, to indicate the demise of Expressionism,[1] magical realism grew to become an important feature of the Boom literature of the 1960s in Latin America (particularly in Gabriel García Márquez's *One Hundred Years of Solitude* of 1967) until it became, by the 1990s, in the words of Homi Bhabha 'the literary language of the emergent postcolonial world'.[2] Unpacking that history is a complex one and beyond the scope of this introductory essay, but a few lines may be drawn in the sand. In *Nach-Expressionismus, Magischer Realismus: Probleme der neuesten Europäischen Malerie (Post-Expressionism, Magical Realism)*, Franz Roh referred to how Post-Expressionism/magical realism embodies the 'calm admiration of the magic of being, of the discovery that things already have their own faces' (p. 20) and, thereby, represents 'in an intuitive way, *the fact, the interior figure, of the exterior world*' (p. 24).[3] In this way, as Roh further suggested, Post-Expressionism 'offers us the miracle of *existence in its imperturbable duration*: the unending miracle of eternally mobile and vibrating molecules. Out of that flux, that constant appearance and disappearance of material, permanent objects somehow appear: in short, the marvel by which a variable commotion crystallizes into a clear set of constants' (Roh, p. 22).

Some of the tension between surface and innerness which is at the core of Roh's essay finds its way into the prologue Alejo Carpentier wrote for his novel,

---

[1] There is an English translation of Roh's 1925 essay, 'Magic Realism: Post-Expressionism', in *Magical Realism: Theory, History, Community*, eds Lois Parkinson Zamora and Wendy B. Faris (Durham, NC: Duke University Press, 1995), pp. 15–31.

[2] Homi Bhabha, 'Introduction', *Nation and Narration* (London: Routledge, 1995), pp. 1–7 (pp. 6–7).

[3] I cite from the English translation, 'Magical Realism: Post-Expressionism', in *Magical Realism: Theory, History, Community*, pp. 15–31.

The Kingdom of this World (1949), in which he described his experience of the marvellous real in Haiti in 1943: 'I was in a land where thousands of men, anxious for freedom, believed in Mackandal's lycanthropic powers to the extent that their collective faith produced a miracle on the day of his execution.'[4] The miracle of the marvellous real, as he clarifies in his essay, 'arises from an unexpected alteration of reality (the miracle), from a privileged revelation of reality, an unaccustomed insight that is singularly favoured by the unexpected richness of reality' (p. 86). Indeed, Carpentier's use of terms such as 'alteration', 'revelation' and 'richness of reality' may be compared to Roh's sense of the 'radiation of magic' (Roh, p. 20), the 'new space' (Roh, p. 25), 'the interior figure' (p. 24), the 'vortex of depth' (p. 27) which is 'throbbing' (Roh, p. 20) within phenomenal reality. It was precisely this event – the description of Mackandal's execution – which Carpentier used as the centrepiece of his novel, but what is remarkable is that the scene is visualized as a split event. The slaves witness his escape: 'The ropes binding him dropped to the floor and the negro's body launched ('se espigó') into the air, flying above their heads before submerging in the black waves of the mass of slaves. A single cry filled the square:– *Mackandal sauvé!*'[5] But the French colonisers and their agents, the Haitian soldiers, see nothing and instead witness his execution; as the third-person narrative informs us: 'few saw that Mackandal, who had been seized by ten soldiers, was rammed into the fire, and that a flame intensified by his burning hair had extinguished his final cry' (p. 41). The expression 'few saw' must be understood to mean that the soldiers, the narrator (and now the reader) witnessed the event, but not the slaves. The statement 'few saw' introduces a note of ocular empiricism into the account, and the reader's first reaction will be to interpret the event as an example of mass delusion. The short sentence which concludes the paragragh – 'There was nothing left to see' (*The Kingdom of this World*, p. 41) – reinforces the impression that the miracle was similar to a dream which fades when we emerge from sleep.

There are, however, a number of events, linguistic and otherwise, which subvert the apparent empiricism of the text. Chapter VI describes Mackandal's metamorphoses: Mackandal is able to change into an animal or a bird or a fish or an insect (*The Kingdom of this World*, p. 33) as if such transformations were a matter of well-known fact ('everyone knew': 'todos sabían'; *The Kingdom of this World*, p. 33). Pointing in a similar direction, the final chapter of the novel describes how Ti Noel 'made use of his extraordinary powers in order to transform himself into a goose' (*The Kingdom of this World*, p. 141) and, as a result of this transformation, achieves an enlightenment which 'explains' the mystery of human creation. It is noteworthy that the most significant chapter from

[4] 'On the Marvellous Real in America', *Magical Realism: Theory, History, Community*, pp. 75–88 (p. 87).
[5] Alejo Carpentier, *El reino de este mundo* (Barcelona: Biblioteca de Bolsillo, 1998), p. 41. All translations are mine.

a structural point of view – the last – should focus on the magical, supernatural subtext operating within the visibly real level of the human condition. In effect, the world of the Afro-Caribbean 'subaltern' becomes the magical black archive hovering within the white, empiricist narrative of a slave rebellion.[6] The knowledge the novel imparts is apocalyptic, revelatory, magical. The archive of the novel is, indeed, not expressed in terms of a syncretistic vision for it runs counter to white history and white knowledge. The novel itself – we may conclude – like the Mackandal flight episode, hovers between the real and the marvellous. It was this vacillation between the two kingdoms – analysed so expertly by Tzvetan Todorov in his *Introduction à la littérature fantastique* (1970)[7] – that was to remain a hallmark of magical realism although the elements within the equation would not remain constant and the relationship between those elements would also change.[8]

Carpentier's *Kingdom of this World*, like Miguel Ángel Asturias's *Men of Maize* published in the same year (1949), is often characterised as an important harbinger of magical realism which in turn is typically seen as achieving its canonical incarnation in Gabriel García Márquez's *One Hundred Years of Solitude* (1967).[9] Clearly *One Hundred Years of Solitude* expresses the same type of split-vision in evidence in Carpentier's novel but the realm of the magical is not locked up within the notion of an atavistic archive (namely, the Colombian equivalent of the Afro-Caribbean subaltern as portrayed in Carpentier's novel). It migrates depending on who the perceiver is; magical realism is born, the novel suggests, in the gap between the belief systems of two very different groups of people. What for the inhabitant of the 'First World' is magical (a woman who ascends to heaven, ghosts who return to earth, priests who can levitate, gypsies who can morph into a puddle of tar) is real and unremarkable for the inhabitant of the 'Third World'. To keep the symmetry, what for the inhabitant of the 'Third

---

[6] The term archive is used here to mean a cultural and linguistic set of knowledge paradigms which allow individuals or social groups or nations to assert and create identity. In the case of the Afro-Cuban archive this cultural identity is contestatory. For further discussion of this term see Michel Foucault, 'The Historical *a priori* and the Archive', in *The Archeology of Knowledge*, trans. A.M. Sheridan Smith (London: Tavistock, 1972), pp. 126–31, and Roberto González Echevarría, *Myth and Archive: Theory of Latin American Narrative* (Cambridge: Cambridge University Press, 1990). The term subaltern is used here in Gayatri Spivak's sense to refer to a subordinate group within a hierarchised society whose voice is rarely if at all heard; for further discussion of Subaltern Studies, see Ileana Rodríguez (ed.), *The Latin American Subaltern Studies Reader* (Durham, NC: Duke University Press, 2001).

[7] Tzvetan Todorov, *Introduction à la littérature fantastique* (Paris: Seuil 1970).

[8] For the application of Todorov's theories to magical realism, see Amaryll Beatrice Chanady, *Magical Realism and the Fantastic: Resolved Versus Unresolved Antinomy* (New York: Garland, 1985). For a discussion of Chanady's approach with particular reference to the differences between the fantastic and magical realism, see Maggie Ann Bower, *Magic(al) Realism* (London: Routledge, 2004), pp. 24–7.

[9] For a discussion of the differences between Carpentier's 'real maravilloso' and García Márquez's magical realism, see Stephen M. Hart, 'Magical Realism in Gabriel García Márquez's *Cien años de soledad*', *Inti*, 16–17 (1982–83), 37–52.

World' is magical (false teeth, magnets, films, trains, ice) is real and unremark-able for the inhabitant of the 'First World': 'Dazzled by so many and such marvellous inventions, the people of Macondo did not know where amazement began.'[10] García Márquez deliberately prevents the reader from taking up an out-sider/insider or Us/Them attitude towards the world of the magical. By using one paradigm, and then reversing it, García Márquez makes sure that the reader is unable to escape from a sense of the world as containing a magical dimension. Macondo does not offer a place to which the reader can retreat, a world that is either just real or just magical. The realism of the real is permeated by magic just as the world of the magical is underpinned by the real.

Once García Márquez has drawn us into this self-consistent and water-tight world and we have let our defences down, then he starts to pull his political punches. He shows us how North American capitalism destroys Macondo, how the military shoot defenceless workers, how the authorities deny that any wrong-doing has been committed ('You must have been dreaming (. . .) Nothing has happened in Macondo, nothing has ever happened in Macondo, and nothing ever will happen. This is a happy town'; p. 252) – in sum, he draws out a political allegory of injustice in Latin America. While *The Kingdom of this World* is Calibanesque (namely, reminiscent of the Carib counter-culture associated with Caliban in Shakespeare's *The Tempest*), *One Hundred Years of Solitude* is not only Calibanesque but also Revolutionary (in a Third-World, Marxist sense).[11] Nevertheless the work of both writers is predicated on a vision of the world as deeply fissured (*The Kingdom of this World*, indeed, revolves around a revolu-tion which occurred in the Caribbean), characterised by a deep divide between the realm of the powerful and the world of the powerless.[12]

---

[10] *One Hundred Years of Solitude*, trans. Gregory Rabassa (London: Picador, 1978), p. 185. García Márquez's novel was published twelve years after the famous Bandung conference of 1955 in which the term 'Third World' gained wide currency. For further discussion of the notion of the Third World see James Manor (ed.), *Rethinking Third World Politics* (London: Longman, 1991). Some of the problems involved in even using the notion of Third World literature are addressed by Aijaz Ahmad, 'Jameson's Rhetoric of Otherness and the "National Allegory"', *The Post-Colonial Studies Reader*, eds Bill Ashcroft, Gareth Griffiths and Helen Tiffin (London: Routledge, 1995), pp. 77–82.

[11] For a politicised reading of Caliban, see Roberto Fernández Retamar, *Caliban and Other Essays*, trans. Edward Baker (Minneapolis: Minnesota University Press, 1989). For some sense of what is intended by a more revolutionary view of fantasy, see Jacques Stephen Alexis, 'Of the Marvellous Realism of the Haitians', and Michael Dash, 'Marvellous Realism: The Way out of Négritude', both in *The Post-Colonial Studies Reader*, eds Bill Ashcroft, Gareth Griffiths and Helen Tiffin, at pp. 194–8, and pp. 199–201.

[12] A similar pattern can be traced in Brazilian literature. From the 'forerunner' of magical realism, Mário de Andrade's *Macunaíma* (1928), as identified by Nancy Gray Díaz (quoted in Charles Perrone, 'Guimarães Rosa through the Prism of Magic Realism', in *Tropical Paths: Essays in Modern Brazilian Literature* (New York: Garland, 1993), pp. 101–22 [p. 114, n. 1]), the movement blossomed in novels such as João Guimarães Rosa's *Grande sertão: veredas* (1956), Jorge Amado's *Dona Flor e Seus Dos Maridos* (1966; *Dona Flor and Her Two Husbands*) and his *Tereza Batista Cansada de Guerra* (1972; *Tereza Batista Home from the*

Once the mould had been set by García Márquez in 1967 – and in effect given the final canonical flourish in 1982 when the Colombian novelist won the Nobel Prize – it led, perhaps predictably, to a number of re-vampings in the Hispanic literary world, notably Isabel Allende's *The House of the Spirits* (1982), Laura Esquivel's *Like Water for Chocolate* (1989), and Luis Sepúlveda's *The Old Man who Read Love Stories* (1993).[13] But perhaps just as significant were the reformulations of the magical-realist mode of narrative which emerged in non-Hispanic countries such as Robert Kroetsch's *What the Crow Said* (1978), Salman Rushdie's *Midnight's Children* (1980), D.M. Thomas's *The White Hotel* (1981), Angela Carter's *The Bloody Chamber and Other Stories* (1981), Nakagami Kenji's *A Thousand Years of Pleasure* (1982), William Kennedy's *Ironweed* (1983), Patrick Süskind's *Perfume* (1985), Tahar Ben Jelloun's *L'Enfant du sable* (*Sand Boy*, 1985), José Saramago's *The Stone Raft* (1986), Amitrav Ghosh's *The Circle of Reason* (1986), Toni Morrison's *Beloved* (1987), Kjarten Flogstad's *Portrett av eit magisk liv: Poeten Claes Gill* (*Portrait of a Magic Life: The Poet Claes Gill*, 1988), Ben Okri's *The Famished Road* (1991), André Brink's *Imaginings of Sand* (1996), Addelkader Benali's *Wedding by the Sea* (1999; published in original Dutch in 1996), and Ciaran Carson's *Fishing for Amber: A Long Story* (1999).[14] Critical theorizations of magical realism during this period also began to reflect its gradually broadening parameters.[15] While early work on magical realism tended to focus on the movement in terms of a technique – the prototypes were Ángel Flores's article in 1955 and Luis Leal's in 1967 – [16] work in the 1980s tended to focus on the ways in which magical realism invoked social practice and ideology,[17] and interacted with issues

---

Wars). For more on these works see the discussion in Charles Perrone, 'Guimarães Rosa through the Prism of Magic Realism', and Daphne Patai, *Myth and Ideologies in Contemporary Brazilian Fiction* (Cranbury, NJ: Associated University Presses, 1983), pp. 111–40.

[13] Isabel Allende, *La casa de los espíritus* (Barcelona: Plaza y Janés, 1982); *The House of the Spirits*, trans. Magda Bodin (New York: Knopf, 1985). Laura Esquivel, *Como agua para chocolate* (Mexico City: Planeta, 1989); *Like Water for Chocolate*, trans. Carol Christensen and Thomas Christensen (New York: Doubleday, 1993). There has been an important film version of the book directed by Alfonso Arau; see Stephen M. Hart, *Companion to Latin American Film* (London: Tamesis, 2004), pp. 171–8. Luis Sepúlveda, *Un viejo que leía novelas de amor* (Barcelona: Tusquets, 1993); *The Old Man who Read Love Stories*, trans. Peter Bush (London: Arcadia, 2002).

[14] I am grateful to Eli Park Sørensen's unpublished essay, 'Scandinavian Magical Realism and Fantastic Literature' for the Norwegian reference.

[15] See, for example, Timothy Brennan's *Salman Rushdie and the Third World* (New York: St Martins, 1989).

[16] Both essays are collected in *Magical Realism: Theory, History, Community*, pp. 109–24.

[17] Some examples of this approach are: Irlemar Chiampi, *El realismo maravilloso: forma e ideología de la novela hispanoamericana* (Caracas: Monte Ávila, 1983); Graciela Ricci della Grisa's monograph, *Realismo mágico y conciencia mítica en América Latina* (Buenos Aires: Cambeiro, 1985); María Elena Angulo, *Magic Realism: Social Context and Discourse* (New York: Garland, 1995).

subtending postcolonial theory; Stephen Slemon's 1988 article, 'Magic Realism as Post-Colonial Discourse', for example, epitomises this trend.[18] The work of Lois Parkinson Zamora and Wendy B. Faris should be highlighted as bringing a distinctly interdisciplinary impetus to the theorization of magical realism; Zamora in her comparisons of Latin American with U.S. literature, Faris in her comparative work on especially García Márquez and Salman Rushdie, and which culminated in their 'canonical' *Magical Realism: Theory, History, Community* (1995).[19] Magical realism is nowadays a complex, global literary phenomenon and there is little indication that it has run out of steam, despite pronouncements that the term has 'neither the specificity nor the theoretical foundation to be (. . .) useful', which underline the gulf between the academy and the praxis of writing more than anything else.[20]

The question inevitably arises: how is it that magical realism has been so successful in migrating to various cultural shores? Why has it seemed able to offer a vehicle for the expression of the tensions within different societal frameworks? Is it really the language par excellence (Bhabha's idea) of the emergent postcolonial world? One of the reasons why it appears to have attracted the attention of a range of writers – Alejo Carpentier, Gabriel García Márquez and Isabel Allende in Latin America, Salman Rushdie, Amitrav Ghosh, Ben Okri, B. Kojo Laing, M.K. Vassanji elsewhere (to give Elleke Boehmer's list)[21] – is its ability to express 'a world fissured, distorted, and made incredible by cultural displacement' (Boehmer, p. 235). As Boehmer further suggests: 'Like the Latin American, they [postcolonial writers in English] combine the supernatural with local legend and imagery derived from colonialist cultures to represent cultures which have been repeatedly unsettled by invasion, occupation, and political corruption. Magic effects, therefore, are used to indict the follies of both empire and

---

[18] Now reprinted in *Magical Realism: Theory, History, Community*, pp. 407–26. See also Román de la Campa, 'Magical Realism and World Literature: A Genre for the Times?', *Revista Canadiense de Estudios Hispánicos*, 23.2 (1999), 205–19; Jean-Pierre Durix, *Mimesis, Genres, and Post-Colonial Discourse: Deconstructing Magic Realism* (New York: St Martins, 1998); Elsa Liguanti, Francesco Casotti and Carmen Concilio (eds), *Coterminous Worlds: Magical Realism and Contemporary Post-Colonial Literature in English* (Amsterdam: Rodopi, 1999).

[19] See Faris's 'Scheherezade's Children: Magical Realism and Postmodern Fiction', and Parkinson Zamora's 'Magical Romance/Magical Realism: Ghosts in U.S. and Latin American Fiction', both in *Magical Realism: Theory, History, Community*, pp. 163–90, pp. 497–550. Other important works by these authors are Zamora's *Writing the Apocalypse: Historical Vision in Contemporary U.S. and Latin American Fiction* (Cambridge: CUP, 1989), and Faris's *Ordinary Enchantments: Magical Realism and the Remystification of Narrative* (Nashville, TN: Vanderbilt University Press, 2004). An interdisciplinary approach is also evident in Jean Weisberger (ed.), *Le Réalisme magique: Roman, peinture et cinéma* (Brussels: Le Centre des Avant-gardes littéraires de l'Université de Bruxelles, 1987).

[20] The phrase appears in Roberto González Echevarría, *Alejo Carpentier: The Pilgrim at Home* (Ithaca: Cornell University Press, 1977), pp. 111–12.

[21] Elleke Boehmer, *Colonial and Postcolonial Literature* (Oxford: Oxford University Press, 1995), p. 235.

its aftermath' (p. 235). As Jean-Pierre Durix memorably puts it: 'Imperialistic powers deprived the colonized people not only of their territories and wealth but also of their imagination.'[22] While it is not the case that magical realism is the only or necessarily the best vehicle with which to express 'cultural displacement'– Dennis Walder's book on postcolonial writing, for example, makes scant reference to magical realism[23] – and since it would be impossible to follow through each branch of this complex flowering I have decided to focus upon two test-cases, one from India, the other from Africa, Salman Rushdie's *Midnight's Children* and Ben Okri's *The Famished Road*.

Before passing to a discussion of these two novels it is important to draw out the implications of the 'fissured' world to which Boehmer alludes (see above). It is necessary to underline that it is precisely because Latin American cultural reality is fundamentally riven that it has been able to offer a model to the writers of other postcolonial nations. Indeed, 'mestizaje' is a misleading metaphor to use in this context.[24] Antonio Cornejo Polar has convincingly argued that 'mestizaje', despite being 'the most powerful and widespread conceptual device with which Latin America has interpreted itself', is predicated on a 'salvational ideology' which promotes a notion of a 'conciliating synthesis of the many mixtures that constitute the social and cultural Latin America corpus'.[25] In the process, Cornejo Polar argues, 'the social asymmetry of the originating contacts' is, in effect, 'obviated' (p. 117). Furthermore, Cornejo Polar argues that 'multiple intercrossings **do not** operate in a syncretistic way, but instead emphasize conflicts and alterities' ('Mestizaje, Transculturation, Heterogeneity', p. 117). Latin American literature, as an embodiment of that culture, is thus characterized by a 'copious, profound, and disturbing conflictiveness' (p. 119). Cornejo Polar therefore proposes heterogeneity as an apt metaphor to capture Latin American cultural reality and the literature which issues from that reality. In that Cornejo Polar's theory of cultural dynamics consistently refuses synthesis and fusion – it is, in effect, radically anti-metaphoric, keeping as two what others wish to see as one – it provides a helpful tool with which to analyse magical realism not only in its local Latin American configuration but also as a globalised literary phenomenon.

---

[22] Jean-Pierre Durix, *Mimesis, Genres and Post-Colonial Discourse: Deconstructing Magic Realism* (London: Macmillan, 1998), p. 187.

[23] Dennis Walder, *Post-colonial Literatures in English* (Oxford: Blackwell, 1998). For a helpful discussion of postcolonial theory, the reader is referred to Peter Childs and Patrick Williams, *An Introduction to Post-Colonial Theory* (New York: Prentice Hall, 1997). An excellent introduction to the historical backdrop of postcolonialism is provided by Robert C. Young, *Postcolonialism: An Historical Introduction* (Oxford: Blackwell, 2001).

[24] For further discussion of this point see Amaryll Chanady, 'Identity, Politics and mestizaje', in *Contemporary Latin American Cultural Studies*, eds Stephen M. Hart and Richard Young (London: Hodder, 2003), pp. 192–02.

[25] 'Mestizaje, Transculturation, Heterogeneity', in *The Latin American Cultural Studies Reader*, eds Ana del Sarto, Alicia Ríos and Abril Trigo (Durham: Duke UP, 2004), pp. 116–19 (p. 116).

Salman Rushdie's *Midnight's Children* (1980) intersects with magical realism as playfully as it traverses postcolonialism. Its magical elements are well-known – one only need recall Saleem's gargantuan nose, the 1,001 children born in India between midnight and 1 a.m. on 15 August 1947 (p. 195), the whore who claims to be 512 years old (p. 319), Saleem's aunt who keeps on seeing ghosts of the past around the house: 'So it's you again; well, why not? Nothing ever seems to go away' (p. 331), Saleem who is able to disappear at will into thin air (p. 380), and the ten thousand women who are in love with Major Shiva (p. 409).[26] Its postcolonial credentials are just as obvious (Wendy Faris calls *Midnight's Children* an 'aggressively postcolonial text' [*Ordinary Enchantments*, p. 29]). Saleem Sinai, the 'I' of the novel was born at precisely the time that India achieved its independence from Britain and thus fulfils the need in postcolonial fiction, as identified by Stephen Slemon, that it should represent 'the foreshortening of history so that the time scheme [of the story] metaphorically contains the long process of colonization and its aftermath' (Slemon, p. 411). Saleem, 'mysteriously handcuffed to history' (p. 9), is also a curious mixture of the colonised and the coloniser: he is like 'an empty pickle jar in a pool of Anglepoised light' (p. 19), or 'a badly-fitting collage' (p. 25). That his identity is not unitary in any sense is suggested by the fact that his first significant memory is that of being a ghost (p. 31), itself a hallmark of the magical-realist mode in that it suggests the apparition of a colonial identity stranded in the netherland of subalternity.[27] This ghostly resonance, though simply a parlour game in the novel, is emblematic of the deliberate syntax of oblivion employed by colonialist discourse: 'We are a nation of forgetters' (p. 37).

It is important to underline in this context that when events are recalled in the text they are not so much remembered as re-cast, becoming in the process the mixed-up 'pickles of history' (p. 461). Thus when the ghost episode is recalled, the sheet Saleem wore as a child is now directly related to the sheet which heralded his birth: 'And that was also the time when I was cast as a ghost in a children's play, and found, in an older leather attaché-case on top of my grandfather's almirah, a sheet which had been chewed by moths, but whose largest hole was man-made: for which discovery I was repaid (you will recall) in roars of grandparental rage' (p. 188). The expression 'you will recall' is deceptive since we **do not** recall the events in precisely this fashion; their inner meaning or 'magic' has now been extrapolated before our eyes. Saleem's birth – the birth of India and Pakistan – was no more, the text suggests, than a phantom. This idea then begins to leak disarmingly into later parts of the text; Saleem's father starts disappearing: 'my father's morning chin began to fade' (p. 201).

Midnight's Children proclaims palimpsestism as a form of archaeological knowledge far more befitting the case of India than the lockstep of syncretistic

---

[26] All references are to *Midnight's Children* (London: Vintage, 1995).

[27] For further discussion of this point, see Stephen M. Hart, 'Magical Realism in the Americas: Politicised Ghosts in *One Hundred Years of Solitude, The House of the Spirits,* and *Beloved*', *Journal of Iberian and Latin American Studies*, 9.2 (2003), 115–23.

logic and its favoured mode of enquiry – the syllogism. The three generations – Aadam Aziz, Dr Aziz and Saleem Sinai – repeat ideas and thoughts such that it becomes difficult for the reader to distinguish between them. This is clearly a nod in García Márquez's direction; Rushdie once referred to the Colombian's magical realism as an expression of a 'genuinely "Third-World" consciousness. It deals with what Naipaul has called "half-made" societies, in which the impossibly old struggles against the appallingly new' (quoted in Faris, *Ordinary Enchantments*, p. 38). The onward 'mill of history' (p. 333) is thereby viewed in *Midnight's Children* not so much as a teleological march towards a given goal but rather as a circular vortex in which layers are superimposed on other layers, and indeed stripped back, to produce a sense of time as a kaleidoscope rather than a line of succession from Genesis to Apocalypse: 'Memory's truth, because memory has its own special kind. It selects, eliminates, alters, exaggerates, minimizes, glorifies, and vilifies also' (p. 211). In some ways Rushdie takes this idea further than García Márquez. For the Colombian as much as the Indian 'cosmopolitan' the sense of time as a revolving rather than a linear experience allows for the history of colonialism – with its teleological focus – to be played with, undermined, rejected. But Rushdie also explores this palimpsestine sense of time in the context of monotheistic religions such as Judaism, Christianity and Islam: 'On Mount Sinai, the prophet Musa or Moses heard disembodied commandments; on Mount Hira, the prophet Muhammed (also known as Mohammed, Mahomet, the Last-but-One, and Mahound) spoke to the Archangel (Gabriel, or Jibreel, as you please)' (p. 163). For some, statements such as these are blasphemous – as Rushdie discovered to his peril when a *fatwa* was decreed as a result of his words – yet they indicate how Rushdie views historical experience as repeatable, layered, palimpsestine.

Yet Rushdie is not simply playing with reality for the sake of it, as the conclusion of the wonderfully amusing intercalated fairy-tale makes quite clear: 'the newspapers – *Jang, Dawn, Pakistan Times* – announced a crushing victory for the President's Muslim League over the Mader-i-Millat's Combined Opposition Party; thus proving to me that I have been only the humblest of jugglers-with-facts; and that, in a country where the truth is what it is instructed to be, reality quite literally ceases to exist, so that everything becomes possible except what we are told is the case' (p. 326). This connection between magic and politics is pursued consistently in the chapter, 'The Shadow of the Mosque', in which the illusionism of communism is compared to conjurors' tricks: 'The problems of the magicians' ghetto were the problems of the Communist movement in India. (. . .) There were Trotskyist tendencies among card-sharpers, and even a Communism-through-the-ballot-box movement among the moderate members of the ventriloquist section' (p. 399). Taking a leaf out of *One Hundred Years of Solitude*, perhaps, Rushdie employs the rhetoric of magic to ram his political point home.

A similar blend of postcolonial rhetoric, magic and politics is evident in Ben Okri's *The Famished Road* (1991). In *Magical Realism in West African Fiction: Seeing with a Third Eye*, Brenda Cooper shows how Okri was able to carve a new African vision out of a genre which sprang from Latin America,[28] and in *Ordinary Enchantments*, Wendy B. Faris points in particular to Azaro's mask – which is so mysterious that the reader cannot tell whether it causes the visions Azaro subsequently experiences or 'forms part of them' (p. 11) – as a classic hallmark of magical realism.[29] *The Famished Road*, indeed, is full of that 'irreducible magic' which 'frequently disrupts the ordinary logic of cause and effect' (*Ordinary Enchantments*, p. 11). Azaro is, indeed, as slippery a narrator as Saleem in *Midnight's Children*. What is curious, though, about Okri's text is the fact that – even while it fuses the magical with the real, and the animal with the human, the spiritual with the material, and the natural with the supernatural – it never loses its political relevance. For Azaro's story is not only about the life of a young child who has spiritual sight; it also functions as an allegory of the trauma of Nigerian nationhood. As Ato Quayson has suggested: 'the *abiku* child is also meant to stand for the fractious postcolonial history of his native Nigeria'.[30] While not a new association ('in this linking of a national history with the condition of the *abiku* Okri echoes a suggestion made by Wole Soyinka in *A Dance of Forests*, which was commissioned specifically to commemorate Independence in 1961'; Quayson, p. 227), Okri's re-working of the trope produces a powerful vision. The *abiku* child's disability (in the sense that his spiritual sight alienates him from 'normal' people on the compound), as much as the visually alarming disability of the spirits Azaro happens across in his travels or the regular customers at Madame Kyoto's restaurant ('spirits who had borrowed bits of human beings to partake of human reality', p. 161)[31] operates as a metaphor of political disempowerment. To quote Quayson:

> The presence of disabled people in postcolonial writing marks more than just the recognition of their obvious presence in the real world of postcolonial existence and the fact that in most cases national economies woefully fail to take care of them. It means much more than that. It also marks the sense of a major problematic: which is nothing less than the difficult encounter with history itself. For colonialism may be said to have been a major force of disabling the

---

[28] *Magical Realism in West African Fiction: Seeing with a Third Eye* (New York: Routledge, 1998).

[29] Other critics who discuss *The Famished Road* in terms of its magical realism are: Edna Eizenberg, '*The Famished Road*: Magical Realism and the Search for Social Equity', *Yearbook of Comparative and General Literature*, 43 (1995), 25–30; and Philip Whyte, 'West African Literature at the Cross-roads: The Magical Realism of Ben Okri', *Commonwealth Essays and Studies*, 5 (2003), 69–79.

[30] 'Looking Awry: Tropes of Disability in Postcolonial Writing', in *Relocating Postcolonialism*, eds David Theo Goldberg and Ato Quayson (Oxford: Blackwell, 2002), pp. 217–30 (p. 227). According to Nigerian folklore an 'abiku' is a spiritually gifted child who is destined to die young.

[31] All references are to Ben Okri, *The Famished Road* (London: Vintage, 2003).

colonized from taking their place in the flow of history other than in a position
of stigmatized underprivilege. (Quayson, p. 228)

Indeed the magical-realist sheen of the style does not in itself deaden the political points that *The Famished Road* makes. The episode in Book II, chapter 4 when
Azaro is bundled into a sack and taken off by some of Madame Kyoto's customers
functions not only as an example of a mishap occurring on the soul's spiritual
journey but also as an allegory of the kidnapping of the subaltern by the forces of
reaction within society. As Azaro cries out: 'Politicians! Politicians are taking me
away!' (p. 131). The evil of this political conspiracy is underlined in the following chapter when the Party of the Rich arrives – with the collusion of the landlord
of the compound – handing out free milk in exchange for votes, and, in the
process, poisoning the population (as the plague of vomiting which ensues vividly
suggests). That the political focalization of the text is from the vantage point of
the poor is suggested by the fact that it is Azaro's father – he 'supported the Party
for the Poor' (p. 151) – who discovers that the collective vomiting has been caused
by the milk (p. 155). Azaro's father is a labourer who lives a life of drudgery, com-
plaining about the heavy load he has to carry, 'his head, his back, his legs' (p. 149);
as he comments: 'If you want to vote for the party that supports the poor, they give
you the heaviest load. I am not much better than a donkey' (p. 96). He is the epit-
ome of all the other workers who seem 'damned, or as if they were working out
an abysmal slavery' (p. 170); Azaro sees him fall to the ground under the weight
of his burdens (p. 176). The rebellion of the compound inhabitants and the subsequent repression is all the more effective by being presented through a child's eyes.
The spirit world is shown, during the period of repression in which the photographer in particular is victimised, to be on the side of the oppressed: 'The dead were
curiously on the side of the innocents' (p. 211). That the world of the spirit is not
separate from the world of politics is made very clear in the closing stages of
Okri's novel. The political struggle is echoed in the fight between the spirits:
'The Party of the Rich drew support from the spirits of the Western world' (p. 568).
In *The Famished Road* Okri is able to combine in an arresting manner a vision of
the supernatural with a sense of the real political problems faced by Africa today.
It was as a result of its intrinsic heterogeneity rather than its syncretism that
the discourse of magical realism was able to migrate from Latin America to various cultural shores around the world. Particularly for writers in countries which
had recently escaped from the clutches of colonialism, magical realism appeared
to offer a literary idiom which could reflect the raw political tensions which
accompanied the movement towards nationhood, this particularly so during the
1980s and early 1990s which may be seen as the highwater mark of globalised
magical realism. But there have been dissenting voices. It is clear, for example,
that for a number of commentators the notion that magical realism is the 'language of the postcolonial world' is a misleading one. Indeed, it is not simply
post-Bhabhian critics who distance themselves from this idea. The Guatemalan
Nobel Prize winner Miguel Ángel Asturias accused Gabriel García Márquez way
back in the 1960s, firstly, of stealing his ideas and, secondly, of gaining success

simply as a result of the astute use of publicity.[32] Asturias's slur failed to stick on the Colombian writer but it has haunted some of the latter's 'imitators'. William Rowe, for example, has argued that Isabel Allende and Angela Carter simply adopted the rhetoric of García Márquez's magical realism – style without substance: 'In the 1980s magical realism became a genre formula, transferable to scenarios that lacked the particular historical characteristics outlined above, and was even adopted as a model by non-Latin American writers (such as Angela Carter). The Chilean novelist Isabel Allende uses in her narratives magic as an amalgam of styles of previous writers like García Márquez.'[33] Raymond L. Williams, for his part, has dismissed Allende's fiction as nothing more than facile imitations of the Colombian's novels.[34] Much the same has been said of Laura Esquivel's fiction; indeed, as Helene Price suggests in her essay in this volume, *Like Water for Chocolate* portrays Mexico in stereotypical terms which suggest that the style rather than the politics of magical realism is being employed in Esquivel's novel and Arau's film. A recent promotion of the Harry Potter series on the official Bloomsbury web-site refers to the novels as 'magical-realist'.[35] If *Harry Potter and the Philosopher's Stone* can be magical-realist, then, the argument goes, surely anything can be part of the discourse of magical realism? Is it the case, as one critic has recently argued, that: 'Writers have been distancing themselves from the term while their publishers have increasingly used the term to describe their works for marketing purposes'?[36] No wonder, then, that John King could complain in 1990 of the 'sloppy use of the term "magical-realist" by western critics eager to bracket and explain away the cultural production of the region [Latin America]'.[37]

One way of addressing this problem would be to argue that works such as *The Kingdom of this World*, *One Hundred Years of Solitude*, *Midnight's Children* and *The Famished Road* are 'authentic', magical-realist novels in Bhabha's sense (i.e. expressions of the 'postcolonial world') whereas others – such as fictional works by Angela Carter, Isabel Allende, Laura Esquivel, and J.K. Rowling – are examples of a stylistic aesthetic emptied of political content.[38] But this

[32] Quoted in José Donoso, *Historia personal del 'Boom'*, 2nd edn (Barcelona: Seix Barral, 1983), p. 15.

[33] William Rowe, 'Magical Realism', *Encyclopedia of Latin American Literature* (Chicago: Dearborn, 1997), pp. 506–7.

[34] Raymond L. Williams, *The Postmodern Novel in Latin America: Politics, Culture, and the Crisis of Truth* (New York: St Martin's Press, 1996), p. 71.

[35] See http://www.bloomsbury.com/ (consulted on 1 November 2003). For further discussion see Stephen M. Hart, 'Cultural Hybridity, Magical Realism, and the Language of Magic in Paulo Coelho's *The Alchemist*', *Romance Quarterly*, 51.4 (2004), 304–12 (p. 305).

[36] Maggie Ann Bowers, *Magic(al) Realism* (London: Routledge, 2004), p. 1.

[37] John King, *Magical Reels: A History of Cinema in Latin America* (London: Verso, 1990), p. 5.

[38] For further discussion of this point, see Stephen M. Hart, 'Cultural Hybridity, Magical Realism, and the Language of Magic in Paulo Coelho's *The Alchemist*', *Romance Quarterly*, 51.4 (2004), 304–12 (pp. 305–9).

manicheistic approach has its problems. What about writers such as Toni Morrison in whose work some critics have discerned magical-realist elements,[39] even if Morrison has distanced herself from the movement? How about Patrick Süskind's *Perfume* which has been seen by critics such as Wendy Faris as magical-realist (see *Ordinary Enchantments*, pp. 83–4, 117–18) but by others as simply revisiting the Gothic tradition? Is Franz Kafka's *The Metamorphosis* a magical-realist novel?[40] How about Günter Grass's *The Tin Drum*? Even if the novel is magical realism, can Germany, or indeed any other Western nation, be legitimately seen as postcolonial?[41] In the sense perhaps that Angela Carter said that Yorkshire is a type of 'Third World' (see the discussion in Sarah Sceats's essay in this volume)? Is the 'Third World' even a valid term since the demise of the 'Second World' with the Fall of the Berlin Wall in 1989? For some critics (Chanady, Durix) the fantastic and magical realism are intimately related, while for others (Lucila-Inés Mena, Bowers) they are distinct.[42] The temptation to adopt a purist-relativist approach (namely, see all incarnations of magical realism as dependent on the cultural context which produced them, and therefore as intrinsically unique and not worth comparing) can become overwhelming.

Magical Realism and Beyond: Ideology of Fantasy

Wen-chin Ouyang

'The concept of magic realism raises many problems, both theoretical and historical', Fredric Jameson thus begins his 1986 essay 'On Magic Realism in Film'.[43] To experts and connoisseurs of contemporary fiction, art and film, the

---

[39] See Stelamaris Coser, *Bridging the Americas: The Literature of Paula Marshall, Toni Morrison, and Gayl Jones* (Philadelphia: Temple University Press, 1994), p. ix, pp. 1–2; and Stephen M. Hart, 'Magical Realism in the Americas: Politicised Ghosts in *One Hundred Years of Solitude, The House of the Spirits*, and *Beloved*', *Journal of Iberian and Latin American Studies*, 9.2 (2003), 115–23 (pp. 119–23).

[40] There are different views on this novel; compare Amaryll Chanady, *Magical Realism and the Fantastic: Resolved Versus Unresolved Antimony*, esp. p. 24, and Maggie Ann Bower, *Magic(al) Realism*, pp. 24–8.

[41] See Wendy Faris for a discussion of *The Tin Drum* as magical-realist; *Ordinary Enchantments*, pp. 92–3.

[42] Chanady, *Magical Realism and the Fantastic: Resolved Versus Unresolved Antimony;* Jean-Pierre Durix, *Mimesis, Genres and Post-Colonial Discourse: Deconstructing Magical Realism* (London: Macmillan, 1998); Lucila-Inés Mena, 'Hacia una formulación teórica del realismo mágico', *Bulletin Hispanique*, 77.3–4 (1975), 517–24; Bowers, *Magic(al) Realism*.

[43] Originally published in *Critical Inquiry*, 12.2 (Winter 1986), 301–25, and later in *Signatures of the Visible* (London and New York: Routledge, 1990), pp. 128–52. All quotations are from the latter.

spread of magical realism across continents and cultures, and more significantly across media of expression and genres, may be a welcome sign that marks the opening up of the global literary, artistic and visual landscapes to diversification held together by a common core. Magical realism, however vaguely this term may explain the composition and effect of a piece of work, has served as the common ground for discussions of many issues pertinent to cultural and identity politics termed as postcolonialism and postmodernism in the past three or four decades, from the 'native' recovering 'local' or 'indigenous' cultures and writing back at empire to creating hybridities that accommodate multiplicities, and from questioning the epistemological premises of European post-Enlightenment realism to remapping the novel and the visual arts. To theorists of culture and literature, the term and the phenomenon it denotes have proven vexingly impossible to pin down, whether in its politics or aesthetics. Magic can mean anything that defies empiricism, including religious beliefs, superstitions, myths, legends, voodoo, or simply what Todorov terms the 'uncanny' and 'marvellous' fantastic. Realism, seen from the perspective of magic, is one or any way of grasping reality outside the matrix of what is by now disdained conventional realism.

The conceptual problems, Jameson points out, 'emerge clearly when one juxtaposes the notion of "magic realism" with competing or overlapping terms: in the beginning, for instance, it was not clear how it was to be distinguished from the vaster category simply called fantastic literature: at this point, what is presumably at issue is a certain type of narrative or representation to be distinguished from "realism"' (p. 128). The terminological complexities are compounded further by the appearance of texts that carry what Jameson calls political or mystificatory value (p. 129). The tri-continental and multi-media labyrinthine genesis of magical realism only adds fuel to the already confusing fanfare of fire for theorists and critics who attempt to make sense of, articulate and contextualize the politics and aesthetics of this alternately named 'mode', 'genre' or 'style' of expression. What a critic calls the 'hollowness' of magical realism, as a meaningful theoretical term, is precisely what makes it so strangely seductive for Jameson; for it allows for numerous ways of engaging with the 'concept' to speak about contemporary narrative and representation (p. 129). Here is where attention is drawn to the critical enterprise itself. In the chapter devoted to magical realism in *Posts and Pasts: A Theory of Postcolonialism*,[44] Alfred J. López sums up the crux of the matter in the widespread use, or misuse, of the 'hollow' term he speaks of, bringing the problem back to the originary act of naming:

> 'Magical realism'. A European term applied to a 'non-European' literature, a literature which, despite the assimilating effects of the 'Third World

---

[44] 'Reason, "The Native," and Desire: A Theory of "Magical Realism"', in *Posts and Pasts: A Theory of Postcolonialism* (Albany: SUNY Press, 2001).

cosmopolitan' status bestowed upon its originary authors, retain its irreducible difference, its mark or alterity, which only begs the question: What of this act of *naming*, of the boundary or mark of a text written by, say, a Latin American author, imposed upon it from without, in a futile European attempt to categorize and thus 'understand' it by this process of naming – which is already itself an act of appropriation, a bid to harness the wild, 'exotic' text within a reasonable European critical framework – to 'master' the other's difficult text? Here the act of naming emerges as the allegory of a colonial fantasy: the mastery of reading as a reading of mastery. (p. 143)

Part of his solution to this critical impasse is to reread the major magical-realist texts from the perspective of postcolonial theories, bringing 'Freudian' or 'Lacanian' desire for authority, legitimacy, alterity and agency, all familiar tropes in postcolonial studies, into a Hegelian reading of both literary and critical texts. Alejo Carpentier's famous prologue to his novel, *The Kingdom of This World*, is seen as embodying paradoxical impulses of on the one hand self-colonization and on the other the creation of a radical alterity. In forwarding Gabriel García Márquez's *One Hundred Years of Solitude* and Salman Rushdie's *Midnight's Children* as expressions of postcolonial desire for alterity that escapes European mastery and of 'the native's' will to self recovery, López dismisses interrogation grounded in postmodernism, such as the kind advocated by Jameson (p. 129), as insufficient in that it attempts to 'reduce to a narrative technique, to explain away as Otherness or political allegory or a naïve "nativism" the movement of a literature which . . . is not apprehended by a neocolonial desire that lies latent in Western practices of reading and classifying texts' (p. 144).

López, though by far the most theoretically sophisticated postcolonial critic of magical realism, is not the first or only critic who champions interrogation of magical realism within the framework of postcolonial theories. In this, he joins forces with postcolonial critics, such as Stephen Slemon and Jean-Pierre Durix (see above), and postmodernist critics, such as Lois Parkinson Zamora, Wendy Faris (see above) and, let us say, Fredric Jameson in attempts to find ways to speak more concretely of a phenomenon that has come to elude specificity. In fact, the trajectory of magical realism has been spiralling out of control since the 1960s. The scope of López's significant contribution to theorizing about magical realism (centred on García Márquez, Coetzee and Rushdie) cannot match that of magical realism itself, which has now become global, invading and setting up colonies in the literary and visual landscapes of, additionally, Africa, Asia and Australia. There is no stopping it. It is everywhere. It is in Arabic, Chinese, English, German, Italian, Japanese, Persian, Portuguese, Spanish, Tibetan and Turkish, to name but a few languages. It is in fiction, film and the arts. The framework for inquiry derived from Latin American Studies or readings, let us say, of Anglophile Indian or African novels from the perspective of Spanish American magical realism (of the postcolonial drive), or comparative analyses of Northern and Southern American texts, or American and European works (of the postmodernist impulse), suddenly seem paradoxically illuminating and obfuscating.

The insights gained from research on Spanish American magical realism, for the importance of which one only needs to look at Zamora and Faris's pioneering volume, have served as the theoretical core for the analysis of non-Spanish American texts that combine the fantastic and the real in speaking of reality. Whether this reality is the postmodern of the so-called 'First World' or the postcolonial of the 'Third World', politics and aesthetics intersect in such a way that the text comes to be a map of conflicting ideologies and desires. Resistance to, subversion and reconfiguration of what may be termed 'modern Western epistemology', whether in the form of empiricism or empire, are uncovered, discussed and packaged as magical realism. These broad theoretical principles, under close scrutiny, are at risk of becoming a straightjacket, especially for non-Spanish American texts, potentially obscuring other equally important theoretical principles. The generalizing drive of the research on magical realism, as in any kind of research, is interestingly obfuscating in an illuminating way. In the very groundedness of these theoretical principles in the specific context of Spanish America lies their global appeal. Here, a new examination of them in a comparative framework that broadens out to include African, Asian and Australian contexts, as well as forms of expression outside the novel, such as film and the arts, may lead to reformulation of the questions behind them, and the formulation of new ones. Let us revisit, as an example, the subject of the source and effect of magic, and try to see if new questions on the politics and aesthetics of magical realism may be raised.

Two generalizations based on juxtaposition of the 'local' or 'indigenous' with the 'West' seem to have found universal sympathy. Magic is derived from the 'supernatural' elements of 'local' or 'indigenous' myths, religions or cultures that speak directly to the imposition of Christianity in addition to post-Enlightenment empiricism on the 'natives' of South America. Christianity and European empiricism, as institutions of knowledge of the empire, have become the symbols of this empire. The novel, itself a 'European' import, necessarily becomes the site of resistance on the ground of which the war of cultural recovery takes place. The process of decolonization, it may be said, entails recovery of histories derived from 'local' or 'indigenous' myths and religions that are not those of the 'West'. The 'West' in this case may be particularized as, let us say, the 'Hispano-Catholic' Europe that has its own articulation of the broader 'Western' institutions of knowledge in tension with those of the rest of Europe and its other empires, such as the British or the French. In what ways is the reformulation, or as some would say 'misuse', of 'local' or 'indigenous' myths and religions a response to Catholicism? What of the particularities of the responses to Anglican or Protestant Christianity? And, would the prior presence of Christianity in the lands that later came to be colonized by the 'West' effect different cultural politics? How do the Christians in the Middle East, for example, respond to 'Western' colonization? How does the colonial encounter problematize discourses about other monotheistic religions, such as Islam in the Middle East, Africa and India? Here, one must pause and pose another question: in what ways has the response to Christianity in non-Christian cultures coloured their resistance to 'Western' secular institutions of knowledge, such as empiricism, and vice versa?

And what of the language of this resistance, of decolonization? English, French and Spanish, to writers from South America, Africa and Asia, are the language of the colonizers and, more importantly, they simultaneously open up and limit creative vistas to a world constructed by these languages in the form of a tradition that has taken shape over the centuries. The importance of this tradition is the clearest in literature where literary texts have a way of getting entangled in dialectical dialogism with preceding texts that embody the epistemological system produced and operative in the same culture. The choice of English, French or Spanish as the language of engagement with colonization, for example, means taking on as well as becoming limited to the literary tradition of each language, including its internalization of the broader 'Western' literary canon. García Márquez, it has been pointed out many times, looks up to as well as subverts classical Greek and Spanish texts. Magic does not only come from the 'supernatural' elements of 'local' myths and religions, but also from pre-realist 'Western' texts. Borges, whether we consider him a precursor or pioneer of magical realism, derives the fantastic from the 'Western' literary tradition.[45] The choice to write in a language that does not belong to the colonizer then affords the writer options to map his texts in completely different ways. This is especially true of languages that come with a long, written literary tradition with a strong component of the fantastic, such as, let us say, Arabic, Chinese, Japanese and Persian. Magic in texts written in these languages may easily be the result of a concoction of materials taken from 'local' myths and religions and the literary tradition effected through strategies of intertextuality.

Intertextuality in contemporary literatures not in the languages of the most recent colonizers, whether of the magical kind or not, it may be argued, is a feature of postcolonial texts driven by an impulse to decolonize. Decolonization in this case involves a return to 'native' traditions. Intertextuality in, for example, the Arabic novel, tells a tale of the ways in which the form, imported from the 'West', founds a genealogy for itself in the Arabic literary tradition in general and 'local' tradition of storytelling in particular in order to overcome its foreignness. In the process of its decolonization it 'invents a tradition' the contours of which are delineated by the borders of the nation-state. 'The invention of tradition' Hobsbawm and Ranger speak of is a cultural artefact of the nation-state, whose newness requires for its legitimation a tradition with roots in the past.[46]

---

[45] The influence of *The Thousand and One Nights* on Borges is well-known. The genealogy of the *Nights* is a problematic one, and it may arguably be considered a 'Western' text in that it has taken shape (in its present form) in the 19th century during the height of the fascination with the Orient during the colonial period in Europe. More important, Borges, not knowing Arabic, could only access the text in translation (Richard Burton's in particular) and, it may be argued, translations are texts in their own right that bear only semblance of resemblance to the original. This is particularly true of the pseudo-translations of 'oriental tales' and the ensuing development of the 'Oriental Tale' in Europe.

[46] See Eric Hobsbawm and Terence Ranger, *The Invention of Tradition* (Cambridge: Cambridge University Press, 1983).

This 'invented tradition' is akin to the 'immemorial past' Anderson identifies as the historical dimension in 'imaginings of community' within the framework of nationalism – the nation is inevitably 'imagined' as 'limited' and 'sovereign' with roots in an 'immemorial past' on the landscape vacated by 'religious community' and 'dynastic realm'.[47] Is the turn, or return, to pre-colonial 'local' or 'indigenous' myths and religions in Spanish American magical realism a part of imaginings of nation? Does magical realism find a precursor in and dialogues with Spanish American romance that took part in imaginings of community?[48] Is magical realism deconstructive only, or is it that and constructive as well? Should Rushdie's *Midnight's Children* be dismissed simply as 'postmodern historiography', as López does, that writes history in a fragmentary, questioning and unreliable fashion all in response to colonial single-voiced, self-assured linear grand narrative? Is it too driven by a desire for an alternative community? If this should be the case, then 'magic' here is no different from the kind of 'fantasy' Jacqueline Rose analyses as both the constructive and troubling source of the nation-state.

Locating her 'Freudian' analysis of the discourses and policies the State of Israel in the overlap, or slippage in another sense, between 'religious community' and 'nation-state', Rose looks at the role of fantasy, as a manifestation of desire, and its frustration in shaping discourse and policy. Playing on the word 'state', as both the condition of desire and its political actualization, she exposes the complex ways in which the Utopian world of a religiously imagined community, present or absent, intrude on the discourses and practices of the nation-state. Is this a possible context for the politics of apocalypse in magical realism? *States of Fantasy*, the title of her book, denotes both states of desire and polit-ical communities the imaginings of which are driven and drawn by desire. Seen in this light, desire is intriguingly political and fantasy profoundly ideological. In *The Fantastic*, a work that has been seminal in the discussions of what constitutes magic in magical realism, Todorov points to the importance of desire in structuring the relationship between the individual and the world, 'self' and 'other' in their infinite varieties, and, more importantly, narrative.[49]

The workings of desire in structuring the politics of longing for community as detailed by Todorov and Rose find a beautiful visual articulation in Wim Wenders' 1987 film, *Wings of Desire* (Der Himmel über Berlin – literally: Heaven Over Berlin). Maggie Ann Bowers locates magical realism of the film in

---

[47] See Benedict Anderson, *Imagined Communities: Reflections on the Origin and Spread of Nationalism* (London and New York: Verso, 1983).

[48] For romance as nationalist narrative, see Doris Sommer, 'Irresistible Romance: the Foundational Fictions of Latin America', *Nation and Narration*, ed. Homi Bhabha (New York and London: Routledge, 1990), pp. 71–98.

[49] See in particular chapters 7 and 8: 'themes of the self', and 'themes of the other', in *The Fantastic: A Structural Approach to a Literary Genre*, trans. Richard Howard (Cornell: Cornell University Press, 1975).

the convergence of the worlds of the angels and humans, and in its interrogation of the nature of reality.[50] The explicit references to the destruction of Berlin towards the end of World War II and the persecution of the Jews before – in the form of film-within-film, however, points the way towards reading the film as political allegory as well. The film is as concerned with history, especially its extreme 'nationalist' misadventure during the Nazi ascendance, and with the German nation's coming to terms with this episode in its history. The film is as much about the reality on the ground as it is about the nature of reality in perception. In this, magical realism and fantasy have much in common. Who would doubt today that J.R.R. Tolkien's *The Lord of the Rings*, defined as fantasy in no uncertain terms, is an allegory of post-World War I Europe and an imagining of an alternative community? Today's magical realism and fantasy seem equally haunted by imperialism and empire, nationalism and nation-state.

Magical realism has resisted being viewed as fantasy in part because of its own desire for territoriality, and in part because of its aspiration to literariness and radical politics – to be taken seriously as literature and epistéme – which may explain the concern with the distinction between 'literature' and 'popular fiction'. The lines between the two 'modes' or 'genres', however, have never really been clearly drawn. Borges is famously claimed by both, so is García Márquez now,[51] let alone writers like Rushdie.[52] There may be some benefit in eschewing the impossible-to-maintain distinction on occasion in order that the insights of both areas of inquiry may be brought together to bear on the texts we try to come to terms with. Aside from the location of the fantastic – that in magical realism it is grafted on reality and in fantasy on a never-land – the motors driving narrative and the trajectories of this narrative are, in a sense, more similar than not. The politics of fantasy, like those of magical realism, are driven by desire at one level to grapple with reality and the epistemological systems in place for knowing it, and at another level to transcend here and now and imagine an alternative world. In its flights of fantasy, it problematizes, as magical realism does, the various social and cultural institutions based in religion, ethnicity, class and gender.[53] It too subverts realism as a mode of narrative.[54] More important,

---

[50] Maggie Ann Bowers, *Magic(al) Realism*, The New Critical Idioms series (London: Routledge, 2004), pp. 111–12.

[51] See Brian Attebery, *Strategies of Fantasy* (Bloomington and Indianapolis: Indiana University Press, 1992), p. 13 and p. 127.

[52] See, for example, Richard Mathews, *Fantasy: The Liberation of Imagination* (New York and London: Routledge, 2002).

[53] For these politically and epistemologically subversive dimensions of fantasy, see Rosemary Jackson's survey of the critical literature on the subject and her own discussion in *Fantasy: The Literature of Subversion* (New York and London: Routledge, 1981), p. 91, 93, 95, 98. The bibliography is extremely useful.

[54] See, for example, Catherine Brooke-Rose, *A Rhetoric of the Unreal: Studies in Narrative and Structure, Especially of the Fantastic* (Cambridge: Cambridge University Press, 1981); W. R. Irwin, *The Game of the Impossible: A Rhetoric of Fantasy* (Urbana, Chicago,

perhaps, is its engagement with subjectivity that has yielded significant insights into the ways in which the workings of desire, conscious or unconscious, structure literary texts. Todorov, it seems, may have some more mileage in magical realism.

In today's global economy, in which production is dictated ever more by consumption, the already fuzzy distinctions among 'genres', 'modes' and 'media', or even 'registers' (such as 'literature' and 'popular fiction') are becoming even fuzzier. The literary field finds itself under the influence of new rules of play as it opens itself up to various forms of migration. Rapid, albeit haphazard, translation has increased the volume and speed of cross-cultural exchange and literary cross-fertilization. The ease of travel from one cosmopolis to another, the spread of internet technology, the reach of Hollywood, to mention but a few features of our contemporary life, are redrawing the map of the literary field everywhere in the world. The migration of story from literature to cinema, for example, has often led to the production of a written text based on the film quite different from the original. In many instances the film version is an improvement on and more popular than the original. Under such circumstances questions of discreteness, definition, category and origin become less important than the workings of a text, be it literary or visual, and the ways in which these relate the text to the world and other texts without necessarily abandoning altogether the familiar articulated categories of knowledge. Perhaps letting the texts speak of their own politics in the multi-cultural, inter-generic and cross-media contexts will lead to some unexpected discoveries.

Familiar Grounds, Novel Trajectories: The Fantastic, the Real and Magical Realism

Stephen M. Hart and Wen-chin Ouyang

Intended as a celebration ten years on of Lois Parkinson Zamora and Wendy B. Faris's landmark volume, *Magical Realism: Theory, History, Community* (1995), this *Companion to Magical Realism* is informed by the scope and parameters delineated by its predecessor but hopes to offer its readers something new at the same time, bringing new themes, issues and writers into the purview of magical realism. It has not been the intention of the editors to impose a Latin American straightjacket reading old or new texts that are the subject of the papers collected in this volume (as if to argue that they depart from the Latin American norm and

London: University of Illinois Press, 1976); and Robert Scholes, *Fabulation and Metafiction* (Urbana, Chicago, London: University of Illinois Press, 1979). For a more recent work informed by contemporary literary and cultural theories, see Lucie Armitt, *Theorising the Fantastic* (London: Arnold, 1996).

thereby betray its authentic roots). Rather, it is hoped that an interdisciplinary and cross-subject interrogation of these texts will allow their subtle nuances to become more discernible, and the complex webs of connections, cultural, literary, historical and political, more visible. Lois Parkinson Zamora's essay, indeed, establishes a line of continuity between literature and art, and Borges's 'poetic objects', García Márquez's 'Baroque objects' and Franz Roh's 'magical objects'; they are linked by what she terms magical realism's 'visualising capacity'. Stephanie Jones's essay on Rushdie's *Satanic Verses* dispels the myth that Rushdie is simply pouring old Marquezian wine into new Indian bottles. Is Rushdie, after all, any less authentic than García Márquez?

Our book sets out to present a reasoned view on familiar contentious issues. Diverging from William Rowe's view, for example, Sarah Sceats argues in this volume that there are clear areas of overlap between the substance of magical realism and Angela Carter's work. Likewise Philip Swanson, in his essay on *La Ciudad de las Bestias* (*City of the Beasts*), shows how Allende employs the motifs of children's literature in her latest novel to significant aesthetic effect. Is this 'plundering' of popular culture less reprehensible than her 'pillaging' of the discourse of magical realism, we might ask? The aim of this companion, thus, is to offer a set of new interlocking and pluralistic readings of magical realism. Some of the essays, for example, re-visit the work of authors whose association with magical realism and the discourse of the fantastic is unquestionably canonical (Asturias, Rulfo, Carpentier, Borges, García Márquez, Allende, Rushdie) and they aspire to open up new perspectives on the masters' voice. Jason Wilson, for example, provides new evidence to demonstrate that Carpentier's 'marvellous real' was closer to surrealism than the Cuban writer was prepared to admit at the time. Evelyn Fishburn offers an innovative reading of the same writer's novel, *The Kingdom of this World*, which focuses on the humour thrown up by the clash between Caribbean and French cultures, as exemplified in particular by Mlle Floridor's antics. Donald Shaw takes a fresh look at how commentators have analysed the role of myth in a selection of Boom novelists.

There are also new readings of the patriarch of magical realism, García Márquez, in this volume. Robin Fiddian, for example, analyses 'Big Mama's Funeral' and identifies the precise point of emergence of the Colombian's distinctive literary style. Lorna Robinson excavates some striking similarities between the imagery of *One Hundred Years of Solitude* and Ovid's *Metamorphoses*. Efraín Kristal, for his part, focuses on García Márquez's recently published memoirs, *Vivir para contarla* (*Living to Tell the Tale*), and meditates on the uncanny ways in which literature and life, the magical and the real, are found to converge. Other essays, such as that by Julia King and Stephen M. Hart on Bombal, Parra, Asturias and Rulfo, and Humberto Núñez-Faraco's essay on José Eustasio Rivera's *The Vortex*, analyse the work of writers who preceded the Boom but whose novels have clear similarities with the hermeneutic strategies subtending magical realism.

This *Companion to Magical Realism* dedicates space to the analysis of magical-realist motifs in the work of writers not readily associated with the movement: John Erickson writes on Tahar Ben Jelloun's work, Michael Berkowitz on contemporary Jewish writers, Alejandra Rengifo on Mayra Montero's *The Red of His Shadow*, Stefan Sperl on Ibrahim al-Kawnī's *The Lunar Eclipse*, Mark Morris on Nakagami Kenji's work, Jonathan Allison on the poetry of W.B. Yeats and Seamus Heaney, David Henn on José Saramago's fiction, Tsila Ratner on Dorit Rabinyan's *Persian Brides*, and Wen-chin Ouyang on Elias Khoury's *Little Ghandi*. This is the first time, indeed, that writers such as W.B. Yeats, Seamus Heaney, José Saramago, Dorit Rabinyan, Ovid, María Luisa Bombal, Ibrahim al-Kawni, Mayra Montero, Nakagami Kenji, José Eustasio Rivera and Elias Khoury have been analysed in the context of magical realism.

The essays are grouped into four distinct though overlapping sections: (i) Genealogies, Myths, Archives, (ii) History, Nightmare, Fantasy, (iii) The Politics of Magic, and (iv) Empire, Nation, Magic. Each section has a short introduction summarising the focus and main points of the essays grouped together. The organization of these sections, and the grouping and sequencing of the essays in each section are guided by the critical observations made and theoretical questions raised earlier in this introduction. Genealogies, Myths, Archives examines the ways in which magical realism invents its own tradition, History, Nightmare, Fantasy explores new forms of magical interaction with realism, The Politics of Magic looks at postcolonial nationalist politics, and Empire, Nation, Magic interrogates the nation-state as magical realism's political framework.

This companion has a Guide to Further Reading, which lists and briefly discusses the most important critical works to date on magical realism. All quotations have been translated into English for the reader's ease.

Part I: Genealogies, Myths, Archives

Introduction

Stephen M. Hart

'Le mythe est un langage' (myth is a language) (Roland Barthes, *Mythologies*)

This section uses three related but distinct motifs – genealogy, myth, and archive – in order to address the foundational moment of magical realism. In 'Swords and Silver Rings: Magical Objects in the Work of Jorge Luis Borges and Gabriel García Márquez', Lois Parkinson Zamora traces the complex genealogy of magic through a set of key figures. She identifies a line of continuity running from Franz Roh's sense of the 'oppositional energy' inherent in the painted objects of magical-realist painting, through Borges's portrayal of objects via an iconography she labels 'magical idealism', up to the 'baroque objects' which populate García Márquez's fiction and, in which, as he suggests, 'magic wells up'. As Zamora concludes: 'Borges and García Márquez are (. . .) equally concerned with the relations of the visible world to invisible meanings, but García Márquez gives priority to the former, from which he infers the latter, whereas Borges proceeds in the opposite direction, starting with the invisible, from which he infers the world' (p. 44). Donald L. Shaw traces another type of genealogy within the discourse of magical realism; now it is myth which acts as a recurring leitmotiv in the work of a set of key figures. In an important study published more than twenty years ago, *La transculturación narrativa en América Latina* (Narrative Transculturation in Latin America, 1982), Ángel Rama had argued that the innovation of the Boom novel derived from its incorporation of the Amerindian archive of myths into a new framework whereby the myths were no longer viewed as exotic and foreign (namely, as if from a Eurocentric perspective), but rather were seen, as it were, from the inside. Donald L. Shaw, in his essay, 'The Presence of Myth in Borges, Carpentier, Asturias, Rulfo and García Márquez', builds on some of Rama's insights but he shows how the myths used by the writers mentioned in fact derived from a number of different sources, not just the Amerindian archive. Borges, for example, has recourse to Classical myths (such as the Minotaur in his *Fictions*), Carpentier employs Classical (Orpheus in *The Lost Steps*) as well as Afro-Caribbean myths (Mackandal in *The Kingdom of this World*), Asturias evokes Mayan folklore (in *Men of Maize*), Juan Rulfo combines Christian with Mesoamerican mythologies (in *Pedro Páramo*), while García Márquez (in *One Hundred Years of Solitude*) expresses a specifically Americanist myth. Furthermore Shaw demonstrates that this set of writers employed these myths not for any truth intrinsic to the myths themselves but as a vehicle allowing for the effective expression of new cultural insights.

Julia King and Stephen M. Hart, for their part, in their essay 'The Earth as Archive in Bombal, Parra, Asturias and Rulfo', use four test-cases to underline the difference between the ways in which male and female authors draw the archive of myth into the purview of their writing. Asturias captures Mayan myth masculinocentrically within *The Men of Maize*, while Rulfo, in *Pedro Páramo*, portrays the encounter with a mythical Beyond (itself the result of a melding of Christian and Amerindian beliefs) as riven by disorientation and confusion. Bombal and Parra, however, de-petrify the very images of women promoted by writers such as Asturias, and delve into the natural world in order to release a new image of an interiorised female consciousness grounded in the body and its sexuality. For his part, Jason Wilson, in 'Alejo Carpentier's Re-invention of América Latina as Real and Marvellous', looks closely at the process whereby the term 'lo real maravilloso' (the marvellous real) as well as the concept underpinning it came to fruition in Carpentier's *oeuvre*. He analyses Carpentier's links with surrealism, focuses on three allegorical journey-moments (the opening chapter of *El reino de este mundo*, the beginning of *Ecué-yamba-o*, and Esteban's journey in *El siglo de las luces*) in order to demonstrate that, when Carpentier coined the term 'lo real maravilloso', he was in effect jettisoning the anachronistic elements of surrealism while simultaneously re-stamping its essence within a new American context.

The two remaining essays in this section focus on the seminal Americanist and Classical myth of the Golden Age. Lorna Robinson, in 'The Golden Age Myth in Gabriel Garcia Marquez's *One Hundred Years of Solitude* and Ovid's *Metamorphoses*', for example, shows how the myth of prelapsarian bliss evoked in *One Hundred Years of Solitude* as a time when the world 'was so recent that many things lacked names', recalls its portrayal in a number of Classical authors ranging from Plato to Ovid to Virgil. Despite the difference of their respective contextual settings – Ovid was writing during a period of peace and prosperity, García Márquez during a time of violence and corruption – *One Hundred Years of Solitude* and the *Metamorphoses* are characterised by a sense of belatedness and literary syncretism. Efraín Kristal, in 'Lessons from the Golden Age in Gabriel García Márquez's *Living to Tell the Tale*', uses García Márquez's autobiography as a means of delving into different articulations of the Latin American archive, including 'popular memory', the story of the growth of the United Fruit Company, García Márquez's family history (and its subsequent transformations within his novels), and the memory of Gaitán's assassination which so traumatized the Colombian nation in 1948. Kristal demonstrates that García Márquez's brand of magical realism grew from his acute awareness of 'the articulated superposition of whole layers of the past within the present' of Latin America. As this section suggests, myths surfaced in different ways from the Latin American archive but, whatever their source, it was the way in which the various mythical strata were overlaid which insured that magical realism offered a strikingly apt vehicle with which to describe the New World.

Swords and Silver Rings: Magical Objects in the Work of Jorge Luis Borges and Gabriel García Márquez

Lois Parkinson Zamora

> In order for a thing to become interesting, one has only to look at it for a long time.
>
> Gustave Flaubert[1]

As is well known, the term 'magical realism' was first applied to the visual arts in 1925, when the German art critic Franz Roh used it to describe a group of painters whom we now categorize generally as Post-Expressionists. The term had been coined more than a century earlier by the German Romantic philosopher Novalis to describe an idealized philosophical protagonist capable of integrating ordinary phenomena and magical meanings.[2] Novalis may have been Roh's source for the term, given certain marked similarities in their arguments, most particularly in their refusal of the either/or structures of instrumental reason and their shared emphasis on the complementarity of opposites. Besides Novalis, there was the great art historian Heinrich Wölfflin, with whom Roh studied in Munich between 1915 and 1919.[3] Wölfflin was the first to define the

---

Note: I want to express my heartfelt gratitude to Evelyn Fishburn for her generous and insightful reading of this essay, and others. An earlier version of this essay, which focuses only on Borges' work, is entitled 'The Visualizing Capacity of Magical Realism: Objects and Expression in the Work of Jorge Luis Borges', *Janus Head: An Interdisciplinary Journal*, 5.2 (2002), 21–37. This issue is devoted wholly to magical realism.

[1] Gustave Flaubert, letter to Le Poittevin, September 1845, *Correspondance* (Paris: Gallimard, 1973), Vol. I, p. 252.

[2] Novalis envisions such a protagonist in notebook entries in 1799. He refers to a 'magical idealist' and a 'magical realist', the latter of whom overarches the oppositions of known and unknown, finite and infinite. Novalis, *Allgemeines Brouillon*, 1798–99, in *Werke*, ed. G. Schultz (Munich: C.H. Beck, 1969), p. 479.

I am indebted for this reference to Irene Guenther, 'Magic Realism in the Weimar Republic', in *Magical Realism: Theory, History, Community*, eds Lois Parkinson Zamora and Wendy B. Faris (Durham, NC: Duke University Press, 1995), pp. 34, 64, n. 15. See also Christopher Warnes, '"Eternal Crevices of Unreason": Magical Realism in its Historical and Cultural Contexts', unpublished manuscript.

[3] Horacio Fernández, et al., *Franz Roh: teórico y fotógrafo* (Valencia: IVAM Centro Julio González, 1997), p. 9. Fernández points out that Roh's parallel lists of twenty-two

Baroque as an artistic style, a salient feature of which was its manipulation of antitheses. According to Wölfflin, the play of contradictions is inherent in Baroque aesthetics, whether in the tension between nature and artifice, sensuality and spirit, absence and abundance, surface and depth or, I am tempted to add, magic and real. It seems to me likely that both Novalis and Wölfflin informed Roh's conception of magical realism, but my focus here at the outset will be on Roh, because it was he who served as the conduit between the European uses of the term and its Latin American literary revisions.

In a work entitled *Nach-Expressionismus, Magischer Realismus: Probleme der neuesten europäischen Malerei*, published in German in 1925, Roh offered the term 'magical realism' to describe (and celebrate) the Post-Expressionists' return to realism after a decade or more of abstraction.[4] In the preface to the expanded Spanish-language book based on Roh's essay, published two years later by José Ortega y Gasset's influential *Revista de Occidente* with the terms of the title tellingly reversed,[5] Roh again emphasized these painters' realistic engagement of the 'everyday', the 'commonplace'. He wrote that 'with the word "magic" as opposed to "mystic", I wish to indicate that the mystery does not descend to the represented world, but rather hides and palpitates behind it'.[6] An alternative term for this style in German painting was *Neue Sachlichkeit*, the New Objectivity, literally the 'new thing-ness', a term that has outlived magical realism as an art historical label, in part because Roh eventually disavowed his own designation. In his 1958 survey of twentieth-century German art, he explicitly retired the term magical realism, tying its demise to the status of the object itself: 'In our day and age [1958], questions about the character of the object . . . have become irrelevant . . . I believe that we can demonstrate that in abstract art the greatest [achievements] are again possible.'[7] In this retrospective survey, then, Roh revises his opposition to abstraction and relegates the 'countermovement' that he had labeled magical realism to '. . . one of those retardations which history likes to throw in as a breathing spell when we have experienced too many innovations' (p. 112).

characteristics in his 1925 essay distinguishing Expressionism from Post-Expressionism (i.e., 'magical realism') follow Wölfflin's strategy of distinguishing between Renaissance Classicism and the Baroque in *Principles of Art History* (1915). See Fernández's essay in this volume, 'La doble cuerda: Franz Roh, teórico y fotógrafo', p. 13.

[4] Leipzig: Klinkhardt and Biermann.

[5] Franz Roh, *Realismo mágico, post expresionismo: problemas de la pintura europea más reciente*, translated from the German by Fernando Vela (Madrid: Revista de Occidente, 1927). In fact, the essay version of Roh's text published in Ortega's magazine omits the term *post expresionismo* altogether. *Revista de Occidente*, 16 (April, May, June 1927), 274–301.

[6] From the preface to *Realismo mágico, post expresionismo*; see Wendy B. Faris' translation in *Magical Realism: Theory, History, Community*, p. 16. Faris' translation does not present Roh's entire text; below I cite a passage from *Realismo mágico* that was not included in this translation.

[7] Franz Roh, *German Art in the 20th Century: Painting, Sculpture, Architecture*, trans. Catherine Hutter (Greenwich, CT: New York Graphic Society, 1968), p. 10. I am grateful to Lily Ann Cunningham for these references and for her insights into Roh's aesthetics of the object.

Franz Roh's 1958 shrug of dismissal has been accepted by literary critics, who have largely preferred to ignore the origins of magical realism in the visual arts. Timing has something to do with it, of course, for just as Roh was performing the last rites, literary critics were beginning to resuscitate the term for use in Latin America. And from the very outset, literary critics chose to reverse Roh's emphasis, focusing on the magic rather than the real of the texts in question.[8] This transatlantic appropriation of magical realism took three decades to occur, and we would do well, five decades later still, to reconsider its historical relation to the visual arts. I say this because texts accurately referred to as 'magical-realist' do indeed raise questions about the visualizing capacity of language in ways that realistic texts do not. While all works of fiction require that we visualize objects, realism requires of objects that they represent only themselves. They may, of course, have symbolic or psychological or metaphysical content, but their signifying function is nonetheless different from the objects in magical realist texts, which must represent not only themselves but also the potential for some kind of alternative reality, some kind of 'magic'.

Think of Clara's three-legged table in Isabel Allende's *The House of the Spirits*, Melquíades' magnets in Gabriel García Márquez's *One Hundred Years of Solitude*, or Saleem's nose in Salman Rushdie's *Midnight's Children*. The 'magic' may inhere in the object, as in these examples or, alternatively, it may precede objects and generate them. Examples of the latter tendency would be Mackandal's spirit force in Alejo Carpentier's *The Kingdom of this World* (1949) and Jorge Luis Borges' idealism in 'Tlön, Uqbar, Orbis Tertius' (1940). In *The Kingdom of this World*, the clash between European and African world-views invests objects (most especially Mackandal's body) with contradictory meanings that co-exist and operate equally within the text – a semantic dupli-city largely foreign to literary realism. The characters in this novel will select one or another of the contradictory meanings according to their own cultural positioning, but the reader must envision them all at once. This process of 'seeing' lies at the heart of Carpentier's conception of *lo real maravilloso americano*.

In Borges' story, 'Tlön, Uqbar, Orbis Tertius', the 'magic' proceeds not from the interactions of multiple cultures but of multiple fictional worlds – a strategy to which Borges calls attention in his title. The clash of disjunctive metaphysics (the 'real' and 'ideal' worlds of the story) serves Borges' counterrealist purposes in ways similar to the clash of disjunctive cultures in Carpentier's fiction. As dif-ferent as these writers are – and we will be exploring some of the differences below – they nonetheless coincide in dramatizing the interpenetration of seem-ingly irreconcilable worlds, a drama (again, largely foreign to literary realism)

---

[8] This shift is apparent in the earliest formulations of magical realism as a literary critical term. See the first two essays on this matter by Ángel Flores, 'Magical Realism in Spanish American Fiction' (1955) and Luis Leal, 'Magical Realism in Spanish American Literature' (1967), reprinted in *Magical Realism: Theory, History, Community*, pp. 109–24.

from which the 'magic' in their fiction emerges. This capacity of magical realism to integrate various kinds of otherness (cultural, metaphysical) without
reconciling their contradictions goes a long way in explaining the current attraction of the mode to postcolonial writers worldwide.

It also points to what I am calling the 'visualizing capacity' of magical realism.
Whether the magic is thought to inhere in the real, or whether it pre-exists the real
according to cultural or philosophical systems of belief, objects in magical-realist
texts operate with symbolic energies that are distinct from those in realistic texts.
Put another way, magical-realist texts often conflate sight and insight, thus collapsing the literal and figurative meanings of 'vision' by making the visible world
the very source of insight. So I propose this generalization at the outset: magical
realism is characterized by its visualizing capacity, that is, its capacity to create
(magical) meanings by envisioning ordinary things in extraordinary ways.

My essay unfolds in three parts; my first section, 'Roh's Magical Objects',
highlights the German critic's understanding of the oppositional energy inherent
in the painted objects of 'magical-realist' painting. In section two, 'Borges'
Poetic Objects', I trace Borges' participation in the Argentine avant garde in the
1920s in ways related to Franz Roh's participation in the German avant garde of
the same decade; the two were contemporaries – Roh was born in 1890, nine
years before Borges. Nonetheless, we will find that Borges' fiction reverses
Roh's understanding of the object in ways that are better labeled magical idealism than magical realism. Section three, called 'García Márquez's Baroque
Objects', locates García Márquez's visualizing procedures in terms of Baroque
aesthetics and iconography by way of Alejo Carpentier's reformulation of the
Latin American Baroque beginning in the 1940s. I will focus on Borges and
García Márquez (via Carpentier) because they seem to me to represent opposite
ends of the spectrum of Latin American magical realism, both in style and substance. Their differences will allow me to range far and wide, from twentieth-
century Post-Expressionism to seventeenth-century Baroque art and back again.
My approach is comparative and interartistic: I will discuss paintings and
painters along with my literary examples to aid us in visualizing the symbolic
seeing in the work of Borges and García Márquez.

Roh's Magical Objects

> And some certain significance lurks in all things, else all
> things are little worth, and the round world itself but an
> empty cipher . . .
>
> Herman Melville, *Moby Dick*[9]

Melville's Ishmael hopes to find 'some certain significance in all things', a desire
fully realized, it seems, by Franz Roh in the 'magical-realist' paintings of Franz

---

[9] Herman Melville, *Moby Dick* (1851; New York: W.W. Norton, 1967), Ch. 99, 'The
Doubloon', p. 358.

Radziwill, Alexander Kanoldt, Otto Dix, George Grosz, Christian Schad, Giorgio de Chirico and Henri Rousseau, among others. As I have already suggested, Roh structures his argument by contrasting these paintings to the Expressionism that preceded them. Indeed, their exaggerated clarity of line and color, their flattened texture and perspective, and their return to human figures and furnishings represent a striking departure from Expressionism, with its abstract forms and kinetic surfaces. Roh asserts that 'in magical-realist paintings . . . we are offered a new style that is thoroughly of this world, that celebrates the mundane'.[10] Objects are endowed with new significance after the 'fantastic dreamscape' (p. 17) of abstraction: 'It seems to us that this fantastic dreamscape has completely vanished and that our real world re-emerges before our eyes – bathed in the clarity of a new day. We recognize this world . . . we look at it with new eyes' (p. 17). Despite having rejected the term 'magical realism' Roh continued to insist upon this point thirty-three years later, in his 1958 survey of German art: 'In opposition to Expressionism, the autonomy of the objective world around us was once more to be enjoyed, the wonder of matter that could crystallize into objects was to be seen anew.'[11] Objects that had been lost to abstraction were now being recuperated by the magical-realists, the world was being made newly available to the senses of the beholder. Roh's formulation echoes the Russian Formalist Victor Shklovsky's famous definition of defamiliarization in his essay 'Art as Technique', written in 1917, eight years before Roh's essay. The renewed apprehension of the familiar world was, for Shklovsky in 1917, as it was for Franz Roh in 1925, not only the function of art, but its very definition.

For Roh, then, the essence of magical realism was to be found in its objects. He titled one section of his essay 'The New Objects', another 'Objectivity', a third 'The Proximity of the Object as Spiritual Creation', and he asserted at the outset that '. . . the new painting separates itself from Expressionism *by means of its objects*' (p. 16, author's emphasis). Consider Roh's development of this assertion:

> . . . Post-Expressionism offers us the miracle of existence in its imperturbable duration: the unending miracle of eternally mobile and vibrating molecules. Out of that flux, the constant appearance and disappearance of material, permanent objects somehow appear: in short, the marvel by which a variable commotion crystallizes into a clear set of constants. This miracle of an apparent persistence and duration in the midst of a demoniacal flux, this enigma of total quietude in the midst of general becoming, of universal dissolution: this is what Post-Expressionism admires and highlights. (p. 22)

Roh continues:

> When . . . Expressionism had crystallized the object's exclusively internal aspect, the unusual opportunity of looking at the object close up from the other

---

[10] Roh, 'Magical Realism: Post-Expressionism', *Magical Realism: Theory, History, Community*, p. 17.

[11] Roh, *German Art in the 20th Century: Painting, Sculpture, Architecture*, p. 112.

side had arrived, in other words, the opportunity of reconstructing the object, starting exclusively from our interiority. (p. 24)

What is striking is Roh's emphasis on 'permanent objects' in the first passage and, in both passages, his emphasis on the *materiality* of the object, the very fact of which, according to Roh, allows us to look at the object 'close up from the other side'.

But what 'other side'? This is a matter for speculation, of course, but it seems to be analogous to the 'magical' content of material objects in magical-realist literature. In his formulation of 'the other side', Roh engages the play of contradictions that literary critics must also address – between magic and real, material and meaning, visible and invisible. Roh was clear about this dual charge of material objects – what he called 'la *compenetración* de ambas posibilidades; no equilibrio, ni menos confusión de los contrarios, sino sutil, y, sin embargo, incesante tensión entre la sumisión al mundo presente y la clara voluntad constructiva frente a él' ('the *penetration* of both possibilities; not equilibrium and even less confusion of contraries, but rather a subtle and nonetheless incessant tension between submitting to the world and confronting it with creative energy').[12] Roh's *compenetración* arises from the materiality of the object, but does he mean to suggest that the more 'close up' the object, the more resonant the meaning of the 'other side'? That the more *objective* the painted image, the more *subjective* its meaning in the mind of the viewer? For Roh, there does seem to be a correlation between the verisimilitude of the visual image and its magical quotient, a correlation that underlines his assertion that 'mystery' wells up from the world as we know it. Roh's 'other side' is impelled by the strangeness in plain sight.

José Ortega y Gasset's influential essay on 'dehumanization' in the arts was written the same year as Roh's essay, and upon rereading it, we see why Ortega immediately had Roh's essay translated into Spanish and published.[13] Their

---

[12] Roh, *Realismo mágico: post expresionismo: problemas de la pintura europea más reciente*, p. 52, my translation.

[13] Ortega's theory of the European avant garde, like Roh's, was strongly influenced by the German art historical discourse of the time. Roberto González Echevarría, in his 1978 article entitled 'Apetitos de Góngora y Lezama', points out that Wilhelm Worringer's *Abstraction and Empathy* (1907) and *Form in Gothic* (1912) were particularly important to Ortega, who, in 1911, wrote a series of articles on Worringer's work in *El Imparcial*, and later published translations from the works mentioned above in *Revista de Occidente*. González Echevarría notes further that Oswald Spenger considered the Gothic and the Baroque to be 'stages of one and the same style', as opposed to René Wellek's later idea that the revival of the Baroque (and Góngora's work in particular) during this period paralleled the taste for Expressionism's chaotic forms. 'Góngora is clearly part of . . . an entire avant-garde aesthetic that sees him as the champion of a pure and hermetic poetry'; see González Echevarría, 'Apetitos de Góngora y Lezama Lima', in *Barroco en América* (Madrid: Ediciones Cultura Hispánica, 1978), p. 560. See also footnote 9, p. 599. This essay will appear in translation in *Baroque New Worlds: Representation, Transculturation, Counterconquest*, eds Lois Parkinson Zamora and Monika Kaup, forthcoming from Duke University Press, 2007.

arguments are parallel: Ortega, too, celebrates a return to objectivity in the literary arts, though it is not abstraction that he considers to have obscured the poetic object but rather the emotionalism of 'romantic art': 'Instead of delighting in *artistic objects* people delight in their own emotions . . .. "Lived" realities are too overpowering not to evoke a sympathy which prevents us from perceiving them in their *objective purity*.'[14] Ortega makes the Symbolist Mallarmé his watershed: after asserting that the poet does not merely reflect the world but *adds* to it, he describes Mallarmé's poems as '. . . small lyrical objects distinct from human fauna and flora' (p. 31); they '. . . present us with figures so extramundane that merely looking at them is delight' (p. 32). Ortega's 'extramundane' parallels Roh's intuition of the 'other side' of the object: magic inheres in the material fabric of the world, and art must embody this fact.

Both Ortega and Roh were responding to (and at the same time defining) European avant garde aesthetics. For both of them, the image (whether visual or verbal) was to be crystalline in structure, a dynamic pattern of intellectual and emotional energies, a sharply focused object whose referent is both in the world and beyond it. Their analogue in English literary criticism was T.E. Hulme, who argued that poetry should be 'all dry and hard',[15] and in fiction, James Joyce, whose conception of epiphany was, he said, 'a revelation of the whatness of a thing' – a sudden, unmediated apprehension of the world. And in poetry, of course, it was Ezra Pound, T.S. Eliot and William Carlos Williams. Pound's Imagist emphasis on metaphor and Eliot's reclamation of the 'metaphysical' conceits of the seventeenth-century English poets John Donne and George Herbert parallel Roh's and Ortega's aesthetics, and they predict the young poet Jorge Luis Borges, who also called for the renovation of figurative language in poetry in an early essay entitled 'Metaphor', where he urges the creation of images that are '. . . verbal objects, pure and independent like a crystal or a silver ring'.[16] Borges aspired to practice the same objectivity that Roh celebrated in the visual arts, and that Ortega and the Anglo-Americans celebrated in literature; his early outlines of *ultraísta* aesthetics consistently addressed the capacity of the poetic image to communicate sensory material in objective, crystalline forms.[17]

By the end of the 1920s, Borges had moved away from his avant garde involvement, and whether he had read Franz Roh is not documented. It does seem likely to me that he would have read the 1927 *Revista de Occidente* translation, because he had by then himself published in the *Revista*. In either case, we can fruitfully

---

[14] José Ortega y Gasset, 'The Dehumanization of Art' (1925), trans. Helene Weyl, in *The Dehumanization of Art and Other Essays on Art, Culture, and Literature* (Princeton: Princeton University Press, 1968), p. 28, my emphasis.

[15] T.E. Hulme, *Speculations: Essays on Humanism and the Philosophy of Art*, ed. Herbert Read (New York: Harcourt and Brace & Co, 1936), p. 126.

[16] Borges, 'La metáfora', in *Obras completas*, p. 382, my translation. Borges is describing the kennings of the Icelandic poet Snorri Sturluson, as we will see shortly.

[17] See Borges' texts in Hugo J. Verani, *Las vanguardias literarias en hispanoamérica (manifiestos, proclamas y otros escritos)* (Rome: Bulzoni Editore, 1986), pp. 265–99.

approach Borges' poetic objects by means of Roh's discussion of magical-realist painting.

Borges' Poetic Objects

> In those days the world of mirrors and the world of men
> were not, as they are now, cut off from each other.
>
> *Jorge Luis Borges*[18]

In his story 'Pascal's Sphere', Borges contemplates the possibility that 'universal history is the history of a few metaphors'.[19] Given the repeating metaphors in his own work, we have reason to accept the premise. Several of Borges' favorite metaphors and narrative devices are intended to call into question visual perception – the mirror, the labyrinth, the dream, the aleph, the *trompe l'oeil*, the *mise en abyme* – and they are also used to signal Borges' great theme, the illusory nature of knowledge itself. In fact, seeing and its related modes of verbal description are often the subject of Borges' essays and stories. His encroaching blindness might account for his particular sensitivity to this matter – certainly it would have – but I also believe that it was his apprenticeship in the avant garde ideas to which I have just referred that caused him, in several essays and stories, to theorize the capacity of language to create visual images in the reader's mind.

Borges' most extended consideration of this question is his 1940 story, 'Tlön, Uqbar, Orbis Tertius'. Consider the objects called *hrönir* in the idealist world described in this story. *Hrönir*, you'll recall, are the objects in Tlön, but we are told they are 'secondary objects' that duplicate lost objects. Like shadows in Plato's cave, they exist by virtue of their relation to prior (lost) entities; they are reflections (reproductions) of something that was once 'real' but no longer is.

Jason Wilson argues that Borges' ultraist aesthetic was designed in part to reject the political involvements of the French avant garde:

> Borges opted for Hispanic, Germanic and Anglo-American modernism, and denigrated Paris-based Dada, and then surrealism, assuming that writing a poem was an aesthetic act that took place on a page and in the mind, *el puro goce estético [pure aesthetic thrill]*. Turning a deaf ear to the relationship of the poet to his times was crucial in Borges's later self-definition, despite writing early poems praising the 1917 Russian Revolution.

Jason Wilson, 'Jorge Luis Borges and the European Avant-Garde', in *Borges and Europe Revisited*, ed. Evelyn Fishburn (London: University of London Institute of Latin American Studies, 1998), p. 69.

See also Beret E. Strong, *The Poetic Avant-Garde: The Groups of Borges, Auden and Breton* (Evanston: Northwestern University Press, 1997).

[18] Jorge Luis Borges, with Margarita Guerrero, 'Fauna of Mirrors', in *The Book of Imaginary Beings*, rev. and trans. Norman Thomas di Giovanni (London: Penguin, 1974), pp. 67–8.

[19] Borges, 'Pascal's Sphere', trans. Suzanne Jill Levine, in *Selected Non-Fictions*, ed. Eliot Weinberger (New York: Viking, 1999), p. 352.

These objects are 'secondary' in the same sense that all visual and verbal representations of material objects are secondary, but the narrator tells us that *hrönir*,
themselves replicas, may also replicate themselves endlessly, each copy thus progressively removed from its 'real' object. *Hrönir* are secondary, and thus by
definition figurative, not material: we are told by the narrator that 'All nouns
(man, coin, Thursday, Wednesday, rain) have only a metaphorical value' (p. 11).
And in Tlön, there is yet another category of secondary object beyond the *hrön*:
the narrator tells us that 'Stranger and more perfect than any *hrön* is the *ur*, which
is a thing produced by suggestion, an object brought into being by hope' (p. 11).
The *ur* is a conceptual object even further removed from the material world than
the *hrön* and thus, it seems, more real. In Tlön, 'real' objects are non-existent;
only ideal objects are real.

'Tlön, Uqbar, Orbis Tertius' is a hilarious send-up of Berkeleyan idealism, and
a send-up, too, of the very notion that ideas and objects can be so neatly separated.
Thus, in the postscript to this story, two Tlönian objects shed their ideal form to
take on material substance and intrude into the 'real' world of the narrator. These
objects, a compass and small metal cone, produce in Borges' narrator 'a feeling of
oppressiveness' and 'a disagreeable impression of repugnance and fear'; the
weight of the tiny cone is described as 'intolerable' and leaves a deep impression
on the palm of the narrator's hand (p. 16, p. 17). Objects, it seems, may magically
change their form and substance according to the world they occupy, but Borges'
narrator remains nostalgic for Tlön's ideal objects and repelled by its real ones.

I would propose that Borges, like the idealists in Tlön, is a universalizer who
must confront the same problem as they: he must write about ideal worlds in
material terms, and describe universals in the relentlessly specific medium of language. Recall that the speakers of Tlön have devised a strategy for dealing with
this problem by undermining the specificity of language: they create 'poetic
objects' by combining adjectives that circle around the thing itself but do not name
it. The narrator explains: 'The noun is formed by an accumulation of adjectives.
One does not say "moon"; but rather "round airy-light on dark" or "pale orange-
of-the-sky" or any other such combination' (p. 9). In Tlön these poetic objects *are*
real objects: we are told that '. . . no one believes in the reality of nouns . . . any
more than in the objects they designate', so they may proliferate and signify without limit. Language has been unanchored from a familiar reality and thus freed to
visualize the magical meanings that have been worn away by time.

This same strategy of circumlocution characterizes the kenning, the medieval
Germanic verbal figure of which Borges was so fond. In Borges' story, 'The
Zahir', the narrator is writing 'a tale of fantasy [that] contained two or three
enigmatic circumlocutions, or "kennings": for example, instead of *blood* it says
sword-water, and *gold* is the *serpent's bed* . . .'[20] This reference to the kenning
is not developed in 'The Zahir', but Borges had already written an essay on these

---

[20] Borges, 'The Zahir', trans. James E. Irby, in *Labyrinths* (New York: New Directions,
1962), p. 197.

'enigmatic circumlocutions' in his 1936 collection *History of Eternity*. He begins this essay by discussing the kennings in the Icelandic sagas of the thirteenth-century Icelandic writer Snorri Sturluson, then moves without transition to the Spanish Baroque poet Baltasar Gracián, whose paraphrastic structures he finds similar to Icelandic kennings in their avoidance of naming, and hence their avoidance of constaining specificity.

In the essay that I have already mentioned, 'Metaphor', from the same 1936 collection, Icelandic sagas are again the subject of Borges' attention. The question here is whether Snorri Sturluson's composite metaphors – his kennings – arise from the intuition of an analogy between *words* or *things*. We are not surprised to learn that Borges considers that they arise from language – from analogies among words – and he praises them for this reason. In his essay on Quevedo in *Other Inquisitions* (1952), he notes that '. . . the metaphor is the momentary contact of two images, not the methodical likening of two things'.[21] Similarly, he invents his own idealizing strategy of selecting adjectives that subvert the substantive nature of nouns: in 'The Circular Ruins', to take just one example, we find a number of insubstantial adjectives joined to nouns: the 'unanimous night', the 'incessant trees', the 'propitious temple', the 'inextricable jungle', the 'vain light of afternoon'.

A related form of 'enigmatic circumlocution' is mentioned in 'Narrative Art and Magic' (1932). This is one of Borges' most discussed essays, but only the second half of the essay has been given much critical attention, whereas it is the first half of the essay that is relevant to our purposes. Here, Borges contemplates at some length the nature of verbal description, more particularly the ways in which certain writers manage to create ideal objects in words. His examples are typically idiosyncratic, and the layers of unreality are typically dizzying, beginning with William Morris' ten thousand line poem 'Life and Death of Jason' (1867), a work that describes the fantastical objects of myth. How does Morris make the reader visualize the 'reality' of the centaur? According to Borges, he does so by referring to the centaur several times before it appears on the fictional scene, and, when it does appear, by describing him as 'a mighty horse, once roan, but now almost white, with long gray locks on his head and a wreath of oak leaves where man was joined to beast'.[22] As specific as this description seems, Borges at once blurs its realism: 'We note, in passing, that it is not essential that Morris give the reader his image of the centaur, or even invite us to have one of our own; what is required is our sustained belief in the fact that he had one' (p. 35). And what of the sirens that Morris also describes? Again Borges marvels at Morris' indirection, even as the poet describes the scene in seemingly realistic fashion: 'The very precision of Morris's colors – the yellow edges of the shore, the golden spray, the gray cliff – move us, for they seem rescued intact from that ancient evening' (p. 35). Borges praises the clarity of line and color of Morris'

[21] Borges, 'Quevedo', in *Other Inquisitions 1937–1952*, trans. Ruth L.C. Simms (Austin: University of Texas Press, 1964), p. 39.

[22] Borges, 'Narrative Art and Magic', trans. Norman Thomas di Giovanni, in *Borges: A Reader*, ed. Emir Rodríguez Monegal and Alastair Reid (New York: E.P. Dutton, 1981), p. 34.

verbal objects: they are like Sturluson's kennings, which we have already heard Borges describe as '. . . pure and independent like a crystal or a silver ring',[23]or like Quevedo's poems, which he describes as '. . . verbal objects, pure and independent like a sword or a silver ring'.[24] Borges proceeds to discuss the color white in Poe's *Narrative of Arthur Gordon Pym* and Melville's *Moby Dick*, and then, like Ortega y Gasset, he cites Mallarmé: 'Mallarmé is said to have remarked that naming an object outright is to suppress three-fourth of a poem's enjoyment, for the pleasure of reading is in anticipation, and the ideal lies in suggestion' (p. 36). If Ortega celebrates Mallarmé's poems themselves as 'small lyrical objects', Borges celebrates something else: Mallarmé's refusal to 'name an object outright' in favor of idealizing evocation.

There are many more strategies of removedness-from-the-real in Borges' fiction. Consider his Aleph and his sphere of Pascal: they are Tlön-like poetic objects made up of many terms that circle around their referent but do not name it. Put another way, these poetic objects are themselves the unnamable universe. Then there is Borges' fondness for allegory, that dual narrative structure in which absent, invisible narratives are more present than the ones we read. And again, there are Borges' parables of *failed* removedness-from-the-real: in 'The Zahir', it is the narrator's fate to be obsessed by a single object, a coin that he no longer possesses but cannot forget, an ideal object gone haywire, a mental image that eliminates all others. This character, like Funes the memorious, suffers from a visual dysfunction. His mind's eye is blinded by a single material object, as Funes is blinded by an infinite proliferation of objects. If 'Tlön, Uqbar, Orbis Tertius' takes idealism to its logical (and absurd) extreme, 'The Zahir' and 'Funes the Memorious' do the same with pragmatism. Recognizing this play of extremes, I would suggest – I already have – that it is the impossible, idealizing language of Tlön to which Borges himself aspires, and the utterly specific language of Funes that he works to subvert in all of his fiction. For Borges, the elusive essence of the real must be approached indirectly, through 'second degree' objects like *hrönir* or his own stories, which do not limit the real because they are strategically removed from it. The universe can only be envisioned, not seen: in Borges' stories, sight becomes insight only when the visible world is overcome.

García Márquez's Baroque Objects

> Household objects, in the fullness of their poetry, flew with
> their own wings through the kitchen sky.
>
> *Gabriel García Márquez*[25]

---

[23] Borges, 'La metáfora', in *Obras completas*, I, p. 382, my translation.

[24] Borges, 'Quevedo', in *Other Inquisitions*, p. 42.

[25] Gabriel García Márquez, 'Light is like Water', in *Strange Pilgrims*, trans. Edith Grossman (New York: Penguin Books, 1993), p. 160.

Whereas Borges explicitly addresses the visualizing capacity of language within his fictions, García Márquez does not, preferring to leave his readers to wonder whether to believe our eyes. If the idealist Borges refuses the magical content of real objects, preferring to locate his magic in 'secondary', Platonic, 'poetic objects', García Márquez's more realistic aesthetic allows for a visible world in which magic does indeed 'hide and palpitate' behind the real (to repeat Franz Roh's phrase). We have only to consider the ice and the magnets at the beginning of *One Hundred Years of Solitude* to find perfect Roh-ian objects. These objects – the ice, the magnets – are described as magical, and are endowed with inner lives. The ice mentioned in the justly famous first sentence of the novel is later described as '. . . an enormous, transparent block with infinite internal needles in which the light of the sunset was broken up into colored stars'.[26] And when José Arcadio becomes overly enthusiastic about the magical capacity of Melquíades' magnets, with which he hopes '. . . to extract gold from the bowels of the earth', Melquíades calms him down by assuring him that 'Things have a life of their own . . . . It's simply a matter of waking up their souls' (p. 11). Franz Roh could not have put it better. Macondo is filled with wonderment that is contained in, and expressed by, material objects.

But unlike the painted objects of the Post-Expressionists, which I have quoted Franz Roh as calling 'enigmas of quietude in the midst of general becoming' (p. 22), García Márquez's verbal objects are anything but quiet. The exuberant enumeration of material objects gives to García Márquez's fictional world a Baroque texture that is sensuous, ornate, dynamic, theatrical. Richness of narrative detail on an immense scale characterizes *One Hundred Years of Solitude*, *The Autumn of the Patriarch*, *Love in the Time of Cholera*, and it is this profusion of things, I am arguing, that gives to his novels their magical substratum. Countless examples could be offered, but here I will give only one, a passage from *Love in the Time of Cholera*, in which Fermina Daza finds herself in the Arcade of the Scribes – 'a place', we are told, 'of perdition that was forbidden to decent young ladies'.[27] Fermina nonetheless directs her steps to the Arcade: '. . . into the hot clamor of the shoeshine boys and the bird sellers, the hawkers of cheap books and the witch doctors and the sellers of sweets' (p. 101). Her attention is drawn to a paper seller hawking 'magic ink', and after considering a rainbow of colors she decides on a bottle of gold ink to write her love letters to Florentino, whereupon she proceeds to the stalls of the candy sellers and chooses six of every kind of candy – 'six angel hair, six tinned milk, six sesame seed bars, six cassava pastries, six chocolate bars, six blancmanges, six tidbits of the queen, six of this and six of that, six of everything' (p. 101) – until the colors and smells and tastes and sheer variety of endless things are said to cast a spell upon her.

---

[26] García Márquez, *One Hundred Years of Solitude*, trans. Gregory Rabassa (New York: Avon, 1970), p. 18.

[27] García Márquez, *Love in the Time of Cholera*, trans. Edith Grossman (New York: Knopf, 1988), p. 100.

Indeed, throughout García Márquez's work, proliferating objects cast spells –
ice, magnets, the tapestries so real that the hens peck at the embroidered plants,
the political enemy served for dinner like a suckling pig with an apple in his
mouth, hair that won't stop growing even after death; furthermore, these proliferating objects often signal prodigious appetites, or prodigious patience, or
prodigious evil, or any number of other prodigies. Excess is characteristic of
Baroque representation, but here my point is to distinguish García Márquez's
ontology of the image from Borges'; whereas Borges' enumerations are designed
to *avoid* naming objects and thus to diminish their material specificity, García
Márquez's enumerations are designed to create something like the opposite
effect: they are intended to *heighten* the specificity – and thus the magic – of their
materiality. For García Márquez as for Franz Roh, magic wells up from the world
as we know it.

Would García Márquez have read Franz Roh? I doubt it, despite their clear
affinities, but if the European avant garde was far removed from Aracataca, the
Baroque was not. In fact, García Márquez *has* acknowledged his debt to Baroque
aesthetics, and it is in this direction – toward the Baroque – that I want to head
in this third part of my essay. I have already noted that Franz Roh studied with
the essential theorist of Baroque aesthetics, Heinrich Wölfflin, and that his definition of 'magical realism' may have been influenced by Wölfflin's discussion
of Baroque aesthetics. Furthermore, the avant garde movements of the 1920s to
which I've already referred coincide with the resuscitation and revalorization of
Baroque art and literature in Europe and Latin America. Besides T.S. Eliot's
recuperation of the English Baroque poets, Federico García Lorca and Dámaso
Alonso were enthusiastically exhuming Spanish Baroque poetry (the Generation
of '27 refers to the tercentenary of Góngora's death in that year), as was the
Mexican intellectual Alfonso Reyes. In Germany, Walter Benjamin published his
book on the German Baroque theatre in 1928,[28] and Borges, too, was intensely
engaged in assessing his Baroque precursors during this period.[29] Perhaps, then,
I am justified in proposing the Baroque as one more branch of our magical-realist
family tree.

[28] Walter Benjamin, *The Origin of German Tragic Drama* (1928), trans. John Osborne
(London: Verso, 1977). This was Benjamin's only book-length study.

[29] Borges' first volume of prose, *Inquisiciones* (1925), contains three essays on Baroque
literature: 'Menoscabo y grandeza de Quevedo', 'Sir Thomas Browne', 'Milton y su
condenación de la rima'. His second, *El tamaño de mi esperanza* (1926) offers 'Examen de
un soneto de Góngora'. And of the fifteen essays in his third collection, *El idioma de los
argentinos* (1928), three are devoted to Baroque writers and subjects: 'El culteranismo', 'Un
soneto de don Francisco de Quevedo', and 'La conducta novelística de Cervantes', none of
which has yet been translated into English. There is also a dour little piece of four short
paragraphs entitled 'Para el centenario de Góngora' in which Borges affirms his distaste for
Góngora and his disdain for the excitement surrounding the tercentenary of his death. Borges
will eventually dismiss the Baroque altogether, though his admiration for Quevedo and
Cervantes will never wane.

It was Alejo Carpentier who first made explicit the connection between Baroque representation and American versions of magical realism. In his 1949 preface to his novel *The Kingdom of this World*, Carpentier referred to *lo real maravilloso americano*, which he defined in negative terms: it is *not* European and it is most especially *not* surrealism. In later interviews, he amplified his definition, saying that the marvelous real consists of '*the strange*, the singular, the unusual'.[30] But what is interesting for our purposes is that, almost immediately after 1949, he began to link his American marvelous real to the Baroque, eventually conflating the two in ways that render them virtually indistinguishable. Carpentier's engagement of a European art historical category – the Baroque – when he was, in fact, aiming to *differentiate* American cultural identity from European cultural models, is noteworthy, and the question is why?

It is my strong sense that Carpentier recognized the need for the Baroque as a counterbalance to his American marvelous real *not* for its elaborate ornamentation or for its dynamics of decentering or its theatrical space or its illusionism or its hyperbole – though all of these Baroque characteristics would prove useful; rather, I believe that he needed the Baroque for its realism. In interviews and essays, Carpentier repeatedly insists upon the realistic character of Baroque representation, and on the importance of Baroque realism to Latin American writers attempting to depict Latin America's histories and people. In a 1964 essay entitled 'Problematics of the Current Latin American Novel', Carpentier cites a contemporary poet as saying, '*Show* me the object; make it with your words so that I can *touch it, value it, feel its weight*', and then he adds, 'The object lives, is seen, lets its weight be felt. But the prose that gives life and substance, weight and measure [to the object] is a Baroque prose, a forcefully Baroque prose.'[31] Carpentier was a lifelong student of the visual arts and art history, and he knew perfectly well that Baroque realism aims not only to replicate the world but also (more importantly) to reveal an invisible realm beyond the real.

---

[30] See Carpentier y Ernesto González Bermejo, 'Alejo Carpentier: "Para mí terminaron los tiempos de la soledad" (1975), *Entrevistas*, p. 285. In this 1975 interview, Carpentier notes that his use of the terms '*maravilloso*' and '*barroco*' has become confused, and he offers clarifications of both. His definition of *lo maravilloso* is as follows:

> . . . lo maravilloso es – en realidad – *lo insólito*, lo singular, lo inhabitual, bello o feo, hermoso o terrible, jubiloso o lúgubre, dondequiera que se le halle . . . . Y no puede negarse que nuestra historia toda se caracteriza, desde sus inicios, por lo *insólito* de sus contingencias y peripecias. (p. 285, Carpentier's emphasis). . . the marvelous is, in reality, *the strange*, the singular, the unusual, beautiful or ugly, handsome or horrible, joyful or lugubrious, wherever it is found . . . . And it cannot be denied that our whole history is characterized from its beginning by the *strangeness* of its contingencies and peripeteias. (my translation, author's emphasis)

[31] Carpentier, 'Problemática de la actual novela latinoamericana', in *Tientos y diferencias* (1964; Montevideo: Editorial Arca, 1967), p. 36, author's emphasis.

The ontology and ideology of the Baroque image are rooted in seventeenth-century Counter Reformation Europe, of course, and during this period the Catholic Church was responding to Protestant attacks on a number of fronts, including iconoclasm. Reformers in northern Europe were destroying paintings, altars, and entire churches, and the Church answered by reaffirming the legitimacy of visual images in Catholic practice and reiterating their correct use.[32] Visual images, far from being obstacles to worship, as the Protestants contended, were understood as a means of visualizing the invisible. Images are *not* spirit themselves, and they certainly are not to be worshipped – that would be idolatry; rather visual images direct the believer to the contemplation of invisible truths. The activity of visualizing divinity became Counter Reformation policy, and the realistic depiction of the visible world became a means of bringing the beholder into mystical communion with disembodied spirit. In Baroque religious art, the phrase 'seeing is believing' is taken literally.

This form of realism, with its transcendental view of reality, was produced throughout Latin America in richly transculturated forms during the entire colonial period; the Baroque extends far longer in Latin America than in Europe – into the last quarter of the eighteenth century. Baroque iconography was the *lingua franca* of the time; visual images were crucial not only to devotional but also to educational purposes, so events and personages had to be clearly identifiable. Prescribed objects (or 'attributes') accompanied portraits of religious figures and communicated their life-and-death stories, as well as the nature of their sanctity. St Peter with his keys, Mary Magdalene with her vessel of oil, St Catherine of Alexandria with her broken wheel, the Mater Dolorosa with her daggers: these attributes are objective correlatives (Eliot's term is apt) that make interiority visible. In Baroque religious portraiture, subjectivity is externalized; human figures are at once individuals and archetypes; their singular stories are also allegories of human traits and tendencies.

The analogy that I'm suggesting to García Márquez's fiction is not that his work is religious or that it embodies Counter Reformation doctrine – far from it – but that his realism is Baroque in nature, and that the magic in his realism proceeds from a view of reality that is essentially Baroque. Consider García Márquez's characters, who are secular saints and martyrs and monsters in a Baroque mode. Can we say that fictional characters are 'objects' in the same sense as ice or magnets or cassava pastries? Certainly they proliferate in ways similar to García Márquez's objects, and they are often objectified by means of attributes and archetypes. In *One Hundred Years of Solitude*, think of the multiplying generations of Aurelianos and José Arcadios, the former all disembodied mind, the latter all erotic energy; or Remedios the Beauty, an archetype of

---

[32] For an excellent overview of contrasting Protestant and Catholic attitudes toward visual images, see Margaret R. Miles, *Images as Insight: Visual Understanding in Western Christianity and Secular Culture* (Boston: Beacon Press, 1985), especially Ch. 5, 'Vision and Sixteenth-Century Protestant and Roman Catholic Reforms', pp. 95–125.

innocence who is surely meant to recall the innumerable Baroque paintings of levitating beauties, whether the Virgin or the saints and angels who float and fly through infinite painted skies. Think, further, of the Patriarch, an archetype of evil in *The Autumn of the Patriarch*, or the amorous excesses of Florentino in *Love in the Time of Cholera*, excesses presented as saintly abstinence. For despite his six hundred and twenty-one women, we are told that Florentino remains a virgin because he loves only Fermina. Furthermore, he has suffered terribly for his devotion to her, suffering that is several times described as his martyrdom.

All of García Márquez's characters are objectified to a greater or lesser extent, and their psychological status is often related to the vivification and proliferation of objects. I have already mentioned several examples, and there are many more: Aureliano Buendía's little gold fishes, Ursula's carmel animals, the Patriarch's objectified body parts (feet like paws, whistling herniated testicle), Sierva María's African necklaces and her recurring dream of eating grapes in *Of Love and Other Demons*. In this regard, consider Octavio Paz's statement contrasting Romanticism and the Baroque, in which he argues that the former represents 'the apotheosis of the subject' and the latter 'the metamorphosis of the object':

> Although the baroque and romanticism are mannerist, the similarities between them cloak very profound differences. Each, reacting against classicism, pro-claimed an aesthetic of the abnormal and the unique; each presented itself as a transgression of norms. But while *the romantic transgression centers on the subject, the baroque transgression focuses on the object*. Romanticism liber-ates the subject; the baroque is the art of the metamorphosis of the object. Romanticism is passionate and passive; the baroque is intellectual and active. Romantic transgression culminates in the apotheosis of the subject or in its fall; baroque transgressions lead to the appearance of an unheard-of-object. Romantic poetics is the negation of the object through passion or irony; *the subject disappears in the baroque object*.[33]

I would propose that García Márquez's counterrealisim is based in part on his capacity to make 'the subject disappear in the baroque object'. He reaches back to a pre-Romantic conception of the self to create selves who are embedded in (sometimes stuck, sometimes rising above) their communal and material cul-tures. His subversion of the modern, singular, psychologized self revivifies the relations of subject and object, and in the process awakens the souls of things.

In this regard, let's return briefly to *Love in the Time of Cholera*. Fermina Daza is an avid collector of things, impelled, it seems, by the same *horror vacui* that characterizes Baroque expressive forms; absence co-exists with abundance as she attempts to fill the void of her marriage. Her world is like a Baroque still life, replete with objects described in such a way that, as in the Arcade of the Scribes,

[33] Octavio Paz, *Sor Juana or, The Traps of Faith*, trans. Margaret Sayers Peden (Cambridge: Harvard University Press, 1988), pp. 53–4, my emphasis.

not only the character but the reader wishes to reach out and touch, smell, taste. And at home, when there is no more space for her things, Fermina resorts to rearranging them but, the narrator tells us, 'Dr Urbino would laugh at her fruitless efforts, for he knew that the emptied spaces were only going to be filled again. But she persisted, because it was true that there was no room for anything else and nothing anywhere served any purpose . . . (pp. 300–1). After her husband's death, Fermina burns everything – she no longer needs to prove to herself that she wants for nothing – but her relation to objects is as it was before; they invade and possess her. The material world has more agency and independence than she does, and she remains an archetype, whether Daughter, Wife, Mother, or Beloved, surrounded by her identifying 'attributes', as Florentino remains an archetype of the Suffering Saint, surrounded by his. This is as it should be in García Márquez's fictional world; the self does not construct the world but is constructed by it. So the author reconstitutes subjectivity in relation to a sumptuous, sensuous, metamorphic world.

Conclusion

> I am convinced that the detective genre, like all genres, thrives on the continuous and delicate infraction of its rules.
>
> Jorge Luis Borges[34]

Borges and García Márquez are, then, equally concerned with the relations of the visible world to invisible meanings, but García Márquez gives priority to the former, from which he infers the latter, whereas Borges proceeds in the opposite direction, starting with the invisible, from which he infers the world. For Borges, ideas precede objects and generate them, whereas for García Márquez, the object *is* the idea. García Márquez's Baroque aesthetics coincide with Franz Roh's avant garde aesthetics in their shared insistence on the invisible meaning inherent in visible artifacts, whereas Borges' idealizing strategies subvert the magic of the material world in favor of the magic of 'secondary' objects, which liberate him from the constraints of the real.

And yet, despite their differences in style and substance, more unites Borges and García Márquez (and Carpentier) than separates them, for what they share, as I asserted at the outset, is their investment in contradictory forms of reality and their narrative modes. Each of these writers engages defamiliarizing strategies in order to renew his readers' appreciation of realism, and the real. How the many, sometimes-magical dimensions of the world can be visualized on the printed page is as urgent a question for Borges as it is for García Márquez.

---

[34] Borges, *Textos cautivos: ensayos y reseñas en El Hogar (1936–1939)*, ed. Enrique Sacerio-Garí and Emir Rodríguez Monegal (Barcelona: Tusquets Editores, 1986), p. 227.

Despite the emphasis of recent literary criticism – my own included – on the magical aspects of the mode, magical realism has, in fact, reinvigorated realistic modes of narration. In the past half century, magical realism has revitalized the novel itself, and we can expect that it will continue to enrich our experience of literary realism, and reality, for some time to come.

The Presence of Myth in Borges, Carpentier, Asturias, Rulfo and García Márquez

Donald L. Shaw

The only critical text which attempts to deal directly with the mythical roots of magical realism is Graciela Ricci's *Realismo mágico y conciencia mítica en América Latina* (Magical Realism and Mythic Consciousness in Latin America, 1983).[1] Unlike Seymour Menton in his *Historia verdadera del realismo mágico* (*True History of Magical Realism*, 1998)[2] she accepts both the 'marvelousness' which is alleged to be inherent in external reality and the marvelousness which derives from the act of perception on the part of a certain category of viewers. Following Carpentier, in his famous prologue to *El reino de este mundo (The Kingdom of This World*, 1949) she affirms that the elements which compose the former are especially prominent in Latin America. But it is the latter which is her main concern; for she contends that the particular form of perception which Carpentier includes under the heading of 'fé' (faith) is in fact a special form of insight 'un tipo de conocimiento sapiencial' (a kind of cognitive knowledge, p. 32), even a 'percepción de la Realidad Nouménica' (perception of Noumenal Reality; Ricci, p. 33). She goes on to assert that this special faculty is deeply rooted in the collective Latin American psyche and manifests itself most visibly in magical-realist narrative. We are left, then, with the notion of a culture-specific pattern of writing in which certain myths are used to bring forth hidden truths. This is simply affirmed as a mystique, that is, without proof, and should not be taken at face value. An inspection of magical-realist narrative reveals something quite different: the mythical elements incorporated into it are not normally there for any truths intrinsic to the myths themselves. On the contrary, they are devices employed by the writers in question to function as a relatively new and effective way of expressing their own attitudes and ideas. This is a crucial distinction.

---

[1] Graciela Ricci, *Realismo mágico y conciencia mítica en América Latina* (Mila: CELA, 1983).
[2] Seymour Menton, *Historia verdadera del realismo mágico* (Mexico: Fondo de Cultura Económica, 1998).

Jorge Luis Borges

On this basis one would normally expect that the myths which the Latin American magical-realist authors make use of would be borrowed from specifically Latin American (presumably indigenous or popular) sources. But this is not always the case. Depending on how comprehensive a view of magical realism one chooses to take, there are really three kinds of myth which come into play: Classical, Christian and indigenous Latin American. Consideration of the first raises the vexed question of whether Borges can or should be classified as a magical-realist writer. Discussion of this issue remains inconclusive. But it is clear that only the narrowest definition of magical realism, such as that of Camayd-Freixas,[3] which relates it almost exclusively to the magico-mythical outlook of the indigenous peoples of Latin America, could exclude him completely. In fact he has been associated with the movement since the term magical realism was originally popularized in Latin American Studies in 1955 by Ángel Flores.[4] The reason is obvious: whether we accept that the 'marvelous' elements of magical realism inhere in reality itself, American or otherwise, or whether we see them as deriving from a certain form of perception, or as merely improbable and sometimes supernatural, we can find them in Borges's stories. His relationship to magical realism rests on his view that, in a world which we are not programmed to understand 'toda estrafalaria cosa es posible' (anything, however outlandish, is possible; *Discusión, Discussion 1932 O.C.*, p. 238).[5] One of the most obvious examples appears at the end of 'El Sur' in *Ficciones (Fictions*, 1944). Menton, in the second chapter of his 1998 book, 'Los cuentos de Jorge Luis Borges ¿fantásticos o mágicorrealistas?' (Jorge Luis Borges's Short Stories: Are They Fantastic or Magical-Realist?), totally fails to understand the mythic stature of the old gaucho who helps Dahlman to make his final and probably fatal choice by throwing him a knife with which to fight the young red-neck who has insulted him. He is not simply an improbable or unexpected onlooker: his *chiripá* and *botas de potro*, items of traditional gaucho dress unthinkable in twentieth-century Argentina, and the description of him as 'como fuera del tiempo' (as if outside time) mark him as figuring the myth of Argentine-ness which is crucial to the level of interpretation of the story which concerns Dahlman's choice between his German and Argentine roots. A somewhat less strong case might be made for the mythicization of Cruz in 'Biografía de Tadeo Isidoro Cruz' (Biography of Tadeo Isidoro Cruz) in *El Aleph (The Aleph,* 1949) in the light of Borges's obvious intention to relate him to a prominent aspect of the myth of an Argentine national character, as he explains in 'Nuestro pobre individualismo' (Our Poor Individualism) in *Otras inquisiciones (Other Inquisitions, O.C.* 1974, pp. 658–9).

---

[3] Erik Camayd-Freixas, *Realismo mágico y primitivismo* (Lanham, New York & Oxford: University Press of America, 1998).

[4] Ángel Flores, 'Magical Realism in Spanish American Fiction', *Hispania*, 38 (1955), 187–92.

[5] Jorge Luis Borges, *Obras completas 1923–1972* (Buenas Aires: Emecé, 1974).

It is not necessary for the myths employed by the Latin American magical-realists to be so intrinsically Latin American. Both Borges and Carpentier also use Classical myths. A notable case in the former's work is 'La Casa de Asterión' (The House of Asterion) in *El Aleph*, which uses the myth of the Minotaur to interpret in this case, not so much Latin American reality, but the state of the universe. It has been argued, notably by Alazraki, that Asterión represents Everyman and his labyrinth the world.[6] But I have suggested elsewhere that the details do not fit.[7] Rather, Borges seems to be using the myth of the Minotaur to explore the loneliness, misery and self-hatred of those who consciously choose evil and destruction as a way to give direction to their lives. Thus the submissiveness of Asterión to Theseus presents in mythical guise the fragile foundations on which dedication to evil and violence (in Borges's opinion) ultimately rests. More interestingly perhaps, the story contains an unexpected shift from Classical mythology to a Redemption myth presented via references to the Bible and to the Lord's Prayer. But Theseus's slaughter of the Minotaur shows that Borges has inverted the myth, as Asturias also does in *El Señor Presidente* (*Mr President*, 1946), Rulfo in *Pedro Páramo* (1955), Roa Bastos in *Hijo de hombre* (*Son of Man*, 1960) and Donoso in *El lugar sin límites* (*Hell has no Limits*, 1966). We must also notice Borges's use, in some stories, including 'El jardín de senderos que se bifurcan' (The Garden of Forking Paths, *Ficciones*), 'La muerte y la brújula' (Death and the Compass, *Ficciones*), 'Tema del traidor y del héroe' (Theme of the Traitor and the Hero, *Ficciones*) and 'El inmortal' (The Immortal, *El Aleph*) of the myth of circular time, which was to reappear in García Márquez's *Cien años de soledad* (*One Hundred Years of Solitude*, 1967). Not all of the above-mentioned texts qualify as magical-realist. What they illustrate is that magical-realist works share with others the use of myth, not only as a vehicle for commentary, but also as a structuring principle of the narrative.

Alejo Carpentier

Carpentier, as we have suggested, does not always use magical realism in the same way. In 'Viaje a la semilla' (Journey Back to the Source) a genuinely supernatural event takes place. But in *El reino de este mundo* the events which nourish one of the most astonishing rebellions in history are rooted in something else: the collective faith of the blacks in a wider dimension of reality than Western rationalism accepts. In Haiti, Carpentier was suddenly struck, not so much by the marvelousness of what he saw around him in 1943, but by the marvelousness of Haitian history in the period of the French Revolution and the rise to power of Henri Cristophe. Part of the magical realism of *El reino de este mundo* derives simply from Carpentier's evocation of this astonishingly improbable process.

---

[6] Jaime Alazraki, 'Thön y Asterión: metáforas epistemológicas', in *Jorge Luis Borges. El escritor y la crítica* (Madrid: Taurus, 1976), pp. 183–200.

[7] *Borges's Narrative Strategy* (Leeds: Francis Cairns, 1992), p. 5.

But a second dimension of magical realism in the novel arises from his presentation of the magico-mythical as a major element in the dynamic, which drove the process forward. Mackandal, from being a crippled slave, is transformed into a *haugán*, a miracle-working representative of the black divinities, who, the blacks believe, save him from being burned alive. The Mackandal-myth, illustrating the superiority of the 'viviente cosmogonía del negro' (living cosmogony of the negro)[8] over the beliefs of the whites, operates after his death to ensure the triumph of the slave revolt. Once more, this is not a case of a myth that is featured in the narrative because of its expression of some deeper truth. In fact Carpentier is at pains to insist that Mackandal actually does suffer the fate that his followers believe he escaped; the myth is an illusion. Carpentier makes use of it to illustrate the important role often played by collective faith, even when it is without foundation, in bringing about historical change.

By far the most important example of the inter-connection of magical realism and myth in Carpentier's work is to be found in *Los pasos perdidos* (*The Lost Steps*, 1953). Like Rulfo's *Pedro Páramo*, Carpentier's novel incorporates a quest which can be seen in terms of Classical mythology. If Juan Preciado can be perceived as a Telemachus-figure, in *Los pasos perdidos* we can recognize a Jason in the narrator, when early in the story, in Mouche's study, he mentions Jason's ship, the Argo. Vassar, in a cogent study, has identified allusions to four other specific Greek myths in the novel: the Sisyphus story, the tale of Prometheus, the *Odyssey* journey and the myth of Orpheus.[9] It is not surprising that although Camayd-Freixas includes Carpentier as one of only four writers he is prepared to accept as true magical-realists, he ignores *Los pasos perdidos*: it does not reflect the primitive outlook of Indians, blacks and rural peasants which he regards as the only valid criterion for belonging to the movement. Once more, as Vassar correctly understands, it is not simply a case of identifying parallels, interesting as these are; the real question is one of function. As we have seen, one important function of myth in magical-realist narrative is to provide a structural principle. Barry sees the mythical past figured forth in the *Odyssey* as providing the basic structural pattern in *Los pasos perdidos*.[10] But it is the other function, that of acting as a method of commentary, bringing out the deeper meaning of the novel, that Vassar emphasizes. At times, she argues, the treatment of myth in the novel seems to postulate a circularity in which 'the cycle not only traps man, but also destroys him'. But at other times 'myth, rather than being a destructive force, is perceived as that which is being destroyed' (p. 216). Recognizing, along with a number of other critics, that Carpentier, far from accepting a repetitive, cyclic vision of history, believed in a slow upward spiral of progress, she concludes that the message conveyed by the treatment of myth in *Los pasos perdidos*

---

[8] Alejo Carpentier, *El reino de este mundo* (Santiago de Chile: Universitaria, 1969), p. 87.

[9] Anne Vassar, 'The Function of Greek Myth in Alejo Carpentier's *Los pasos perdidos*', *Neophilologus*, 76 (1992), 212–23.

[10] John Barry, 'Tiempo mítico en la novela contemporánea', *Explicación de Textos Literarios*, 11.2 (1982–83), 69–79 (pp. 73–4).

is that 'Modern humanity may not be completely free from the mythic cycle, but it is not operating in a totally closed system where myths are destined to exact repetition' (p. 221). This is one of the clearest accounts of the role of myth in a specific magical-realist novel that we possess.

Miguel Ángel Asturias

In the case of Asturias, we have to distinguish between his use of mythological elements for explicit social and existential commentary, as in *El Señor Presidente* (1946) and his use of Central American mythology in *Hombres de maíz* (*Men of Maize*, 1949) and *Mulata de tal* (*A Certain Mulatto Woman*, 1963). Whether we are prepared to accept *El Señor Presidente* as a magical-realist novel or not depends very largely on the degree to which we think that in it Asturias depicts a Central American dictatorship in magico-mythical terms. Before the crucial articles of Yepes Boscán and Osorio it was possible to see *El Señor Presidente* basically as a novel of protest against presidential tyranny.[11] But the work of these two critics and others (such as Verdugo and Walker) has totally altered the interpretation of the work from that of one more protest against brutal power to that of an allegory of the human condition.[12] The central structuring myths of the novel are those of Tohil, a non-redemptive, cruel and bloodthirsty tribal God of Central America, and the myth of Lucifer, which, in a world dominated by Tohil, is ironically reversed. The figure of El Pelele ('INRI-idiota'; INRI-idiot) is clearly intended to parody that of Christ, just as Cara de Angel's fate parodies that of Lucifer. While the above-mentioned critics are not specifically concerned with the work as magical-realist, the mythical elements that they identify, together with the work's general atmosphere, link it closely with magical realism.

El Señor Presidente is, in fact, the first major novel to illustrate Camayd-Freixas's assertion that 'El arte de Carpentier y Asturias, como más tarde el de Rulfo y García Márquez, descubre en las funciones del mito posibles confluencias de lo autóctono y lo universal' (The art of Carpentier and Asturias, as later on that of Rulfo and García Márquez, discovers in the myth possible convergences of the autochthonous and the universal, p. 11). His affirmation on the same page that this constitutes an 'americanismo de la forma' (americanism of form) is, however, only half-true, since the myths the magical realists make use of include Classical and biblical ones. But what a mythical reading of *El Señor Presidente* fully confirms is that in magical realism it is normally not what the myths are, but what they are

---

[11] Nelson Osorio, 'Lenguaje narrativo y estructura significativa de *El Señor Presidente* de Asturias', *Escritura* (Caracas), 5/6 (1978), 99–156; Guillermo Yepes-Boscán, 'Asturias, un pretexto del mito', *Aportes*, 8 (1968), 100–16.

[12] Iber Verdugo, '*El Señor Presidente*, lectura estructural', in Miguel Ángel Asturias, *El Señor Presidente, Obras completas* (Paris and Mexico: Klincksieck and Fondo de Cultura Económica, 1978), III, pp. clv–ccxii; John Walker, 'The Role of the Idiot in Asturias' *El Señor Presidente*', *Romance Notes*, 12 (1970), 1–6.

used for, that matters. Even when in *Hombres de maíz* and *Mulata de tal* autochthonous myths are employed to represent a pre-modern outlook and render it interesting and comprehensible to the modern reader, introducing him or her to the otherness of native Latin Americans as part of the area's marvelousness, there still emerges, as Prieto insists, a blend of 'Mayan mythology, surrealist rhetoric, and, above all, [Asturias's] keenly developed sociopolitical consciousness'.[13] Similarly, Gerald Martin, in the section on myth in his comprehensive study of *Hombres de maíz*, concludes that 'Asturias, al tratar los mitos, pretende enseñarnos las relaciones materiales entre la evolución de los mitos y el desarrollo de la sociedad' (Asturias, when he handles myths, attempts to reveal to us the material relationships between the evolution of the myths and social development).[14]

Juan Rulfo

Rulfo's *Pedro Páramo* (1955), which is sometimes compared to Asturias's *El Señor Presidente* because of the mythical presentation of the two central figures, confirms what we have seen so far. The principal difference between Rulfo on the one hand and Asturias and Carpentier on the other is that while the latter relate some of the mythical elements in the relevant parts of their work to the indigenous Indian outlook or to that of the Caribbean blacks, Rulfo situates them simply in rural Jalisco. Once more we can identify the presence of Classical, biblical and local myths. Thus Camayd-Freixas's contention that Rulfo resolves the contradiction he sees in Carpentier and Asturias, between a cultured narrator and the primitive outlook of the characters, falls to the ground: the mythical substructure of the novel is just as indebted to Western culture as was the case in the work of the other two novelists. But there is no need to postulate a contradiction: the authocthonous mythical elements provide an Americanist dimension to the texts while the Classical and biblical ones provide a more universal one.

Like the President in *El Señor Presidente*, *Pedro Páramo* represents a myth of omnipotence. This has been interpreted by Ferrer Chivite and others in terms of the almighty (oppressive) Mexican state, i.e. as the mythicization of a historical situation.[15] But, equally, there are other levels of myth involved. Given Paz's assertion in *El laberinto de la soledad* (p. 18) that all Mexican history is dominated by a search for 'filiación' (filiation), Juan Preciado's quest can be seen as a search for a mythic Mexican national identity.[16] Carlos Fuentes in *La nueva novela hispanoamericana* (*The New Spanish American Novel*, p. 16) has noticed

---

[13] René Prieto, *Miguel Angel Asturias: Archeology of Return* (Cambridge: Cambridge University Press, 1993), p. 249.

[14] 'Estudio general' in Miguel Angel Asturias, *Hombres de maíz, Obras completas* (Paris and Mexico: Klincksieck and Fondo de Cultura Económica, 1981), IV, pp. xxi-ccxliv (p. ccxlii).

[15] Manuel Ferrer Chivite, *El laberinto de México de/en Juan Rulfo* (Mexico: Novarro, 1972).

[16] Octavio Paz, *El laberinto de la soledad* (Mexico: Fondo de Cultura Económica, 1982).

obvious links with Greek mythology.[17] The notion of the dead surviving as 'ánimas en pena' (souls in torment) is borrowed from popular mythology. Above all, George Freeman (p. 68) has identified in the pivotal episode of the incestuous couple in the centre of the novel 'sugerencias que se relacionan con el relato bíblico de la caída de la gracia del hombre' (suggestions that are related to the biblical story of man's fall from grace).[18] Like *El Señor Presidente*, *Pedro Páramo* incorporates a mythico-religious metaphor of the human condition. But it is a metaphor that parodies Christian beliefs by inverting them.[19] Juan Preciado's return to Comala, which he thinks of as green and fertile under his father's rule, plainly alludes to man's search for a loving, fatherly God presiding over a lost edenic existence. What he finds instead is a hell dominated by a cruel and vengeful, all powerful, God-figure, inhabited by lost souls for whom even death brings no peace, and by an incestuous Adam-and-Eve couple who represent a parody of the Genesis-myth. Whereas the Christian conception is that of a God of love, Pedro Páramo is ironically pictured as a God yearning for love but denied it. Whereas God is thought of in the West as sending his only son to redeem men by sacrificing his life for them, Miguel Páramo is seen as a rapist and ne'er-do-well, and Pedro is murdered by another of his sons in a transparent reference to the Death of God. Once the mythic substructure of the novel is understood, it ceases to be the work viewed by Mexicanist critics as an unconvincing Beauty-and-the-Beast story transferred to a pseudo-realistic Mexican rural setting and tricked out with gimmickry borrowed from the Mexican cult of death. Instead it incorporates, like *El Señor Presidente*, a parodic mythico-religious metaphor of the Human Condition.

Gabriel García Márquez

Almost all critics who have dealt with the presence of myth in magical realism have recognized in García Márquez's *Cien años de soledad* the work in which that presence is most obtrusive and developed. On the one hand, it operates to challenge a positive vision of Columbian and by extension Latin American history by reducing it to a succession of repetitive cycles. As Lucila Mena (p. 131) puts it: 'La linealidad de la historia desemboca en la circularidad del mito' (the linearity of history leads into the circularity of myth).[20] On the other hand, once more by incorporating biblical elements, it attempts to confer universal significance on the story of Macondo. Camayd-Freixas (p. 273) suggests that the net

[17] Carlos Fuentes, *La nueva novela hispanoamericana* (Mexico: Mortiz, 1972).

[18] George Freeman, 'La caída de la gracia: clave arquetípico de *Pedro Páramo*', in *La narrativa de Juan Rulfo*, ed. Joseph Sommers (Mexico: Sepsetentas, 1974), pp. 67–87.

[19] See Donald L. Shaw, 'Inverted Christian Imagery and Symbolism in Modern Spanish American Fiction', *Romance Studies*, 10 (1987), 71–82.

[20] Lucila Mena, *La función de la historia en 'Cien años de soledad'* (Barcelona: Plaza y Janes, 1979).

result is to present the reader of *Cien años de soledad* with examples of 'el mito degradado' (degraded myth). But this is not quite accurate. Myth in García Márquez's novel is no more 'degraded' that it is in *El Señor Presidente* or *Pedro Páramo*. What Camayd-Freixas seems to be referring to is the now familiar process by which magical-realist authors use mythical elements to express, in this case, a negative vision of reality.

Where we see this emerge prominently at an earlier date is in 'Los funerales de la Mamá Grande' (Big Mama's Funeral, 1962) in which García Márquez employs the death of the mythicized figure of la Mamá Grande to depict the end of the feudal era in Colombian history. The magical-realist dimension of the story is created by the apparently straight-faced enunciation by the narrator of the incredible power and wealth of La Mamá, which are believed to extend to the ownership of every telegraph pole in the country, all present and future water-rights and even the regulation of the sunshine. The mythical figure thus evoked is then carnavalized for purposes of socio-political commentary. But, as in *Cien años de soledad*, behind the hilarity lies a deep and bitter pessimism. La Mamá and her unequalled patrimony have passed away, but it will take centuries to clear up the mess her passing has left behind.

This is a specifically Americanist myth. But in *Cien años de soledad* the frame of reference is greatly extended. González Echevarría (p. 19) writes:

> It seems clear that myth appears in the novel in the following guises: (1) there are stories that resemble classical or biblical myths, most notably the Flood, but also Paradise, the Seven Plagues, the Apocalypse, and the proliferation of the family, which with its complicated genealogy, has an Old Testament ring to it; (2) there are characters who are reminiscent of mythical heroes: José Arcadio Buendía, who is a sort of Moses; Rebecca, who is like a female Perseus; Remedios, who ascends in a flutter of white sheets in a scene that is suggestive, not just of the Ascension of the Virgin, but more specifically of the popular renditions of that event in religious prints; (3) certain stories have a general mythic character in that they contain supernatural elements, as in the case just mentioned, and also when José Arcadio's blood returns to Ursula; (4) the beginning of the whole story, which is found, as in myth, in a tale of violence and incest. All four, of course, co-mingle, and because *Cien años de soledad* tells a tale of foundations or origins, the entire novel has a mythical air about it. No single myth or mythology prevails.[21]

Nor does any interpretation of the mythical elements in the novel prevail. Everything depends on the meaning we ascribe to the Apocalypse at the end: the Rushing, Mighty Wind that carries Macondo away from the face of the earth. To some critics what matters is that the biblical myths, which structure the text, do not involve a myth of final Redemption. Mena, Williamson and others see history

---

[21] Roberto González Echevarría, *Myth and Archive. A Theory of Latin American Narrative* (Cambridge: Cambridge University Press, 1990).

as finally devoured by myth.[22] Gerald Martin, on the other hand, insists that the myths exist in the minds of the characters, rather than in the mind of the author and that critics fail to differentiate between the two.[23] García Márquez is on record as stating 'la realidad es también los mitos de la gente, es las creencias, es sus leyendas' (reality is also people's myths, it is their beliefs, it is their legends; quoted in Kline, p. 125).[24] It can be argued that when Gabriel leaves Macondo at the end, he escapes from its mythical mentality and achieves what Williamson (p. 60) calls 'salvation'.

Clearly, myth has at least three important functions in magical-realist narratives. It offers, in certain cases a novel, exotic, primitive vision of reality in the context of what Camayd-Freixas (p. 215) calls 'América como encuentro imprevisto de culturas' (America as an unforseen meeting-place of cultures). But behind this we perceive its use by the various authors to express their outlook on aspects of Latin American reality, including myths of nationality and mythic representations of socio-political or historical forces for purposes of interpretation, criticism or protest. Finally, we find myths employed to express the author's wider view of the Human Condition generally.

---

[22] Edwin Williamson, 'Magical Realism and the Theme of Incest in *One Hundred Years of Solitude*', in *Gabriel García Márquez. New Readings*, eds Bernard McGuirk and Richard Cardwell (Cambridge: Cambridge University Press, 1987), pp. 45–63.

[23] Gerald Martin, 'On "Magical" and Social Realism in García Márquez', in *Gabriel García Márquez. New Readings*, pp. 95–116.

[24] Carmenza Kline, *Los orígenes del relato: los lazos entre ficción y realidad en la obra de Gabriel García Márquez* (Bogotá: Ceiba, 1992).

The Earth as Archive
in Bombal, Parra, Asturias and Rulfo

Julia King and Stephen M. Hart

The term 'archive' is common currency in criticism on Latin American litera-ture,[1] and especially in the analysis of magical realism.[2] The term has often been used to locate early twentieth-century Latin American novels in relation to their successors during the 1960s Boom generation. In this way the archive constitutes a residual reference point from which the so-called Latin American legacy[3] can be extracted. In this essay, however, the term 'archive' takes on a different mean-ing, becoming an active source which cannot be conceived of in its entirety. It is an archive similar to that referred to by Foucault since it 'emerges in fragments, regions and levels' and its

> threshold of existence is established by the discontinuity that separates us from what we can no longer say, and from that which falls outside our discursive practice; it begins with the outside of our language (*langage*).[4]

The archive is oblique and the authors studied here locate it within nature. In fact archive as embodied in the earth becomes a subterranean *tesoro* (treasure) which the writers excavate with the tools of imagination and language. Since Foucault conceives of archive as active and a life-source on its own terms, nature is a par-ticularly appropriate embodiment of this idea and, as we shall see, is employed pre-cisely to demonstrate the visceral materiality of life and death, culture and myth.

---

[1] See Roberto González Echeverría, *Myth and Archive: A Theory of Latin American Narrative* (Cambridge: Cambridge University Press, 1990).

[2] See Ángel Rama, *La transculturación narrativa en América Latina* (México: Siglo Veintiuno, 1982).

[3] Magical realism was originally conceived of as a literary or artistic style which had its roots in the particulars of the Latin American social, natural and cultural landscape. The earlier writing lay the foundations for these specific indicators of Latin Americanness. For a fuller discussion on this point, see Ángel Rama, *La ciudad letrada* (Hanover, NH: Ediciones del Norte, 1984).

[4] Michel Foucault, *The Archaeology of Knowledge*, translated by A.M. Sheridan Smith, (London: Routledge, 1989), p. 130.

The texts studied here were written by María Luisa Bombal, Teresa de la Parra, Miguel Ángel Asturias and Juan Rulfo. While texts by the latter two authors are seen by most critics as paradigms of magical realism, the work of the other two authors – despite Flores's suggestion in 1955 that Bombal's 'oneiric stories' were direct precursors of magical realism's 'magnificent flowering'[5] – are nowadays seen as only tangentially related to the movement; they nevertheless provide important new insights into the pre-history of magical realism.

1: María Luisa Bombal

Viewing earth as archive is especially revealing when considering the work of María Luisa Bombal. Critics have yet to uncover her literary archive and little is known about the writers or literary traditions which influenced her work. The most striking literary genre which permeates her work is Romanticism. Women in Romantic texts are often objectified, petrified: a common trope for French Romantic poets such as Baudelaire is the perfection of a woman's petrified, death-like state.[6] Images of Nature proliferate in Bombal's work and there are instances when women are depicted as beautiful, muse-like creatures as, for example, when the protagonist of *La última niebla* is seen bathing in the lake by a man passing by through the woods in a horse-drawn carriage.[7] An important distinction must be drawn between Bombal and the Romantics, however, despite their common interest in natural motifs. Bombal inverts the subject-object relationship, whether the key term is woman or nature, and offers the reader an insight into the interiorised landscape of both. Their living roots and originary sources are made manifest, and are no longer a superficial veneer seen through the Romantic gaze. The most explicit example of this inversion of the subject/object dichotomy is found in *La amortajada* (*The Shrouded Woman*) where the protagonist, Ana María, is a dead woman covered in a shroud. For the male Romantic artist this would be an image of the petrified woman in her moment of perfection when she can be dominated and mastered by the masculine gaze. But Bombal does not allow this to happen and the dead body becomes a subject with memories, and gains power over men on re-entering the womb of the earth at the end of the novel. On entering the site of her burial the reader is offered a privileged view of the earth from a subterranean vantage-point. The

---

[5] Ángel Flores, 'Magical Realism in Spanish American Fiction', *Hispania*, 38.2 (1955), 187–9, is quoted here via the reprinted version in *Magical Realism: Theory, History, Community*, eds Lois Parkinson Zamora and Wendy B. Faris (Durham, NC: Duke University Press, 1995), pp. 109–17 (p. 113).

[6] See by way of example, 'Une Charogne' and 'Alchimie de la douleur', in *Les Fleurs du Mal*, ed. Raymond Decesse (Paris: Bordas, 1971), pp. 64–5, and p. 107.

[7] María Luisa Bombal; *La última niebla, La amortajada* (Barcelona: Seix Barral, 2001), p. 26.

fusion of Ana María with the earth is significant since it is one of the many instances in Bombal's work where the subjectivity of women is activated, aligned and often merged with the earth; in so doing Nature is feminised.

Interestingly the only texts which Bombal claims to have had a strong impact on her are the fairy tales which her mother read to her as a child. *La última niebla* demonstrates an interiorised deposit of fairy tales to be generated and drawn out. If Bombal had an archive of some sort it would appear to have been a personal, interiorised and almost subterranean archive linked to the spirit of femininity. Catherine Boyle writes: 'When she [Bombal] was in fact asked about the intentions of her work, if she had intended to denounce the role of women in society, she would reply: "Yo tenía pasión por lo personal, lo interno, el corazón, el arte, la naturaleza. No yo no perseguía nada . . ." ' (I was passionate about the personal, the inner world, the heart, art, nature. I wasn't pursuing anything . . .).[8]

The main objective behind Bombal's work appears to be the desire to depict an uncovered *tesoro* which would chart the interiorised space of feminine imagination. Every one of her stories or novels, except for *Lo secreto* (*The Secret Part*), revolves around a female protagonist who is depicted as having a supernatural connection with the earth, and natural images become a backdrop for a journey into the feminine imagination. Bombal said, as quoted above by Catherine Boyle, that she was not interested in denouncing women's position in society, which may have been so. This does not invalidate her work in the context of Latin American women's writing; Bombal seeks to unearth the foundations of an as yet uncharted feminine archive. Evidently her work cannot oppose all those conceits surrounding femininity left by various literary movements such as Romanticism but what is important is that we view the feminine archive from within, from a female subject's point of view.[9]

Nature is an important character in many of Bombal's stories and novels. However the stage for natural landscapes is often truncated; it is the garden, a lone tree outside Brígida's window, the hacienda grounds, not the vast pampas traversed by people on horseback or the endless labyrinth of the jungle.[10] Bombal's depictions of nature are domesticated since they reflect woman's physical immobility. Having said that, her depiction of nature is infused with a sense of mystery, myth and magic so that it is elevated beyond the purely functional plane of the domestic sphere; a fusion of domesticity with the transcendental powers of the imagination.

---

[8] Catherine Boyle, 'The Fragile Perfection of the Shrouded Rebellion (Re-reading Passivity in María Luisa Bombal)', in *Women Writers in Twentieth-Century Spain and Spanish America*, ed. Catherine Davies (London: The Edwin Mellen Press, 1993), pp. 27–42 (p. 37). Translation provided by authors unless otherwise specified.

[9] For further discussion of the feminine archive, see Emilie Bergmann *et al*, *Women, Culture, and Politics in Latin America* (Berkeley: University of California Press, 1990).

[10] This refers to the tropes in the *novela de la tierra* tradition; see Doris Sommer, *Foundational Fictions: The National Romances of Latin America* (Berkeley: University of California Press, 1991) for further discussion; in particular see p. 259, p. 391 n. 7.

That the natural world is familiarised and personalised is demonstrated by its proximity to the domestic sphere. More typically, though, the earth stands in for the female protagonist's subjectivity; nature becomes emblematic of a feminine interior landscape or 'inscape'. In *La última niebla* it is never clear whether it is the trickery of the mist or of the protagonist's imagination which shrouds the story in mystery and uncertainty; they are often one and the same thing. Lucía Guerra Cunningham has commented on the 'búsqueda' that takes place in Bombal's work, stating: 'Sin embargo, es importante notar que, a diferencia de un héroe problemático como Don Quijote, quien se enfrenta al mundo en una búsqueda hacia afuera, la aventura de nuestra protagonista tiene las característi- cas de una búsqueda interior, alejada de un verdadero enfrentamiento' (However, it is important to underline that, unlike a problematic hero such as Don Quixote who confronts the world in a search which is directed towards the external world, the adventure of our protagonist is characterised by a journey inwards which does not involve any real confrontation).[11] This observation by Lucía Guerra is particularly revealing since it alludes to an interior journey. The novels written by men during this period often revolved around a journey into the Latin American outback in search of the 'true' Latin American archive.[12] This legacy suggests that images of nature could be associated with the idea of a journey; in Bombal's novel, though, it is a journey into female subjectivity. The natural images are signposts as the protagonist travel deeper into a feminine memory, archive and identity. The protagonist of *La última niebla* explores the natural world around her and in doing so discovers consciousness of her identity, her body and her sexuality.

Archive as documented memory is something which has only become available to women relatively recently.[13] At the time when Bombal was working she had to draw on myth and mystical impulses similar to the partially attainable archive described by Foucault to discover a feminine archive which would help her bet- ter understand women's subjectivity. The imagined or mythical archive is high- lighted in *Las islas nuevas*[14] where Yolanda is depicted as a mythical relic from a previous era. She dreams of 'helechos gigantes' from her experience in some kind of primordial, pre-socialised space, and her atrophic wing is symbolic of severance from that space and the excision of female memory or archive therein. That the memory being archived and documented by Bombal should be

---

[11] Lucía Guerra Cunningham, *La narrativa de María Luisa Bombal: una visión de la existencia femenina* (Madrid: Nova Scholar, 1980), p. 51.

[12] For further discussion see Gerald Martin, *Journeys Through the Labyrinth: Latin American Fiction in the Twentieth Century* (London: Routledge, 1989); Doris Sommer, *Foundational Fictions*; and Roberto González Echeverría, *The Voice of the Masters: Writing and Authority in Modern Latin American Literature* (Austin, TX: University of Texas Press, 1985).

[13] For further discussion see Francine Masiello, 'Women, State, and Family in Latin American Literature of the 1920s', in Emilie Bergmann *et al*, *Women, Culture, and Politics in Latin America* (Berkeley: University of California Press, 1990), pp. 27–47.

[14] Bombal: *La amortajada*, pp. 71–92.

mythical, derived from her own literary experience with fables and fairy tales, does not invalidate it. Indeed many of her contemporaries also draw on popular myth, folklore and the myths of pre-Hispanic origins to create an autochthonous Latin American archive, which would inspire the Boom generation in the 1960s.

2: Teresa de la Parra

In both of Teresa de la Parra's novels, *Ifigenia* (1924) and *Las Memorias de Mamá Blanca* (1929; *Mama Blanca's Memoirs*), nature and the Latin American landscape play a significant role. Whether these texts can be incorporated into the Latin American literary canon is hard to say. Parra seems to have had a different agenda, one which was highly feminised, in her depiction of nature and landscape. Her agenda is distinct to that of Bombal; Teresa de la Parra's fictional natural space often depicts an idealised realm associated with the pre-socialised space of childhood or adolescence. In this context 'pre-socialised' refers to women's experience before marriage since this was the threshold when women officially entered into a socially acceptable role in the 1920s in Venezuela. In this way nature is not directly linked to a collective feminine memory or archive of the female body but it depicts rather a sense of nostalgia for a naïve or uncorrupted contact with nature, symbolic perhaps of the freedom and independence a woman could experience outside marriage.

The most significant episode in *Ifigenia* in terms of revealing the significance and feminisation of the Venezuelan landscape occurs when María Eugenia is staying at the family *hacienda* outside Caracas. Here we see her partake in an almost pagan ritual of spiritual transcendence on entry into the river and this is also where her sensuality and love for Gabriel Olmedo is awakened. The episode reads as follows:

> yo, sola y desnuda, creyendo ser el alma viva del paisaje, me hundía en la ansiada frescura de mi pozo predilecto. Y recuerdo que aquel día sumergida en el pozo, perdí como nunca la noción de mi existencia, porque el rodar del agua me tenía la piel adormecida en no sé que misteriosa delicia, y porque mis ojos vagando por la altura, olvidados de sí mismos, se habían puesto a interpretar todos los amores de aquella muchedumbre de ramas que se abrazan y se besan sobre su lecho del río . . .[15]

> (Alone and naked, believing that I was the living soul of this landscape, I submerged myself in the freshness of my delectable water hole. I can remember that on that day as I was submerged in the water hole I completely lost all notion of my existence because the rolling water had lulled my skin into a mysterious ecstasy and because my eyes roaming all around and forgetting

[15] Teresa de la Parra, *Ifigenia*, ed. Francisco Rivera (Caracas: Monte Ávila, 19XX), I, p. 275.

themselves had begun to interpret all the love present between that swathe of branches which kiss and embrace above their river bed . . .)

Following this intimate contact with nature María Eugenia plays out a series of fantasies in her imagination of how it will be next time she sees Gabriel, often substituting Perucho for the absent Gabriel. She also writes him a letter in that very spot by the river. It is a significant moment in the book, if only transient, since it reveals the consciousness of the spiritual transcendence made possible on contact with nature. It is also significant since the scene depicts a sexual awakening on contact with nature in which the protagonist is the active agent. The scene may not be as explicit as those in Bombal but the idea is the same; unlike the Romantics' conceits, here a woman is the protagonist engaged in a sensual if not sexual awakening. Indeed Louis Antoine Lemaître has noted: 'Like Parra, who experienced contact "with the universal soul" while bathing in the river at Macuto, María Eugenia describes for us her own rite of water-borne nature worship.'[16] This is, however, a parenthetical and transitory episode within the book and this sensual fusion with nature is certainly not a recurring trope as is the case in Bombal's work. In Parra's view, elevation beyond the material constraints of society cannot be constant and there may only be a few points in one's life where this plane reveals itself. The spiritual is tied up with the sensual, the sacred merges with the profane, rendering the moment one of pagan ritual as noted by Lemaître. But it is a fragmented and parenthetical moment, given Parra's social and political conscience, based on the recognition that woman's duty to Venezuelan society in the early twentieth century was to get married and lead an honourable life.

Once a woman is married, it would seem, she loses her innocence (literally she loses her virginity and her sexuality is awakened by a husband), a topic which María Eugenia discusses (*Ifigenia*, pp. 196–9), as she begins to understand the meaning of words such as duty and honour. It appears that these ideas do not marry with those of an awakened sensuality or physical contact with the natural world. Despite the fact that María Eugenia demonstrates such disdain for her family and the role they carve out for her, she ultimately chooses to conform and leave behind more sensual desires which would become nostalgia were she to reflect on them.

Las Memorias de Mamá Blanca is clearly a novel based on a feminine experience but that of girls who are pre-adolescent and so not incorporating sexuality overtly into the text. However, Elizabeth Garrels has discussed the matter of sexuality in the book noting:

One of the signs the novel uses to discuss female sexuality is the novel *Paul et Virginie* (1787), by the French writer Bernard de Saint-Pierre. (. . .) A recasting of the myth of paradise (like *Mama Blanca's Memoirs*), *Paul et Virginie*

---

[16] Louis Antoine Lemaître, *Between Flight and Longing: The Journey of Teresa de la Parra* (New York: Vantage Press, 1986), p. 80.

establishes rigid equivalences among innocence, happiness, childhood, and the colonial island countryside, on the one hand, and, on the other, among sin, suffering, maturity, and Europe (the immoral 'city' of the topos *beatus ille*).[17]

As the girls approach puberty (the signifier of their awakened sexuality) they move to Caracas and so nature becomes a memory set against a pre-social and pre-sexual backdrop. The same could be said of María Eugenia who experiences a physical and sensual relationship with nature whilst still a virgin. It would appear that nature in Parra's work has the ability to awaken a feminine, self-reflexive sensuality where men are not necessary but which will remain a dormant memory feeding nostalgia on the awakening of female sexuality in the conventional context.

The natural world of Piedra Azul is governed by the mother and it is her influence that demarcates the territory as pre-social and non-conformist as made manifest by the strong contrast with the subsequent owner's rendering of the land.[18] Here we see an enclosed natural world and the activities therein all take place within the safe boundaries of Piedra Azul; it is a domesticised nature and not the great landscape which engulfs man or which he must tame as in the case in much contemporary Latin American literary production.[19] Parra depicts, therefore, a feminised, pre-social world which exists amongst the shelter and comfort of the dense foliage of a hacienda looked over by a woman. It evokes strong childhood memories, resulting in nostalgia, but does not offer the possibility of this almost prelapsarian bliss lasting into adulthood. The city is synonymous with conformity and rigidity as regards women's options in life and thus simultaneously she loses those more instinctive contacts with nature and with her inner self, something which Bombal exteriorises in her work through a sensual depiction of the body and desires which are brought to the forefront of consciousness in a playful sensuality with nature. Nature always flirts and sows the seeds of desire but it never engages sexually nor entraps women within conformity as is the case in society.

Motherhood eventually replaces the childlike or adolescent contact with nature; the reader is not privy to a glance at María Eugenia's later life but both Mamá Blanca and her own mother are indeed mothers and significant creative forces in Parra's own book. Blanca Nieves stamps her mark on the hacienda and on her children with their ostentatious names and hairstyles, and she is also depicted as a great story teller, like Mamá Blanca. The loss of sensual and pre-socialised intimacy with nature is replaced, thus, by a generative activity which leads to children, stories and writing. The feminine archive in Parra's work is presented quite explicitly as a partial sphere which 'overhangs' the protagonists

---

[17] Elizabeth Garrels, 'Piedra Azul, or the Colonial Paradise of Women', in *Teresa de la Parra: Mama Blanca's Memoirs*, ed. Doris Sommer, trans. Harriet de Onís (Pittsburgh: Pittsburgh University Press, 1993), pp. 136–50 (p. 146).

[18] See Elizabeth Garrels for a discussion of men's role in the colonial hacienda, p. 140.

[19] See Doris Sommer, *Foundational Fictions*, pp. 257–89.

in the text. The archive is embodied in the memoirs which Mamá Blanca writes
and in the stories her mother told her as a child. They are peripheral to societal
activity, taking place in the boudoir or passing from hand to hand and never seeking to be published. They exist as tangential to the present, not attempting to fill
or dominate a discourse which perhaps is ruled by a different order. Throughout
Parra's work there is a nostalgic mood – and indeed her own life was marked by
nostalgia for the colonial legacy and her ancestry – whilst at the same time
acknowledging her desire to be a modern and independent woman.[20] Perhaps
nostalgia and constant negotiation between the past and the present are the creative impulses behind the literary creativity of Parra and her female protagonists.

3: Miguel Ángel Asturias

It would be difficult to think of a novel which, at first glance, appears more distinct from Bombal's and Parra's work than Miguel Ángel Asturias's *Hombres de
maíz* (1949; *Men of Maize*). Called the 'first great "magical-realist" novel' by
Gerald Martin,[21] *Men of Maize* delves self-consciously into Mayan folklore,
sacred lore and mythology in a way which differs radically from the layer of fairy
tales which subtend, for example, Bombal's fiction. Yet there is a similarity in
that for the Guatemalan writer as much as for Bombal and Parra nature becomes
an archive which aims to produce corporeal self-knowledge. The first section of
the novel is set towards the end of the nineteenth century and recounts the story
of one Gaspar Ilóm, the leader of a group of native Mayan Indian tribesman who
are struggling in vain to keep control over their ancestral homeland in the mountain forests of Guatemala. Encroachment of their land is being directed by the
Liberal government then in power which was selling communal indigenous territories to farmers. Deliberately subverting the epistemological simplicity of the
Realist novel, *Men of Maize* opens *in medias res* with the portrayal of Gaspar
Ilóm's thoughts as he lies dead and buried beneath the surface of the earth:
'Gaspar Ilóm shook his head from side to side. To deny, to grind the accusation
of the soil where he lay sleeping with his reed mat, his shadow and his woman,
where he lay buried with his dead ones and his umbilicus, unable to free himself
from a serpent of six hundred thousand coils of mud, moon, forests, rainstorms,
mountains, birds and echoes he could feel around his body' (p. 1). As the first
chapter gradually unfolds it is clear that the individual designated by the name
of Gaspar Ilóm is at once a nineteenth-century Indian insurgent who struggled
against the rapacious 'criollos' in Guatemala and also a spiritual deity whose

[20] See Lemaître, *Between Flight and Longing*, p. 15.
[21] 'Introduction', in *Men of Maize*, translated by Gerald Martin (London: Verso, 1988),
pp. v-xvi (p. xvii); for further discussion of the role of magical realism in *Men of Maize*, see
Ray Verzasconi, *Magical Realism and the Literary World of Miguel Ángel Asturias* (Seattle:
University of Washington Press, 1965).

consciousness lives on in the earth and aspires to enact revenge on the new colonists who are felling the trees in his heartland. Gaspar Ilóm is not a local deity for he comes to stand – in the manner of a synecdoche – for the spirit of the Mayan people and their sense – as expressed in the holy book of the Mayas, *The Popol Vuh*, that man is made of maize: 'Bare earth, wakeful earth, sleepy maize-growing earth, Gaspar falling from where the earth falls, maize-growing earth bathed by rivers of water fetid from being so long awake, water freed from the wakefulness of the forests sacrificed by the maize made man the sower of maize' (p. 2). Asturias gives this fundamental Mayan metaphor a contemporary, postcolonial relevance by evoking the destructiveness of the modern settlers who raze the forest to the ground with fire: 'The air of Ilóm was heavy with the smell of newly felled trees, the ashes of trees burned to clear the ground' (p. 3). In his essay, 'Magical Realism as Postcolonial Discourse', Stephen Slemon suggests that a fundamental feature of postcolonial fiction is that history is foreshortened 'so that the time scheme of the novel metaphorically contains the long process of colonization and its aftermath',[22] and this seems particularly pertinent to Asturias's novel. The novel is not only about how Gaspar Ilóm 'lives' within the ground, or indeed about how man is 'made of maize', but instead we might say it uses ideas such as these in order to present a politically-inflected narrative about the cruel removal of subaltern arable farmers from their land in modern-day (i.e. post-Independence) Guatemala. It is the earth, though, wherein the drama of postcoloniality is staged.

It is important to underline that the figure of the subaltern in *Men of Maize* is associated with the world of myth and magic. When, for example, the indigenes are being massacred by the ladinos under Colonel Gonzalo Godoy's command – the firefly wizards are hacked to death while they sleep, and Gaspar Ilóm dies from poison – Nicho the Postman manages to escape and he does so by changing into his 'nagual' (animal spirit) form as the Curer-Deer of the Seventh Fire: '"I survived the massacre", the curer went on, a swarm of mosquitoes was flying close by his ear, "because I had time to turn back into what I am, to bring out my four paws"' (*Men of Maize*, p. 303). This has important implications for how the narrative style has been moulded in order to complement the world-view of each of the warring groups. Chapter VIII which focuses on the man who is leading the attack on the Mayan peasants, Colonel Chalo Godoy, is noticeably more realist in tone and expression than chapter X which focuses on Nicho the Postman's lost wife, María Tecún. The opening sentence of the latter chapter ('From his liana tongue, from his teeth of coyote's milk, from the roots of his weeping the rumbling earthslides of his cries were riven'; *Men of Maize*, p. 103) is typical of the Modernist/poetic/stream-of-consciousness style used to evoke Nicho the Postman's desperate search for María Tecún. Not only is the style

---

[22] Stephen Slemon, 'Magic Realism as Postcolonial Discourse', *Magical Realism: Theory, History, Community*, eds Lois Parkinson Zamora and Wendy B. Faris (Durham, NC: Duke University Press, 1995), pp. 407–26 (pp. 411–12).

different. There is also a clear demarcation line drawn in the novel between the oppressors and the oppressed in terms of their access to the world of magic, and particularly the ability to change from human to animal form and vice-versa. It is the oppressed – Gaspar Ilóm, Nicho the Postman, María Tecún – who are able to morph, while the oppressors have no access to this magical world. In chapter XVIII, for example, we read of how the postman and the curer descend to the caves in order to witness the emergence of the animal spirit, the 'nagual', 'which presents itself to them alive, exactly as it is deep within the tenebrous dampness of their skin' (*Men of Maize*, p. 298). This shamanistic knowledge – which emerges only in the vaulted caves beneath the earth – must be kept secret: 'And those who have succeeded in going beyond the subterranean darkness, when they return tell that they have seen nothing, and keep a constrained silence, letting it be known that they understand the secrets of the world hidden beneath the mountains' (*Men of Maize*, p. 297). This 'world hidden beneath the mountains' is an archive which the likes of Colonel Chalo Godoy and his ladino henchmen have no knowledge of nor interest in. This cultural knowledge, rooted in the earth and in the Mayan lore with which it becomes almost synonymous, is recuperated within the novel and comes to form the archival substratum within which the flowers of magical realism – the mixing of the magical-organicist beliefs of the Maya and the historical struggle of Guatemalan peasants in the modern era – germinate and flower.

4: Juan Rulfo

Juan Rulfo's *Pedro Páramo* (1955), like *Men of Maize*, has been associated by a number of critics with magical realism,[23] and, like the other texts analysed in this essay, it takes its point of departure from the land. In an important essay Lois Parkinson Zamora shows how the ghosts which inhabit Rulfo's fiction are similar to those we find in the work of Elena Garro and William Goyen in that they 'live underground, in an earth inhabited by ancestral inhabitants. Their novels are American books of the dead, necrogeographies of the buried traces of indigenous cultural identity in a shared region of America.'[24] The novel opens with the description of Juan Preciado journeying downwards to Comala in what – it soon becomes clear – is a journey to the nether regions of death. But here the similarity with Asturias's novel ends. While *Men of Maize* is a novel which enacts

---

[23] For more on the history of the term magical realism, the reader is referred to Stephen M. Hart, *Reading Magic Realism from Latin America* (London: Bloomsbury, 2001), Internet:ISBN:0747556202;
http://www.Bloomsbury.com/BookCatalog/ProductItem.asp?S=&sku=1213813&EmailMe
=&mscssid=B3RQTNGSSBVL9LPWUA28C06G31570S9A.

[24] Lois Parkinson Zamora, 'Magical Romance/Magical Realism', *Magical Realism: Theory, History, Community*, eds Lois Parkinson Zamora and Wendy B. Faris (Durham, NC: Duke University Press, 1995), pp. 498–550 (pp. 499–500).

a recuperative, metaphorical gesture bringing the cultural realities of the past into communion with the present (ancient Mayan wisdom throwing light on the dilemmas of the present), *Pedro Páramo* re-creates a journey towards cultural origins which is frustrated at every turn.

This is, indeed, the alarming thing about *Pedro Páramo* for its portrayal of a process of infinite regress is anything but a knowledge-bearing visit to the fires of Christian hell, or the land of the dead according to the Nahual-speaking peoples, Mictlan.[25] The space conjured up by Comala has some close parallels, of course, with the Catholic notion of Purgatory. Thus the inhabitants of Comala ask Father Rentería to bless Miguel Páramo but he refuses, claiming that God will be annoyed with him if he intercedes on his behalf (p. 29; see also p. 81).[26] This notion is echoed by Dorotea's dream in which she is told by an angel in a dream to return to earth in order to rest and thereby make sure 'that your purgatory will be shorter' (*Pedro Páramo*, p. 65; all translations are by authors). Without the sacraments, as one of the characters points out, you are forced to wander the earth as a lost soul ('penando'; *Pedro Páramo*, p. 116). The novel also makes some clear allusions to the Mexican religious practices associated with El Día de los Muertos, a ceremony in which relatives visit the cemetery where their loved ones are buried, light candles, say prayers and leave food offerings.[27] This practice is re-created in the scene in which Susana scales down a mine for her father, and finds a skull at the bottom; the allusion to popular Mexican culture is made explicit by the detail that 'the jaw came off as if it was made of sugar' (*Pedro Páramo*, p. 95).

Unlike the visit by Nicho and Gaspar Ilóm which leads to a shamanistic knowledge in *Men of Maize*, the encounter with the Beyond in Rulfo's novel leads to disorientation and confusion. The following conversation is typical:

> – Aren't you dead? – I asked them.
> And the woman smiled. The man looked at me with a serious look on his face.
> – He's drunk – said the man.
> – All he is is scared – said the woman. (*Pedro Páramo*, p. 51)

The reader will find it difficult to decide which of the following possibilities is the 'correct' reading: (i) Juan Preciado is alive and the couple are dead; (ii) Juan Preciado is dead and the couple are alive; (iii) Juan Preciado and the couple are dead; or (iv) Juan Preciado and the couple are alive. The inevitable answer is that

[25] For further discussion of this motif in Rulfo's work, see Stephen M. Hart, '*Pedro Páramo* and the Dream of the Dead Father', in *The Other Scene: Psychoanalytic Readings in Modern Spanish and Latin-American Literature* (Boulder, CO: Society of Spanish and Spanish-American Studies, 1992), pp. 51–62.

[26] All references are to Juan Rulfo, *Pedro Páramo* (Mexico: Fondo de Cultura Económica, 1977).

[27] See Elizabeth Carmicheal and Chloë Sayer, *The Skeleton at the Feast: The Day of the Dead in Mexico* (London: British Museum, 1991).

the characters themselves are in a state of unknowing about themselves as much as about others. Rulfo perceives the world of mythic resonance in terms of loss, absence, synecdoche. Rather than the voices of the dead, we hear their whispers. The human presence is reduced to an echo; the room in which Juan Preciado is sleeping was where Toribio Aldrete was hanged and Juan hears his scream (*Pedro Páramo*, p. 37). Damiana tells Juan: 'this town is full of echoes' (*Pedro Páramo*, p. 45), and Juan even blames his death on the whispering voices: 'The murmurs killed me' (*Pedro Páramo*, p. 62). He confuses his interlocutor's gender, believing Dorotea to be a man, calling her Doroteo (*Pedro Páramo*, p. 62):

> – What do you understand?
> – Nothing – I said – Each time I understand less. (*Pedro Páramo*, p. 57)

Rulfo's ghosts are lost in an archive without meaning. Rather than ontology *Pedro Páramo* deals in hauntology.

It is important to underline that the metaphysical dimension of Rulfo's novel works in concert with the political resonance the novel possesses. One example is the boundary dispute between Toribio Alderete and Pedro Páramo – as transpires during the latter's conversation with Fulgor (*Pedro Páramo*, p. 44); in a later conversation with Fulgor, the matter is referred to as 'dealt with' (*Pedro Páramo*, p. 45), and we know that this means Toribio Alderete was murdered for trying to stand in Pedro Páramo's way (*Pedro Páramo*, p. 37). When Comala is described as 'a town without grace' (*Pedro Páramo*, p. 87), thus, this can be interpreted as much in a metaphysical as a political sense.

While both *Men of Maize* and *Pedro Páramo* portray dramas which are played out within the archive of the earth, the former novel employs a rhetorical strategy which is recuperative and metaphorical while Rulfo's novel portrays a world which is shorn off from its roots, thereby creating a climate of radical metonymic unknowledge. Despite their differences, though, Asturias and Rulfo have recourse to masculinocentric strategies which attempt to master the earth. Bombal and Parra, however, unlike the male writers studied in this essay, seek to recover a space within Nature which is feminocentric and allows for the creation of an as yet uncharted feminine archive.

Alejo Carpentier's Re-invention of América Latina as Real and Marvellous

Jason Wilson

'Marvellous! The marvellous beauty and fascination of natural wild things! The horror of man's unnatural life, his heaped-up civilization', D.H. Lawrence, *St Mawr*[1]

The work of the Cuban novelist and musicologist Alejo Carpentier (1901–1980) was a nodal point in the debate about how to define Latin American uniqueness. His fiction struggled to identify this Latin American cultural uniqueness within the long-standing history of Latin American dependence on and mimicry of Europe – in essence, Paris. Paris, as is often cited, was the capital of the nineteenth century,[2] where the life of the mind vibrated most contagiously, to paraphrase Nicaraguan poet Rubén Darío,[3] famously accused by the Spanish critic Juan Valera in 1888 of having adopted a French mindset. A crucial moment in this history of Gallic cultural dominance was the Parisian-based surrealist movement, which developed out of post first-world-war Dada despair into an organized group, energetically controlled by André Breton with the first surrealist manifesto of 1924. Surrealism ushered in a poetics based on unpredictability, magic, primitivism and surprise that in fiction became loosely called magical realism.

The French Connection

Alejo Carpentier's creative tussle with André Breton and French cultural domination has been well studied and I intend to review this briefly.[4] Parisian surrealism welcomed foreign painters into the group. The visual image transcends

---

[1] D.H. Lawrence, *St Mawr* (New York: Vintage, 1953), p. 128.

[2] Walter Benjamin, *The Arcades Project*, trans. Howard Eiland and Kevin McLaughlin (Cambridge, Mass: The Belknap Press of Harvard University Press, 2002).

[3] Rubén Darío, 'Las letras hispanoamericanas en París', in Rubén Darío, *La caravana pasa*, ed. Gunther Schmigalle (Berlin: Verlag Walter Frey, 2001), p. 69.

[4] Klaus Müller-Bergh, 'Corrientes vanguardistas y surrealismo en la obra de Alejo Carpentier', *Revista Hispánica Moderna* (October–December 1969), 323–40; Stephen Henighan,

the language barrier. The Hispanic contribution to surrealist painting has been enormous, as just listing names like Miró, Dalí, Domínguez, Matta, Varo and Lam (whom I will discuss in greater detail later) suffices to indicate. In the case of writing, the Latin American 'viaje a París' (journey to Paris; *the literal translations are mine*) rarely resulted in a change of language from Spanish to French, but it did lead to bilingualism in Latin American attempts to be recognised and accepted abroad in Paris. The Chilean experimental poet Vicente Huidobro, who invented his own rival theory of poetry against surrealism, called 'creacionismo', but lacked the group energy of Breton's surrealists, duplicated what he wrote in Spanish in the 1920s in French, modifying his name as Vincent Huidobro. A Peruvian poet pseudonymously called César Moro, the sole Latin American writer to publish in one of Breton's main journals (*Le Surréalisme au service de la Révolution* in 1933), went one step further and wrote his poetry in French, despite living in Peru and Mexico. The Ecuadorian poet, Alfredo Gangotena, who accompanied Henri Michaux around Ecuador in the 1920s, also wrote in French.[5] From the periphery, it seemed that cultural life could only happen in certain magic spaces inside Paris, often cafés, and seeking Parisian approval.

Carpentier and Desnos's Critique of Surrealism

Carpentier was brought up speaking French; he wrote French well and could have become a French writer from the Caribbean, like Saint-John Perse or Aimé Césaire. Pablo Neruda mischievously referred to him as 'el escritor francés' (the French writer).[6] Carpentier contributed to fringe surrealist magazines in French, though usually as a spokesman for the Caribbean, and as a translator. In 1928 he arrived in Paris as a 24-year-old Cuban on the run from five months in the Prado prison under dictator Gerardo Machado, escaping on the surrealist poet Robert Desnos's journalist's documents. Desnos was his quick entry into surrealism and he couldn't have found a better guide. In fact, Carpentier's attitudes to and critiques of Breton closely follow Desnos's. Robert Desnos was the most active member of the group in the 1920s, during the period of self-induced trances as a means of liberating the unconscious. André Breton called him the most surrealist of the surrealists.[7] Desnos travelled to Havana by boat with many Latin

---

'The Pope's Errant Son: Breton and Alejo Carpentier', in *André Breton. The Power of Language*, ed. Ramona Fotiade (Exeter: Elm Bank Publications, 2000), pp. 139–48. See also Roberto González Echevarría, *Alejo Carpentier. The Pilgrim at Home* (Ithaca: Cornell University Press, 1977) and Leonardo Padura Fuentes, 'Carpentier y el surrealismo', *Cuadernos hispanoamericanos*, 649–50 (July-August 2004), 35–41.

[5] Adriana Castillo de Berchenku, *Alfredo Gangotena, poète équatorien (1904–1944) ou l'Écriture partagée* (Perpignan: Presses Universitaires de Perpignan, 1992). See my 'Spanish American Surrealist Poetry', in *A Companion to Spanish Surrealism*, ed. Robert Havard (Woodbridge: Tamesis, 2004), pp. 253–76.

[6] Pablo Neruda, *Confieso que he vivido. Memorias* (Buenos Aires: Losada, 1974), p. 171.

[7] Dominique Desanti, *Robert Desnos. Le roman d'une vie* (Paris: Mercure de France, 1999), p. 128.

American journalists, including the Mexican poet and critic Jorge Cuesta and the Guatemalan Miguel Ángel Asturias, representing an Argentine newspaper *La Razón*, for the seventh congress of Latin American journalism. Carpentier and Desnos immediately became friends, and Desnos learnt about Cuba through his friend's knowledge of music, *santería* and the sugar business. Back home in Paris, Desnos wrote five articles on his Cuban trip.[8] However, Desnos (with Prévert and Leiris), and despite his special role in the group, was publicly expelled by Breton in his 1929 second surrealist manifesto. According to Breton, Desnos was not sufficiently militant politically (he had refused to join the French Communist Party), was an individualist, was reported quoting Racine while in Cuba, was involved in a nightclub in Montparnasse called Maldoror (thus besmirching Lautréamont), and, worst of all, was a journalist.[9] At that time, Breton began to be compared to the Pope as the surrealist group was split apart by arguments about political involvement. Desnos contributed to a group protest, *Un cadavre* (referring to the surrealist game, *Un cadavre exquis* and to Breton as a corpse), mocking the leader Breton in 1930. In his piece, Desnos imperson-ated Breton, confessing that he (Breton) had lied, deceived his friends, hated ped-erasts, written stupid sentences, faked everything, and mistreated his best friend Desnos. Thus spoke the 'fantôme puant d'André Breton' (the stinking ghost of André Breton).[10] As Desnos's friend, Carpentier, never a surrealist and thus not expelled, wrote the closing piece in the pamphlet. In it he admits that he only ever met Breton once when he had told him that surrealism in Latin America was essentially Paul Éluard's poetry. Breton replied by saying that if that was really so, then surrealism was 'foutu' (screwed), and repeated the word several times. Breton went on to say that Éluard's poetry was the opposite of real poetry, and that he couldn't understand what was happening in Latin America. Carpentier swore that this dialogue took place, and named his witness Jorge Cuesta (who wrote up his interview with Breton in the Mexican magazine *Contemporáneos* in 1931). A cunningly placed epigraph cites Breton praising Eluard's poetry. Carpentier's piece highlighted Breton's vanity. How could Éluard represent sur-realism? What about Breton's own poetry, his novel *Nadja*, his essays? Thanks to Carpentier's wit, Breton seemed a careerist, moved by envy for his rival Éluard (Pierre, p. 148). In April 1930 Carpentier wrote a chronicle about the nightclub Maldoror, where he said that Breton, with his abundant hair, looked like Titta Ruffo (a well-known male baritone), and acted like a dictator, a Mussolini.[11] In 1975, Carpentier evoked his close friend Desnos. They saw each other nearly every day between 1929 and 1939, even sharing a pair of shoes during the worst

---

[8] Vásquez, Carmen, *Robert Desnos et Cuba. Un carrefour du monde* (Paris: L'Harmattan, 1999).

[9] *Manifiestes du Surréalisme* (Paris: Jean-Jacques Pauvert, 1962), pp. 196–202.

[10] José Pierre (ed.), *Tracts surréalistes et déclarations collectives 1922–1939* (Paris: Le Terrain Vague, 1980), pp. 143–4.

[11] Alejo Carpentier, 'El escándalo de Maldoror', *Obras Completas*, Vol 8, (México: Siglo Veintiuno Editores, 1985), pp. 256–8.

post-Crash days. Desnos exalted love and friendship, and even while a surrealist had never failed to have Sunday lunch with his parents. Carpentier found him
to be secretive, very private, never talking about his writing.[12]

The surrealist map of the world was based on a grid of exoticism and a desire
for the freedom of the unknown; the less the surrealists knew about a distant culture the more they admired it, sure that it would produce natural surrealists.[13]
Breton visited Mexico in 1938 to meet, and draw up a manifesto, with Trotsky,
but which was signed instead by Diego Rivera, Trotsky's host.[14] In Mexico,
Breton discovered Frida Kahlo, who, though she had studied in Paris, was
deemed to be naturally surrealist.[15] Earlier, in Paris, Breton had discovered
Mexican jumping beans, that led to Roger Caillois being expelled as he challenged Breton's willed self-delusion about Mexico and magic. Caillois simply
cut open a bean to reveal the worm inside.[16] Later, in exile from Vichy France,
Breton travelled to Haiti, provoked a revolt, and then north to Nova Scotia
exploring tribal culture, extending his surrealist belief in the periphery being
more vital, more surprising than the cultural centres of Paris and New York that
he knew so well.[17]

Carpentier and Breton's Surrealism

Carpentier appropriated two terms from Breton's vocabulary, and used them
against Breton, as Stephen Henighan has argued from a more psychological
position. The first was 'le merveilleux', a code word for the thrill of the chance
encounter where a frisson or epiphany is sparked by the clash between subjectivity and the objective world of things and other people. Carpentier located a
specific Latin American 'maravilloso' in tropical Caribbean nature and the history that is grounded in it, arguing that the Parisian marvellous was simply mental, vicarious and bookish. This is a trick, because some of the crucial surrealist
text were grounded in journeys into the odd and bizarre, especially Breton's
Nadja, 1928, with its Paris street itineraries and 44 photos, and Aragon's
Le Paysan de Paris, 1926, in its elegy for the lawless arcades. However, the surrealist 'merveilleux' remained urban. As many critics have shown, Carpentier
developed a natural surrealism, located in tropical excess, adopting an exotic
view of his own culture. He called this the uniqueness of the Latin American
experience. He could discount the surrealist marvellous because he linked urban
with reason, and tropical nature with the unpredictable and 'desmesura' (excess)

[12] 'Robert Desnos' *Le Monde,* 10 January 1975, 15.
[13] Louise Tythacott, *Surrealism and the Exotic* (London: Routledge, 2003).
[14] Clarence Lambert, 'André Breton en México', *Vuelta,* 148 (March 1989), 9–16.
[15] André Breton, 'Souvenirs du Méxique', *Minotaure* (1939), 30–51.
[16] Roger Caillois, *Cases d'un échiquier* (Paris: Gallimard, 1970), pp. 122–8.
[17] Martin Sawin, *Surrealism in Exile and the Beginning of the New York School*
(Cambridge, Mass: The MIT Press, 1995).

so that whatever happened in Paris was based on will, on choice, on the emotional poverty of rationalism.[18]

The second term he appropriated – 'pas' or 'pasos' – comes in the title of Carpentier's quest novel *Los pasos perdidos*, 1953 (*The Lost Steps*, 1956), a title which appropriates (and ultimately subverts) André Breton's 1924 collection of essays *Les Pas perdus* (Lost Steps). In the novel, a jaded musicologist journeys up the mythical Orinoco. He dumps his left-bank, surrealist-addicted mistress called Mouche for a real South American woman called Rosario, to find that he cannot remain in the jungle and history's tribal origins that South American culture still contains. The once lost, but now-found, steps back into the beginnings of art and social order contrast with Breton's lost steps, which are simply his avant-garde *anti-passatismo*.[19] The rotten past is no guide to the future and surrealism must start the whole enterprise from a violent *tabula rasa*. Carpentier discovered the richness and complexity of Latin American history, therefore the steps are not lost through surrealism; Breton rejected history for revolution and a new start, therefore the steps are lost.

In his initiatory novel *Los pasos perdidos*, 1953, about a musician making sense of real Latin America located in its deep Amazonian jungle, and then being forced to abandon paradise to be a witness to the twentieth century's existential crises, Carpentier had created an intellectualised musician a bit like himself. This nameless narrator who rediscovers the thrill of being a Latin American is involved in relationships with three women. The first is his dull actress wife, abandoned in New York. It is the second that concerns me, his mistress, Mouche, French for fly, also alluding to the title of Jean-Paul Sartre's play *Les Mouches*, 1943. For Mouche is a latter day Nadja, only ridiculed, an arty surrealist type invented to bash Breton. She is made so grotesque in comparison to his third woman from the interior, Rosario, that she becomes the most interesting character.

Mouche is an astrologist, has published a collection of poems illustrated by photomontage, she's bookish, and had been formed by the 'gran baratillo surrealista' (the great surrealist junkshop),[20] which she dogmatically defended. She boasts about her dreams, voices the surrealist clichés about chance encounters, the unknown, shooting into a crowd, slapping corpses, suicide, and constantly cites Rimbaud's 'bateau ivre', as did Breton (p. 35). She is stale in a literary way while in the tropics of South America. Nothing in Mouche was direct, felt; every opinion was second-hand, literary, fashionable. She can't leave her 'terrenos del surrealismo, astrología, interpretación de los sueños' (surrealist terrain, astrology, dream interpretation) behind her (p. 74), and look at and appreciate what is

---

[18] *Tientos y diferencias* (Montevideo: Arca, 1967), p. 25.

[19] Renato Poggiolo, *The Theory of the Avant-Guard* (Cambridge, Mass: Harvard University Press, 1968), p. 55.

[20] Alejo Carpentier, *Los pasos perdidos* (México: Compañía General de Ediciones, 1959), p. 18.

really new. She's made so *contra natura* that she becomes a lesbian (p. 156), and more and more ugly to the narrator until she makes him puke. Finally, he makes love with his third woman, Rosario, under the hammock in which a sick and dirty Mouche, looking like the Gorgon, leans over and watches the fornicators, screaming 'pigs, pigs' (p. 158).

Carpentier spent eleven long years in Paris (1928–39), where he refused to write for Breton's magazine, though he bumped into one surrealist or another every day. He did write for dissident surrealist magazines edited by Bataille, but Carpentier assured an interviewer that surrealism merely ignited a spark, that surrealism made him Latin American. When Breton was in Haiti in 1941, with his doctor friend Pierre Mabille (who delivered Breton's daughter Aube), he watched a voodoo ceremony, and almost fainted, saying 'C'est horrible'. Thus was the Great Pope of Surrealism, in Carpentier's irony, unable to bear Latin American reality.[21]

Journeys to and from Europe

Much of Carpentier's fiction, and thinking through fiction, is accomplished on different kinds of journeys to and from Europe that he conceptualised musically as counterpoint. There are the actual journeys across the Atlantic that in the case of *El reino de este mundo* (1949, *The Kingdom of this World*, 1957), see Paulina Bonaparte liberate herself from European inner models or Solimán her black masseur discover dead, white culture in Rome, to the journeys to and from European-type cities already mentioned in *Los pasos perdidos*, and the complex journeys that French revolutionary ideas take in Carpentier's masterpiece *El siglo de las luces* (1962, *Explosion in a Cathedral*, 1963) to the journeys that his dictator takes in *El recurso del método* (1974, *Reasons of State*, 1976). Each journey offers a new insight for the reader and for the characters, but not for Carpentier. My guess is that Carpentier became, early on, a writer of parables and allegories, that he had worked out his theory before writing his fiction, and did not write fiction to find out what he thought; he is a master of Baroque lists and anecdotal examples illustrating his thesis. He could not be further from automatic writing, or believing that the unconscious dictates meaning. The basic parable surfaces constantly in his work and illustrates his primal, and compensatory insight about the vitality of the Caribbean in counterpoint to grey, urban, rational Paris. Carpentier was aware in the 1940s that he was going against the Latin American grain of trying to make Europeans understand Latin American culture by travelling to Paris. Instead, he brought 'ciertas verdades europeas a las latitudes que son nuestras' (certain European truths to our latitudes), and these truths were surrealist.

---

[21] Ernesto González Bermejo, 'Alejo Carpentier', *Crisis*, 22 (March 1975), p. 44.

Carpentier, Haiti and the Surrealist Gaze

The clearest example of the exoticist surrealist gaze employed by Carpentier to re-interpret his own culture comes with his first visit to Haiti where he saw the ruins of King Henri Christophe's sacked Sans Souci palace and the mountain top fortified Citadelle Laferrière. He breathed in the strange atmosphere and found Christophe's deeds 'mucho más sorprendentes que todos los reyes crueles inventados por los surrealistas, muy afectos a tiranías imaginarias, aunque no padecidos' (much more surprising than all the cruel kings invented by the surrealists, prone to imaginary, but not suffered tyrannies). This traveller's experience was the seed of his theory of 'lo real maravilloso', not just rooted in Haiti, but common to all Latin America (*Tientos y diferencias*, p. 119, Touches and Differences, not translated). The grid of his heretical surrealist gaze is obvious: what counts is what surprises, as opposed to the banality of what is just invented in the mind, where no actual experience of suffering is involved. Christophe's palace was real, suffered, mind-baffling. This exoticist perception was developed in his novel *El reino de este mundo* with King Christophe's downfall due to his ignoring of black, animist culture. Years later, in an interview, Carpentier decoded his own theory thus: 'lo maravilloso es, en realidad, lo insólito, lo singular, lo inhabitual' (the marvellous is, in reality, the unexpected, the singular, the exceptional) (González Bermejo, p. 44). Carpentier's vision matched that of a tourist like Alec Waugh whose travel book *Hot Countries*, 1930, has these same ruins become the eighth wonder of the world; James Ferguson still found the complex 'awesome' in 1997.[22]

Carpentier returned to the tourist's sense of shocked surprise at discovering the ruined Sans Souci palace and the Citadelle Laferrière through the black slave Ti Noel in his novel *El reino de este mundo*: 'Pero ahora el viejo se había detenido, maravillado por el espectáculo más inesperado, más imponente que hubiera visto en su larga existencia' (But now the old man, amazed by the most unexpected, most imposing spectacle that he had ever seen in his long life). 'Lo más inesperado' reveals the clear surrealist aesthetics of shock – and leads into a long description of the imagined pink fantasy palace with its domes and columns and gardens and lakes to realise that 'ese mundo prodigioso' (this prodigious world) was peopled by blacks mimicking French court life. Ti Noel was witnessing King Henri Christophe's palace before it had been sacked, and fallen into the ruins that Carpentier the tourist had found so exciting.[23] Ti Noel was forced into helping build the extraordinary castle, with its drawbridge, and room for 15,000 soldiers. In his eyes, it was 'una obra inverosímil' (implausible work), straight from Piranesi (*El reino de este mundo*, pp. 98–9).

---

[22] James Ferguson, *Traveller's Literary Companion to the Caribbean* (Lincolnwood, Ill: Passport Books, 1997), p. 91.
[23] *El reino de este mundo* (Barcelona: Editorial Seix Barral, 1967), pp. 88–90.

Parables of Belonging

I want to place Carpentier's appropriation of the surrealist exotic within the conventional parable of belonging enacted by Latin Americans from the 1880s to the 1920s, that is, by his precursors. I have chosen a version from Rubén Darío. In 1903 Darío published a poem titled 'Caracol' (Shell) in Buenos Aires. The poem turns a shell into a confession of love. The parable is colonial – only what crosses the ocean from Europe, 'de ultramar', matters. The title's metaphoric shift from *caracol* to *corazón* (shell to heart) suggests that listening to what arrives from overseas is converted into heart, that is, love, passion. Darío is a lover of imported cultural goods and beauty. The poet finds a golden shell, decorated with pearls, on a beach. It has been touched by Europe, crossing the seas on the mythic bull; Zeus, in the form of a white bull, had raped Europa.[24] The poet brings his lips to the 'caracol sonoro' (sonorous shell) and hears that 'me han cantado en voz / baja su secreto tesoro' (they have sung its secret treasure to me in a low voice). The poem concludes by binding the metaphors: '(El caracol la forma tiene de un corazón)' (the shell is heart-shaped), that is, the heart is a sonorous shell whispering its secret, European treasures to the poet as his muse, his inspiration.[25]

Against this one-way colonial journey towards the centre, Carpentier proposes a counter voyage. I want to comment on three allegorical journey-moments. The first is a macro-allegory, the opening chapter of *El reino de este mundo* where the black Caribbean slave world clashes with the white French colonial world. The chapter is titled 'Cabezas de cera' (wax heads) and can be divided into discrete scenes. It opens with a description of two types of horse: the slave Ti Noel's horse and the master Lenormand de Mezy's, where the horses represent their riders and reverse the master-slave relationship. Mezy rides into town to be shaved. His slave notices four wax heads in the barber's shop and then next door, thanks to a 'graciosa casualidad' (amusing chance) that is only amusingly chance-like for Ti Noel and the reader, but not for Carpentier (this is allegory), a butcher's shop with 'cabezas de ternero' (calf heads) that seem wax-like ('cerosas'), with wigs of lettuce. Ti Noel fantasies that these are 'cabezas de blanco' (white men's heads) on a table. We now have the far from free-associations: white / wax / dead / food. This static opening piece slips from realistic description into allegory. In the next shop on the other side of the barber's Ti Noel sees prints of white kings, with one showing an African king. When the master Mezy comes out from the barber shaved, Ti Noel realises that Mezy looks, surprisingly (but it's no surprise) like a wax head. Mezy then buys a 'cabeza de ternero' from the butcher, Ti Noel fingers it and thinks that it feels like his master's bald head under his wig. So white colonial French is linked to wax, dead calf, meat, and perhaps revolution and execution. Three shops in a row produce meanings based on

---

[24] Robert Graves, *The Greek Myths* (Harmondsworth: Penguin Books, 1955), pp. 194–5.
[25] *Cantos de vida y esperanza, los cisnes y otros poemas*, ed. Francisco J. Díez de Revenga (Salamanca: Ediciones Almar, 2001), pp. 139–40.

artificial 'amusing coincidences' and 'surprising' analogies; this is a surrealist tableaux, linking outrageous metaphors of the sewing machine and the umbrella on the dissection table kind beloved of the surrealists (*El reino de este mundo*, pp. 9–14).

The next allegory is embedded in a perception from the opening page of Carpentier's first novel *Écue-Yamba-Ó* (1933, Lord Praised be Thou):

> El viejo Usebio Cué había visto crecer el hongo de acero, palastro y concreto sobre las ruinas de trapiches antiguos, asistiendo año tras año, con una suerte de espanto admirativo, a las conquistas de espacio realizadas por la fábrica. Para él la caña no encerraba el menor misterio. Apenas asomaba entre los cuajarones de tierra negra, se seguía su desarrollo sin sorpresas. El saludo de la primera hoja . . . La locomotora arrastra millares de sacos llenos de cristalitos rojos que todavía saben a tierra, pezuñas y malas palabras. La refinería extranjera los devolverá pálidos, sin vida, después de un viaje sobre mares descoloridos.

> (Old Usebio had watched the steel, plaster and concrete fungus grow above the ruins of old sugar mills, witnessing, year after year, with a kind of shocked admiration, the conquest of space carried out by the factory. For him, sugar cane held no mystery. From as soon as it grew out of the lumps of black earth, he would follow its development without surprises. The wave of the first leaf . . . The train dragged thousands of sacks filled with little red crystals which still tasted of earth, hooves and swear words. The foreign refinery would send them back pale and lifeless, after a journey across colourless seas.)[26]

Carpentier thinks through Cué, accustomed to the mystery of extracting sugar from sugar-cane, where the journey of red-crystal sugar, suggesting blood, and tasting of earth, hooves and swear words, is turned by the sea-crossing to Europe into pale and lifeless, white sugar, suggesting death. As in the later *El reino de este mundo*, the 'viaje a París' has become one towards death. Latin American culture, when received by Europeans in Europe, looses its taste of soil and toil, its reality.

My final micro-parable within the larger parable of the novels comes from *El siglo de las luces*:

> De sorpresa en sorpresa descubría Esteban la pluralidad de las playas donde el Mar, tres siglos después del Descubrimiento, comenzaba a depositar sus primeros vidrios pulidos; vidrios inventados en Europa, desconocidos en América; vidrios de botellas, de frascos, de bombonas, cuyas formas habían sido ignoradas en el Nuevo Continente; vidrios verdes, con opacidadas y burbujas; vidrios finos destinados a catedrales nacientes, cuyas hagiografías hubiera borrado el agua; vidrios que, caídos de barcos, rescatados de naufragios, habían sido arrojados a esta ribera del Océano como misteriosa novedad,

---

[26] Carpentier, *Écue-Yamba-Ó* (Montevideo: Editorial Sandino, 1973), p. 5.

y ahora empezaban a subir a la tierra, pulidos por olas con mañas de tornero
y de orfebre que devolvían una luz a sus matices extenuados.[27]

(From surprise to surprise, Esteban discovered the plurality of beaches where
the Sea, three centuries after the Discovery, began to deposit the first pieces of
polished glass; glass invented in Europe, unknown in America, glass from bottles, jars, canisters whose shapes had never been seen on the New Continent;
green glass, with opacities and bubbles; fine glass destined for new cathedrals
with hagiographies effaced by water; pieces of glass that, fallen from ships and
rescued by ship-wrecked sailors, had been hurled on to this Ocean shore like
a mysterious novelty and now began to rise on to dry land, polished by waves
with the skills of lathes and jewellers that restored light to its exhausted hues.)

Another journey, this time from Europe to Latin America, where polished
European glass is washed up on Latin American shores as mysterious novelty, is
recreated, like a surrealist 'objet trouvé', a natural surrealist metamorphosis. The
Ocean is an Unconscious that recreates a magic lost in rational, sterile Europe.
In this passage about appropriation, or transculturation, I hear Carpentier sub-
verting Darío's poem.

The surrealist exotic of the late 1940s can be linked to what was happening to
André Breton's group after his return to Paris from exile in New York in 1946.
Post second-world-war Paris was dominated by resistance polemics, the Camus /
Sartre debate about the writer's task, the revelations of Stalin's death camps, post-
war poverty, the Cold War and so on, but despite and because of all this (and
more) Paris remained a cultural capital in Darío's terms. However, surrealism no
longer dominated the cultural scene; indeed, Sartre, the new *maître à penser*,
demolished the movement in his polemic *Qu'est que la littérature?* (1948), when
he objected to Duchamp's birdcage with sugar-lumps as vacuous, gestural
shock.[28] Carpentier's 1930s animosity to Breton, inherited from his friend Robert
Desnos, and part of the foreigner-in-Paris's resentment at not being accepted, simply could not continue to develop along the same lines, as surrealism itself
became marginalised. However, it continued underground in Carpentier's perceptions about what made Latin America unique.

Carpentier, Lam and Surrealism in American Exile

One last example of surrealism's re-interpretation of Latin America emerges in
Carpentier's attempt to reveal the movement's 'imaginative poverty' by contrasting André Masson's paintings of a jungle Masson could not really understand – despite being in exile in Martinique – with Wifredo Lam's jungle.
Carpentier claimed that it had to be a painter from *América*, the Cuban Lam, who

---

[27] *El siglo de las luces* (Buenos Aires: Editorial Galerna, 1967), p. 211.
[28] Jean-Paul Sartre, *Situations, II. Qu'est-ce que la littérature?* (Paris: Gallimard, 1948),
pp. 318–24.

would teach the world about 'la magia de la vegetación tropical' (the magic of tropical vegetation), not a Frenchman (*Tientos y diferencias*, p. 117). Now, Lam might be Cuban, but he was also a surrealist. Lam would teach Latin Americans how to grasp tropical nature's incredible interlacing lianas and promiscuous fruit. There are strange parallels with Carpentier. Lam was born a mulatto on a sugar estate in Cuba, of a Chinese father aged eighty-four and a mulatto mother, like Carpentier an outsider on the island. He studied art in Havana, travelled to Madrid in 1924, then Barcelona, discovering African art in 1928. He fought in Madrid during the Spanish Civil War in 1937–38. Through a close friendship with Picasso he became friendly with André Breton and joined the surrealist group in 1940 on the eve of its exodus from Marseille to Martinique and then New York on board a ship with André Breton, Claude Lévi-Strauss and Victor Serge. While detained in Martinique, Lam and Breton met Aimé Césaire and discussed *négritude* theories, which Lam later adopted. After 17 years abroad, and unable to proceed to New York, he finally returned to Cuba in August 1941. He painted the famous picture *La jungla* in 1943 in Mariano, a suburb of Havana in Cuba, and exhibited it in New York. He later visited Haiti for the first time in 1944, with André Breton (and later on a second visit stayed for 6 months). In January 1946, Breton wrote a catalogue note on Lam in Haiti as the inheritor of African roots, with dreams of Eden, and able to paint the marvellous, ever-changing glow from tropical nature's stained-glass window, in a spirit freed from all influences, releasing hidden gods. In an age of atomic disintegration, wrote Breton, Lam has tapped into the source, the mystery tree of human nature.[29] All this is close to Carpentier's views on Lam. For Breton in 1946, Lam was surrealism's best hope. Breton's magnetism was irresistible, said Lam later.[30]

Like Carpentier, Lam's surrealist experiences enabled him to re-view Cuba, Haiti and the Caribbean through the lens of voodoo and *santería*, that is, those aspects of the Caribbean experience that he knew at first hand and that had been re-valued by the surrealists themselves in their rejection of the rotten Christian West.[31]

Lam told Fouchet that the Cuba he rediscovered was a hell, with pleasure-drunk tourists, over 60,000 whores and the Cuban blacks still living in slave-like conditions. He sought to paint the drama of his country by 'expressing the Negro spirit'; his art would surprise and disturb the dreams of the exploiters (Fouchet, p. 30). Out of this encounter grew 'La jungla', 1942–43. Fouchet evoked the painting's rhythm, like drums in the suffocating heat of a tropical forest. But what strikes me is the way the jungle, the bamboos, the sugar cane stalks and leaves metamorphose into figures, and sensual fragments with mask-like faces, the scary but invisible spirits from the Yoruban past. Lam absorbed Douanier Rousseau's exotic

---

[29] *Le Surréalisme et la Peinture* (Paris: Gallimard, 1965), pp. 169–72.
[30] Lowery Stokes Sims, *Wifredo Lam and the International Avant-Garde 1923–1982* (Austin: University of Texas Press, 2002), p. 64.
[31] Max-Pol Fouchet, *Wifredo Lam* (Barcelona: Ediciones Polígrafa, 1986).

jungle, even Max Ernst's tangled, weird 'The Joys of Living' (1936), where the eye has to figure out what lies hidden in the thick foliage. Lam also claimed that Cuba had no jungle, that he was out to convey a 'psychic' state. Only in 1957 did he actually visit the Amazonian jungle (Stokes Sims, p. 64). The painting has been interpreted many ways, but Breton best summarised its appeal as a combination of a marvellous primitivism, with acute artistic consciousness; quite different from the *art naïf* that Breton had admired in Haiti (*Le Surréalisme et la Peinture*, p. 169). The living African realities seen in Cuba, and especially in Haiti, are transformed through surrealism's fascination with dark forces, the occult, the unconscious into a metaphor where jungle is as Jungian as it is botanical.

Surrealism offered Carpentier and Lam an image of soul-less, urban modernity devoured by natural frenzy, Benjamin Péret's photo of the locomotive swamped by the living, animated jungle, Dalí's taxi overgrown with plants and snails, the Spanish galleon grounded in García Márquez's Macondan jungle. The two poles of this metaphor are artificiality and rationality subverted by natural energy, in the form of hidden or invisible gods and creativity, all that escapes reason's vigilant, censoring eye. Surrealism's mutation into magical realism in the peripheries simply illustrates this seductive image that links the jaded metropolitan reader with the empowered magical periphery and this link is embodied in the creative contradictions of Carpentier and Lam, in their biographies as much as in their work.

Conclusion on Surrealism and the Marvellous

I conclude by speculating why Carpentier refused to admit his surrealist filiation when re-conceiving Latin America's differences with Europe. Not only did Carpentier take sides with his friend Desnos against Breton in the 1930s, but, furthermore, by the 1940s, surrealism was no longer the privileged space for debating modernity, not only as a result of Jean-Paul Sartre's demolition of surrealism in 1948; Sartre became the defining voice on the role of writing and the writer, through his *engagement*, in what a critic has recently called 'le siècle de Sartre' (Sartre's century).[32] Carpentier argued with Sartre, the new star in Paris, in essays and within his fiction (the endings of *El reino de este mundo* and *Los pasos perdidos* are Sartrian codas to the artist's 'task' [*tarea*]). Surrealism had lost its aura, its challenging and provocative position just when it began to be adopted in Latin America, and Carpentier did not want to seem *démodé* like his fellow Latin Americans. For example, in Buenos Aires, the writer Julio Cortázar was defending Artaud and surrealist values in 1949, the same year the poet Octavio Paz joined Breton's group in Paris, while Enrique Molina founded his surrealist journal *A partir de cero* in Buenos Aires in 1951. Carpentier, meanwhile, asserted that surrealism was over in Paris, and yet was being poorly imitated in Latin America (*Tientos y diferencias*, p. 26). He could not endorse a surrealist view without seeming anachronistic. He called it 'lo real maravilloso'.

---

[32] Bernard-Henri Lévy, *Le Siècle de Sartre. Enquête philosophique* (Paris: Grasset, 2000).

The Golden Age Myth in Gabriel García Márquez's *One Hundred Years of Solitude* and Ovid's *Metamorphoses*

Lorna Robinson

In the prologue to his novel *El reino de este mundo,*[1] the Cuban novelist Alejo Carpentier writes the following: 'Because of the virginity of the land, our upbringing, our ontology, the Faustian presence of the Indian and the black man, the revelation constituted by its recent discovery, its fecund racial mixing, America is far from using up its wealth of mythologies. After all, what is the entire history of America if not a chronicle of the marvellous real?' (Carpentier, p. 88). Carpentier's formulation of magical realism, as a mode of literature emerging essentially from the largely untapped and Baroque magnificence of his continent's geography, history, diversity and mythology, has been taken by many scholars as seminal. Indeed, magical realism is still often regarded, several decades later, as primarily a Latin American phenomenon, despite the international success of novels such as Salman Rushdie's *Midnight's Children* and Toni Morrison's *Song of Solomon*, amongst others, which are regularly cited as skilful examples of magical-realist texts.

In this essay, I examine the territorial claim, echoed by prominent writers such as Miguel Ángel Asturias and Gabriel García Márquez,[2] by applying their literary assertions to the text and background of Ovid's *Metamorphoses*. This work lies far behind the muddied waters of contemporary literary movements and influences, and is positioned prominently in the Classical Western tradition against which Latin American magical-realists regard themselves as reacting. By observing

---

[1] Alejo Carpentier, 'On the Marvellous Real in America', in *Magical Realism: Theory, History, Community*, ed. Wendy B. Faris and Lois Parkinson Zamora (Durham, NC: Duke University Press, 1995), pp. 75–88.

[2] Amaryll Chanady speaks of Miguel Ángel Asturias' territorialisation of magical realism, quoting him as saying that it has 'a direct relationship to the original mentality of the Indians', in 'Territorialization of the Imaginary: Self-Affirmation and Resistance to Metropolitan Paradigms' in Faris and Zamora, p. 140. In the same essay, she also writes of García

how Ovid's *Metamorphoses*,[3] completed in 7 A.D. Rome, uses magical-realist modes to represent its political, mythological, geographical and literary settings, and by examining García Márquez's *One Hundred Years of Solitude*,[4] a novel with a very different background, I aim to deepen an understanding of magical-realist writing's potential relation to the author's external reality.

Two New Worlds

> At that time Macondo was a village of twenty adobe houses, built on the bank of a river of clear water that ran along a bed of polished stones, which were white and enormous like prehistoric eggs. The world was so recent that many things lacked names, and in order to indicate them it was necessary to point. (*One Hundred Years of Solitude*, p. 9)

> Golden was that first age which unconstrained,
> With heart and soul, obedient to no law,
> Gave honour to good faith and righteousness.
> No punishment they knew, no fear; they read
> No penalties engraved on plates of bronze;
> (*Metamorphoses* 1.89–93.)

The opening paragraph of García Márquez's novel presents an idyllic picture; in fact, there is something distinctly ancient and mythical in his portrayal of the early Macondo that harks back to a world of innocence and unblemished natural beauty. Sparse population and clear flowing water are conspicuous symbols of a lost paradise, particularly in these modern times of sprawling cities and pollution; the simile of the stones as being like prehistoric eggs emphasises the primeval quality of this setting, invoking the notions of ancient and new in the very fecund symbol of the egg. The most obvious link to a mythic beginning is the narrator's observation that the newness of things meant that words had not yet been invented for them, a remark that inevitably invokes the biblical topos of God naming the world, and granting man the gift of naming each living creature.[5] Fusion of art and nature, which runs as a theme throughout the first paragraphs of the novel, expands upon these implied parallels: the stones are described as 'polished', a word that suggests the conscious effort of an artistic demiurge as much as the natural and incidental actions of the environment upon

---

Márquez: '[he] effects an analogous legitimation and territorialization when he explains that Latin America, "that boundless realm of haunted men and historic women", that "outsized reality", "nourishes a source of insatiable creativity" more adequate for the representation of the continent's excesses than the "rational talents" of Europe', p. 133.

[3] Edition used is *Metamorphoses* (Oxford: Oxford University Press, 1987).

[4] Edition used is *One Hundred Years of Solitude* (London: Picador, 1978).

[5] *Genesis* 1:3–27 and 2:19–20.

the stones.[6] This fusion foregrounds the concept of a 'freshly minted' world forged perhaps by a creating divinity, with a nod towards the creative powers of the author himself. It is a world, so far, steeped in mythical themes, giving a universal and momentous tone to the opening descriptions.

The careful crafting of a newly emerged environment has already been undermined by the very first line of text, however: 'Many years later, as he faced the firing squad, Colonel Aureliano Buendía was to remember that distant afternoon when his father took him to discover ice' (p. 9). Less than a lifetime later, firing squads and armies are in currency, a fact that conflicts with the evocation of a paradisiacal land that follows the opening statement. It also suggests the realities of decline through the negative developments of human civilization, startling because of its close proximity to humanity's mythical primordial existence. This new world appears to be a façade, hiding a much longer ancestry than its innocently idyllic atmosphere suggests. It is also a distinctive signifier of the status of the text as magical-realist: it portrays a mingling of unreal and mythical elements in a world that is otherwise apparently the reader's own.

Ovid, early in *Metamorphoses*, also depicts the first age of mankind, an age of abundance and serene bliss in an idyllic environment, 'the golden age'.[7] It forms part of an extended account of the four ages of man, a traditional notion in Classical literature that first occurs in Hesiod's *Works and Days*. Ovid evokes the blissful serenity of this age by an abundance of end-stop lines, which create a sense of completeness and harmony; words denoting safety and innocence proliferate: 'safe', 'secure', 'unharmed' and 'untouched'. The first eleven lines of his account recall this world of innocence primarily by the absence of certain elements, in much the same manner as the chaos before creation was pictured in terms of its lack of things. In the creation episode the missing items were considered things of positive worth; however, in this account, the missing constituents are negative and man-made: 'with no avenger, . . . lawlesss . . . the absence of punishment and fear, and no threatening words to be read on bronze tablets' (1.89–93). Laws, judges and punishments, as well as armour, swords and other war paraphernalia, are all earmarked as negative aspects of contemporary Roman life that happily did not exist in that legendary time. This suggests a nostalgic and therefore partially fictitious re-creation from a perspective governed by awareness of loss. Certainly it is an account moulded into its distinct form by the contemporary culture of Rome: a poet conjuring a golden age today would be more likely to list nuclear and biological weapons, rather than swords and helmets, as the negative developments of civilization. The ideal of an unblemished landscape is

---

[6] Later examples of this conflation in *One Hundred Years of Solitude* of nature and artistry include the fifteenth-century suit of armour 'soldered together with rust' (p. 10), and the Spanish galleon 'adorned with orchids' (p. 17). Interestingly, both these examples are cases of nature asserting its power over the creations of men.

[7] For further discussion of this topos see Levin Harry, *The Myth of the Golden Age in the Renaissance* (Oxford: Oxford University Press, 1969).

expressed: 'not yet had the pine tree, cut down from its mountains, descended into the liquid waters to see the world' (1.94–5). Here the notion expands to encompass a moral transgression, not just of violating nature, but also of exploring the world.

The second half of the account of the golden age accentuates the abundant fertility of the earth, which gives freely, 'the earth herself, without compulsion, untouched by hoe or ploughshare, gave all things spontaneously' (1.101–2). A long list of the fruits of the land is given, with repeated emphasis upon the magical spontaneity of these gifts: 'with no force . . . flowers without seed . . . unploughed . . . with unfallowed field' (l.103–10). Ovid uses examples of the fruits and plants that were common in his time: strawberries, plentiful in the hills of Italy and Sicily, and acorns, similarly native to the region. A warm and soothing breeze, 'zephyri', is depicted caressing the opulent land. These details display a regionalist interpretation of the myth, focusing upon the natural wonders of a specifically Italian environment.

The narrator relates the account of the earth's golden age as if it really happened: it is presented in a straightforward manner, and it forms a part of world history that Ovid weaves into his continuous verse spanning from the dawn of time up to his own era. This was his explicit intention at the start of his poem: 'breathe on these my undertakings, and spin out my song in unbroken strains from the world's very beginning up to the present time' (1.3–4). It imbues his creation with a magical ambience, not explicable or reducible to any rationalisation, whether religious or scientific. As with García Márquez's novel, Ovid's poem creates a world in magical-realist terms.

Two Contexts

While Ovid was composing *Metamorphoses*, the miseries of the late Republic had finally settled under Augustus, and the Roman Empire was being heralded as a new golden age. Ovid's great predecessor, Virgil, who had lived through the civil wars, did a great deal to reflect this backdrop in his poetry. His work influenced Ovid, and the golden age theme has clear debts to Virgil's poem, the *Georgics*, which strove to recreate Italy as an idyllic pastoral community.[8] The *Georgics* purports to be a didactic treatise on farming life, and it offers comparisons between the simple agricultural existence that its narrator is advocating and the golden age: 'Before Jove's day no tillers subdued the land. Even to mark the field or divide it with bounds was unlawful. Men made gain for the common store, and Earth yielded all, of herself, more freely, when none begged her' (*Georg.*1.125–8). Virgil conflates golden age archetypes with his ideal of a pastoral life, declaring the existence of his imaginary Italian farmer to be

[8] Edition used is Virgil, *Eclogues, Georgics, Aeneid 1–6* (London: Heinemann, Loeb Classical Library, 1922).

a blessed one: 'Oh happy farmers! Too happy, should they come to know their blessings! For whom, far from the clash of arms, most righteous Earth, unbidden pours forth from her soil and easy sustenance' (*Georg*.II.458–60). He uses the myth as an example in an ostensibly didactic poem, both to decorate and strengthen his case for the simple farming life. The reader is not meant to take such references to the golden age as realities that actually existed, and his presentation of the idyllic agricultural life is often undermined by darker political and philosophical themes.

Ovid recalls Virgil in his version of the four ages, but produces an account of the golden age that is presented as an historical reality, albeit one that eludes explanation; in a typically magical-realist manoeuvre, he relativises the historical paradigm of truth by foregrounding a mythological account of time. Virgil's images are tempered with realism. It has already been noted that the early Greek poet Hesiod first recorded in extant Classical literature the myth of the decline of man through metallic ages. In his *Works and Days* the golden age involved complete rest and no one worked; yet Virgil emphasises the value of work, making it central to his golden age ideal. Ovid bypasses Virgil and alludes directly to the original Hesiodic model, reincorporating the idea of a world entirely free from toil into the *Metamorphoses*' golden age. This suggests that Ovid is flaunting his literary learnedness by incorporating different elements from his models; it also indicates that he has little interest in using the myth, as Virgil does, to make any profound comment on Roman society. Also noteworthy is that Virgil has set his golden age in the framework of an awesome Jupiter who governs mankind carefully and wisely; Ovid's Jupiter is capricious, ultimately at the mercy of the mysterious transformative power that the poem places at the origin of the universe.[9]

Ovid also consulted as a source the scientific poet Lucretius, whose didactic poem *De Rerum Natura* strove to free men from fear of death and gods by converting them to Epicureanism. In book five he speculates about the creation of the world and the development of human society, stating his opinion that the world is newly made, for civilization and scientific inquiry are still in their infancy. Lucretius' account of early man contains some features similar to Ovid's, but the tone is different. For example, Lucretius describes the nourishment of this first era: 'Their hearts were well content to accept as a free gift what the sun and showers had given and the earth had produced unsolicited. Often they stayed their hunger among the acorn-laden oaks' (V.937–40). However, his account lacks the whimsical nostalgia of either Virgil's or Ovid's version. Lucretius describes this first state of man as akin to animals, mindless and uncomfortable: 'They were relatively insensitive to heat and cold, to unaccustomed diet and bodily ailments in general. Through many decades of the

---

[9] Virgil's Jupiter created the seasons and alters the ideal golden age in order to sharpen the wits of mankind (*Georg*.I.121–4); yet Ovid's Jupiter appears to act arbitrarily and to no higher purpose (*Met*.I.116–18).

sun's cyclic course they lived out their lives in the fashion of wild beasts roaming at large' (V.928–32).

Ovid not only alludes to Lucretius' poem but also reverses its original premise. In representing the early world, Ovid uses Lucretian terminology, but twists it to reflect his own intentions: so the vocabulary of science is incorporated into what is essentially a magical version of creation. Lucretius' 'semina rerum' represent 'atoms', which in his philosophy were the basic constituents of his purely material and explicable universe.[10] Ovid shifts this phrase into his account of an intrinsically protean and mysteriously animate universe.

In summary, Ovid takes the elements of golden age longing, cynicism and nostalgia in his predecessors, and expands them into a fully realised chronological epoch of the beginning of the world, giving both his text and the world it invokes a magical basis constructed on previous literary interpretations. This overt use of literary predecessors' conceptions foregrounds the artificiality of the account: the Roman reader would recognize Virgilian and Lucretian echoes as an implicit commentary by Ovid's text. The mingling of contradictory aspects from earlier versions introduces a strong sense of aestheticism in the poem and suggests that Ovid's primary motivations were not especially political, philosophical or historical.

It is well known that Classical texts placed a great emphasis upon literary emulation and tradition; however, *One Hundred Years of Solitude* comes from a very different context. The nameless state of many things that appears at the opening of García Márquez's novel is markedly similar to words written to Charles V by Hernán Cortés: 'As I do not know what to call these things, I cannot express them . . . There is no human tongue that can explain its grandeurs and peculiarities.'[11] When the Spaniards first came to the New World, they chronicled their discoveries in awe-struck terms, astonished at the peoples and places they encountered.

Europe was then in the Renaissance years, an era of increased literary freedom from religious dogma, and the Classical writers were championed and greatly imitated by writers, rather than plundered for potential Christian allegory or rejected entirely. Poets frequently alluded to these texts, creating the notion of an idyllic place, 'Arcadia', constructed from the landscapes of Virgil's *Eclogues* and Ovid's *Metamorphoses*. These poems were seen as expressing a bygone ideal age of culture and beauty that Europe in the fifteenth century strove to resurrect. The discovery of the New World had fuelled the cultural atmosphere of the time, and the language of the Chroniclers echoes the ideals of the Classical

---

[10] The Epicureans believed that only two basic realities existed: void and matter. Matter was constituted by infinite and indestructible particles. There was no room for supernatural causes: everything happened according to the behaviour of these particles. See C.D.N.Costa, *Lucretius: De Rerum Natura V* (Oxford: Oxford University Press, 1984).

[11] Hernán Cortés, *Five Letters 1519–1526*, trans. J. Bayard Morris (London: George Routledge, 1928), p. 89. See also p. 23, p. 50, p. 62, and p. 85.

golden age as they sought to express their new experiences and locate their romantic ideals in a spatial rather than chronological framework. This often led to quite fantastical notions appearing in their accounts.

García Márquez constructs early Macondo in just these terms: 'Since the time of its founding, José Arcadio Buendía had built traps and cages. In a short time he filled not only his own house but all of those in the village with troupials, canaries, bee eaters and redbreasts . . . The first time that Melquíades' tribe arrived, selling glass balls for headaches, everyone was surprised that they had been able to find that village lost in the drowsiness of the swamp, and the gypsies confessed that they had found their way by the song of the birds' (p. 15). This passage invokes the journals of Christopher Columbus, who repeatedly noted the intense music of the songbirds in the regions he came upon;[12] García Márquez exaggerates by having such an abundance of birdsong in early Macondo that one inhabitant resorts to putting beeswax in her ears (p. 15). Likewise, Columbus' descriptions of orderly houses, 'swept clean and near to running fresh water, twelve to fifteen in a village', are recalled by the 'twenty mud and cane houses' and their nearby stream in Macondo.

Yet the arrangement of the houses has another literary precedent in its symmetrical perfection. The narrator describes: 'the others had been built in its image and likeness. (Each) had a small, well-lighted living-room, a dining-room in the shape of a terrace with gaily-coloured flowers, two bedrooms, a courtyard . . . and a corral where goats, pigs and hens lived in peaceful communion . . . from all of (the houses) one could reach the river and draw water with the same effort, and he had lined up the streets with such good sense that no house got more sun than another during the hot time of the day'(p. 15). These details mirror the orderly ideal community in Thomas More's *Utopia*, which depicted the kind of symmetrical planning included as an inevitable feature of all utopias in literature from Plato's *Republic* onwards. More's two books were written in 1516, around the time of the New World's discovery, and they both expressed and parodied the hopeful fervour of the times, whilst displaying clear debts to the Classical golden age in many self-conscious allusions.

In *One Hundred Years of Solitude* the dream of a perfect commune of existence, that the colonists perceived among the native Indians or attempted themselves to establish, is expressed in concrete form. It is represented in the first chapter: 'Within a few years Macondo was a village that was more orderly and hard-working than any known until then by its three hundred inhabitants. It was a truly happy village where no one was over thirty years of age and where no one had died' (p. 15). A remarkably Virgilian influence occurs in this chapter that can be traced to a passage in the *Georgics*, where in the pastoral utopia envisaged there, Virgil imagines the ancient armour of a soldier being discovered,

---

[12] 'The nightingale and other small birds were singing as they do in that month in Spain, and he says it was the greatest delight in the world'; see J.M. Cohen (ed.), *The Four Voyages of Christopher Columbus* (London: Century Hutchinson, 1988), p. 174; see also p. 70.

overgrown by nature and representing the decay and redundancy of by-gone wartime (*Georg*.1.493–7). When the founder of Macondo attempts to use magnets to locate gold, he uncovers a calcified skeleton in its rusted armour, a symbol of the past days of the Spanish Conquest (p. 10). It is a further indicator that the people of Macondo are depicted as actually occupying the Classical utopia of which writers such as Virgil only dreamed.

So why is García Márquez using Classical literary themes as well as alluding to the writings of the Conquest in his creation of early Macondo? The Mexican poet Octavio Paz has an answer. He describes Latin America as a chapter in the history of European utopias in *The Labyrinth of Solitude*;[13] García Márquez's construction of Macondo based upon inherited literary ideals acknowledges this disconcerting sense of being a victim of someone else's dream. By invoking these previous literary interpretations the novel both reflects and subverts their notions.

García Márquez's golden age theme develops continually throughout, in contrast to Ovid's brief self-sealed account in book one of his poem. Macondo succumbs slowly to the influences of the outside world which appear to precipitate its fall: the gypsies bring knowledge that fills the founder's head with flighty dreams and distracts him from his duties; before long a magistrate by the government, who arrives quietly but rapidly, becomes a source of corruption and strife. Later in the novel, lawyers are depicted as benders of reality and sanctifiers of lies, flitting around like crows, traditionally sinister birds. Civilisation is seen as descending from outside, as Macondo is invaded, exploited and finally abandoned. Expressed in the microcosm of Macondo is Latin America's sense of being victim of a European dream, envisioned as an earthly paradise, populated and exploited for its resources, and left at the mercy of other continents' economies and whims. The golden age myth, with its irredeemable remoteness and futile nostalgia, mirrors the dream of the Renaissance Europeans, constructed from previous fictional ideals; and it is not just the Spanish explorers that have their myth exploded, but also the Creole inhabitants whom García Márquez's central characters represent. They retreat into the unreality of myth and fail to connect with history, and so remain inside the deluded idyll of a golden age.

Conclusions

The background of *One Hundred Years of Solitude* is quite different from Ovid's Rome: violence, corruption and exploitation were the chief characteristics of contemporary Colombia while García Márquez was writing his novel; peace and comfortable wealth were Ovid's experiences while composing his poem.

---

[13] Octavio Paz, *The Labyrinth of Solitude*, trans. Lysander Kemp (New York: Grove Press, 1985), p. 97.

Likewise, Rome's temperate climate and pleasant Mediterranean habitat contrast wildly with the extremities of the tropical regions of Colombia.

That both Ovid and García Márquez have used magical realism to express their myth suggests that magical realism flourishes irrespective of cultural and geographical context. This conclusion invalidates Carpentier's claim of the essential links of the mode with geographical and historical setting. While environment no doubt impacts greatly on the literature produced, it cannot be the whole picture; in this instance, literary tradition seems just as significant a factor in its emergence. This essay also shows how magical realism can be used by authors in very different ways: political, historical and aesthetic. This is a topic that requires further analysis, but I will close this study by observing something important to these arenas for defining and comprehending magical realism: it is notable that each text is affected by a strong sense of belatedness and literary syncretism, which in turn produce a strong sense of fiction with all its fabulous and deceptive qualities. These features undoubtedly reflect the fact that both authors felt they were writing under a veritable or oppressive shadow of tradition; for García Márquez the Western European heritage, for Ovid, the glittering examples of Greek and Roman genius that he was continuously emulating. The absorption of previous works into an all-encompassing framework is one way of transcending any sense of inferiority and newness on the scene; by realising their realities as one of many other realities inside the text, this relativises the canonical importance of any one piece of work. Such an explanation fits neatly with Ovid's text, as it is the expression of his literary ingenuity and learning that is often paramount; for García Márquez, his version of magical realism is also used to express the inherent sense of unreality for people who feel they are living another's dream.

Lessons from the Golden Age
in Gabriel García Márquez's *Living to Tell the Tale*

Efraín Kristal

One April day in 1950 the 22-year-old writer, eaten up with nerves, offers the rough typescript of his first novel to the old Catalan dramatist, Don Ramón Vinyes, leading spirit of their bohemian group. Putting on his spectacles, Don Ramón smooths the pages out on the café table and reads, without any variation in his expression, the opening section of what would become *Leaf Storm*. Then, replacing his spectacles in their case, and the case in his breast pocket, he makes a few comments on the novelist's handling of time – which was, as García Márquez admits here, 'my life-or-death problem'; without doubt, the 'most difficult of all'.[1]

Resolving the Problem of Time

This portrait of the artist as a young man is no late, lazy memoir but a literary work in its own right, which recounts – or recreates – the process of García Márquez's formation as a writer within a highly wrought temporal framework. *Living to Tell the Tale* opens two months earlier, *in medias res*, as the author's mother, in mourning garb, threads her way lightly between the tables of the Mundo bookshop in Barranquilla, a stone's throw from Don Ramón's café, to confront her errant son with a mischievous smile: 'before I could react she said, "I'm your mother." And next, in her customary, ceremonial way: "I've come to ask you to please go with me to sell the house"' (*Living to Tell the Tale*, p. 3).

From here, time will double forward and back. The slow journey towards the old family home in Aracataca opens up vistas on to the past:

> The Sierra Nevada de Santa María and its white peaks seemed to come right down to the Banana plantations on the other side of the river. From there you could see the Arawak Indians moving in lines like ants along the cliffs of the

[1] Gabriel García Márquez, *Living to Tell the Tale*, trans. Edith Grossman (New York: Knopf, 2003), p. 142.

sierra, carrying sacks of ginger on their backs and chewing pellets of coca to make life bearable. As children we dreamed of parched, burning streets. For the heat was so implausible, in particular at siesta time, that the adults complained as if it were a daily surprise. From the day I was born I had heard it said, over and over again, that the rail lines and camps of the United Fruit Company had been built at night because during the day the sun made the tools too hot to pick up. (*Living to Tell the Tale*, p. 5)

But it also, of course, anticipates the future – the moment in 1965, still ten years ahead at the end of this book – when, driving his family to Acapulco on holiday, García Márquez finds one of the twentieth-century's most famous first sentences forming in his head: 'Many years later, facing the firing squad, Colonel Aureliano Buendía was to remember that distant afternoon when his father took him to discover ice.'[2] He turns the car round and roars back to Mexico City, locks himself in his room for eighteen months, smoking cigarettes stump to tip, and writes *One Hundred Years of Solitude*.

Yet in another sense, *Living to Tell the Tale* begins long after the wind at the end of that novel has blown everything away. The old house in Aracataca has gone to rack and ruin by the time García Márquez and his mother arrive there, peopled by unevictable tenants; they are unable to make a cent from it. Echoing one of the most recurrent, indeed predictable, patterns in García Márquez's fiction, what was intended is not fulfilled as one had expected, but as destiny wills. Instead of money, the journey provides García Márquez with his principal literary inspiration. He sees the arid little square in Ciénaga where, in 1928, the Colombian army had mown down the striking banana workers – in his grandfather's version, as recounted in *One Hundred Years of Solitude*: the three thousand men, women and children motionless under the savage sun, as the officer in charge gives them five minutes to clear the streets. He hears the stories of his parents' courtship – the beautiful daughter of the élite Liberal family pursued by an ambitious Conservative telegraph operator; his colleagues conspiring to tap out love messages down the wires, as her parents whisk her to safety – that inspired both *Leaf Storm* and *Love in the Time of Cholera*. He recalls his close relationship with his grandfather, who had fought in Colombia's devastating civil wars and who resurfaces in several fictional characters, including *No One Writes to the Colonel*. Gazing from the train window as they pull slowly through the green silence of the banana groves, García Márquez is taken with the name of an old plantation, 'Macondo', which will feature as the tropical town in so many of his tales and novels.

The centrepiece of the journey back is a Proustian experience, as he and his mother are invited to lunch at the home of the poor but dignified family doctor:

---

[2] Gabriel García Márquez, *One Hundred Years of Solitude*, trans. Gregory Rabassa (London: Picador, 1978), p. 9.

> From the moment I tasted the soup, I had the sensation that an entire sleeping world was waking in my memory. Tastes that had been mine in childhood and that I had lost when I left the town reappeared intact with each spoonful, and they gripped my heart. (*Living to Tell the Tale*, p. 39)

But if the raw material for his fiction was to be the *real maravilloso* of the Colombian Caribbean, what of its form? García Márquez has often told the story of discovering, in Kafka's 'Metamorphosis', the same impassive narration of the extraordinary that he remembered from his maternal grandmother's tales. There is further homage to Tranquilina Iguarán here, as to his aunts and to Doña Juana de Freytes, who would retell stories for the children drawn from the *Odyssey*, *Orlando Furioso*, *Don Quixote* and *The Count of Monte Cristo*. The 'popular memory' of Aracataca's inhabitants, he found, would often correct or contradict official accounts of historical events. At school and college, first in Barranquilla and then Bogotá (where 'an insomniac rain had been falling since the beginning of the sixteenth century'), his time was devoted to 'reading whatever I could get my hands on, and reciting from memory the unrepeatable poetry of the Spanish Golden Age' (*Living to Tell the Tale*, p. 301).

In the Shadow of Poetry

After 1948, fleeing the violence and repression that swept Bogotá following the assassination of the Liberal leader Jorge Eliécer Gaitán, García Márquez returned to Barranquilla, one of the safest cities in the country. It was at this stage that he fell in with the group around Don Ramón Vinyes. 'It is difficult to imagine the degree to which people lived then in the shadow of poetry' (*Living to Tell the Tale*, p. 311), he writes here of his literary education:

> We not only believed in poetry, and would have died for it, but we also knew with certainty – as Luis Cardoza y Aragón wrote – that 'poetry is the only concrete proof of the existence of man'. The world belonged to the poets. Their new works were more important for my generation than the political news, which was more and more depressing. (*Living to Tell the Tale*, pp. 301–2)

Of equal importance were the Modernist writers, newly available to a Spanish reading public in the translations produced by Jorge Luis Borges and his circle in Buenos Aires – 'we waited for the traveling salesmen from the Argentine publishers as if they were envoys from heaven' (*Living to Tell the Tale*, pp. 246–7; see also p. 352). Faulkner, Woolf, Conrad, Graham Greene, Joyce, Gide, Kafka, Mann and Borges himself were devoured by the Barranquilla group, along with the Greek classics that would inform, for example, the Sophoclean *Chronicle of a Death Foretold*.

It was here in Barranquilla under the vicious regime of Laureano Gómez that García Márquez began to develop his *métier* as a writer, published his first short stories and gained his initial literary reputation, while eking out an existence as a journalist. His life as a reporter became progressively more difficult as, under Rojas Pinilla, the censorship increased still further. In 1954, his serialized 'Story of a Shipwrecked Sailor' – an account of a Colombian navy vessel that had sunk on its way back from Alabama – attracted the wrath of the authorities. According to the official version, the ship had been wrecked in a terrible storm, and the drowned sailors were made national heroes. On interviewing a survivor, however, García Márquez discovered that there had been no storm; but the officers had so overloaded the boat with contraband household appliances that it had capsized, leaving the Everyman hero adrift on his raft in the ocean. García Márquez and his editor at *El Espectador* were both aware that the articles would embarrass the armed forces; but the reaction was more sordid than anticipated. García Márquez was dogged by a man who claimed to admire his writing, but warned that 'he was doing a disfavour to his country by supporting the Communists' and that his informant had 'infiltrated the Armed Forces in the service of the Soviet Union' (*Living to Tell the Tale*, p. 569). *Living to Tell the Tale* takes the story up to 1955 when, after a series of such incidents, García Márquez leaves Colombia for a four-year exile in Europe, where he would write *In Evil Hour*. It ends with a cliffhanger that points towards the life to come in Volume Two: the letter of reply from Mercedes Barcha, his future wife.

Many of these details – the family history and its recreation in his later work; initiations into literature, sex, journalism and politics; the insights about his creative methods – have already been documented, in *The Fragrance of Guava* and elsewhere.[3] But the portrait of the writer that emerges remains an engaging one, steady and self-assured; even the most intimate admissions reveal a man content with a life he considers well lived. From the vantage point of his seventy-five years, García Márquez pays homage to friends, lovers and mentors; makes some disarming confessions regarding his phobias and manias; and gracefully settles a few old scores.

There are many fond memories of the bordellos where he would carouse with friends and colleagues, and of the kindness of the prostitutes with whom he shared the town's cheapest hotel. Sex, and its free celebration, constitute an important part of García Márquez's self-identity, as of his vision of political liberation. Though he objects to his father's and grandfather's patriarchal attitudes towards their daughters – whose own sexuality is reduced to a matter of paternal honour – he applauds their virility in siring innumerable children, before and after wedlock, with the grudging acquiescence of their wives; both of whom eventually welcomed these illegitimate offspring into their households. But his claim that women 'sustain the world while we men mess it up with our

---

[3] Plinio Apuleyo Mendoza, *The Fragrance of Guava: Conversations with Gabriel García Márquez*, trans. Ann Wright (London and Boston: Faber Faber, 1988).

historical brutality' (*Living to Tell the Tale*, p. 89) can scarcely suffice as a politically aware account of the mass degradation forced upon lower-class Colombian women by the population displacements of the civil wars and *La Violencia*; and now again, with Uribe's counter-insurgency and fumigation campaigns. Keenly aware of the plight of the young men who came to peaceful Barranquilla as political refugees from the violence of other cities, García Márquez seems to overlook that of their sisters – many of whom became prostitutes as widows or orphans as a result of the same repression, driven from their homes to fill the bars and brothels he frequents.[4]

In many places, *Living to Tell the Tale* reads like a novel – fashioned with the same humour, themes, structures and poetic inflections as García Márquez's narrative fiction. If some of the rhetorical devices feel a little stale – there must be over a hundred uses of 'not this, but that' constructions to emphasize the unexpected – there are passages here as riveting as any that he has put on paper. Perhaps even more so, in his account of the assassination of Gaitán or of his own struggles against censorship, where the urgency of the historical moment, the combined sense of personal risk and social significance, is not mitigated or diffused by the subterfuges of magical realism. There is something refreshing about these sections, which deploy García Márquez's considerable literary resources stripped of any flights of fancy.

García Márquez's Magical Realism

In general, though, it is the aesthetic of magical realism that is exemplified; underscoring García Márquez's claim that, in Latin America and the Caribbean, 'artists have had to invent very little, and perhaps their problem has been the exact opposite: to make their reality credible'.[5] Many of the characters he recalls from childhood hold the wildest fantasies as firm beliefs, while he affects a tone, tiresome at times, of accepting them as reality himself; or of having experienced a few fantasies of his own. Yet as Fredric Jameson has suggested for the works of fiction, this brand of magical realism was born in an environment in which precapitalist and nascent capitalist modes overlap, involving – and this is another insight on García Márquez's handling of time – 'the articulated superposition of whole layers of the past within the present'[6]: Indian or pre-Columbian realities, the colonial era and slavery, the Bolivarian struggle for independence, *caudillismo*, the War of a Thousand Days, the period of direct American domination. Indeed, the story of Aracataca and of his family can only be understood in terms

---

[4] For a sobering picture of the exploitation and abuse of Colombian prostitutes in the 1950s see Saturnino Sepúlveda Niño, *La prostitución en Colombia. Una quiebra de las estructuras sociales* (Bogotá: Editorial Andes, 1970).

[5] Gabriel García Márquez, 'Fantasía y creación artística', *Notas de prensa, 1980–1984* (Bogotá: Editorial Norma, 1988), p. 147. All translations from the Spanish are my own.

[6] Fredric Jameson has speculated that magical realism 'depends on a content which betrays the overlap or the coexistence of precapitalist with nascent capitalist or technological

of the false sense of progress brought by the United Fruit Company, before it devastated the region's economy and ecology.

One might extend Jameson's point by suggesting an activist intention of sorts, perhaps underwritten by García Márquez's own emphasis on the Spanish classics. This brand of magical realism could be seen as a political secularization of a central theme of Golden Age literature – in *Don Quixote* of course, but in Baroque poetry as well: the realization that, if life is a dream, nevertheless the blurring of boundaries between fantasy and reality does not exonerate humanity from its moral commitments. It goes without saying that morality, for García Márquez, translates into social and political rather than religious terms. But the point can still be made: for García Márquez, literature is a vehicle through which to understand a given reality; his brand of magical realism is informed by his political commitment. How he first began to make connexions between the two is one of the underlying themes of this memoir.

The Political Education

Elements of García Márquez's political education are powerfully reconstructed here. A visceral anti-imperialist sentiment was implanted early, by his grandfather's descriptions of the 1928 massacre of the striking United Fruit Company workers. The same viewpoint underlies his interpretation of Colombia's geopolitical predicament:

> Colombia had always been a country with a Caribbean identity which opened to the world by means of the umbilical cord of Panamá. Its forced amputation condemned us to be what we are today: a nation with an Andean mentality whose circumstances favour the canal between two oceans belonging not to us but to the United States. (*Living to Tell the Tale*, p. 538)

At the boarding school in Zipaquirá, on the outskirts of Bogotá, García Márquez recalls some of his progressive teachers as living expressions of magical realism – Manuel Cuello del Río, for example, a radical Marxist who 'admired Lin Yutang and believed in apparitions of the dead' (*Living to Tell the Tale*, p. 232). One of them lent him a book in which he found a citation, attributed to Lenin,

---

features. [. . .] Not a realism to be transfigured by the "supplement" of a magical perspective but a reality which is already in and of itself magical or fantastic. Whence the insistence of both Carpentier and García Márquez that in the social reality of Latin America, "realism" is already "magical realism". [. . .] the articulated superposition of whole layers of the past within the present (Indian or pre-Columbian realities, the colonial era, the wars of independence, caudillismo, the period of American domination [. . .] is the formal precondition of this new narrative style.' See Fredric Jameson, 'On magical realism in film', *Critical Inquiry*, 12 (Winter 1986), p. 311.

that he would never forget: 'if you do not become involved in politics, politics will eventually become involved in you' (*Living to Tell the Tale*, p. 249). At this stage, however, literature still appeared as an escape from a depressing social reality, rather than an engagement with it. In retrospect at least, Pablo Neruda's arrival in the late 1940s – bringing to Bogotá the conviction that 'poetry had to be a political weapon' (*Living to Tell the Tale*, p. 305) – was a challenge to this quietism. García Márquez considers it 'a heartening symptom of the power of poetry during those years' (*Living to Tell the Tale*, p. 305) that the satirical sonnets Neruda composed in Bogotá on the subject of local intellectuals were taken so seriously; especially those that poked fun at Laureano Gómez's reactionary politics, even before he became Colombia's head of state.

But it was the events of 9 April 1948 and after that would signal his political coming of age. The most gripping section of *Living to Tell the Tale* is its account of Gaitán's assassination on that day, which triggered the furious protests and brutal repression of the *Bogotazo* – one of the defining moments of the decades palsied by *La Violencia*, during which at least 200,000 people were reputed killed (García Márquez suggests the figure might be much higher). Hobsbawm and others have argued that the conflicts can only be understood in the context of a frustrated social revolution – when 'revolutionary tensions are neither dissipated by peaceful economic development, nor redirected to create new and revolutionary structures. The armies of death, the scores of uprooted, the physically and mentally mutilated, are the price Colombia has paid for that failure.'[7] Though García Márquez would come to interpret the events along similar lines, he had initially been sceptical – 'I had allowed myself the arrogance of not believing in Gaitán' (*Living to Tell the Tale*, p. 331), as he puts it; but on hearing him speak, 'I understood all at once that he had gone beyond the Spanish country and was inventing a lingua franca for everyone' (*Living to Tell the Tale*, p. 331). The 20-year-old, then a cub reporter on the Bogotá *Espectador*, took part in the 'march of silence' against government repression, organized by Gaitán some months before the assassination – his first political act: 'I had come without political conviction, drawn by the curiosity of the silence, and the sudden knot of tears in my throat took me by surprise' (*Living to Tell the Tale*, p. 333). With hindsight, he sees Gaitán as having radicalized his election campaign of the previous year in a way

> that went beyond the historic division of the country into Liberals and Conservatives, [to make] a more realistic distinction between the exploiters and the exploited. With his historic slogan, 'Let's get them!', and his supernatural energy, he sowed the seeds of resistance even in the most remote places with a gigantic campaign of agitation that continued gaining ground until . . . it was on the verge of being an authentic social revolution. (*Living to Tell the Tale*, p. 330)

---

[7] E.J. Hobsbawm, 'La anatomía de "La violencia" en Colombia', in Hobsbawm, *et al*, *Once ensayos sobre La Violencia* (Bogotá: Centro Gaitán, 1985), p. 23.

Gaitán had been on his way to lunch with *El Espectador*'s editor on the morning of the assassination. García Márquez heard the news within minutes and rushed to the scene of the crime. Angry bootblacks were already using their wooden boxes to bang down the gates of the chemist's shop where the police had locked the assailant, to protect him from the mob. 'A tall man, very much in control of himself and wearing an irreproachable grey suit as if he were going to a wedding, urged them on with well-calculated shouts' – and was driven away in a 'too new' car, as soon as Gaitán's apparent killer had been dragged off by the crowd.

It was only later that 'it occurred to me that the man had managed to have a false assassin killed, in order to protect the identity of the real one' (*Living to Tell the Tale*, p. 338). García Márquez recalls the rebellion that ensued:

> The smoke from the fires had darkened the air, and the clouded sky was a sinister blanket. Maddened hordes, armed with machetes and all kinds of tools stolen from the hardware stores, set fire to the businesses along Carrera Séptima, with the help of mutinous police officers . . . Wherever we went we stumbled across household appliances, over bottles of expensive brands of whisky and all kinds of exotic drinks that the mobs beheaded with their machetes. (*Living to Tell the Tale*, p. 338)

Government troops raked the Plaza de Bolívar with machine-gun fire. A group of Gaitán supporters from the University proclaimed themselves a revolutionary *junta*. The Communists – 'the only ones who seemed to act with any political sense' (*Living to Tell the Tale*, p. 346) – directed the crowd, 'like traffic police', towards the centres of power. In this chaos, who should appear but the 20-year-old Fidel Castro, in Bogotá as a University of Havana delegate to a progressive students' congress, and with an appointment to meet Gaitán that afternoon. Castro, who can do no wrong in García Márquez's eyes, is presented as a sensible pragmatist, trying to help stop the killings in the streets: 'One would have to know him to imagine his desperation' (*Living to Tell the Tale*, p. 356). He rushes to a pro-Gaitán police division, holed up in their garrison, and tries to persuade them, without success, that any force that stays in its barracks is lost: 'He proposed that they take their men out to struggle in the streets for the maintenance of order and a more equitable system' (*Living to Tell the Tale*, p. 357).

The Image of a Literary Life

Living to Tell the Tale suggests that García Márquez's intentions as a novelist, journalist and political activist constitute a coherent project; but a lot is left unsaid, and much might be read between the lines. The official image is of the most famous of all living Latin American writers, who has happily reconciled his literary vocation and global prestige with his political commitments: Caribbean *joie de vivre* goes hand in hand with a broad sense of compassion for hunger, poverty, human misery and social injustice. To the right-wing media – enamoured of his fiction but contemptuous of his affiliations – he has written: 'as a man, I am indivisible and my political position reflects the same ideology with which I write my books'.[8] But although he has often declared himself a sympathizer of the Colombian Communist Party, García Márquez has also wanted to maintain a safe distance from political militancy – explaining, in *The Fragrance of Guava*: 'My relationship with the Communists has had many ups and downs. We've often been at loggerheads because every time I adopt a stance they don't like, their newspapers really have a go at me. But I've never publicly condemned them, even at the worst moments.'[9]

Another, still more sanitized reading could show him as a man who values friendship over politics, and whose public interventions have stressed 'reconciliation' in the interests of peace. There are anecdotes here to suggest that his Nobel Prize status has made him a statesman of sorts, with access to political players across the spectrum from Castro to Kissinger and Clinton. It is clear that he wants to be seen as a man who has been able to reach – by virtue of his craft or prestige – spheres that might have otherwise been averse to the significance of his underlying message. And if he sometimes plays the naïve by leaving hidden the full thrust of his political views, he has been sanctioned in so doing by the most important leaders of the Latin American Left. There is a telling moment in the early 1950s when Gilberto Vieira – 'the most prominent of the founders of the Communist Party . . . the man most wanted by the country's secret services' – contacts García Márquez from his clandestine hideout in Bogotá to let him know that he has been reading his newspaper articles with great attention, and has even identified the young journalist's anonymous pieces in order to 'interpret their hidden meanings'. It is from Vieira himself that García Márquez is exonerated from joining the Party, or from any direct political involvement: 'he agreed that the best service I could offer the country was to continue in the same way without compromising myself with anyone in any kind of political militancy' (*Living to Tell the Tale*, p. 556).

But if several meanings can be read from García Márquez's statements of his political positions, it is impossible to pin him down. Though he makes little of the years he spent as a law student it is clear that he is also mounting a pre-emptive defence in *Living to Tell the Tale* against those who might accuse him of either too much or too little radicalism. Perhaps something

[8] Gabriel García Márquez, *Notas de prensa, 1980–1984*, p. 112.
[9] Plinio Apuleyo Mendoza, *The Fragrance of Guava. Conversations with Gabriel García Márquez*, p. 97.

similar could be said of his literary achievements which, if one reads carefully between the lines, can be interpreted either as what Gerald Martin has described, in *Journeys Through the Labyrinth*,[10] as depictions of 'the prehistory before the dawn of proletarian consciousness'; or as wild expressions of the Latin American imagination, if one would prefer.

[10] Gerald Martin's *Journeys Through the Labyrinth. Latin American Fiction in the Twentieth Century* (Verso, London and New York, 1989) is arguably the most compelling case for reading the Latin American novel as a response to social and political predicaments, and the high point of the book is the analysis of *One Hundred Years of Solitude*. Martin argues that García Márquez's novel signals 'the end of primitive neocolonialism, its conscious or unconscious collaborators, and an epoch of illusions' (p. 233). The famous deciphering episode of a parchment in Sanskrit, at the end of the novel, which links Aureliano (the decipherer) and his friend Gabriel (García Márquez writes himself into the novel to indicate his complicity with a character whose understanding of the world is taken to be wild fantasies by all those around him) signifies, for Martin, nothing short of 'the prehistory before the dawn of proletarian consciousness' (p. 233). And indeed, Martin rounds off his main contention by indicating that the implicit, optimistic hope that the new Latin American novel 'itself was proof of the end of neocolonialism and the beginning of true liberation' (p. 233).

Part II: History, Nightmare, Fantasy

Introduction

Stephen M. Hart

'la metafísica es una rama de la literatura fantástica'
(metaphysics is a branch of fantastic literature)
(Jorge Luis Borges, 'Tlön, Uqbar, Orbis Tertius', *Ficciones*)

It was Stephen Dedalus, a character in Joyce's *Ulysses* (1922), who once famously stated that 'history is a nightmare from which I am trying to awake', and some of the edge of Dedalus's idea animates the essays brought together in this section. One of the most contentious areas surrounding the analysis of magical realism is the intrinsic depth attached to the use of fantasy in magical-realist novels. Is fantasy, for example, simply a case of escapism or does it voice a concrete political critique? Does the fantasy in a magical-realist novel indicate the hallucinations of an artist who is in the process of retreating from the world around him, or does it embody the desire for a more just political world? This is the Janus-like dilemma which the essays in this section attempt to address. David Henn, in his essay 'History and the Fantastic in José Saramago's Fiction', for example, focuses on three of the Nobel prize-winner's novels, *Raised from the Earth* (1980), *Baltasar and Blimunda, The Year of the Death of Ricardo Reis* (1984), and *The Stone Raft* (1986), which helped to secure the Portuguese writer's international reputation. Whether describing the construction in 1717 of a 'flying machine', or the empiric survival of a poet's *nom de plume* (Ricardo Reis) after the poet's actual death (Fernando Pessoa), or the uncoupling of the Iberian Peninsula from France and its subsequent floating across the Atlantic towards America, Saramago is able to root his descriptions within the realm of the historical and the everyday – a hallmark, as Henn underlines, of the playful trappings of magical realism. In 'Magical-realist Elements in José Eustasio Rivera's *The Vortex*', Humberto Núñez demonstrates that Rivera's masterpiece contains a number of characteristics which locate it squarely as a forerunner of the evolution of magical realism in Latin America. These include the use of myth and legend, the reference to magic and the supernatural, allusions to ethnic and cultural heterogeneity, the presence of the jungle's flora and fauna, and the denunciation of social injustice and criminality. For her part, Alejandra Rengifo, in 'Beyond Magical Realism in *The Red of His Shadow* by Mayra Montero', shows how Montero underpins her depiction of a harsh, everyday reality in Haiti with a brooding sense of the supernatural. *The Red of His Shadow* alludes to some of the repertoire pieces of magical realism – an impossible day when snow falls on an island in the Caribbean – but, just as important, Montero is keen to point to the ways in which Voodoo animates, controls and sometimes destroys the lives of ordinary people in Haiti.

The concluding two essays in this section probe the ways in which fantasy upturns bourgeois norms. Michael Berkowitz, in 'Cops, Robbers, and Anarcho-terrorists: Crime and Magical Realism's Jewish Question', for example, focuses on the novels of two Israelis – *The Zigzag Kid* by David Grossman and *Four Mothers* by Shifra Horn – and four by American Jews: *Leviathan* by Paul Auster, *Bee Season* by Mylka Goldberg, *The Escape Artist* by Judith Katz, and *The Isaac Quartet* by Jerome Charyn. Berkowitz shows how the shadow of Borges's Funes el memorioso (Funes the Memorious), his sense of 'inner violence and betrayal', hovers over this set of Israeli and Jewish-American novels, thereby intersecting at various levels with the themes and techniques of magical realism, particularly when viewed through the lens of criminality. Sarah Sceats, for her part, in 'Flights of Fancy: Angela Carter's Trangressive Narratives', shows how the English novelist employs fantasy and symbolism in order to offer a slyly sub-versive view of the world around us. *The Bloody Chamber*, for example, offers a reworking of the Bluebeard story in which the traditional role ascribed to women is overturned, while *Nights at the Circus*, in evoking some of the basic tropes of magical realism (a girl with eyes in her nipples, and shards of broken mirror which are too hot to touch because they have absorbed a troupe of tigers), manages to fundamentally de-stabilise the gendered categories which police the relationship between the fantastic and the real. The literary works studied in this section – ranging from Portuguese novels such as *The Stone Raft* to Latin American works such as *The Vortex* and *The Red of His Shadow*, from Israeli novels such as *The Zigzag Kid* to English fiction like *The Bloody Chamber* – evoke the praeternatural in uniquely personal ways, but they join hands in their portrayal of the process whereby the laws of the empirical world by which we live our everyday lives are turned upside-down. In their work the supernatural walks the tightrope between the miracle and the nightmare.

History and the Fantastic in José Saramago's Fiction

David Henn

Historical Reality and Flights of Fancy

In Lisbon, during the second half of 1709, a Brazilian-born priest and inventor, Bartolomeu Lourenço de Gusmão, made a number of attempts to launch a balloon-type apparatus. Eventually the craft, popularly known as the *Passarola* (Great Bird), took off from the heights of St George's castle, overlooking the centre of the city, and apparently carried Lourenço down to the vicinity of the River Tagus – a distance of about one kilometre.[1]

Father Bartolomeu Lourenço, who was referred to in his day as 'the flying man' (Corrêa Neves, p. 19), is one of the principal characters of José Saramago's *Baltasar and Blimunda* (1982).[2] In the novel, his *Passarola*, now evolved into a craft with the appearance of a bird-cum-boat, is shown to be capable of flying many kilometres, at speed, and at a considerable height. In an interview published in 1986, Saramago noted that, although he saw himself as very much a realist writer, his novels all revealed some element of the fantastic.[3] But he has also stressed the importance of history to works of fiction, asserting that every novel is, in a sense, a historical novel.[4] Indeed, in his novels of the 1980s – *Raised from the Earth* (1980), *Baltasar and Blimunda*, *The Year of the Death of Ricardo Reis* (1984),[5] *The Stone Raft* (1986),[6] and *The History of the Siege of Lisbon* (1989) – Saramago draws, at times heavily, on historical material. Thus the narrative action of both *Baltasar and Blimunda* and *The Year of the Death of Ricardo Reis*, two of the three works I wish to look at in terms of history,

---

[1] For details of these various attempts, see Gustavo Corrêa Neves, *As Experiências Aerostáticas de Bartholomeu Lourenço de Gusmão* (Lisbon: Aero-Club de Portugal, 1911), pp. 36–7.

[2] José Saramago, *Baltasar and Blimunda*, trans. Giovanni Pontiero (London: Picador, 1989).

[3] See Perfecto E. Cuadrado, '*Objecto Quase* y el estatuto de las "Obras menores"', *Insula: José Saramago; Escritura abierta*, No 663 (March 2002), 28–30 (p. 29).

[4] Carlos Reis, *Diálogos com José Saramago* (Lisbon: Caminho, 1998), p. 139.

[5] *The Year of the Death of Ricardo Reis*, trans. Giovanni Pontiero (London: Harvill Press, 1999).

[6] *The Stone Raft*, trans. Giovanni Pontiero (London: Harvill Press, 1999).

the fantastic, and magical realism, is firmly pegged to specific events of clearly defined historical periods. *Baltasar and Blimunda*, which contains numerous, precise historical and chronological markers, covers much of the first half of the eighteenth century. The narrative development of *The Year of the Death of Ricardo Reis*, although chronologically much more restricted (covering the period from the closing days of December 1935 to the end of August 1936), reveals, by means of the introduction of news stories and the comments of various characters, political and historical events of those eight months. In the third novel I shall consider, *The Stone Raft*, contemporary politics emerge in terms of pressures and interests, rather than through specific historical occurrences; here, the sheer magnitude of the fantastical element is overwhelming.

Saramago's three novels of 1982–86 are the works that established the author's international reputation. They mark his movement away from the almost total neo-realism of *Raised from the Earth* (which details the lives of three generations of a family of Portuguese peasants and covers the period from World War I to the revolution of April 1974) and into narratives that derive much of their impact from the juxtaposition of historical (and quotidian) reality with elements of the fantastic. To date, critics of the three novels I shall discuss have been rather timid with regard to Saramago's exploitation and manipulation of the fantastic in these works. For example, addressing principally *Raised from the Earth*, *Baltasar and Blimunda*, and *The Stone Raft*, David Frier focuses on the ideological beliefs of the author and simply refers in passing to 'seductive flights of fancy' in Saramago's works such as *Baltasar and Blimunda* and mentions 'the implausibity of the plot' of *The Stone Raft*.[7] And in his study of *The Year of the Death of Ricardo Reis*, Giovanni Pontiero pays no attention to the dramatic impact of the post-burial manifestation of the poet Fernando Pessoa and the incarnation of his heteronym, Ricardo Reis. Indeed, Pontiero's critical focus is largely on Saramago's portrayal of Pessoa and Reis, the narrative importance of fate in this work, issues of reading, writing, and narrating, and Borgesian resonances in the novel.[8]

More recently, Saramago's Spanish translator has referred to *Baltasar and Blimunda* as simply a 'prodigious love story'.[9] However, another Spaniard, after focusing on the historical and factual backdrop to *The Year of the Death of Ricardo Reis*, and suggesting that the year 1936 is the 'authentic protagonist' of the work, later observes that bringing the dead poet back to 'life' for nine months

[7] David Frier, 'Ascent and Consent: Hierarchy and Popular Emancipation in the Novels of José Saramago', *Bulletin of Hispanic Studies: Portugal; Its Culture, Influence and Civilization*, 71 (1994), 125–38 (p. 129).

[8] Giovanni Pontiero, 'José Saramago and *O Ano da Morte de Ricardo Reis*: The Making of a Masterpiece', *Bulletin of Hispanic Studies: Portugal; Its Culture, Influence and Civilization*, 139–48.

[9] Basilio Losada, 'Figuras de mujer', *Insula: José Saramago; Escritura abierta*, 3–4 (p. 3).

is 'an element of "magical realism" in the style of the great Latin-American narrators'. The critic then immediately adds that this narrative device is a 'concession to the fantastic' in a work that he regards as a blend of journalistic and historical fact presented in a realist mode.[10] This is indeed some 'concession'. Finally, in the same special issue of *Insula*, the Portuguese critic Maria Fernanda Abreu deals with *The Stone Raft* in terms of the 'journey motif'. At the same time, and without being at all distracted by the narrative presentation of the Iberian peninsula making its stately way around the Atlantic, she pursues the connection between Saramago's novel and *Don Quixote*.[11]

As was noted earlier, Saramago has acknowledged the importance of the fantastic to his fiction; he also observed that for him the fantastic was 'not an end – but a means'.[12] What I now propose to examine is the way in which, in the three novels under consideration, Saramago makes use, often in a spectacular fashion, of fantastical, inexplicable elements and how, by combining these with both historical and everyday reality, he develops narratives that belong in the literary realm of magical realism.

A Monastery-Palace on the Ground and a Craft in the Air

Baltasar and Blimunda opens in 1711, with the early pages focusing on the ritual and pageant surrounding the bedchamber encounters of King John V and his Austrian queen. After two years of marriage without issue, anxiety and gossip are widespread at court. The king vows that if an heir is born within a year, then he will build a monastery for the Franciscan order at the village of Mafra, forty kilometres northwest of Lisbon. The vow is proclaimed, children are later born to the royal couple, and the narrative duly records that in 1717 work begins on the religious house. At this time, Baltasar Mateus, an inhabitant of Mafra who is intermittently involved in the construction of Father Lourenço's flying machine, notes the digging of the foundations for the monastery.

The Portuguese title of the novel is, in fact, *Memorial do Convento* (Chronicle of the Monastery) and reflects the narrative's foregrounding of the construction of the massive monastery-palace at Mafra. Originally intended as a small religious house for thirteen Franciscan friars, the scheme was gradually enlarged until, when it was completed in 1735, the huge building, with a 220-metre façade and an area only slightly smaller than that of the Escorial, could accommodate 280 friars and well over 100 novices. One of the great architectural monuments

[10] Manuel Angel Vázquez Medel, 'Pessoa revisitado: *El año de la muerte de Ricardo Reis*, de José Saramago', *Insula: José Saramago; Escritura abierta*, 5–9 (pp. 5, 9).

[11] Maria Fernanda Abreu, 'Dos Caballos-Rocinante o el viaje en *La balsa de piedra* leída por *El Quijote*', *Insula: José Saramago; Escritura abierta*, 10–11.

[12] Perfecto E. Cuadrado, p. 29.

of Portugal and the most striking legacy of John V, the monastery-palace is also a reminder of the wealth of Brazil, from which it was financed, and of the heyday of the Portuguese Empire. Yet Saramago does not address the construction of this vast and ornate building in terms of the vision of a monarch, the designs of his German architect, or the magnificence of the structure and its contents. The Mafra focus is almost entirely on the ordinary men, labourers and craftsmen, who toiled and sometimes died so that the king's project could be completed.

Elsewhere in his novel, Saramago alights on affairs of state – wars, peace treaties, colonial problems, dynastic marriages, and so on. At the same time, the narrative repeatedly contrasts such nationally important events, what might be termed the showcase of history, with the existences and concerns of the ordinary people caught up in, or indirectly affected by, the policies and plans of the powerful. In particular, he gives generous recognition to the anonymous workers at Mafra, where at times there were as many as 20,000 men engaged on the site. For a period, Baltasar is one of these and, in this context, the reality of his day-to-day existence largely reflects that of his fellows. The ex-soldier lives with Blimunda who, for much of her time, pursues a humdrum domestic routine. However, these two lovers and companions, whose story commands approximately one half of the narrative, are also involved in activities that provide a dramatic contrast with the normally bleak and arduous reality of those around them. With her gift of clairvoyance, Blimunda is able to see, for example, an unborn child, a tumour in a man, gravel and granite beneath the soil, or the skeleton of a huge fish in an underground reservoir (*Baltasar and Blimunda*, p. 66).[13] This ability enables her to look for cracks in the canework or air bubbles in the metal of the flying machine that Baltasar is helping the priest to build. Furthermore, it permits her to see people's spirits or wills (a small, dark cloud inside the individual) and to collect them when they are about to leave the body, for the machine is to be powered by the effect of sunlight on glass globes containing human wills.

With these elements that show natural laws being defied by a woman exercising clairvoyance and a flying machine that is powered by captured human spirits, Saramago's novel adequately satisfies Tzvetan Todorov's preliminary definition of 'the fantastic' in literature: the occurrence of 'an event that cannot be explained by the laws of the world with which we are familiar'.[14] Subsequently, Todorov qualifies this definition. He proposes the terms 'fantastique-étrange' (fantastic-uncanny) for events that are initially perceived by the reader as manifestations of the supernatural but which, in the end, have a rational explanation and 'fantastique-merveilleux' (fantastic-marvellous) for those happenings that

---

[13] Written accounts mention a young woman who lived in Lisbon during the reign of John V and who apparently possessed such powers. See Ana Paula Arnaut, '*Memorial do Convento*': *História, ficção e ideologia* (Coimbra: Fora do Texto, 1996), pp. 63–6.

[14] Tzvetan Todorov, *Introduction à la littérature fantastique* (Paris: Éditions du Seuil, 1970), p. 29.

have no such explanation and, ultimately, require the reader to accept occurrences that are not governed by known laws of Nature (Todorov, pp. 46–62). The fantastic-marvellous is therefore the 'sub-genre', as Todorov terms it, that involves what we have come to label as 'magical realism'.

In Saramago's novel, the fabulous craft does indeed fly. On the first occasion, the eponymous protagonists accompany the priest as he flees from the Inquisition. Soaring over Mafra, the three aviators note the site where the monastery-palace is being built, while the appearance of the *Passarola* causes widespread panic on the ground (*Baltasar and Blimunda*, pp. 178–84). Then, a good while later, the machine again takes to the air. Hidden away in the hills, it is being examined by Baltasar when its spirit-globes are accidentally exposed to the sun. The craft ascends with its solitary passenger who is not seen again until some nine years later, when Blimunda watches Baltasar being led to the stake to be burned on the orders of the Inquisition. Before he dies, she captures his will.

In this work, the author has developed a narrative that accommodates the events of history, the legacies and monuments of those events, the cast of historical celebrities involved, the power and wealth of the monarchy, and the sinister presence of the Church. In addition, the novel acknowledges the role of countless anonymous soldiers, servants, builders, and other ordinary citizens of the period. It does this by presenting the daily routine of the lives of those so often overlooked by the record of history. Through this canvas of historical and social reality, Saramago weaves three main fantastical threads: clairvoyance, the collecting and harnessing of people's wills, and air travel by humans. These are sufficiently fabulous and dramatic to provide a prodigious contrast with the sheer mundanity and physicality of the buildings, the masses of people, the opulence at court, the squalor of the poor, the landscapes, and, above all, the massive structure so painstakingly rising by the village of Mafra.

Poets and Politics in the Year of 1936

With *The Year of the Death of Ricardo Reis*, the author also looks, although far less searchingly, at some of the humble participants in the historical process. However, his main focus is on the unwillingness of two artists and intellectuals to address the menacing events taking place in the world around them. In particular, Saramago presents his educated and cultured eponymous protagonist as a mildly curious but overwhelmingly passive spectator of the rise of Fascism in Portugal and elsewhere. The name Ricardo Reis is one of the three heteronyms used by Portugal's leading twentieth-century poet, Fernando Pessoa. However, these heteronyms were not intended to be simply pseudonyms attached to parts of Pessoa's poetic output. Each denotes a distinctive poetic voice and personality. Indeed, Pessoa provided short biographies of his three creations. Thus Reis was supposedly born in Oporto in 1887 and educated by the Jesuits before studying medicine and entering general practice. He knew Latin and taught himself

Greek, and in 1919 Reis, a confirmed monarchist, left the Portuguese republic to settle in Brazil.

Fernando Pessoa died on 30 November 1935. The opening scene of Saramago's novel takes place a month later, on 29 December, as Ricardo Reis sails into Lisbon and sets foot in his home country for the first time in sixteen years. Under the 1933 constitution of the so-called New State, Portugal was by then a right-wing, pro-Catholic, nationalist dictatorship.

The first of the novel's three epigraphs is the opening line of an untitled ode, dated June 1914, by Ricardo Reis: 'Wise is the man who contents himself with the spectacle of the world.' Reis's poetry, with its many classical and pagan resonances, constantly reveals a belief in the power of Fate and proposes equanimity and serenity when one is confronted with the uncertainties and irrationalities of the world around. This single line of poetry, with its proclamation of the wisdom of detachment and passive observation, has been dismissed by Saramago as 'idiocy'.[15] Consequently, it comes as no surprise to find that the epigraph announces an intellectual posture that Saramago's novel will come to expose and implicitly condemn.

On his return to Lisbon, Ricardo Reis finds a suitable hotel, which he describes as 'a neutral place requiring no commitment' (*The Year of the Death of Ricardo Reis*, p. 11), and the next day, without explanation, he goes to the Lisbon cemetery where Fernando Pessoa is buried. He finds the grave, looks at it, reads the inscription, reveals no emotion, and then decides to have lunch. Just over a day later, and half an hour into the New Year of 1936, Reis returns to his hotel room and finds that the cemetery visit has been reciprocated. Sitting on the sofa, with the light on, is the dead poet. Reis simply says 'Hello'. After an exchange of pleasantries, Pessoa explains that he has until the end of August to wander around as he pleases: 'The usual period is nine months, the same length of time we spend in our mother's womb, I believe it's a question of symmetry [. . .] and apart from exceptional cases it takes nine months to achieve total oblivion' (*The Year of the Death of Ricardo Reis*, p. 64).

The unreality of this situation, indeed the slightly comic absurdity of it, with Pessoa sitting on a hotel sofa dressed in his sombre burial suit, might entitle the reader to expect a rational explanation (that Reis is dreaming or hallucinating) and what Todorov would describe as an example of the 'fantastic-uncanny' (Todorov, pp. 49–51). However, by the end of the narrative, and after a series of almost mundane appearances by the dead poet, it transpires that there is no natural explanation for these interventions in the life of Ricardo Reis. Accordingly, they constitute examples of Todorov's the 'fantastic-marvellous' (Todorov, pp. 57–8).

Throughout *The Year of the Death of Ricardo Reis*, the eponymous protagonist's detached observations of the real world and his supernatural encounters with his creator and former literary colleague, the deceased poet, are presented

<hr>

[15] Carlos Reis, *Diálogos com José Saramago*, p. 160.

against a background of the ominous reality of the events of 1936. Frequent references are made to Mussolini's imperial adventures in Africa, Nazi Germany's occupation of the Rhineland, political turmoil in republican Spain, the destruction of Addis Ababa, German designs on Danzig and Czechoslovakia, the insurrection of army officers in Japan, the uprising of right-wing generals in Spain in July 1936 and that country's descent into civil war. Concerning Portugal, there are, for example, references to the New State, the vigilance of the police force, censorship, celebrations of the eighth anniversary of the dictator António de Oliveira Salazar's accession to power, a visit by members of the Hitler Youth, and the existence of the equally disturbing Portuguese Youth Movement.

At times Reis expresses his right-wing sympathies and at times he wearies of the propaganda. But basically he is an observer of the minutiae of everyday life in Lisbon and frequently looks away from ominous events in Portugal and elsewhere: 'Ricardo Reis takes stock of his own ambitions and concludes that he craves nothing, that he is content to watch the river and the passing ships, the mountains and the peace that reigns there' (*The Year of the Death of Ricardo Reis*, p. 278). Reis also watches people: at the hotel, in the streets, and in other public places. His various conversations with the dead poet range over such subjects as existence, death, multiple personalities, Reis's poetry, artistic sincerity, Portugal's colonies, Portugal's national poet, Camões, love, artistic creativity, women, and scruples. Politics and the state of contemporary Europe are rarely on the agenda. When they do figure they elicit only a superficial, acquiescent response.

The fact that Reis and the dead poet occasionally talk of women and love is largely because of Reis's association, during the course of the narrative, with two females. These are the hotel chambermaid, Lydia, with whom he has a regular, but passionless sexual relationship, and Marcenda, the elegant but neurotic upper middle-class young woman who, with her withered arm, is regarded by Reis as a vulnerable as well as an elusive ideal. In fact, by using the names Lydia and Marcenda for these two characters, who play a significant part in Reis's reacquaintance with Lisbon, Saramago is providing an intertextual link with Ricardo Reis's poetry. In his verse there are four named women who are addressed by the poet and invited to be his companion. And while Marcenda figures in just one poem, the name of Lydia is used in well over twenty of the 200 or so poems attributed to Reis. However, the Lydia that Saramago puts into Reis's hotel bed is a far cry from the bucolic ideal and chaste companion evoked in so many of the odes. She is a lusty, honest, affectionate and hard-working young woman of humble origins. When she informs Reis that she is pregnant, his reaction is one of indifference, although his attitude softens a little before his 'death'. This occurs at the end of August 1936. When Pessoa's nine transitional months have run their course, Reis accompanies him to oblivion.

In this novel, Saramago exposes and implicitly condemns two literary, intellectual figures for their failure to confront and reject the pernicious ideologies of nationalism and Fascism. To this end he resurrects a dead poet and adds a new chapter to the biography of one of the poet's literary voices, one of his 'fictions'. The result is a work in which the fantastic is used to display the intellectual posturing and the passivity of Pessoa and Reis in the presence of the sinister, historical realities of the mid-1930s. In his following novel, *The Stone Raft*, the author moves from the use of the fantastic in the case of two individuals to the stunning spectacle of half a million square kilometres of southern Europe detaching itself and moving away into the Atlantic.

Iberia Adrift: Magical Realism
Writ Large and Small

With this 1986 novel, the specificity of historical events is abandoned. Moreover, the opening phase of the narrative is carefully developed as a manifestation of the fantastic. Without a logical or natural explanation, a massive crack appears along the length of the Pyrenees. In the early pages of the novel, the fissure is associated with the strange experiences of a handful of people in various parts of the Iberian Peninsula and with the unexpected behaviour of some dogs and a large flock of birds. Thus, the narrative begins with a Portuguese woman marking a line in the ground with a piece of elm branch. In the French district of Cerbère, in the eastern Pyrenees, where for centuries the area's dogs have remained silent, there is panic among the inhabitants when the animals start to bark. According to local legend, the barking of these dogs will herald the end of the universe. Elsewhere, on a beach in northern Portugal, a man picks up a heavy stone and heaves it into the sea. But instead of plunging beneath the waves it bounces high, descends and bounces high again, all the while travelling into the distance before sinking. In a small town in Andalusia, a pharmacist rises from his chair and feels the earth shake, a movement apparently not perceived by anyone else in the vicinity. Back in Portugal, a large flock of starlings flies above a man, following him as he strolls through the countryside, while in another Portuguese location a woman decides to unpick an old, blue, wool sock but finds the task never-ending and the sock getting no smaller.

By deploying a series of mysterious incidents that readily recall some of the playful trappings of magical realism, the narrator quickly invites the reader to accept that the massive geological disruption that will soon see the separation of Spain and Portugal from their continent is somehow part of an inexplicable, fantastical process. As the narrative develops and the peninsula moves slowly westward into the ocean, those characters encountered in the opening pages as unknowingly associated with the catastrophic event make contact and come together to try to understand their possible role in what has happened. They also attempt to come to terms with these new circumstances and adjust to their developing relationships. And as the 'stone raft' begins its voyage around the Atlantic Ocean, so these central characters undertake their own odyssey – first to the north to witness and confirm the massive fracture, and then around various parts of Spain and Portugal.

During the course of their travels they witness the extensive disruption of life in Iberia – including the panic of many and the exodus of the rich – as the peninsula seems certain to collide with the Azores. And while the two Iberian governments can only respond to the situation in a limited way, the international reaction is often less than sympathetic and sometimes wholly opportunistic. At first, the European Community solemnly reaffirms the validity of all treaties with the two countries currently adrift, while NATO equivocates on the issue of Atlantic solidarity. Subsequently, though, European governments become disturbed as their own citizens show solidarity with the floating Spaniards and Portuguese by proclaiming in various European tongues: 'We are Iberians too' (*The Stone Raft*, p. 126). Also, there is talk of international pressures being brought to bear on the two hapless governments 'to bring the situation to an end' (*The Stone Raft*, p. 129). While the United States is initially helpful, providing fuel and food, it soon becomes clear that it has its own geopolitical agenda – seeing the strategic possibilities of a mid-Atlantic Iberia if the collision with the Azores takes place. Then, when the peninsula changes course and moves towards Newfoundland, the Americans at first see the possibility of a new international grouping but subsequently express relief that Canada appears to be the destination. Indeed, fearing immigration problems, both Canada and the United States soon realize that they do not want Iberia too close to their shores.

In the meantime, the small group of travellers moves on. Romantic relationships develop and two of the women become pregnant. The oldest man in the group dies. Thus while one life comes to a conclusion, others take new directions. Floating Iberia also changes course. After rotating for a while, the stone raft heads south and at the close of the narrative has come to a halt in the ocean between the Americas and Africa – away from Europe and away from the United States, and in a location that for Portugal has powerful historical and symbolic resonances. The travellers, the reader is informed, will continue their journey.

In the introduction to her recent, wide-ranging study of magical realism, Wendy B. Faris briefly refers to this novel, suggesting that 'the magical severance' of Iberia from the European mainland 'dramatizes the sense of cultural isolation experienced by Spaniards and Portuguese in relation to the rest of Western Europe'. The critic then proposes that the image of this 'chasm' is, in addition, 'extended in a more general and cosmic sense to encompass divisions between people, and existential questions of connection'.[16] In *The Stone Raft*, images and issues of division, as well as of connection and community, are certainly prominent. However, what Faris does not find room to mention in the single paragraph that she devotes to Saramago's novel is the *political* divide – between governments and their people – that the novel also signals. Indeed, she makes no reference to the political context of the work.

---

[16] Wendy B. Faris, *Ordinary Enchantments: Magical Realism and the Remystification of Narrative* (Nashville, TN: Vanderbilt University Press, 2004), pp. 9–10.

Despite its imaginative power and implausibility, this narrative would not be considered by Todorov as an example of literature of the fantastic. This is because the author has conceived and developed the novel as an allegory. Once recognized, an allegory does, of course, refer the reader back to the reality of the world (Todorov, pp. 37–8). Earlier I mentioned the lack of historical specificity of *The Stone Raft*. Yet the novel has considerable political, economic, and cultural depths. It was published in 1986, the year in which Portugal and Spain joined the European Community, an organization that Saramago has criticised on democratic as well as economic grounds.[17] The physical breaking away from Europe of the Iberian peninsula, so graphically and wittily described in *The Stone Raft*, is thus a creative response to a kind of reverse process, at least in the political and economic sense, the *joining* of Portugal and Spain, in 1986, to the Europe of the EC. The broader reality that Saramago also wishes to signal is the power and self-interest of other, larger states (European and non-European) and the willingness of governments to take their countries in certain directions, regardless of the wishes or welfare of the citizens. These citizens are simply expected to adjust to the new circumstances.

In effect, the strange series of events witnessed in the opening pages of the novel – the line marked on the ground, the barking dogs, the bouncing stone, the woollen sock, the flocking birds, and so on – are just parodic and ludic diversions. These mysterious occurrences initially steer the reader towards a particular kind of reception of the narrative as literature of the fantastic, with the drifting peninsula providing a spectacular visual image that is possibly unmatched in the literature of magical realism. The historical and political processes, so vividly and precisely illustrated in *Baltasar and Blimunda* and *The Year of the Death of Ricardo Reis*, although not readily apparent in *The Stone Raft*, are figuratively lurking beneath the surface of an Iberian peninsula that Saramago would regard not as being adrift in some kind of fantastical way, but rather as being sailed from one unacceptable place to another.

Conclusion: Magical Realism and Reality in Saramago's Novels

In *Baltasar and Blimunda*, the craft that takes to the air thanks to the effect of sunlight on captured human spirits, and for a while flies spectacularly, is an unforgettable aspect of the narrative development of the work. Similarly, Blimunda's oft-demonstrated gift (or curse) of clairvoyance is significant not only in terms of the practical application of her extraordinary visual powers but also constitutes the other element in the text that defies the laws of mechanics or Nature and, as with the flight of the *Passarola*, provides a vivid element of magical realism to a work that owes much of its impact to the weight of historical detail and the physicality of its characters, locations, and monuments.

---

[17] See Reis, pp. 146–8, and also Juan Arias, *José Saramago: O Amor Possível*, trans. Carlos Aboim de Brito (Lisbon: Dom Quixote, 2000), pp. 85–9.

Yet it could be argued that the spirit-powered craft and Blimunda's transvision are no more than important dramatic aspects of a narrative that could still function effectively (although less flamboyantly and with less symbolic resonance) without their presence. With *The Year of the Death of Ricardo Reis* and *The Stone Raft*, on the other hand, the element of the inexplicable, of the fantastic-marvellous, of magical realism furnishes, in each case, a device that dominates the narrative rather than being simply an aspect of it – a poet brought back from the tomb and one of his heteronyms made flesh, and in the 1986 novel a huge peninsula afloat and on the move in the Atlantic Ocean. With these two novels the reader is presented not with a 'real' world from which excursions are occasionally made into the realms of the fantastic or of magical realism, but largely the reverse. Now the magical realist element is all encompassing and plot-driving, with historical and everyday realities seen either from the perspective of two recreated poets or from within the confines of a free-floating peninsula.

Magical-realist Elements
in José Eustasio Rivera's *The Vortex*

Humberto Núñez-Faraco

José Eustasio Rivera published his only novel, *The Vortex*, four years before his untimely death in 1928. It is now considered the greatest novel of the jungle and one of the most influential books in the development of Spanish American narrative during the first half of the century. It describes the cruelties and injustice endured by rubber workers at a time when the growing demand for rubber from Europe and North America had made it a profitable enterprise in a region which, up to then, had been virtually ignored by the Colombian civil authorities. I refer to the forests of the Amazon, shared between Venezuela, Brazil, Peru and Colombia.

In 1922, Rivera was appointed secretary of the Boundary Commission which eventually settled the line of demarcation between Venezuela and Colombia during the conservative administration of Pedro Nel Ospina. This gave Rivera the opportunity to travel to the wilds of Casanare, where he learned about its geography and the mentality of its inhabitants. There he heard about the atrocities and enslavement suffered by the rubber tappers at the hands of unscrupulous landowners, who had gradually come to dominate the exploitation of vast rubber tree plantations in the south of the country. Indeed the issue at stake was humanitarian as well as political, since the advances of Peruvian settlers inside Colombian territory constituted a serious threat to national sovereignty in the region. This is exemplified by Casa Arana (formerly the Peruvian Amazon Company), whose abuses were denounced by the English media during the late 1900s. Rivera was already acquainted with the socio-political situation in the region and it became for him a matter of exalted patriotism to raise an outcry not only against the arbitrariness of the Peruvians but also against the Colombian government. He felt that the former were encouraging the activities of Casa Arana in breach of international law, and that the Colombian Ministry of Foreign Affairs was turning a blind eye to the problem. Rivera's accusations must have created great embarrassment to a conservative government that was supposed to profess the defense of national values and the creation of a national sentiment both in the political and cultural sphere.

When *The Vortex* was published in 1924 it was acclaimed as a literary masterpiece throughout Spanish America. Although it has been classified as regionalist, the novel actually represents a curious blend of styles and narrative techniques, including Classical, Romantic, and *modernista* elements. In addition, we find the fragmentation of the authorial voice which is so typical of the postmodern novel.[1] In this respect critics have noted a certain lack of structural and stylistic coherence in *The Vortex*, an issue which I do not intend to dispute here. It is clear that Rivera had not reached a mature narrative technique when he began to write the novel, and that its division into three parts is unsatisfactory in terms of internal coherence.[2] What is important to note, however, is the degree of self-consciousness that the novel achieves in its own making, allowing it to call into question the various literary models that constitute it. From this perspective, the jungle can be read as a textual metaphor in so far as *The Vortex* incessantly depletes and reconstructs its own narrative and stylistic resources. Thus, at the end of the first part, through the symbolical conflagration of the plains and the subsequent flight to the jungle, the protagonist witnesses the failure of the Romantic project once cherished by him in the idyllic landscape of the Casanare:

> Where is that solitude poets sing of? Where are those butterflies like translucent flowers, the magic birds, those singing streams? Poor fantasies of those who know only domesticated retreats! (p. 270)[3]

Themes

There are two main aspects in *The Vortex* which I would like to highlight with respect to the creation of an ideology and the transformation of a literary genre. These two aspects are interrelated in the novel, but to what extent their conjunction can be attributed to the development of magical realism as a whole is a question that remains outside the scope of this paper.

In the first instance, the novel displays a number of thematic features that clearly anticipate the rise of magical realism in Spanish America. These include

---

[1] See Montserrat Ordóñez Vila, ' "La vorágine": La voz rota de Arturo Cova', in *Manual de literatura colombiana* (Bogotá: Procultura y Planeta, 1988) pp. 433–518; Raymond Leslie Williams, *The Colombian Novel, 1844 -1987* (Austin, Texas: University of Texas Press, 1991), pp. 69–70; Silvia Molloy, 'Contagio narrativo y gesticulación retórica en *La vorágine*', in *La vorágine: Textos críticos*, ed. Montserrat Ordóñez Vila (Bogotá: Alianza Editorial Colombiana, 1987), pp. 489–513.

[2] For a positive evaluation of the romantic and historical elements in the make-up of the novel, see Clara Román-Odio, 'Space as a Theme in *La Vorágine*', in http://tell.fll.purdue.edu/RLA-archive/1989/SpanishHart-html/Odio-FF.htm.

[3] All quotations are taken from José Eustasio Rivera, *The Vortex*, trans. by E.K. James (London: Putnam, 1935).

(1) the use of myth and legend, (2) the reference to magic and the supernatural, (3) the inclusion of ethnic and cultural heterogeneity, (4) the overwhelming presence of the jungle and its fauna, both of which are frequently described in fantastic terms, and (5) the denunciation of social injustice and criminality, which are fostered by the lack of an effective civil law in the region and the arbitrariness of the political administration on both sides of the frontier.

I would like to propose a Borgesian reading of the novel, taking as a point of departure Borges's (together with T.S. Eliot's) statement that a writer 'modifies our conception of the past, as it will inevitably modify the future'.[4] Rivera had no links with the European and North American avant-garde of the 1920s, and he was probably unaware of the surrealists' growing interest in primitive art as an expression of the 'marvellous'. Unlike Carpentier, therefore, he had no need to validate his poetic creed against the European avant-garde, with its mystification of the eccentric and the instinctive in primitive art.[5] Furthermore, although Carpentier defined the 'marvellous real' ('lo real maravilloso') partly as a deliberate attempt to overcome the limitations of the regionalist or telluric novel in Latin America,[6] the historical development of both the marvellous real and magical realism was actually determined by the regionalist writer's perception of reality as being suffused with a magical essence, an aspect which in turn constitutes a fundamental ingredient of the popular imagination. Thus Rivera effectively incorporates elements in the narrative that belong to the realm of magic, myth, and legend without always questioning their logical validity with regards to the worldview of the protagonist, who represents Western rationality and its cultural values. Of course, this is not to say that *The Vortex* is a magical-realist novel but simply that it can enrich our appreciation of its literary development by presenting a number of motifs that were exploited later on by authors such as Carpentier, Asturias, and García Márquez.[7]

One of the most surprising passages in the novel recounts the legend of the little Indian priestess Mapiripana, 'the priestess of the silent places, the keeper

---

[4] See Jorge Luis Borges, 'Kafka y sus precursores', in *Obras completas*, 3 vols (Barcelona: Emecé, 1989) II, pp. 88–90 (p. 90): 'Su labor modifica nuestra concepción del pasado, como ha de modificar el futuro' (my translation). See T.S. Eliot, 'Tradition and the Individual Talent', in *Selected Prose of T. S. Eliot*, ed. Frank Kermode (London: Faber & Faber, 1975), p. 39.

[5] As is well known, Alejo Carpentier's two seminal novels, *The Kingdom of This World* and *The Lost Steps*, reveal the social and historical dilemmas created by the aesthetics of the marvellous. On this issue see Irlemar Chiampi, *El realismo maravilloso: forma e ideología en la novela hispanoamericana*, trans. by Agustín Martínez and Márgara Russotto (Caracas: Monte Avila Editores, 1983).

[6] See Carpentier's remarks in his latter prologue to *Écue-Yamba-Ó* (Madrid: Alianza Editorial, 2002), pp. 9–11; see Arturo Uslar Pietri, *Godos, insurgentes y visionarios* (Barcelona: Seix Barral, 1985), pp. 40–1.

[7] The presence of the magical and the marvellous in the novel's make-up was also perceived by Rivera's contemporaries; see 'Una hora con Rivera', *El Tiempo*, Suplemento Semanal, 7 February 1926, p. 1: 'En los labios de Rivera la selva toma cierto acento evocador y maravilloso. [. . .] Nadie tenía conciencia de que allí, a cuatro pasos de la frontera, er

of springs and lakes' (p. 180).[8] The story relates her revenge on a lascivious Spanish missionary who, driven by the desire to defy Mapiripana's powers and destroy the Indians' superstitious beliefs, attempts to capture and burn her alive at the stake. The episode confronts the supposed moral superiority of the Spanish *conquistadores* and, more specifically, the legitimacy of the Catholic Church in its ambition to replace the cultural and religious principles of the American Indians. Contrary to his expectation, the friar is overpowered by Mapiripana, who subjects him to a nightmarish expiation in which he becomes the victim of his own shameful acts. From a cultural viewpoint, the triumph of the Indian girl constitutes an affirmation of myth over the presumed superiority of the intruder (see Arrington, p. 714). Note also the magical aura at the end of the story, which suspends the normal parameters of experience in order to introduce the uncanny as something that remains outside the realm of the novel's realist background. By allowing the two world views to coexist Rivera attempts to destabilize the notion of an objective reality, although the final medical explanation does suggest a strictly rational solution to the episode:

> From that time on [. . .] he devoted himself to prayer and penitence, and died old and emaciated. Just before he died Mapiripana found him lying on a miserable bed of leaves and lichens, moving his hands in wild delirium, as though trying to catch his own soul floating in the air. And as he passed away, a butterfly of blue wings, immense and luminous as an archangel, fluttered around the cave, the last vision of all those who die of fever in these regions. (pp. 182–3)

We are faced with a similar situation in Rivera's description of the mentality of the inhabitant of the Orinoco region. In several instances, his belief in the magical power of prayer and ritual is presented in the novel as a matter of fact and not simply as a superstitious element, which the urban reader would be prompt to dismiss. While the protagonist, Arturo Cova, may find it difficult to accept the supernatural as an objective force, this does not imply its negation as a factor at work in the metaphysical framework of the novel. In other words, Rivera endeavours to depict the natives' mentality with an objectivity that may leave untouched his faith in the supernatural. Indeed Cova's own disbelief is put into question as he himself fears the possibility of falling under the magical spell of the *vengavenga*, a love potion prepared from 'the bark of a tree that makes people fall in love' (p. 72). By the same token, the belief in the magical power

---

territorio nacional, existiera ese conjunto maravilloso, que parece extraído de un país de leyenda' (I quote from Hilda Pachón Farias (ed.), *José Eustasio Rivera intelectual* (Bogotá: Universidad Nacional de Colombia, 1991), p. 98.

[8] See Margarita Mateo Palmer, 'Valor y función del mito de origen americano en *La vorágine*', *Casa de las Américas*, 167 (1988), 24–31; Melvin S. Arrington's entry in the *Encyclopedia of Latin American Literature*, ed. Verity Smith (Chicago and London: Fitzroy Dearborn Publishers, 1997), pp. 714–15, 'Rivera'.

of the *piapoco* – a little bird whose song can produce such yearning for the homeland that a man may die of sadness on not being able to return – is reinforced by
proving its effect on one of the characters, who becomes homesick on hearing
the bird's song. Also, in the following passage, the novel anticipates the motif of
metamorphosis which was to be exploited later on by Carpentier in *The Kingdom
of This World*, the work that claims for itself the merit of having revealed the
existence of the marvellous real in Latin American literature:

> I looked at Clarita with surprise, unable to believe that the whole business was
> serious. But she, too, was a convinced believer in the incantations. '*Gua
> chico!*' she explained. 'Mauco knows of medicines. He's the one who kills the
> worms in the animals' sores, praying at them. He cures persons and animals.'
> 'Not only that', added the grotesque fellow. 'I know many prayers for all
> things: to find lost cattle, to find buried treasures, to make myself invisible to
> my enemies. When they were getting recruits for the big war they came to take
> me, but I made myself into a banana tree. Once they grabbed me before I had
> finished the prayer and locked me up in a room under double key; but I turned
> myself into an ant and escaped.' (p. 90)

The assertion that magical realism begins with the chronicles of the Spanish
Conquest of the Indies is now commonplace, but it was far beyond Rivera's
aesthetic horizon when he wrote *The Vortex*.[9] And yet he employed the themes
of Conquest and Discovery in a way that foreshadows the emergence of magical
realism in Spanish America. This takes place in the second and third parts of the
novel, in which the protagonist ventures into the jungle together with a handful
of wretched men: 'Over the hostile regions we marched barefooted, like the legendary heroes of the Conquest' (p. 169). It is here, in the 'green cell' of the
Amazon, that Rivera's depiction of nature acquires an extraordinary dimension.
On the one hand he exploits its mythical potential, as in the first part of the novel,
where 'fantastic cities seemed to tower on the horizon' (p. 28) – a theme
exploited later on in Carpentier's book of the jungle, *The Lost Steps*. On the
other, it possesses a terrible, oppressive, and inhuman law: 'O jungle, wedded to
silence, mother of solitude and mists! What malignant fate imprisoned me within
your green walls?' (p. 143). As an attribute of the jungle, in Rivera's mythical
representation, silence becomes the manifestation of nature in its harmonious

---

[9] For a useful compilation of texts from the Spanish chroniclers, see Mario Germán
Romero (ed.), *América. De lo real maravilloso* (Bogotá: Instituto Caro y Cuervo, 1992); Juan
José Amate Blanco, 'El realismo mágico en la expedición amazónica de Orellana', *Cuadernos
Hispanoamericanos*, 510 (1992), 61–72. See also Gabriel García Márquez's speech of
acceptance upon receiving the Nobel Prize for literature (*El Tiempo*, 9 December 1982,
p. 6-A), together with Iris Zavala's '*One Hundred Years of Solitude* as Chronicle of the Indies',
in Gabriel García Márquez's *One Hundred Years of Solitude*, ed. Gene H. Bell-Villada
(Oxford and New York: Oxford University Press, 2002), pp. 109–25 (esp. pp. 109–15).

existence. Thus man's destruction of the natural world is symbolized by the sinful transgression of quietness. In this way, the novel foretells an apocalyptic finale in which Nature will avenge man's greed and arrogance.

Indeed, Rivera's jungle is imbued with an amazed horror, a vision that springs from the engrossed contemplation of the strange beings that inhabit it. Take, for instance, the episode of the *tambochas*, the giant ants which, marching in millions, devour everything they find in their way, 'stripping the bones of flesh like some fast-dissolving acid' (p. 289); or the description of the *caribes*, the small fish which can reveal the white skeleton of their victim 'with the celerity of hungry chickens that lay bare a cob of corn' (p. 376); the hordes of insects that float in buzzing clouds; the rains that change the fertile savannas into desolate swamps; and the narcotic qualities of *yagé*, a plant whose distilled juices bring 'clairvoyant dreams' to the man who drinks of it, dreams in which thousand-year-old trees unite in their condemnation of man's destruction of the rainforest. Indeed, Rivera's ecological outcry could not be more vigorous:

> The visions of the dreamer proved extravagant; processions of alligators and tortoises, swamps filled with people, flowers that cried aloud. He spoke of the trees of the forest as paralysed giants that at night called to each other and made gestures. They wanted to escape with the clouds, but the earth held them fast by their ankles, motionless for ever. They complained of the hand that scored them, the axe that felled them. [. . .] Pipa understood their bitter voices, heard that some day they were to cover the fields, plains and cities, until the last trace of man was wiped from the earth. (pp. 166–7)

On the other hand, Rivera's depiction of the Indian's religious beliefs (such as the notion of a supernatural power that controls the destiny of the soul) is met with scorn on the part of his protagonist. This is an attitude which has always been the characteristic mark of the White urban population vis-à-vis the American Indian. To be sure, Rivera's socio-political message in the novel is an appeal to the creation of a national sentiment among the various ethnic groups dispersed throughout the Colombian territory. At this point, therefore, it is necessary to distinguish between author and narrator. As a representative of urban positivist ideology, Arturo Cova endorses the traditional treatment of the Indian cultural heritage as something which is inevitably at odds with progress and modernity. And yet, it is clear that the novel raises a humanitarian cry of protest with regard to the atrocities committed against the Indians of the Amazon. It also draws attention to the fact that the existence of ethnic and cultural heterogeneity in Colombia is a historical reality that must be recognised by the central government. Consider the following passage:

> Throughout their orgiastic carousal the atrocious liquor ran like water, and the cries of the women and children added to the bacchanalian turmoil. [. . .] It seemed more the sluggish plodding of fettered prisoners than a dance – prisoners in slow-paced rotation around the fire, forced to tread an only path, eyes on the ground, shackled by the mournful wail of the chirim'a flute

and the grave throbbing of the drums. [. . .] I watched the strange performance, glad that my companions had also joined the drunken celebration. [. . .] *Yet soon I realised they were wailing like the natives, and their lament revealed the same deep-hidden pain, as though one single sadness gnawed the souls of all.* Their cry held all the grief and dull despair of conquered peoples; and it sounded like the sobbing of my own heart, a sobbing that echoed there unuttered by my lips: *A-a-a-a-h-y . . . O-h-é-é . . .!* (pp. 163–4; my emphasis)

Style

The second aspect of the novel that I would like to highlight, in relation to the development of magical realism, is related to style. *The Vortex* betrays a stylistic feature already noted by one of its first critics, Eduardo Castillo. He maintained rather cynically that Rivera's novel was guaranteed great success for the 'red aura of blood and crime' that characterised it and which, in his opinion, was clearly intended to arouse the melodramatic curiosity of the common reader.[10] This populist and sensationalistic element is undoubtedly present in the make-up of the novel. Although Rivera's descriptions of the landscape in the plains of Casanare betray an exquisite mastery in the handling of *modernista* imagery, and despite his magnificent expression of the horrific within the overwhelming presence of the Amazon jungle, *The Vortex* displays such a large number of violent and thrilling episodes that one is tempted to include it among the finest examples of melodramatic literature in Latin America. Indeed the themes of love and violence are announced from the outset: 'Long before I ever fell passionately in love with any woman, I had gambled away my heart and Violence had won it.' Such violent episodes can be distinguished from the serial newspaper novels of Eduardo Gutiérrez – who popularized with bold realism the horrors committed during Rosas' despotic regime in 19th-century Argentina – only by Rivera's superior skill of rhetorical language and poetic imagination. A few examples will suffice to prove the point:

> A gigantic water-serpent, thick as a two-foot beam, had emerged mouth agape. It sank as I fired at it with my revolver, stirring the swamp violently, pulsing the water so the waves overflowed the confines of the pool. (p. 30)
>
> 'Do you think, wretch, that this old man is alone?' I broke out, grasping a knife. (p. 43)

---

[10] '*La vorágine* [. . .] es una novela que nació predestinada a un éxito ruidoso. [. . .] La novela que nos brinda el parnásida de *Tierra de promisión* viene envuelta en un como halo rojo de crimen y de sangre muy propio para excitar la curiosidad de los lectores de folletín' ('La vorágine', in *La vorágine: Textos críticos*, pp. 41–43 (p. 41). On this issue, see David Viñas, '"La vorágine": Crisis, populismo y mirada', *Hispamérica*, 8 (1974), 3–21; Doris Sommer, *Foundational Fictions: The National Romances of Latin America* (Berkeley: University of California Press, 1991), pp. 259–60 and *passim*; Williams, *The Colombian Novel*, pp. 40–1.

But with brutal kicks I broke the cords, grasped Griselda by the hair, and dragged her into the patio. [. . .] And I struck her in the face with a blow that drew blood. (p. 82)

'Don't go out!' she pleaded. 'They'll riddle you with bullets!' [. . .] I had been stabbed in the left arm. [. . .] Those outside were trying to break the door down. I started firing through it, changing my position constantly, as shots were coming in from outside. (pp. 87–8)

Although aggression is the manifestation of a human emotion which in itself is independent of social character, it can be said that in Colombia – one of the most violent countries in the world for the last twenty-five years – violence has become a national trait, one that has permeated the entire history of the country since its independence from Spain in 1819. Nevertheless, it was only during the first decades of the twentieth century that it became a dominant literary theme. In this respect, *The Vortex* can be seen as one of the foundational novels of violence in Colombia. More specifically, behind its violent scenery lies a patriotic programme which aims to boost an aggressive and nationalistic fervour against the Peruvian invasion of the Amazon region. This, in Rivera's view, required firm and decisive action on behalf of the Colombian civil and military authorities. Thus, the main male characters of the novel, all of whom boast about their national sentiment as Colombian citizens over and above their regional identity, can be seen as a deliberate attempt to provide a model of courage and determination in Rivera's heroic campaign against the common enemy. That is to say, the populist and melodramatic ingredients of the work are not only determined by the emergence of a national conscience but also by the need to create a heroic stereotype, one that would be prepared to fight and, if necessary, to die for his country. From this perspective, Alicia and Griselda can be seen as symbols of the mother country whose apparent betrayal must be avenged by their lovers at all costs; indeed Cova's restored dignity, together with the full realization of his paternity, dominate the final pages of the novel.

In his political campaign for the defense of the country's national sovereignty, Rivera opted for the mystification of the individual who struggles against the enslavement and murder of the Colombian rubber workers at the hands of unscrupulous Peruvian settlers. At the same time, the distressing social background of the novel, including the massacre in San Fernando de Atabapo, a small town in the border with Venezuela, could no longer sustain the poetics of enchantment Rivera had once cherished in his precious *modernista* style (see his collection of poems, *Tierra de promisión*, published a few years earlier). Rather, it demanded the recourse to the loathsome and satanic as its only conceivable mode of expression. With the rise of magical realism in Spanish America some years later, the jungle regained the enigmatic and exotic qualities it had previously enjoyed in the European imagination, namely, its position as a *locus amoenus*, the space in which the dream of return to a lost Arcadia would be realized. However, although the political and economic motives that triggered

Rivera's denunciation are no longer relevant, the social and moral aspects, which lie at the heart of the novel, remain an unresolved problem. At least in this respect Rivera may have come closer to the truth. Far from the distorted mystification of the Spanish American world carried out by the poetics of the marvellous real, Rivera may have understood that its reality is not magical or miraculous, but rather that it is tremendously cruel, absurd, and grotesque.

Beyond Magical Realism in
The Red of His Shadow by Mayra Montero

Alejandra Rengifo

It is not obvious at first glance why a writer like Mayra Montero should be included in a volume of this kind. Yet the oblique manner in which the legacy of writers such as Carpentier and García Márquez operates in some of the works of this Cuban-Puerto Rican novelist is precisely what makes her novels rich and, in a very particular way, has allowed her to re-theorize magical realism within her texts. The purpose of this study is to see how, through the portrayal of Voodoo practices, beliefs and rituals Montero conjures up, especially in *El rojo de su sombra / The Red of His Shadow* (1993), a world which is at once magical and real. Before I go further into this topic I will briefly address Montero's literary trajectory to better appreciate the value of her work.

Montero as Caribbean Writer

A journalist by profession, Montero has shown herself to be a very prolific and versatile author. Born in Cuba in 1952, she migrated to Puerto Rico with her family while in her teens. Nowadays she is best known for her portrayals of what critics such as Antonio Benítez Rojo has called Caribbeanness:

> the Antilles are an island bridge connecting, in 'anothor way', North and South America. This geographical accident gives the entire area, including its continental foci, the character of an archipelago, that is, a discontinuous conjunction (of what?): unstable condensations, turbulences, whirlpools, clumps of bubbles, frayed seaweed, sunken galleons, crashing breakers, flying fish, seagull squawks, downpours, night-time phosphorescences, eddies and pools, uncertain voyages of signification; in short, a field of observation quite in tune with the objectives of Chaos.[1]

---

[1] Antonio Benítez-Rojo, *Repeating Island: The Caribbean and the Postmodern Perspective* (Durham: Duke UP, 1996), p. 2.

Montero is, then, an author who explores her surrounding world from the perspective of an insider; she is part of that community, that island bridge, which has given the world writers of the stature of García Márquez and Carpentier. This is why her writings – whether they treat music, ethnicity, religion, identity, even eroticism – always have a Caribbean tint to them. It is worth noting that Montero is one of the only Caribbean female writers to have ventured into the genre of the erotic novel, writing her first novel of this kind in 1991, *La última noche que pasé contigo/The Last Night I Spent with You*. To Montero's surprise this text was a finalist for the XIII Sonrisa Vertical Prize of Erotic Narrative series.[2] It is the story of a middle-aged couple, Celia and Fernando, who go off on a cruise after the marriage of their only daughter. The description of their sexual experiences is balanced by the portrayal of their innermost longings in the present and their memories of their respective pasts. As a result of the success of this novel, Montero participated once more in the 2000 edition of *La Sonrisa Vertical* and, this time, won first prize with her novel *Purpura profundo / Deep Purple (2000)*. Her three most recent novels are *Como un mensajero tuyo/The Messenger* (1999), *El capitán de los dormidos / The Captain of the Sleep* (2002) and the as yet untranslated, *Vana ilusión* (2003).

The Messenger takes as its point of departure the famous Italian tenor Enrico Caruso's visit to Havana in 1920. Montero focuses on what happened to him as a result of an explosion that occurred in the Teatro Nacional in the Cuban capital, and thereby creates a historiographic metafiction narrated as if it were testimonial. Masterfully written, *The Messenger* has recourse to the earthier backdrop of *santería*,[3] in order to emphasize Caruso's love affair with Aida Petrirena Cheng, the daughter of a mulata and a Chinese man. *The Captain of the Sleep* is a love story set against a political backdrop, describing the only attempt by a Puerto Rican group to seize the island of Vieques and initiate an independence movement. The story of a Captain, the owners of a hotel and their son, gives Montero the opportunity to explore a topic she firmly believes in: the sovereignty of Puerto Rico. Once again Montero mixes the explosive combination of love, sex and politics. Her latest book, *Vana ilusión*, takes the form of 'memorias noveladas' (novelised memoirs) of the famous Puerto Rican piano player, Narciso Figueroa. The life story of the struggles of Narciso Figueroa and his family to become the most prominent musical family on the island is delicately narrated, masterfully threading together fiction and real life such that the fine line between the two is blurred and ultimately dissolves.

There is more, though, to Montero's work than simply love and sex. In particular three of her earlier novels focus on a rather different component of human experience, namely, the supernatural. These are *La trenza de la hermosa luna: Narrativas hispánicas/The Braid of the Beautiful Moon: Hispanic Narratives* (1987), *El rojo de su sombra/The Red of His Shadow* (New York:

---

[2] Premio Sonrisa Vertical is an award given to erotic narrative. It was created by Editorial Tusquets in 1979.

[3] *Santería* is a syncretistic religion that combines the worship and beliefs of the Orishas, gods from the Yoruba and Bantu people, and the Roman Catholic rites devoted to to saints and God.

The Ecco Press, 2001; original Spanish edition 1993) and *Tú, la oscuridad/In the Palm of Darkness* (trans. Edith Grossman, 1997; original Spanish edition 1995). *The Braid of the Beautiful Moon* and *In the Palm of Darkness* are set in Haiti, *The Red of His Shadow* in the neighbouring Dominican Republic. Haiti was, indeed, a crucial melting pot of experience for Montero; from her acquaintance as a young girl with a French woman who taught her about Haiti, its people, its religion and its culture, she derived her fascination for Voodoo religion and rituals. *The Braid of the Beautiful Moon*, for example, tells the life story of Jean Leroy, a Haitian who returns to his homeland to help an old friend complete some unfinished business. The action of the novel unfolds during the Duvalier dictatorship and focuses on the tumultuous months that led to his demise. The personal story of Jean Leroy is subtly crosscut with the political-cum-social history of the country at the time. Since Montero uses real people and real historical events, she is able in this novel to cover her depiction of the magical world of Voodoo deities, *tontons macoutes*, potions, spells and incantations, with a veneer of verisimilitude.[4] *In the Palm of Darkness* is also set in the Haiti of the Duvalier dictatorship. The novel tells the story of two men – the herpetologist Victor Grigg and his Haitian guide Thierry Adrien – who are searching for the already mythical and magical 'grenouille du sang', a blood-red *Eleutherodactylus sanguineus*, namely an elusive, near-extinct species of amphibian. Their search for the amphibian takes them deep into the realm of nature as well as the mire of the corruption of the Haitian government. They form a close friendship in a land haunted by superstition, legend, and death, and finally die in a shipwreck.[5]

'The Red of His Shadow', and Magical Realism

In between *The Braid of the Beautiful Moon* and *In the Palm of Darkness*, in between the *tontons macoutes*, the Duvalier dictatorship, the 'grenouilles du sang', and the sex and politics that surface in both stories, Mayra Montero wrote *The Red of His Shadow*, a novel offering a highly complex exploration of the interplay of the real and the supernatural via striking imagery that throws new light on the world of the downtrodden Haitian immigrants who work in the sugar cane fields of the Dominican Republic. This novel gives the reader a glimpse into the harsh world of modern-day Haitian Voodoo by focusing on historical events

---

[4] The *tontons macoutes* were a special police force the Duvalier leaders had created to maintain the population of Haiti under their control.

[5] Montero has published to date eight fictional works. They are: *The Messenger* (New York: Harper Flamingo, 1999); *In the Palm of Darkness* (New York: Harper Collins, 1997); *La trenza de la hermosa luna* (Barcelona: Editorial Anagrama, 1992); *Del rojo de su sombra* (Barcelona: Editorial Tusquets, 1995); *Tú, la oscuridad* (Barcelona: Editorial Tusquets, 1995); *La última noche que pasé contigo* (Barcelona: Editorial Tusquets, 1991); *Púrpura Profundo* (Barcelona: Editorial Tusquets, 2000); *El capitán de los dormidos* (Barcelona: Editorial Tusquets, 2002).

which took place in the Dominican Republic. It takes us to a place full of envy, hate, jealousy and greed, where the population has the power to cast spells which torture and kill others, and bring back the dead; witchcraft becomes merely another way of surviving in a community marked by the supernatural. As a matter of fact it is with this novel, and its portrayal of a real world filled with so many magical elements based on Voodoo practices, that the question arises as to Montero's insertion into the canon of magical realism. Indeed, the reader will ask: is *The Red of His Shadow* a magical-realist text?

Luis Leal proposed the following classical definition of magical-realist fiction:

> magical realism does not use dream motifs; neither does it distort reality or create imagined worlds, as writers of fantastic literature or science fiction do [. . .]. Magical realism is not magic literature either. Magical realism is, more than anything else, an attitude toward reality that can be expressed in popular or cultured forms, in elaborate or rustic styles, in closed or open structures. [. . .] In magical realism the writer confronts reality and tries to untangle it, to discover what is mysterious in things, in life, in human acts (. . .)[6]

Applying Leal's definition to *The Red of His Shadow* leads to the view that it exhibits some important elements of magical-realist discourse, although this should not be taken to mean Montero is a magical-realist writer. Indeed the version of reality portrayed in her novel is close in some key respects to the notion of 'marvellous real' coined by Alejo Carpentier in his prologue to *The Kingdom of this World* (1949):

> the marvellous begins to be unmistakably marvellous when it arises from an unexpected alteration of reality (the miracle), from a privileged revelation of reality, an unusual insight that particularly favours the unexpected richness of reality or an amplification of the scale and categories of reality, a reality thus perceived with special intensity by virtue of an exaltation of the spirit that leads it to a kind of extreme state [*estado límite*].[7]

It is important, however, not to attempt to apply this theory lock, stock and barrel to Montero's novel. As Donald Shaw comments:

> [o]ne tends to think of magical realism as a rather tired term which scholars have consigned to the critical trash can. And yet, as recently as 1995, Zamora and Faris could publish a well-known symposium on the subject and now we have

    [6] Luis Leal, 'Magical Realism in Spanish America', in *Magical Realism: Theory, History, Community*, eds Lois Parkinson Zamora and Wendy B. Faris (Durham, NC: Duke University Press, 1995), p. 120–4 (p. 121).
    [7] Alejo Carpentier, 'On the Marvelous Real in America', in *Magical Realism: Theory, History, Community*, pp. 75–88 (p. 86)

these two new substantial books. Not only will magical realism not go away, but it keeps expanding, and has even invaded, for example, Galdós criticism.[8]

Furthermore, Shaw insists that 'it is necessary to get beyond Carpentier's assertion that "lo real maravilloso" is something present and actually observable in Latin America' (p. 577). As it shall be seen, the magical real becomes, in Montero's hands, a technique with which to open up new visions about contemporary socio-political realities in Haiti transcending and mixing with those in the Dominican Republic.

Voodoo in Haiti

Before I move on to a discussion of the novel it will be necessary to make some preliminary points about Voodoo in Haiti, where this religion has been practiced since the arrival of the first slaves in the Caribbean. Through the years Voodoo has been seen as a mysterious and taboo religion. Voodoo has always lived in the shadow of Catholicism in the New World. Voodoo has had many faces in the Caribbean: *santería, candomble*, rastafarianism, to mention but a few. It has inspired major slave revolts, as in Haiti in 1804 (the setting for Carpentier's novel, *The Kingdom of this World*). Voodoo, as Ishmael Reed points out, has 'the profound beauty and appeal of a faith older than Christianity, Buddhism, and Islam'; it is 'a faith that has survived in spite of its horrendously bad reputation and the persecution of its followers'.[9] Voodoo, as we shall see, lies at the centre of *The Red of His Shadow*.

It is important to emphasize that, despite its interest in the supernatural, *The Red of His Shadow* is primarily concerned with the daily life in the Caribbean island of the Dominican Republic; we see the main characters Zulé, Similá, Jeremie Candé against the backdrop of the sugar cane fields of the island. Montero's artistry consists in her ability to transform that everyday *tranche de vie* into a depiction of a harsh but magical life. Montero allows us to enter imaginatively into the esoteric world of Voodoo and *santería* by embedding the insights of these religions in the collective memory of the characters in her stories. Here she does so through Zulé and her gagá, a socio-religious community of worship particular to the Haitian and Dominican population in the sugar-growing regions of the Dominican Republic, as explained in the glossary of the novel. Voodoo is the faith that gives shape and cohesion to the lives of the characters in this story.

---

[8] Donald L. Shaw, 'Review of *Historia verdadera del realismo mágico* by Seymor Menton and *Realismo mágico y primitivismo: relecturas de Carpentier, Asturias, Rulfo y García Márquez*, by Erik Camayd-Freixas', *Hispanic Review*, 4 (1999), 577–9 (p. 577).

[9] Ishmael Reed, 'Foreword', in Zora Neale Hurston, *Tell My Horse: Voodoo and Life in Haiti and Jamaica* (New York: Harper and Row, 1990), p. xv.

The gagá of Queen Zulé is ready to start Holy Week celebrations. This year the tension is building because a Voodoo priest of a neighbouring Colonia, the bokor Similá Bolosse, who has sworn to kill the Queen Zulé at the precise moment their gagás cross paths. While this tension builds in the present tense of the novel, *The Red of His Shadow* allows Queen Zulé Revé and her gagá's past to emerge into the narrative. Zulé left her native Haiti with her father when she was very young because she had 'un amarre al agua', a bond to the water. Zulé's grandmother, her mother, and her two brothers died as a result of events related to water. Since all the other children have died in water, her father decides to attempt to save her by sending her away to the Dominican Republic; but the latter becomes a space of salvation as well as condemnation. Zulé is a precocious girl who shows an aptitude for religion very soon after her arrival in the new country. After being tested by fire in a Voodoo ceremony, Zulé Revé's eyes are opened and she goes down to the land of the dead; on her return her family 'grew accustomed to her uncontrolled fits of weeping and her impenetrable babbling with the dead' (Montero, p. 59).[10] The reader is soon initiated into a world of 'amarres', trips to the land of the dead, blood baths, Holy Week celebrations in the sugar cane fields of the Dominican Republic it is not processions with the statues of Virgin Mary and the enactment of the passion of Christ that we witness, but the mambos and houngans and their joy. As an initiate Zulé now becomes the Queen of her own gagá while still in her twenties, an honour that shows the strength of character of this Mambo forced to bypass a normal adolescence. Zulé grew up learning about 'amarres', potions and rituals but nothing at all about life, womanhood and especially love.

The Magical and the Real

Zulé's love life seems more magical than real. Married off as a young virgin to Papa Coridon, a man who is as old as her father and the master of one of the most powerful gagás of the region, she then sleeps with her stepson before falling in love with Similá Bolosse, a man with yellow eyes who seems to be almost the incarnation of a 'loa'.[11] In her hut Zulé nurses Similá after he is injured while escaping from the chaos which erupted when Baby Doc was deposed in Haiti. Rejecting everybody's advice, especially that of Anacaona, her stepmother, Zulé welcomes the stranger into her home, feeds him, helps him, cures him and finally becomes pregnant with his child. After ten days living at his mistress's expense, Similá suddenly leaves Colonia Engracia one snowy day. Here is indeed a classic magical-realist detail; on the precise day that Similá abandoned his beloved a meteorological impossibility occurs: it snowed in Colonia Engracia. The snowy

---

[10] All references are to *The Red of His Shadow* (New York: The Ecco Press, 2001).
[11] The 'loa' is a term for a god from the Haitian Voodoo pantheon.

effect is introduced into the story in a very natural way, via the description of the nesting of more than a hundred parrots in the only ceiba tree in the region:

> [t]hey had nested nearby in the past, but this was the first time they had taken refuge in the ceiba tree on the path to the cane fields, the only ceiba still standing for many kilometres around. There were more than a hundred parrots, and they made the usual racket, but this time they also pulled apart the pods on the tree, filling the air with a fluff that cutters would have compared to snow if any of them had ever seen it. (Montero, pp. 76–7)

The day is one of ill omen, all the more so because

> [o]n the eve of Similá's departure, the first, almost insignificant tufts began to fall, and by noon the next day the downpour had become so heavy that women had to cover their faces like outlaws in order to carry lunch to the labourers. Hidden inside her house, looking out through a crack, Zulé saw Anacaona pass by, covered from head to foot, dragging her lameness as if it were a dead man and muttering curses at the swirling fluff that clouded her sight. (Montero, p. 77)

The people of the batey are not even surprised by this incredible event; their reaction is similar to that of the inhabitants of Macondo, in García Márquez's *One Hundred Years of Solitude*, when Mauricio Babilonia's yellow butterflies arrive in town. Their reaction is not to marvel at a miracle; rather they get annoyed because they cannot go about their daily business. It seems that all the elements in the universe are disposed in such a way as to foreshadow, somehow, what is going to happen; yet no one reads anything into such extraordinary events because anything can happen in a world that is bound by the magical. This is also Anacaona's attitude in Montero's novel.

The characters' lives are immersed in a culture that is meticulously bound by the magical. The arrival of the parrots coupled with Similá's disappearance is the prelude to the arrival of Bull Belecou, Erzulie Freda and Carfú. The day Similá leaves Colonia Engracia he goes out of the hut and returns to Zulé with

> the flying tufts [that] had stuck to his face, and now he looked exactly like the most feared and rancorous mystery in the Pantheon: it was the face of Bull Belecou. He contemplated his image, solemn and ecstatic, proud because the invincible mask had been returned to him. [. . .] He began to walk away, not saying a word and not wiping the snow from his face, and the mistress followed him to the edge of the batey. (Montero, p. 77)

Zulé has to let Similá go. She is left standing in the blazing sunlight 'weeping and whorish like Metresa Freda, submissive and great like the Virgin of Erzulie' (Montero, p. 78). Up to this point in the narration – the middle of the story – the reader has been scarcely made aware of the existence of the Voodoo Pantheon, but from this point onwards the Voodoo presence becomes more and more oppressive. This is the first time in the novel that the characters are explicitly equated to gods and it will not be until the end of the story that they will meet again – but under very different circumstances.

After Similá leaves, life in Colonia Engracia changes radically and the story lurches towards its surprising dénouement. Chapter by chapter the narrative of Zulé's life moves inexorably toward the moment when her gagá and that of Similá eventually meet on their pilgrimage through the different sugar cane mills (in effect the present tense of the novel). The day has arrived and, in spite of all the pleas, the reader feels sure that Zulé is going to meet her destiny. The anticipation of where and when Zulé's and Similá's gagás are going to cross paths is woven effectively into the storyline. The narration has taken the reader from Holy Thursday, the day Zulé is preparing her gagá to start the pilgrimage through the fields that surround the colonia, to Easter Sunday, when all the festivities come to an end. This is the chronological time that has elapsed in the story of mistress Zulé's life but it has been interspersed with a sequence of flashbacks to Zulé's early years in the batey, the accompanying festivities, the period when she met Similá Bolosse, the deaths of her uncle and her husband, her coronation as Queen, and so forth. The overlapping of the past and present of Zulé's life, along with the resulting suspense that surrounds the imminent encounter with the Colonia Engracia draws the reader into the narrative. Against all the odds it is not Bull Belecou, a rancorous and vengeful God, that kills Erzulie Freda, the Goddess of love and beauty, but Carfú, the patron of sorcery. Zulé's fate lies in the hands of her own stepson, faithful servant, and ex-lover, Jeremie Candé. But – following the logic of the Voodoo universe – the gods need human agents in order to accomplish their goals and, to do so, they 'possess' them. In this case a triad of well-known gods have possessed three of the main characters of the novel and use their bodies to carry out their wishes. Once again, as we saw with events such as the snow in the Caribbean and Zulé's descent into the world of the dead, the people of the Colonia are not surprised by what happens – they mourn the death of their mistress and life goes on as usual.

The Red of His Shadow focuses on the endurance of a woman in a patriarchal world: the men control this world as much as the next, the novel suggests, and Zulé is fighting against this. *The Red of His Shadow* thereby uses a slice of life in order to focus on the broader ideological and religious tensions in the Caribbean. The figure of Zulé becomes the locus for the cultural context and the religious beliefs of a vast region, where invisible gods and the power of Voodoo set the dominant order, converge. Mayra Montero is a writer of a post-Boom generation and, as such, she has recourse on occasion to some of the language, concepts and style of magical realism. This does not in itself mean, as we have seen, that she is a magical-realist writer. By focusing on Voodoo's control over the popular imagination in Haiti and the Dominican Republic, Montero goes beyond the use of magical realism simply as a technique. The magical and the supernatural appear in her work where they retain a revelatory, religious significance.

Cops, Robbers, and Anarcho-terrorists: Crime and Magical Realism's Jewish Question

Michael Berkowitz

This essay considers the novels of two Israelis, *The Zigzag Kid* (1994, Eng. trans., 1997) by David Grossman[1] and *Four Mothers* (1996, Eng. trans., 1999) by Shifra Horn,[2] and four by American Jews: *Leviathan* (1992) by Paul Auster,[3] *Bee Season* (2000) by Myla Goldberg,[4] *The Escape Artist* (1997) by Judith Katz,[5] and *The Isaac Quartet* (orig. 1974; most recent compilation, 2002) by Jerome Charyn.[6] My aims in this essay are threefold: first, to call attention to the fact that there are a number of contemporary Jewish authors who may be understood and appreciated through the lens of magical realism. Although the genre is typically associated with the steamier climes of Latin America, magical realism nevertheless thrives on the streets of Brooklyn, Tel Aviv, and even Jewish suburbia which is found in most medium-to-large cities in the United States. Second, I wish to situate the above-mentioned self-consciously Jewish novels in the realm of magical realism, and, third, to explore how the notion of Jewish criminality – intertwined with magical realism – unsettles the discourses of respectability which intersect each of these works. Jews in the modern, western, world (including Israel) are for the most part predictable and conventional members of the societies of which they are a part. These novels to be considered are worth exploring because they imagine Jews as straying (or being led astray) from their typical roles, and the approaches of the respective

---

[1] David Grossman, *The Zigzag Kid*, trans. Betsy Rosenberg (London: Bloomsbury, 1998), originally published in Hebrew in 1994 by Ha Sifyriya HaHadash/HaKibbutz MaMeuchad, Tel Aviv, as *Yesh yeladim zigag*.

[2] Shifra Horn, *Four Mothers*, trans. Dalya Bilu (London: Piatkus, 1999), originally published in Hebrew as *Arba 'Imahot*, 1997.

[3] Paul Auster, *Leviathan* (New York: Viking, 1992).

[4] Myla Goldberg, *Bee Season* (London: Flamingo, 2001).

[5] Judith Katz, *The Escape Artist* (Ithaca, NY: Firebrand, 1997).

[6] Jerome Charyn, *The Isaac Quartet: Blue Eyes, Marilyn the Wild, The Education of Patrick Silver, Secret Isaac* (New York and London: Four Walls Eight Windows, 2002).

authors afford a different take on Jewish characters and situations than most 'realistic' Jewish fiction, such as in the novels of Philip Roth and A.B. Yehoshua. Despite the fact that at least two of the authors, Paul Auster and David Grossman, are well-known to the general public and consistently received as serious writers, subject to intense scholarly scrutiny, one finds little – if any – critical comment that touches upon the authors' engagement with magical realism. That is, there is scant reflection of the requirement that readers must suspend belief in notions such as cause and effect, the universality of time, the force of gravity, and the accidental nature of coincidence – and assume that inexplicable and irrational forces, taking on a life of their own, animate the unfolding events.

The Centrality of Crime in *The Zigzag Kid* and *Four Mothers*

In David Grossman's novel, *The Zigzag Kid*, one of the leading characters is a con-man, who kidnaps his grandson whom he's never met, and leads him on a series of adventures. Grossman's persona of thirteen-year-old Nonny writes – or boasts – of his maternal grandfather, that Felix Glick

> had once been the most notorious criminal in Israel.
> He had squandered his millions, after robbing banks
> all over the world and swindling governments and
> shaming the police. He had a private yacht, and a
> thousand mistresses. (p. 105)

Complicating this encounter is the fact that the boy's father is a policeman, and his mother, Zohara, became acquainted with her future husband because of her tendency to inhabit the other side of the law. 'I was the son', Grossman writes, 'of a policeman and a criminal' (p. 228).

In responding to her grandson Nonny's question, 'whether his mother, Zohara, knew her father was a criminal', Lola, Nonny's mostly-absent grandmother, offers the following:

> 'There are all sorts of grandmothers in this world . . .
> You have one sort of grandmother on your father's
> side, I believe, and I'm sure she's very dear to you.
> But I myself am a very different sort of grandmother.'
> 'What do you mean, different?'
> 'I have different ideas, different standards of
> behavior – Everybody's different, right?' (p. 275)

Her own standards involve a tolerance for the 'wild' side (p. 275). Yet in addition to detailing behaviours that violate standards of bourgeois respectability, the fantasy-like settings, and interweaving of coincidences that could not possibly be coincidences separates *The Zigzag Kid* from more earth-bound novels of Grossman, such as *Someone to Run With* (2000, Eng. trans. 2003).[7]

Shifra Horn herself stated that her work, *Four Mothers*, might be best approached via the genre of magical realism, as was suggested by critics, and she found herself rather pleased with this characterization. *Four Mothers* opens with one of the characters lying about having a policeman for a father, in no small part to try to obfuscate the family's position which crosses respectability and legality. Amalya, Horn's narrator, recalls that:

> Questions about my father became particularly
> important to me during my school days, when I had to
> fill in forms from the Education Ministry at the
> beginning of every year. I had no trouble filling in
> my mother's name and occupation – Geula, lawyer – but
> when I came to my father's name I hestitated between
> Moshe and Ya'akov. I decided on Moshe, and as his
> occupation I chose policeman. All the children in my
> class wanted their father to be a policeman, but only
> I could permit myself to proudly write it down. I
> would boast of my policeman father and talk about his
> peaked cap and pistol and handcuffs, and how all the
> crooks in town trembled at the mention of his name. I
> explained his absence by saying that he was busy
> chasing burglars all day and only came home late at
> night. . . . My father the policeman played a
> starring role in my life until the third grade, until
> the moment when the homeroom teacher asked me to bring
> him to class so that he could tell us about his work.
> When I evaded the issue with all kinds of excuses, she
> phoned my mother. (pp. 18–19)

The motif of crime and punishment does not end there. The lawyer mother of Amal (Amalya), Geula, was known to her daughter as strenuously working to defend the underdogs, especially the Arabs, who, she told me,

> had been robbed of their land by the state to build
> railways and roads that bisected their villages and
> cut through their fields, and whom she helped even
> when the authorities suspected them of nefarious
> deeds. (pp. 23–4)

---

[7] David Grossman, *Someone to Run With*, trans. Vered Almog and Maya Gurantz (London: Bloomsbury, 2003); orignally *Meeshehu larutz ito* (Tel Aviv: ha-Kibuts ha-me'uhad, 2000).

The irony of Amal-Amalya's imagination of a policeman-father is further intensified because her own birth was the result of her mother being raped. It is not a 'normal' rape, but a particularly surprising gang-rape perpetrated by Yeshiva students in an academy known for the brilliance of its pupils, who were thought to have especially 'pure souls' (pp. 275–8). Amal's mother Geula is the victim of a brutal crime, which appears not simply to be the work of an individual or even a group – but of inexplicable, sinister 'hidden forces' (p. 305). Edward, the loving boyfriend of Sara, another of the four mothers, is killed when a rock is heaved at his car – which was intended for someone else – by an ultra-Orthodox boy. The hidden-forces further magnify and exert themselves, as the hole from which the rock was pried causes the collapse of a café in Jerusalem's Old City, which kills the murderer along with several innocents. I suspect that many readers began reading Horn's *Four Mothers* expecting a relatively genteel book, in which there would be strong emotions – but not necessarily the level of graphic violence that plays so central a role in the novel.

Magic, Politics and Crime on the Streets of New York

Paul Auster is not known as an author who deals with Jewishness explicitly, as does, say, Philip Roth, Cynthia Ozick, and Saul Bellow. He is more akin to Anita Brookner, a novelist who often features Jewish characters, but does not overtly probe Jewish religious or ethnic identity, preferring to be evasive rather than confessional. Despite a number of signals that he wishes his characters not to be seen as 'too Jewish' – such as the fact that the mother of the protagonist, Benjamin Sachs, is Irish (p. 27) – in Auster's *Leviathan* the main characters are unmistakably New York Jewish intellectuals. The novel retrospectively reconstructs the relationship between a fictionalized version of Auster, Peter Aaron, and his friend, Sachs. We are told, quite early in the novel, that Benjamin Sachs has spent time in prison, and that he regarded it as something of a not totally unpleasant learning experience (pp. 21–3). His crime was of the best sort: jailed for demonstrating in the name of a good cause, a form of civil disobedience.

In turning his 'belief that there was a moral justification for certain forms of political violence' into an academic project, Sachs had illuminated the career and writings of Alexander Berkman (1870–1936). In 1892, during the Homestead, Pennsylvania steel strike, workers were killed by private detectives hired by the company. Berkman tried to assassinate Henry Clay Frick, then superintendent of the Carnegie Steel Company, and was sentenced to twenty-two years in prison; he was released, however, in 1906, and then was deported from the United States, with Emma Goldman and 247 other 'alien radicals' in 1919. Both Berkman and Goldman eventually soured on the Soviet Union as oppressive, especially in light of its stance toward anarchism. Although neither Goldman nor Berkman are usually examined in light of their Jewishness, Berkman himself was explicit about the tie between his understanding of Jewish messianism and revolutionary socialism.[8] Clearly, he saw himself as a 'Jewish Anarchist'.[9]

Sach's tragic undoing, though, comes when he turns to crime per se – although he is still considered by many to be more on the side of do-gooding rather than law-breaking. Benjamin Sachs, partly as a result of a particular childhood experience, decides to protest the betrayal of the American dream by blowing up replicas of the Statue of Liberty all over the United States. He is a romantic adventurer, but also a tortured soul. Magical realism functions in the novel in the form of Sach's escapades, as well as in the ways that he imagines his acts and his thoughts.

Auster, as Peter Aaron, in the book's longest paragraph, encapsulates Benjamin Sachs' life as follows:

> He was born August 6, 1945. I remember the date
> because he always made a point of mentioning it,
> referring to himself in various conversations as
> 'America's first Hiroshima baby', 'the original bomb
> child', 'the first white man to draw breath in the
> nuclear age'. He used to claim that the doctor had
> delivered him at the precise moment Fat Man was
> released from the bowels of the Enola Gay, but that
> always struck me as an exaggeration. . . . He was a
> great one for turning facts into metaphors, and since
> he always had an abundance of facts at his disposal,
> he could bombard you with a never-ending supply of
> strange historical connections, yoking together the
> most far-flung people and events. Once, for example,
> he told me that during Peter Kropotkin's first visit
> to the United States in the 1890s, Mrs. Jefferson
> Davis, the widow of the Confederate president,
> requested a meeting with the famous anarchist prince.
> That was bizarre enough, Sachs said, but then, just a
> few minutes after Kropotkin arrived at Mrs. Davis's
> house, who else should turn up but Booker T.
> Washington? Washington announced that he was looking
> for the man who had accompanied Kropotkin (a mutual
> friend), and when Mrs. Davis learned that he was
> standing in the entrance hall, she sent word that he
> should come in and join them. So for the next hour
> this unlikely trio sat around drinking tea and making
> polite conversation: the Russian nobleman who sought

---

[8] Alexander Berkman, *Prison Memoirs of an Anarchist* [1912] (New York: New York Review Books, 1999), pp. 227–8.

[9] Berkman, pp. 83, 206–7.

> to bring down all organized government, the ex-slave
> turned writer and educator, and the wife of the man
> who led America into its bloodiest war, in defense of
> the institution of slavery. Only Sachs could have
> known something like that. . . . Sachs loved these
> ironies, the vast follies and contradictions of
> history, the way in which facts were constantly
> turning themselves on their head. By gorging himself
> on those facts, he was able to read the world as if it
> were a work of the imagination, turning documented
> events into literary symbols, tropes that pointed to
> some dark, complex pattern embedded in the real. I
> could never be quite sure how seriously he took this
> game, but he played it often, and at times it was
> almost as if he were unable to stop himself. The
> business about his birth was part of this same
> compulsion. On the one hand, it was a form of
> gallows humor, but it was also an attempt to define
> who he was, a way of implicating himself in the
> horrors of his own time. (pp. 26–7)

Ultimately, this 'mixed-up world . . . took root inside him and proliferated beyond his control', (p. 27) leading to his being blown to bits at a Wisconsin roadside.

Myra Goldberg's *Bee Season* involves a Jewish family, the Naumanns, that appears, at first glance, to be quite conventional. It is not terribly important where they live, geographically, as they seem to conform to well-worn Jewish templates: A lawyer mother, Miriam, a rabbi father, Saul, a boy, Aaron, and a girl, Eliza; the children are in the pangs of adolescence. Eliza is not esteemed by the family for her intelligence at the outset of the novel; her brother, Aaron, is far more promising in this way. Eliza, though, demonstrates an incredible gift for spelling in her first 'Spelling Bee', and her father decides to cultivate this talent. Moreover, he sees his daughter's acumen as dovetailing his own personal obsession with Jewish mysticism, especially the thought of Abraham Abulafia. While spending more time and energy on grooming his daughter for increasingly competitive Spelling Bees – hence the title – the son, Aaron, is more and more adrift. He turns to the Hare Krishna sect for his spiritual sustenance. The mother, Miriam, who seems to be the most stable of the principal characters, turns out to be the most unsettled, and anarchic.

Similar to the bizarre behavior of Paul Auster's Benjamin Sachs, Myla Goldberg's woman lawyer, Miriam Naumann, decides to undermine convention and destabilize the world on a more microscopic level: by entering into people's homes and stealing relatively inexpensive, but possibly personally meaningful possessions, from the houses of total strangers. Her professional life, we learn, has been a total sham. She had not been regularly employed, let alone fulfilling a 'normal' lawyer's obligations, for years. She has, however, secured a private space in which she stores the objects she has stolen, and reconfigures them into strange installations – as an act of 'Tikkun Olam' – 'fixing the world' (p. 236). She is, in a word, mad. But she is also a criminal. Her crimes are a result, there is no doubt, of her mental illness, but she is nonetheless an officer of the court who has been incessantly, chronically guilty of trespassing and theft. Probably to some critics' taste, the novel is heavy-handed in revealing each character's parallel struggle to come to terms with him and her-self. The characters are complex, but the message that obsession with one's own life journey can lead to disaster lacks subtlety. Still, it is a powerful novel because the characters, though odd, are very well known in Jewish life and literature. All of them are examined from the inside, and, in the process, turned inside out. The flowering of the mother's madness coincides with the denouement reached by the rest of the family.

The 'Isaac' novels of Jerome Charyn and Judith Katz's *The Escape Artist* are less difficult to situate in relation to magical realism, because both authors depict a South American environment associated with the genre and refer explicitly to characters (and families) who follow irrational- and counter-historical paths. The double-heroines of *The Escape Artist* are Sofia Teitelbaum, from Russian Poland, who is conned into a life of prostitution in a Buenos Aires brothel, and her lesbian lover, Hankus – formerly Hannah Lubarsky. Ironically, this is in many respects the most conventional of the books considered – the most straight-forward love story – except that the lovers happen both to be women. Hankus's utter mastery, however, of magic, illusion, and escape, lift the story into a picaresque realm. Tutsik Goldenberg, who hoped to make a fortune off his 'boy', Hankus, *kvelled* to his disbelieving sister, the matron of the brothel:

> Parlor tricks? Simple-minded? Tutsik was absolutely
> indignant, his face beet-colored. 'That boy doesn't
> do parlor tricks. You, you women do parlor tricks!
> What my boy Lubarsky does is art, capital *A* art. The
> man is a *magician*. A *juggler*. An *Escape Artist*.
> You've seen it with your own eyes here and in the
> synagogue. The boy is a *genius*.' (p. 151)

Charyn's novels – which also deal with modern incarnations of white slavery – center on the milieu and career of a New York City policeman, Isaac Sidel, who in the course of Charyn's novels graduates from a detective to Police Commissioner to the Mayor of New York. Although Isaac's immediate family comes from Eastern Europe by way of England and Ireland (p. 192), Isaac often imagines himself though the prism of Babel's notorious Jewish gangster, Benya Krik. Isaac, with his 'bull-neck', 'had torn out the eye of a bandit from East New York, broken the arms of suspicious characters, [and] survived gunfights with Puerto Ricans and hardened Jews' (p. 178). Although Isaac is widely regarded as a hero (p. 443), as much as he sinks into depression, ill-health, and a nearly vagabond existence, the most heinous evil doers in the novel also spring from Jewry: the Guzmann family, from Spain, Columbia, Peru, Mexico, Palestine, and more recently, the Catskills and New York City. Although the family is 'as much

Muslim and Christian as Jew' (p. 77), their primordial nature is Marrano-Jews who outwardly practiced Catholicism but secretly observed Jewish customs and held to Jewish belief during Spain's Inquisition. Charyn suggests that this led to a kind of schizophrenia that resulted in the family becoming a driving force in international prostitution, continuing the alleged Jewish propensity for White Slavery (pp. 93, 149):

> Isaac might never have started with the Guzmanns.
> Papa's numbers mill didn't disturb him. As a lodge
> brother and information minister of the Hands of Esau
> [an analogue to the Jewish policemen's association,
> the Shomrim], he was ashamed to admit that a family of
> Jews could monopolize a portion of the Bronx, but he
> consoled himself with the knowledge that the Guzmanns
> were false Jews, Marranos who accepted Moses as their
> Christ, ridiculed the concept of marriage, and ate
> pork. Then stories, rotten stories, filtered down to
> Isaac by way of his Manhattan stoolies that a policy
> combine in the Bronx was moving into white slavery,
> that its agents as the bus terminals didn't even have
> the character to distinguish between gentile runaways
> and Jewish ones. The Guzmanns were no longer quaint
> people, retards with policy slips who worshiped at
> home in a candy store; they were 'meateaters' (buyers
> of human flesh), a family of insects preying on
> Isaac's boroughs. He sent his deputies into the
> terminals . . . They couldn't link the Guzmanns to
> terminal traffic. The pimps working the bus routes
> had to ask, who's Cesar, who's Papa, who's Jeronimo?
> And Isaac was made to realize that he couldn't trap
> the Guzmanns with old coordinates and shitty spies. (p. 149)

Yet the Jewish women in Isaac's universe are not simply victims. They can be among the most dangerous criminals themselves – such as Esther Rose, who'd 'come out of a Yeshiva in Brownsville that would only accept the daughters of the Sephardim of Brooklyn' (p. 228). One of Isaac's lovers, Sylvia Berkowitz – wife of the Professor Marshall Berkowitz, Dean of Columbia University's undergraduate college – offers to help him settle a personal and professional vendetta:

> 'I'll help you kill the bastard. I swear . . . We
> won't tell Marsh [the Dean-husband] . . . Marsh is
> a chickenshit . . . I'll go up to Dermott in my
> raincoat . . . get him to visit me in your room . . .
> we'll club him with a pair of lamps . . . hide him
> under the bed . . . how will we get rid of the body?'
> . . . Murder drew her close to Isaac. (p. 474)

Recalling the curse of Borges' 'Funes the Memorious', Isaac was himself responsible for mentally-anarchic-overload in his role as Professor at New York's City University:

> Each Thursday morning in September a blue limousine
> would park outside the John Jay College of Criminal
> Justice to deliver Father Isaac. The Chief had to
> make his eleven o'clock class. He was lecturing on
> the sociology of crime. His students were a
> privileged lot. Patrolmen, firemen, and sanitation
> boys, they had never sat in a class with the First
> Deputy Police Commissioner of New York. They were
> crazy for Isaac. He would talk to them about
> Aeschylus, with a gun sticking out of his pants. They
> would go dizzy from his insights, his remembrance of
> poets, hangmen, crooks, politicians, and carnival
> freaks. (p. 415)

Conclusion

In all of these novels, Jews' relationships to criminality serve to unsettle discourses of respectability in general, and undermine late twentieth-century western expectations of Jewish thought and behavior – especially with regard to gender. The 'Jewish mothers' in some of them – rather than being an anchor to tradition and beacon of morality – emerge as cultural and moral anarchists. (This is opposed to 'Anarchism' as a turn-of-the-century political stream, which was committed to the principles of freeing society from all forms of coercion and exploitation.) Yet there also may be deeper motives, on the part of these authors, in portraying Jews as crooks, instigators of violence, and cut-throats: to assert that Jews are 'normal' – that is, like everyone else. Indeed, one of the better known aphorisms of the pre-state Zionist movement, attributed to David Ben-Gurion, runs that 'when in the future the Jews would attain a nation-state, their "normalcy" could only be said to have begun "when the first Jewish cop arrests the first Jewish criminal"'. Alternatively, throwing a spotlight on lawlessness might reflect a tendency to imagine Jews as animated by buried but influential sub-currents in Jewish history, such as those deemed 'counter-historical' with regard to the scholarship of Gershom Scholem on Jewish mysticism.[10]

I believe that the combination of magical realism and crime operates in these and other self-consciously Jewish novels[11] as a means of acknowledging and

---

[10] See David Biale, *Gershom Scholem: Kabbalah and Counter-History* (Cambridge, MA: Harvard University Press, 1982).

[11] See especially Rachel Rubin, *Jewish Gangsters of Modern Literature* (Urbana and Chicago: University of Illinois Press, 2000), with its extensive references. However, the works of Jerome Charyn and other pertinent authors are apparently unknown to the author.

even interacting with earlier traditions of Jewish writing, such as tales of Hasidic masters and stories of Y.L. Peretz, Isaac Babel, and I.B. Singer.[12] Furthermore, the blurring of boundaries between the real and the imagined, and detailing the interaction between mysterious realms and human activity, is a means of engaging a recognized genre which was particularly popularized through Latin American literature, which also intersects Jewish history and literature. The underworlds (both literal and figurative), heavenly spheres, and gnostic recesses evinced in these novels frequently manifest themselves though violence and crime to radically change the lives of characters and otherwise impinge on the world.

It is no coincidence that the most significant post-1945 analysis of Jewish historiography, Yosef H. Yerushalmi's *Zakhor: Jewish History and Jewish Memory*, concludes with a reference to a story of Jorge Luis Borges, *Funes el memorioso* ('Funes the Memorious'), which Yerushalmi says 'haunts' him because of what it infers about the writing of history. 'It is a tale', Yerushalmi writes:

> about an Argentinian, Ireneo Funes, who, as a result
> of a fall from a horse at the age of nineteen, found
> that henceforth he could forget nothing, absolutely
> nothing. He tells Borges: 'I have more memories in
> myself alone than all men have had since the world was
> a world . . .,

Borges continues:

> We, in a glance, perceive three wine glasses on the
> table; Funes saw all the shoots, clusters, and grapes
> of the vine. He remembered the shapes of the clouds
> in the south at dawn on the 30th of April 1882, and he
> could compare them in his recollection with the
> marbled grain in the design of a leather-bound book he
> had seen only once, and with the lines of the spray
> which an oar raised in the Rio Negro in the battle of
> the Quebracho . . .
>   In effect, Funes remembered not only every leaf
> on every tree of every wood, but every one of the
> times he had perceived or imagined it. He determined
> to reduce all of his experiences to some seventy
> thousand recollections, which he would later define
> numerically. Two considerations dissuaded him: the
> thought that the task was interminable and the thought

---

[12] See, for example, *The I.L. Peretz Reader*, edited and with an introduction by Ruth R. Wisse (New Haven: Yale University Press, 2002), pp. 218–24.

that it was useless. He knew that at the hour of his
death he would scarcely have finished classifying even
all the memories of his childhood . . .

Yerushalmi contends that the 'shadow of Funes the Memorious hovers over us all'. The price of historical understanding, of conceiving 'a time' when people think and act differently from ourselves, entails 'inner violence and betrayal'.[13] This is not criminal violence per se, but a kind of extreme mental anarchy, which is played out several times in these novels, and is reflected even in the work of the suave Paul Auster.

Crime, in no small part because it was a part of the ethnic experience of Jews at certain points in their communal development, appears in many other novels as well – such as Philip Roth's *American Pastoral* (1997), E.L. Doctorow's *Ragtime* (1977) and *Billy Bathgate* (1989), Saul Bellow's *The Adventures of Augie March* (1953), John Le Carré's *A Small Town in Germany* (1968), *The Tailor of Panama* (1996), and *The Constant Gardener* (2001), Reggie Nadelson's 'Artie Cohen' series (1995–2004), and several of Mordechai Richler's works – including *The Apprenticeship of Duddy Kravitz* (1959), *Solomon Gursky was Here* (1991), *Joshua Then and Now* (1980) and *Barney's Version* (1997). Less violent forms of crime are also writ large in Jerome Weidman's *I Can Get It for You Wholesale* (1959) and Budd Schulberg's *What Makes Sammy Run?* (1941). In the last, Sammy is one Sammy Glick – he shares the same surname as Nonny's grandfather in *The Zigzag Kid*. The name is most likely a deliberate signifier in both cases – as Glick is yiddish for luck. This last group of works mentioned, however, do not exhibit the kind of mystical realist dimension as evident in the works I've dealt with here. But there is every indication that this trend, of depicting Jews in a criminal nexus, and of combining mystical realism with crime, is far from abating.

---

[13] Yerushalmi, *Zakhor: Jewish History and Jewish Memory* (Seattle: University of Washington Press, 1982), pp. 102–3. See Jorge Louis Borges, 'Funes el memorioso', in his *Ficciones* (Buenos Aires: Losada, 1956), pp. 123, 125. The English translation is by Anthony Kerrigan in his edition of *Ficciones* (New York: Knofp, 1962), pp. 112, 114.

Flights of Fancy:
Angela Carter's Transgressive Narratives

Sarah Sceats

Angela Carter (1940–1992) is on the face of it an unlikely candidate for inclusion in this volume. The perspective from which she writes, however, is a peculiar one. Stimulated by her sojourn in Japan in 1969–72 (where she claims to have become radicalised) and by travels in Australia, Asia, Europe and the United States, she adopts the 'view from elsewhere', seeing British culture as wonderfully strange, peculiar, exotic. In her journalism especially, she anatomises cultural detail – clothing, fashion, make-up, food, shops, politicians, pop music – with the defamiliarising eye of a poet. On one particularly involving trip, to Doncaster, she comments sardonically that 'It's very tiring, not being alienated from your environment' and elsewhere proclaims that 'alienated is the only way to be, after all'.[1] At the same time, she makes promiscuous use of European and other cultures; drawing on philosophy, fairy tales, high art, kitsch, Shakespeare and cinema, she juggles England with the rest of the world without batting an eyelid. 'Maybe Yorkshire never really left the third World', she writes, and compares the surroundings of Ilkley to Transylvania, Habitat stores to a caravanserai, Empire Day to the Nuremberg rally (*Shaking a Leg*, pp. 172, 174). Nothing is sacred: all regions and nations contribute to the cultural dressing-up box that in her view is there for the plundering.

This approach is consistent with what Carter herself described as her tendency – inherited in part from her Scottish father and Yorkshire grandmother – to be awkward, argumentative: 'bolshy', as she herself puts it.[2] It also suggests a multi-cultural and interdisciplinary impetus. Carter's perspective is fundamentally political, emphatically and often subversively on the side of the disempowered and disenfranchised. We are, she claims, the creatures of history, from which nothing offers a refuge. She rejects essentialist notions and focuses on the forces

---

[1] Angela Carter, 'The Donnie Ferrets', in *Shaking a Leg*, ed. Jenny Uglow (London: Vintage, 1998), pp. 169–73 (p. 173); 'The Mother Lode', in *Shaking a Leg*, pp. 2–15 (p.12). Both articles were written in 1976.

[2] See John Haffenden, *Novelists in Interview* (London and New York: Methuen 1985).

and processes that position us in society. She seeks to subvert received truths and conventional thinking on many levels and in diverse areas. This is particularly so both in gender relations and their intersections with class and race and also in terms of the radical potential of literary and popular genres. 'I am all for putting new wine in old bottles', she says, 'especially if the pressure of the new wine makes the old bottles explode.'[3] For Carter, everything is to be counted, both the material world and the products of our imaginations, and most especially what is uncomfortable: freaks, outlaws, cannibals, fairies, monsters, symbols – whatever we normally edit out from 'reality'.

Disturbing Rewritings: Carter's Provocative Fairy Tales

This thumbnail sketch of Carter's attitudes is intended to frame the proposal that in her fiction she uses fantasy and symbolism (alongside psychological and political plausibility) to offer a deliberately disturbing view of what is 'real'. I use 'disturbing' in both senses here, for she aims, I think, to disrupt and provoke thought and consequently often disquiets and alarms. Consider, for example, the fairy tale, a disturbing form in the first place. There seem to be two schools of thought concerning the 'purpose' of fairy tales: that they are moral or cautionary tales; or that they enable psychological transitions from childhood to adult worlds. In a 1976 article Carter approvingly cites Charles Perrault as championing the view that fairy tales exist as 'a project for worldly instruction' in the most practical sense.[4] Eschewing connections with sexual trauma and awakening, Carter says, he draws morals to do with hard work, ingenuity and self-advancement. Bruno Bettleheim, by contrast, famously offers Freudian interpretations of a variety of fairy tales as paradigms of initiation into fearful, sexualised, adult understanding.[5] It might fairly be said that both of these models assume functionality in the fairy tale, whether this is born of the Protestant Ethic and a taken-for-granted bourgeois ideology or is a manifestation of post-Freudian emphasis on self and identity. Inherent in the fairy tale form, these interpretations suggest, is either a model of instruction or an assumption of difficult but desirable knowledge about the darker side of human desire and aspiration, about how the world works.

---

[3] Angela Carter, 'Notes from the Front Line', in *Shaking a Leg*, pp. 36–43 (p. 37). This article was written in 1983.

[4] 'Charles Perault, academician, folklorist, pedant, but clearly neither nutter nor regressive, takes a healthily abrasive attitude to his material. Cut the crap about richly nurturing the imagination. *This* world is all that is to the point.' Angela Carter, 'The Better to Eat You With', in *Shaking a Leg*, pp. 451–5 (pp. 452–3).

[5] See Burno Bettleheim, *The Uses of Enchantment: The Meaning and Importance of Fairy Tales* (Harmondsworth: Penguin, 1978).

It seems reasonable to assume that readers will approach Carter's own reworking of various folk and fairy tales with some such foreknowledge or precon-
ceptions. While Carter's stories in *The Bloody Chamber* are clearly different
from traditional tales (being highly literary and certainly not written for children)
there is nevertheless a degree of commonality with the more traditional tale, evident in a kind of intersection, between tradition, ideology, expectations and the
shock of the new. And of course they also constitute the meeting place of readers and writer. What Carter does is to exploit the potential for contradiction, challenge and ambivalence. The title tale of *The Bloody Chamber* is a reworking of
the Bluebeard story, a tale in which wifely curiosity overcomes a promise of
obedience with near fatal consequences. Carter makes various changes to the
traditional version, the most obvious being the ending, in which the about-to-be-
beheaded wife is rescued by her feisty mother rather than by her brothers (a feminist substitution that nevertheless disempowers and infantilises the protagonist).
More interestingly, Carter insinuates the suggestion that the wife has a 'capacity
for corruption', is stirred by her husband's objectifying gaze and rampant,
murderous sexuality, and thus in fact colludes in some way with him. (You can
see why she managed to irk not a few fellow feminists.)

This story, placed at the beginning of the collection, establishes the prevailing
themes of sexualisation and empowerment, which challenge the traditions
expressed by both Perrault and Bettleheim (especially Bettleheim). Carter offers
two versions of 'Beauty and the Beast', for example. The first ('The Courtship
of Mr Lyon') is a beautifully written 'straight' version of the story, interwoven
with symbols of virginity and objectification to suggest that Beauty at first avoids
and then succumbs to the contract of marital surrender. The economic subtext
(for Beauty is an object of exchange between her father and the Beast) remains
more or less implicit. In the second story ('The Tiger's Bride'), however, economic factors are overt from the very first line, 'My father lost me to the Beast
at cards', and in further financially-drenched formulations such as 'my own skin
was my sole capital in the world and today I'd make my first investment'. [6]

The second striking difference in this story is that it moves right out of any
pretence at a realist framework and into a fabulous or magical one. The power
play between Beauty and the Beast is concluded here by an extraordinary equality, the reverse of the Beast's traditional transformation into a man. Beauty is told
she may return to her father but sends a simulacrum in her place. Shrugging off
her fur cloak, which resolves into a pack of rats, she seeks out the Beast, who
has meanwhile relinquished human disguise and revealed his fearful symmetry.
When Beauty casts herself before him his great rasping tongue progressively
licks off her skins to reveal the tiger beneath.

This dénouement is much more radical than the vignette of Mr and Mrs Lyon
strolling under the trees at the end of the previous story. It refutes the deal

---

[6] Angela Carter, *The Bloody Chamber and other Stories* (London: Penguin Books,
1981), p. 56.

between father and suitor (that is: marriage, in which, Carter cynically avers else-where, wives 'of necessity fuck by contract') as impossibly unequal.[7] The tiger, she says, will never lie down with the lamb; it is up to the lamb to learn to run with tigers. One of her reworkings of 'Little Red Riding Hood' similarly pro-poses that a canny girl needs no rescue by woodcutter or father; that the ideal solution is for Little Red Riding Hood to get into bed with the wolf, notwith-standing Granny's posthumous disapproval. Carter disappoints the expectations established by the well-known tales, indeed by the genre itself (for familiar pat-terns and elements make for predictable endings).[8] Carter's reversals, bestial transformations and use of Gothic subtly redefine the conventions of the genre at the same time as challenging gender ideologies.

Carter's stories lend themselves to interpretations in terms of class or ethnicity as well as gender. While I would be loath to argue for such a reading of all the tales, it is true that the Marquis in 'The Bloody Chamber' and both Beasts are solid, wealthy, property-owning (even ennobled) citizens and there are intimations in 'The Bloody Chamber' of the brutal exploitation of peasants. Most of the tales feature exiles and outsiders, human or otherwise, who may be seen as peripheral to the cultural and political mainstream. In the final story, 'Wolf Alice', the pro-tagonists are quite outside society: Alice is a wolf-girl who has avoided all but the most rudimentary socialisation. Spurned by and spurning the village, she becomes the house servant of the Duke, a vampiric, lycanthropic creature of the night. When out seeking his dinner in the graveyard – for he draws his sustenance from dead human flesh – he is shot by local vigilantes.[9] As a result of Alice's caring attention the Duke is brought into focus, literally, in the mirror. He thus achieves an identity. The most abstract and oblique of the stories, 'Wolf Alice' may, I think, be read as offering a perverse ideal deriving from the extra-social. The Duke is described as having gone through the mirror, living on the far side, while Alice's reaction to the mirror is playful and explorative. If the collection as a whole offers male brutality as the thesis, female sexualisation and economic empowerment the antithesis, then gender equality with reciprocity is the synthesis. The crucial fac-tor is that this synthesis does not arise out of gender paradigms constructed by society, for Alice and the Duke are both, as it were, beyond the mirror. In the 'real' world, of course, such communicative asociality is impossible; hence the potency of fairy tales exploring literally 'impossible' situations.

One final thought about these tales. I have suggested reading the collection as a whole in terms of gender, but it is not a great leap to consider it also in global terms: for male brutality read colonisation, for female empowerment read eman-cipation. The antithesis, notably, comes from the periphery, a resolution from

[7] Angela Carter, *The Sadeian Woman* (London: Virago, 1979), p. 9.

[8] See Vladimir Propp, *Morphology of the Folktale*, ed. Louis A. Wagner, trans. Laurence Scott (Austin: University of Texas Press, 1968).

[9] The best joke in the collection is that a corpse prophylactically stuffed with garlic to keep the Duke away only appeals all the more as '*cadavre provençal*'.

outside the system. But it would be cheating to base an argument entirely on Carter's fairy tales, for they are more wholly magical than the combination of prosaic and surreal associated with magic realism. The fairy tale form traditionally allows for metamorphoses and infractions of the laws of physics. If Carter's narratives are generically transgressive it will be more clearly seen in relation to the novel form, and what better novel to choose than *Nights at the Circus*, a text as dense and intricately plotted as a nineteenth-century novel, that posits at its centre a larger-than-life cockney trapeze artist from whose shoulders sprout a large pair of wings.

Truth or Reality: the Celebratory Transgression of Nights at the Circus

I want here to interject a comment by Carter herself. In a television interview shortly before her death she asserted that however real or plausible her characters might seem, however much they might 'leap off the page' they were in fact always inclined to be 'telling you something'.[10] What the something might be of course varies, but I think it is fair to say that it is often suggestive and interrogative rather than categorical. This idea is apparent in a 1982 address to a science fiction convention in which Carter outlines her opposition to bourgeois mimesis:

> The idea that first gripped me when I was a little kid and read *The Day of the Triffids* in the newspaper, that the literal truth might not be the whole truth, turned into a conviction that one way of asking questions – because I think that one of the functions of fiction is to ask questions that can't be asked in any other way – is through constructing imaginary worlds in which ideas can be discussed. And speculations about the nature of our experience on this planet be conducted without crap about the imitation of life getting in the way, because whose life are you supposed to be imitating? Obviously a trapeze artist has got as much claim to be alive as a solicitor.[11]

That the literal truth might not be the whole truth is of the essence in *Nights at the Circus*. Indeed, Carter seems far more interested in exploring what is true than what is demonstrably real. To this end she produces her trapeze artist, but 'imitates' her life with what might be called extreme poetic license against a wonderfully and dreadfully energised reality, one that is 'magical'.

The novel begins in Fevvers' London dressing room as she narrates her larger-than-life-story to Walser, a sceptical young American journalist who seeks an answer to the question 'Is she fact or is she fiction?' for his series 'Great

---

[10] *Angela Carter's Curious Room*, dir. Kim Evans. Omnibus Series, BBC Television, 15 September 1992.

[11] Angela Carter, 'Fools are my Theme', in *Shaking a Leg*, pp. 31–6 (pp. 34–5).

Humbugs of the World'. [12] The ambiguity of Fevvers' nature – not only whether she is 'freak or fraud' but who she is and what she is true to – is maintained throughout the book. Even at the end of the novel, her comment to Walser, 'I fooled you', is ambiguous: it might refer to her wings, or to her pretended virginity, or to the pervasive proto-Butleresque implication that she constitutes herself through performance, since she adds that 'there's nothing like confidence' (pp. 294–5). [13] It probably even refers to the confidence trick pulled off by Carter in getting us to believe in her at all.

There is not space here to go into the intricacies of the plot, but I will summarise a little, so as to indicate something of the novel's structure and use of magical-realist elements. What fuels the action is that, overwhelmed by the drama and intrigue of Fevvers' story and by the bizarrely erotic power of her physicality, Walser determines to join the circus incognito and follow Fevvers on her world tour. (Walser is inducted into a more than realist world from the outset, for Fevvers' initial monologue is enhanced by some magical tampering with time by her sidekick and mentor, the revolutionary Lizzie. [14]) Part 2 of the novel, centred on the circus in St Petersburg, sees Walser become a clown, dance with tigers and suffer innumerable humiliations, Lizzie engage in political subterfuge and Fevvers' greed almost culminate in her being miniaturised and entrapped in a Fabergé egg. She only escapes by the boldest of narratorial strategies, a magical-realist *coup de théâtre* that is worth pausing over for a moment.

Carter traps Fevvers with a Grand Duke of superhuman strength, ingenuity and libido who displays his collection to her. These include both an egg containing a miniature Trans-Siberian Express and one with a jewelled birdcage, ready and waiting for Fevvers herself. She is entranced with the miniature train and despite the Grand Duke's strictures she picks it up. As the danger mounts, in an act thoroughly in character and in keeping with Carter's line on the economics of gender relations, Fevvers resorts to sexual distraction to keep the Grand Duke at bay, using her free hand to masturbate him 'as if her life depended on it', all the time regretfully visualising her anticipated diamonds and riches receding into the distance. Now comes the magical-realist stroke:

> [There] came a wet crash and clatter as the ice-carving of herself collapsed into the remains of the caviar in the room below, casting the necklace which had tempted her amongst the dirty supper things. The bitter knowledge she'd been fooled spurred Fevvers into action. She dropped the toy train on the Isfahan runner – mercifully, it landed on its wheels – as, with a grunt and whistle of expelled breath, the Grand Duke ejaculated.

[12] Angela Carter, *Nights at the Circus* (London: Picador, 1985), p. 7.

[13] I refer, of course, to Judith Butler's *Gender Trouble* (London: Routledge, 1989), which incidentally succeeds *Nights at the Circus* by some six years.

[14] Lizzie's magic ceases later on with the loss of her handbag. This presumably hints at the potency of a woman's bag of tricks, but in this case the bag also contains political pamphlets, thus neatly bringing together several ideological and thematic strands of the novel.

> In those few seconds of his lapse of consciousness, Fevvers ran helter-skelter down the platform, opened the door of the first-class compartment and clambered aboard. (p. 192)

The transition, like a sleight of hand, effects a transformation of tone, plot, scene, character and geography. From here the narrative progresses into part 3, the trans-Siberian trip, on which the train is blown up, the characters dispersed and the tightly controlled narrative begins to fall apart.

Carter's use of magic realism at this point is both inventive and traditional. It is, after all, a *deus ex machina*, albeit without the *deus*. But it is also exciting, funny, impossibly bold and mischievous. And it releases the narrative from its tight, intricately plotted, urban character, into something much more apparently disorganised, in both content and structure, with threads running off in all directions. Only after many adventures in the Russian taiga are Fevvers and Walser reunited and their relationship consummated – with Fevvers incidentally in the 'woman on top' position for which nature (or Carter) has equipped her.

It is fairly obvious that Fevvers is an aspirational figure of female empowerment, a New Woman come to demonstrate the desirability of transgressing the rules and conventions. She is huge; she belches, farts and yawns with vulgar abandon, has an appetite to match her size and 'Elizabethan' table manners; she can fly, albeit slowly; she 'spreads' her wings most provocatively, effecting a calculated erotic disturbance in men; and most of the time she is putting on some kind of bravura performance. She has an ebullient personality that embodies libido, the life force. She is a feminist role model of sorts, and – for this reader at least – a positive incitement to kick over the traces and become larger than life.

I think I am safe, therefore, in claiming that *Nights at the Circus* is transgressive, in terms of its central figure at least, and it might be added that, originating from an egg – or so she claims – Fevvers is a quintessential outsider. In addition, the novel itself is difficult to place generically. It is a sort of picaresque romance, encompassing numerous embedded narratives (largely of peripheral, 'freakish', disempowered or exploited women or in one case a symbolically mouthless black servant, significantly called Toussaint). It has gothic passages. It is comic both in voice and resolution. It exploits the conventions of folk tale and animal stories (there are monkeys who study, a tiger who falls in love and a pig who can spell). It is carnivalesque. It is a novel that seems to relish its own diversity. And as suggested earlier what starts out as a tightly (and magically) controlled narrative in London moves into densely plotted adventure and intrigue in St Petersburg, thence unravelling in chaos in Siberia.

And Magic Realism?

What, then, is the status and significance of magic realism in this text? The orgasmic transition related above is not just a brilliant *deus ex machina*. It certainly bears a structural function, but also has thematic significance. It is one of a chapter of disasters or near-disasters to befall the hitherto hermetic world of the circus and involves the loss of Fevvers' phallic power (her sword gets broken in the struggle with the Grand Duke), her relinquishing of material acquisitiveness and the beginnings of the disintegration of her persona. The toy train offers her an escape (from enslavement to the aristocracy) but projects her into the unknown, wild territory of the second world. Fevvers escapes the gilded cage but is released into the foreign, mapless territory of the taiga. It is only after losing Walser (whose own ordeals rob him of spectator status and turn him into a 'real' person) and the disintegration of her colourful persona that she is reconstituted as the source of a carnival laughter that 'shudder[s] across the entire globe' (p. 295).

Carter's magic realism is integral to the novel: she deploys it structurally, thematically and symbolically – not to mention dramatically. Fevvers' great wings, initially suspect, by the end of the novel are simply and clearly a part of her character and physique; her brief and ungainly flight, like that of an overladen bumble bee, is multiply metaphorical, literally impossible and yet of the essence. (There is, incidentally, some fakery, for Fevvers dyes, both hair and plumage.) Thus this central character embodies aspirations on behalf of the most lumpen and least likely to take flight. Coupled with the geographical compass of Fevvers' influence, Lizzie's championing of the world's oppressed, and the hierarchical inversions attendant on carnival (however transient), the fantastic heroine suggests a radical refashioning of the *fin de siècle* and what it promises.

There are numerous embedded narratives in the novel, from a girl with eyes in her nipples to shards of broken mirror too hot to touch because they have absorbed a troupe of tigers. These narratives, along with the rich and complex ramifications of plot, interweave the plausibly real and the impossible, feeding into the overall critique of gender relations and oppressive ideologies at large. There is wry ideological comment, for example in the scene where Walser is silently prevailed upon by a group of self-improving apes to strip and present himself as a naked model for their biology lesson (to give Carter's comic impulse its due: as Walser speculates, they are grappling with Darwin's theory, but from another perspective).

Finally, I would say that Carter uses magic realism, here and elsewhere, to explore existential issues that may or may not be ideological. Becoming a circus clown, for example, offers Walser the 'freedom that lies behind the mask, within dissimulation, the freedom to juggle with being' (p. 103). The idea of being able to deconstruct the self and juggle the elements alternatively is an idea Carter plays with in a number of texts and connects with her anti-essentialist position. Here Walser's freedom to juggle parallels Fevvers' construction through performance. It is a vertiginous and dangerous freedom though, for not only does Walser relinquish his impervious self, he is twice almost wholly obliterated, once by a jealous tiger and again when Buffo the Master Clown succumbs to psychotic despair and attacks him with a carving knife. In a similar way, Carter sets up the clowns, who are, of course, implicated in Walser's deconstruction, to represent the antithesis of Fevvers. She, as I have suggested, is the embodiment of Eros; they manifest negation, entropy and death. When the circus troupe is dispersed they appropriately conjure up their own entropic wind, which blows them all away, leaving just a few shreds of coloured fabric, a broken fiddle and a little dog (p. 243). It is Eros, in this ultimately comic novel, that has the last word.[15]

Does Carter thus re-write history, from the margins? I would say the answer is a qualified 'no'. Of course she (re)invents. But she does not offer an alternative history so much as call into question the ways we read – or ignore – it. What she does achieve, I believe, is to challenge and subvert some of the existing narratives by destabilising relationships between the 'fantastic' and the 'real', so that it becomes difficult or even pointless to attempt to distinguish between them. What is true is multiple and slippery. The great strength of Carter's writing is its capacity to hold this slippery multiplicity.

---

[15] Performance might equally be said to prevail over deconstruction.

Part III: The Politics of Magic

Introduction

Wen-chin Ouyang

> The realities of power and authority – as well as the resist-
> ances offered by men, women and the social movements to
> institutions, authorities, and orthodoxies – are the realities
> that make texts possible, that deliver them to their readers,
> that solicit the attentions of critics.
>
> – Edward Said

There is perhaps no need to reiterate that magical realism is inherently political
concerned not only with the continuing influence of empire in the postcolonial
world but also with the corruption of political authority set up in the postindependence nation-states, not to mention the attendant cultural politics that partake in the formulation of a plausible postcolonial national identity. But there is
politics and there is politics. All roads may lead to empire and nation, but not
all forms of power politics chip at the grand narratives in the same way. For one
thing, there is that mysterious discourse driving ideology that determines the
direction of identity politics and the position from other discourses, and, for
another, there are those numerous articulated categories of knowledge embedded in any grand narrative that require dismantling one by one. And then there
is the style of discourse and the genre in which the discourse is cast. The minute
differences in the selection for engagement of one or any number of articulated
categories of knowledge subject to interrogation can produce subtle nuances in
producing and apprehending cultural and identity politics. The literary texts
analyzed in this Section may be situated within the broader context of postcolonial national politics on culture and identity, but each of them identifies its
own interlocutor and participates in cultural and identity politics in a unique
fashion.

Evelyn Fishburn takes a familiar text and casts new light on it in 'Humour and
Magical Realism in *El reino de este mundo*'. Humour in Alejo Carpentier's
famous novel, *The Kingdom of this World*, Fishburn argues, is political and, more
importantly, it 'provide[s] the space for the unsayable to be said', whether that
pertains to culture, religion or race. Philip Swanson looks at subversion in children's literature in 'Magical Realism and Children's Literature: Isabel Allende's
La Cuidad de las Bestias' and uncovers the ways in which a story written for

children follows the political trajectory of any magical realist novel written for adults, exposing the fallacy of hierarchized polarity between 'North' and 'South', 'First World' and 'Third Word', 'Civilization' and 'Barbarism', and 'Primitivism' and 'Innocence', and giving a moral lesson to 'First World' children. Helene Price, on the other hand, takes Laura Esquivel and her one-time husband Alfonso Arau to task for their neo-'colonial' politics in her novel, *Like Water for Chocolate*, and in his cinematic rendition of it. Looking at gender, class, race and nation as the loci of their political discourse, Price argues in 'Unsavoury Representations in Laura Esquivel's *Like Water for Chocolate*' that both texts, the novel and the film, regurgitate 'conservative', in fact, colonial ideologies that reinforce patriarchy, racism, class distinction and empire. This very conservative political agenda is, however, subject to subversion in Tsila A. Ratner's 'Not So Innocent – An Israeli Tale of Subversion: Dorit Rabinyan's *Persian Brides*'. Basing her discussion on gender and ethnicity in the configuration of the newly founded State of Israel, Ratner demonstrates how by locating the story in the Orient (Persia) of the past and dousing the text with magic the author in fact calls into question the legitimacy of the state's policy of racial discrimination and of orthodoxy's practice of oppressing women. Magical realism can play a constructive role as well. It is part of a strategy of evasion in the works of Nakagami Kenji, Mark Morris argues in 'Magical Realism as Ideology: Narrative Evasions in the Work of Nakagami Kenji', through which the text avoids taking an explicit stance in cultural politics of 'imperial' Japan. There is, however, more to this than meets the eye. Underneath the veneer of a seemingly apolitical text, there is a narrative that transforms what may be called Japanese 'ghetto' into an ideal community. Robin Fiddian makes a similar observation of an early work by García Márquez in 'Legend, Fantasy and the Birth of the New in *Los funerales de la Mamá Grande* by Gabriel García Márquez'. In a postcolonial reading of magical realism that picks apart the world of Mamá Grande dominated by tyranny and corruption, Fiddian shows how the text simultaneously deconstructs an old world and 'heralds the birth of a new political order'.

Humour and Magical Realism in
El reino de este mundo

Evelyn Fishburn

Conflicting Juxtapositions

The episode of the burning at the stake of Makandal encapsulates perfectly what I consider to be the principal and distinguishing feature of Latin American magical realism: the juxtaposition of European and native American or Afro-American perceptions of events. It also serves as a key example of 'bisociative shock', a neologism invented by Arthur Koestler to describe what he considers an important trigger of humour. In this pivotal chapter of *El reino de este mundo* (*The Kingdom of this World*), the scene is set for the *auto da fe* of the runaway slave, an event which will be understood very differently by the two factions watching it. The narrative focuses on the completely different expectations and perceptions of this occurrence and it is this clash rather than the horror of what is happening which is imprinted on the page, and on the reader's mind. I shall return to this later.

The comic always participates in the category of contradiction. To argue the relationship between the underlying principles of humour and of magical realism I shall first focus on oppositional duality as the mainspring for both: humour as resulting from the clash or collision when two contrasting or habitually incompatible associative contexts meet, and magical realism as deriving from 'the cultural sparks which fly from the juxaposition and clash of different cultures at different levels of development'.[1] This definition can equally be applied to Koestler's notion of 'bisociative shock', which denotes the collision between two contradictory levels of association. Koestler focuses on the oppositional nature of humour resulting from 'universes of discourses colliding, frames getting entangled, or contexts getting confused' arguing that the pattern underlying all varieties of humour is essentially 'bisociative'.[2] Koestler's idea

---

[1] Gerald Martin, *Journeys Through the Labyrinth* (London and New York: Verso, 1989), p. 142. Martin usefully clarifies that the contradictions inherent in 'magical realism' differentiate this mode of writing from 'mythical realism'.

[2] See Koestler, *The Act of Creation* (New York: Dell, 1967), pp. 35–40.

can be traced back to Freud's identification of humour as ensuing from the coupling of two dissimilar things bringing to light an 'appropriate incongruity' which in this case exists between two aesthetic systems or modes of thought.[3] There is, and can be, no comprehensive definition of humour, a category that constantly overlaps with other disjunctive systems such as irony, parody, satire and sarcasm. One important distinction is that humour depends on brevity and momentary surprise for its effect. It is a particular way of looking at the world with various degrees of derision or aggression, yet lacking the corrective faith of satire and sarcasm. Irony, the category with which humour is most often confused, differs from it in that it is more reflective and evaluative. A useful distinction is made by Northrop Frye, who argues that 'irony is a vision of ethos concerned with the ideal, the good that ought to be, whereas humour is primordially engaged with the real, with what is'.[4] My reading concentrates largely on humour, but some of the same incidents I analyze from the perspective of humour can be interpreted differently if looked at from the position of irony.

Magical realism, too, is acknowledged and characterized as being principally concerned with the oppositional co-existence of conflicting matrices of thought or behaviour though the debate surrounding its definition is fierce and ongoing.[5] For my purposes here I will accept and limit myself to an understanding of magical realism as a literary movement dealing with the cultural plurality of Latin America in such a way as to present both European and Afro-American based belief systems as valid knowledge, and argue that their stark contrast, heightened through having been accorded equal status, often has a humorous effect. To put it in words which summarize the foregoing, their often explicit or implicit collision causes a *bisociative shock* complete with *flying sparks*.

Both Freud and Koestler saw the relationship between the workings of humour and of creative art. However, the connection between the oppositional elements of humour and of magical realism has so far not received much critical attention, as relevant bibliographies and searches of specialist databases such as MLA,

---

[3] Freud's ideas on humour are found principally in *Jokes and Their Relation to the Unconscious* and his essay 'Humour' (Harmondsworth: The Penguin Freud Library, 1991), vol. 6, and vol. 13, pp. 425–34 respectively.

[4] Northrop Frye, *The Anatomy of Criticism* (Princeton: Princeton University Press, 1971), p. 286. I discuss different aspects of humour more fully in 'From Black to Pink: Shades of Humour in Borgesís Fictions', *Variaciones Borges: Journal of Philosophy, Semiotics and Literature*, 12 (2001), 7–27.

[5] There is, of course, no consistent definition of magical realism, as is evident from the different uses to which the term is put in the essays in this volume. In support of this definition, see W.Rowe's entry 'Magical realism' in *Encyclopedia of Latin American Literature*, ed. V. Smith (London, Chicago: Fitzroy Dearborn Publishers, 1997), pp. 506–7, and Stephen Slemon's definition ('the battle between oppositional systems . . . that is often the matrix of magical realism'), discussed by Wendy Faris in 'The Question of the Other', *Janus Head*, 5.2 (Fall 2002), Special Issue on *Magical Realism,* 103–5.

HLAS and HAPI confirm.[6] The connection between Carpentier and humour, on the other hand, has been both positively denied and even ignored. For instance, in 'Laughing is a Serious Matter' José Oviedo offered Carpentier as an obvious example of the lack of humour in Latin American literature, saying that 'he never found the critical power of humour that would have lightened the monumental gravity of his narratives' and adding that 'for many long years, our letters were incapable of a good laugh, not the laugh of a casual joke but the one that arrives from a *comic vision* of the world' (emphasis in the original).[7] Rodriguez Monegal, for his part, omits Carpentier from the list of humorous Latin American authors he discusses in an important article on 'Traditions of Laughter'.[8] I hope that my discussion of *El reino de este mundo* will prove both these positions to be misguided, and show that Carpentier's short novel is full of humorous situations, or rather serious situations which are depicted humorously.

I wish to argue that Carpentier's vision of the world, which in *El reino de este mundo* I interpret as essentially pessimistic (though some critics have considered it optimistic),[9] draws consistently on the comic as its preferred means of expression. This is not in order to lessen in any way the gravity of the content of his novel, but should be seen rather as a distancing device employed by the author to convey a complex and often tragic reality; this is, at best, a spiral of failed revolutions and, at worst, a cycle of ever-repeating enforcements of brutality by those who have acceded to power. 'For with what does humor deal save with that which isn't funny . . .. tragedy and comedy have a common root, whose name at last I think I know. Desperation': thus wrote the North American humorist De Vries.[10]

Carpentier considered cultural hybridity to be the salient feature of the Latin American reality and that which sets it apart as a continent. As he states in his Prologue to *El reino de este mundo*, the singular history of the black king, Henri Christophe, the sight of a replica of the rococó palace of *Sans Souci* in the midst of the Haitian jungle, as well as the Piranesi-like ruins of La Ferrière citadel and the still-felt presence of Pauline Bonaparte in the tropics led him to

---

[6] There are individual studies of humour in the work of authors usually considered magic realists, but not from this perspective. Bravo's article on *El harpa y la sombra* discusses the humour of clashing isopies (Greimas). See V. Bravo, 'El arpa y la sombra de Alejo Carpentier: La urdimbre de la mentira', *Escritura: Revista de Teoría y Crítica Literarias* (Caracas, Venezuela), vol. 9, nos. 17–18 (Jan–Dec 1984), 117–25.

[7] *Latin American Literature and Arts* (New York, NY), 35.7 (July–Dec 1985), a volume dedicated especially to Humour in Latin American literature.

[8] *Latin American Literature and Arts*, pp. 3–6.

[9] For example, J. Labanyi, 'Nature and the Historical Process in Carpentier's *El siglo de las luces*', *Bulletin of Hispanic Studies*, 57 (1980), 55–66; and R.A.Young, *Carpentier: El reino de este mundo* (London: Grant and Cutler, 1983), particularly pp. 102–4.

[10] This quotation appeared in *The New Yorker* (24 May 2004), p. 48. I thank Lois Zamora Parkinson most warmly for bringing this author to my attention, and for her insightful and constructive reading of a draft version of the present article.

the realization that the famous juxtapositions of the European surrealist movement were artificial whereas in America they were an actuality, a part of its everyday reality.[11] The perception of this 'privileged revelation of reality' he famously called by the paradox 'lo real maravilloso' (the marvellous real).[12] It is not necessary to repeat the finer points of the distinction between marvellous reality and magical realism, which have been argued extensively elsewhere.[13] My focus lies on the overlap between the terms, which allows for the conflation of Carpentier's ontological perception of what he terms the marvellous reality of Latin America and his use of magical realism as a literary mode to represent this reality. Carpentier believed that the apparent incongruity of such combinations of different cultures called for a new writing in Latin America, and his own response to this lies in the double focalization in the narrative of *El reino de este mundo*. Two contrasting mindsets, which I shall label provisionally as the European and the Afro-American, are displayed in contrapuntal dissonance: there is no hierarchy between them, and each plays the leading tune in unmarked succession. To extend the metaphor, this does not mean that there is not a home key, for this is determined by the author's European background and the Spanish discourse in which the novel is cast, but it concentrates on Carpentier's groundbreaking awareness of the need to decentre the European account of history through the presentation of alternative accounts as equally valid. The point has often been made that this is ultimately a European attempt to present the Afro-American mind, but this is not at issue here: what is, is that two different mindsets are given centre stage at key moments in the novel mainly through the use of unmediated indirect free speech.[14]

Cultural Tensions: Decentring the Dominant

The first chapter of the novel is seminal in that it presents magical realism's cultural tensions in three different ways, each also illustrating a different mechanism of humour: the perception of hidden connections between dissimilar things, the unmasking of authority, and cultural misreadings. It begins with the implicit contrast between French colonialist and African values through the

---

[11] Jason Wilson discusses Carpentier's relationship with surrealism in the present volume (pp. 67–78).

[12] These views are amplified in 'De lo real maravilloso americano', *Tientos y diferencias* (Mexico City: UNAM, 1964), pp. 112–20; particularly p. 116.

[13] See Roberto González Echeverría, *The Pilgrim at Home* (Ithaca: Cornell University Press, 1977), pp. 107–29.

[14] Double focalization is extensively discussed in Young, pp. 87–97; and S. Bell, 'Carpentier's *El reino de este mundo* in a New Light: Toward a Theory of the Fantastic', *Journal of Spanish Studies*, 8 (1980), 29–43 (pp. 34–9).

thoughts of master and slave. For Lenormand de Mézy, wigs are a refinement worn by the high-born to hide the grossness of natural hair; for Ti Noel, the expressionless wigged headstands displayed at his master's barber's shop are not very different from the dressed calves' heads at the butcher's next door, and he playfully and iconoclastically imagines such a coiffured head on a banqueting table. The tone is not rancorous but one of amusement:

> Ti Noel se divertía pensando que, al lado de las cabezas descoloridas de los terneros se servían cabezas de blancos señores en el mantel de la misma mesa . . . con sus mejor acondicionadas pelucas. No les faltaba más que una orla de hojas de lechuga o de rábanos abiertos en flor de lis. (p. 10)

> (It amused Ti Noël to think that alongside the pale calves' heads, heads of white men were served on the same tablecloth . . . with their best wigs. All that was lacking was a border of lettuce leaves or radishes cut in the shape of lilies.) (p. 11)[15]

Free from the anthropocentric constraints of the European mindset, Ti Noel has blurred the demarcation lines separating people, particularly members of the aristocracy, from cattle and unwittingly exposed the absurdity of French fashion through this irreverent fantasizing.[16] There are more contrasting heads, now in engravings. These are of the French king and of high dignitaries, all resplendent in their wigs, but further on Ti Noel's attention is captured by an alternative vision, that of a black king seated on the throne, and occupying centre stage while receiving some French dignitary. Ti Noel's appreciation of these prints shows a countercultural position. He sees the effigies of the great French kings as 'soberanos cubiertos de pelos ajenos . . . que sólo sabían *hacer de dioses* en los escenarios de sus teatros de corte, luciendo amaricada la pierna al compás del rigodón' (p. 12; my emphasis) ('those sovereigns wigged in false hair who . . . *were gods only* when they strutted the stage of their court theatres, effeminately pointing a leg in the measures of a rigadoon', p. 14; my emphasis), thus putting a different and highly subversive interpretation upon the great infrastructure of the French empire. For him, these effigies are simply a sign of the physical and moral weakness of its monarch.

---

[15] All page references are to *El reino de este mundo* (Barcelona: Biblioteca Breve de Bolsillo, Seix Barral, Barcelona, 1969), and to *The Kingdom of this World,* translated by Harriet de Onís (New York: Knopf, 1957).

[16] An examination of irony in the novel would note a more sinister reading underlies the description of the wigs, anticipating the impending menace of the guillotine: 'Los rizos de las pelucas enmarcaban semblantes inmóviles, antes de abrirse, en un remanso de bucles sobre el tapete encarnado' (p. 10) (The curls of the wigs, opening into a pool of ringlets on the red baize, framed expressionless faces, p. 10).

The artificial or metaphoric power of the French king, a figurehead who needs an army, a judiciary and the church in order to rule is contrasted unfavourably to the embodied, cosmic power of the African leader, whose supernatural powers are taken for granted and presented as natural. The narrative point of view assumes this mindset unproblematically:

> Allá en cambio – el *Gran Allá* –, había príncipes duros como el yunque, y príncipes que *eran* el leopardo, y príncipes que *conocían* el lenguaje de los árboles, y príncipes que *mandaban* sobre los cuatro puntos cardinales, dueños de la nube, de la semilla, del bronce y del fuego. (p. 13; my emphasis)
>
> (Whereas Back There there were princes as hard as anvils, and princes who *were* leopards, and princes who *knew* the language of the forest, and princes who *ruled* the four points of the compass, lords of the clouds, of the seed, of bronze, of fire.) (p. 15; my emphasis)

Ti Noel's musings are humorous because they constitute an inversion of the usual values embodied in a novel written in Spanish; the effect of this inversion is to unmask the authority of the colonial power. Bergson considers an important cause of comic effect to be the corrective fresh look on the habitual when something alive, spontaneous, instinctive attacks the rigid and encrusted ('l'automatique plaqué sur du vivant'; something mechanical encrusted upon the living), and Ti Noel's views can be seen not only as clashing with but also as challenging and disturbing the automatic (assumptions) of European discourse.[17]

Another important function of humour is to provide the space for the unsayable to be said, and a telling example of this can be found in Ti Noel's crude explanation of the Sacrament of Infant Baptism. His understanding of the theology concerning the rejection of the unbaptised brings to light the doctrine's essential cruelty and intransigence through naming it:

> cuyas mujeres . . . enterraban fetos infantes en un convento cuyos sótanos estaban llenos de esqueletos rechazados por el cielo verdadero, donde no se querían muertos ignorantes de los dioses verdaderos. (p. 14)
>
> (whose wives . . . buried foetuses in a convent whose cellars were filled with skeletons that had been rejected by the true heaven, which wanted nothing to do with those who died ignoring the true gods.) (pp. 16–17)

The dead-pan presentation of this alternative elucidation of Christianity has a comic effect, initially, at least: first, in the reader's 'superior' realisation of the

---

[17] Henri Bergson, *Le Rire. Essai sur la signification du comique* (Paris, Editions Alcan, 1924), p. 23.

black slaves' misunderstanding of Christian practice; then in the (shocked) realisation of the possible truth of this literal account.

Continuities and Discontinuities

I have quoted rather extensively from this perhaps too well-known first chapter because it offers the clearest example of an alternative mindset displacing and decentring the dominant one. It deals mainly with the discontinuities between the two cultures. In what follows I shall examine the presence of different humorous clashes in the rest of the novel from religious, racial and cultural perspectives, noting, when appropriate, Carpentier's suggestions of continuities underlying the apparent oppositions.[18] I have already referred to the scene depicting the death of Mackandal as emblematic of the cultural clashes permeating this work. Now, I should like to return briefly to this incident to examine the subversive and blasphemous implications that underlie the slaves' joyful reaction to the burning of their leader. Their unflinching belief in his power to mock the authorities, escape and return as their political saviour hints at an oblique comparison with Christian belief in the resurrection of Christ for the spiritual redemption of mankind. I am not arguing for a crude identification of Mackandal with Christ, as much as showing suggested similarities in the faith of the white Christians and the African slaves, and, thereby, an iconoclastic decentring of the uniqueness of Christ as Saviour.

What is funny about this? Nothing in the sense of outright hilarity, but there is a distinct satirical aggression against a single cultural position of white superiority and the assumed hierarchies between the faith of a 'true' religion and the 'false' beliefs of superstitions. If magical realism is concerned with the subversion of such distinctions, humour, too, is concerned with desacralization, and the suggested parallels between the political and the spiritual can be seen as a *parodia sacra*, a blasphemous perversion of sacred liturgy. And the teasing goes further when the reader's assumed and invited belief in the empirical reality of the slave's death ('muy pocos vieron que Mackandal, agarrado por diez soldados, era metido en el fuego, y que una llama crecida por el pelo encendido ahogaba su último grito', p. 41) ('very few saw that Mackandal, held by ten soldiers, had been thrust head first into the fire, and that a flame fed by his burning hair had drowned his last cry', p. 52), is set against the pragmatic truth of the slaves' faith in the supernatural power of their leader, since ultimately the spirit of Mackandal did bring about the successful revolt of the negro slaves. According to Bergson, 'Une

---

[18] For a penetrating study of the (eventually synchretic) relationship between the two cultures see Steven Boldy, 'Realidad y realeza en *El reino de este mundo* de Alejo Carpentier', *Bulletin Hispanique*, LXXXVIII.3–4 (1986), 409–38.

situation est toujours comique quand elle appartient en même temps à deux séries d'événements absolument indépendantes, et qu'elle peut s'interpréter à la fois dans deux sens tout différents' (A situation is invariably comic when it belongs simultaneously to two altogether independent series of events and is capable of being interpreted in two entirely different meanings at the same time).[19]

The economy of humour, and its capacity for overdetermination, has allowed Carpentier to demonstrate at one stroke the differences and similarities between the two cultures. Whilst my first reading focuses on the opposite values and beliefs of both cultures which are therefore decentred and relativized, the second incurs the 'blasphemy' of seeing a link between them. The 'blasphemy' is continued by suggested similarities also between Ti Noel and Christ. These build up imperceptibly throughout the text, until an inescapable identification is reached in the last part of the novel: 'Cuando las mujeres lo veían aparecer en un sendero agitaban paños claros, en señal de reverencia, como las palmas que un domingo habían festejado a Jesús' (p. 135) ('When the women saw him approaching, they waved bright cloths in sign of reverence, like the palm spread before Jesus one Sunday', p. 170). There are many biblical allusions used in a non-Judeo-Christian setting, either highlighting their difference and/or suggesting hidden similarities, and indeed, the last chapter is headed Agnus Dei, a title used as an indirect and, I suggest, bleakly jocular, reference to Ti Noel's understanding of his mission as mankind's saviour in this world.[20] In this chapter 'el Reino de los Cielos' (the Kingdom of Heaven) (Revelation, 11:15) is contrasted to the here and now salvation in 'el Reino de este Mundo' (p. 144) ('the Kingdom of this World', p. 185). Interestingly, the Apocalyptic description in Revelation, 11:19 of how this will come about coincides almost exactly with the Voodoo beliefs that inspired the first black revolution. Compare 'and there were thunderings, and an earthquake, and great hail' with 'los Señores de Allá . . . traerían el rayo y el trueno, para desencadenar el ciclón que completaría la obra de los hombres' (p. 33) ('the Lords of Back There . . . would bring the thunder and lightening and unleash the cyclone that would round off the work of men's hands', p. 42). Of course, the poetic ending of the novel can be read as a sign of redemptive hope, or as a positive implication of religious synchretism, but, in the light of the novel's history of failed revolutions, I see it as another instance of the darkest humour, eliciting a smile of despair at yet another doomed belief in a fairer society.

Neither humour nor magical realism seek for a consoling purpose, but are concerned, rather, with bringing new perceptions to light. More startling, more explicit, and more immediately funny, are the cultural clashes based on racial

[19] Bergson, p. 45.

[20] See particularly the Latin quotations in the chapter entitled 'Crónica del 15 de agosto' in contrapuntal opposition to the underlying voodoo beliefs of the black congregation. For a discussion of incongruous juxtapositions in the relationship between chapter headings and their content as well as in other intertextual allusions see Young, pp. 97–110.

difference. These often work through inversion, or an upside-down depiction of society. The behaviour of one group in terms of another serves an aggressive purpose which can be heightened if presented humorously. The scene depicting the replica of the palace of Sans Souci against 'un fondo de mantañas estriadas de violeta' (p. 89) ('Against a background of mountains violet-striped', p. 113), with Henri Christophe's retinue of black slaves solemnly dressed in Napoleonic costumes, aping the manners of the Napoleonic court is a clear example of hostile humour. As such, it is both grotesque, and funny: 'Porque negras eran aquellas señoras, de firme nalgatorio, . . ., negros aquellos dos ministros de medias blancas, que descendían, con la cartera de becerro debajo del brazo, la escalinata de honor; . . . negros aquellos húsares . . .; negros aquellos lacayos de *peluca blanca* . . .'(p. 90, my emphasis) (Because those hadsome, firm-buttocked ladies . . . were Negresses; those two white-hosed ministers descending the main stairway with leather dispatch cases under their arms were Negroes; . . . those hussars . . . were Negroes; those footmen in *white wigs* . . . were Negroes; p. 115). Though the initial target of derision is undoubtedly Henri Christophe's pretentiousness, the butt of the joke seems to lie in the subversive mimicry of the French court. The display of an appropriate incongruity (the world turned topsy-turvy) is a recognized tactic to effect ridicule and one of the consequences of seeing former black slaves grotesquely dressed in the manner of the French empire is to accentuate the absurdity of Napoleonic pomp even in its own context.[21]

There are other incidents in which racial difference is dealt with humorously. For instance, when the black ex-slave Solimán goes to Rome, the Europeans touch him to see if his sweat is black; he, on the other hand, mocks their credulity by pretending to be a nephew of the ex-king of Haiti (pp. 126–7). Racial and cultural clashes often take the form of cultural misreadings, and there are copious examples of this, both on the part of the French, and of the Africans. The French continuously ignore or misread the signs of the impending revolt, as, for example, regarding the place of ophidiolatry in Voodoo culture: '¿Pero acaso una persona culta podía haberse preocupado por las salvajes creencias de gentes que adoraban una serpiente?'(p. 62) ('But could a civilized person have been expected to concern himself with the savage beliefs of people who worshipped a snake?', p. 79). There is added piquancy in the information that there are no more serpents in the Caribbean. This is mentioned in the memoirs of Madame d'Abrantès, and serves to illustrate the gulf between the American reality and its perception in Europe: 'que les serpents ne devraient lui faire aucune peur, attendu qu'il n'y en avait pas dans les Antilles: que les sauvages n'étaient plus à craindre' (p. 43) ('that she need not fear snakes, for there are no snakes in the Antilles; that the savages are not to be feared', p. 55). Voodoo belief in animism

---

[21] The grotesque mixing of this scene can usefully be discussed in the context of Bakhtin's theory of the Carnival. See M. Bakhtin, *Rabelais and His World*, trans. Hélène Iswolsky (Bloomington: Indiana University Press, 1984).

is also ridiculed in Solimán's attempt to bring his ex-mistress Pauline Bonaparte to life by massaging Canova's statue of Venus (Pauline was its model), yet a subtle web of allusions links the African belief in animism with the Greek legend of Galatea, the statue brought to life to satisfy Pygmalion's love.[22] Once again, underlying Carpentier's obvious preoccupation with the discontinuities separating the European and the Afro-American cultures, there lies a humorous and deeply subversive exposition of their continuities.

Phèdre in the Tropics

The place in the novel where the preoccupations of magical realism with cultural hybridity are presented with the greatest humour is in the chapter entitled 'La hija de Minos y Pasifae' (The Daughter of Minos and Pasiphaë). The misunderstandings that can arise when two cultures are confronted, particularly when an elaborate or high culture is 'read' or creatively 'misread' by an unlettered mindset are here enacted with increasing complexity. Bergson's observation on the potential for humour when something can be interpreted in two entirely different ways is here exploited to the full.[23]

Throughout his work Carpentier draws imaginatively on what had been an accepted 'scientific' idea for much of the eighteenth and nineteenth centuries, namely, the degenerating effect of America, a theory which is humorously illustrated by the figure of Mlle Floridor.[24] A failed actress on the Parisian stage, she returns triumphantly to the Cap accompanying the rich colonist Lenormand de Mezy and, like other 'true Parisian actresses' who sing arias by Rousseau, 'secándose el sudor al marcar un hemistiquio' (p. 46) ('pausing between hemistichs to wipe the sweat from their brows', p. 58), Mlle Floridor suffers the ravages of the tropical climate: 'ajada y mordida por el paludismo' (faded and gnawed by malaria), she now declaims her verses 'entre eructos de malvasía' (p. 47) ('between belches of malmsey' [an aromatic grape], p. 60).

The continent's cultural degradation is obliquely hinted at in that the third rate confidante is here able to assume the leading role. Dressed in her modest veils, these being her only theatrical wardrobe, Floridor declaims the noble verses of

---

[22] The naked sight of Pauline Bonaparte evokes the figure of Galatea (p. 72). There is a statue of Galatea attributed to Canova for which Pauline Bonaparte had posed.

[23] See above p. 158–61 of this article. Cultural misreading is a topos of satirical Latin American literature, notably of the gauchesque genre. The description of the plot of *Faust* in Estanislao del Campo's eponymous poem of 1866 is an excellent example.

[24] 'The Europeans who pass into America degenerate, as do the animals: a proof that the climate is unfavourable to the improvement of either man or animal. . . . The degradation of humanity must be imputed to the vitiated qualities of the air stagnated in their immense forests, and corrupted by noxious vapours from standing waters and uncultivated grounds.' Cornelius de Pauw, quoted in E. Fishburn, *The Portrayal of Immigration in Nineteenth Century Argentine Fiction (1845–1902)* (Berlin: Colloquium Verlag, 1981), p. 35, and discussed pp. 35–6.

Racine's most famous female role to an illiterate audience of plantation slaves. A well-known humorous strategy is the incongruity between speaker and spoken word, a device cruelly put to use in this instance by the way in which the interpreter of *Phèdre, une tragédie* is set up as a stocktype of classical comedy, the figure of the 'alazon' or boaster who will ultimately be victimized.[25] Floridor is victimized by being ridiculed for her exaggerated pretensions to being driven in a *berlina* with ten mulattas in tow singing 'en gran tremolina de hembras al viento' (p. 47) ('twittering incessantly [while their blue petticoats] fluttered in the wind', p. 60); she is also consistently referred to as *la cómica*, a term used ostensibly as a linguistic 'fausse amie' or mistranslation of the French word 'comédienne' whilst punning on the word's Spanish acceptance of *cómica* as comic actress and comic figure.

The conflation of interpreter and role, the *person* and the *personae*, has been set up to provide a distancing comic backdrop to the Racinian text, whose recitation is here denuded of the conventions of the theatrical tradition. Mlle Floridor declaims:

> Mes crimes désormais ont comblé la mesure:
> Je respire à la fois l'inceste et l'imposture;
> Mes homicides mains, promptes à me venger,
> Dans le sang innocent brûlent de se plonger. (p.48)

> (My sins are heaped
> Already to overflowing. I am seeped
> At once in incest and hypocrisy.
> My murderous hands, hot for avenging me,
> Are fain to plunge themselves in guiltless blood.) (p. 61)

The audience does not suspend disbelief, and the slaves, recongnizing the key words – 'crimes', 'inceste', 'imposture', 'juge' – arrive at the logical conclusion that their mistress, exiled from France for her immorality, is here openly confessing her personal sins. Interestingly, the African slaves interpret the line 'Je respire à la fois l'inceste et l'imposture' accurately when they understand these sins as literally emanating from their mistress for in the seventeenth century 'respirer' meant to exhale or exude. It is unlikely that Carpentier would not have known this.

Phèdre's declaration that her arms are burning to be bathed in blood ('Dans le sang innocent brûlent de se plonger') is normally taken as poetic metaphor but not by this audience who recognize it as part of an accepted ritual. It is what they do to spur themselves to action, as described in the novel when, 'luego de mojarse los brazos en la sangre del blanco' (p. 56) ('after bathing their arms in the blood of the white man', p. 73), they pillage de Mézy's house and Ti Noel rapes Mlle Floridor. This deliberate confusion of the metaphoric and the literal serves one of humour's

---

[25] For a wider discussion of the alazon, see Frye, pp. 39–40, and pp. 226–8.

basic functions, to unmask and bring to the surface what has been repressed during the 'civilizing process'.[26] Finally, the line, 'Minos juge aux enfers tous les pâles humains' (p. 48) ('Minos, below, judges the souls of men', p. 62) is interpreted by the Africans through a (mis)understanding of their rudimentary Christian instruction, which allows them to adopt an attitude of righteous satisfaction at their mistress's fate and anticipate with glee the punishment of all her compatriots. 'Les pâles humains' are, to them, specifically the French white colonisers.

'La hija de Minos y Pasifae' is a veritable minefield of cultural miscegenation. By mentioning not Phaedra but her supernatural parents in the title, attention is drawn to the heroine's mythical origins. These, which are rendered inconspicuous in the Racinian text, draw attention to its links with the beliefs of the African audience.[27] The play itself was inspired by the dramatic treatment of Phaedra by Euripides and by Seneca, and unites Greek, Roman and classical French culture; transplanted to the Caribbean, its French lines are quoted within a Spanish narrative commenting on their understanding in *Créole*. The dynamics of humour depend not only on the source but also the target and Lloyd King, a reader versed in the basic structures of Haitian Créole, expressed amusement in finding the thoughts of a slave functioning in a restricted code such as Créole rendered in the elaborated code of Spanish.[28] *Phèdre* is generally considered the highpoint of French classical drama. In an analysis of the work prefacing the authoritative Classique Larousse series, the editor notes 'Et c'est aussi pour cela qu'aucun spectateur ne lui refuse son indulgence ni sa pitié' (Which is why everyone in the audience would grant it their pity and forebearance).[29] Through the sufferings of his heroine, Racine wanted to achieve the cathartic effect of Greek tragedy, but instead of inspiring pity and terror in his audience, his work, set in the wrong context, provokes derision and contempt.

Carpentier's humour seldom has only one aim. The hilarity of this narrative describing the cultural clashes that form part of everyday existence serves to undermine the cultural certainties of both the whites and the blacks. The latter are ridiculed not only for their literal reaction to Floridor's performance but also for believing they understand a culture foreign to their own. Yet their confidence can be seen, ironically, as the faint reverse image of the Europeans' own consistent failure to allow for the possibility of a cultural 'otherness'.[30] Finally, what is

[26] Freud discusses the unmasking effect of the comic in *Jokes*, pp. 261–4.

[27] The title is taken from Racine's play, Act I, Sc 1, l. 36. Although the supernatural elements are mentioned in the French version they are, in Racine's words in the Preface, 'des ornements' in a story which is concerned principally with human moral weakness.

[28] See Lloyd King, 'Ambiguities in Caribbean Humour', *Humour in Spanish Caribbean literature*, Conference Papers, Seventh Conference of Hispanists (Barbados: University of the West Indies, 1984), pp. 9–18, and p. 12.

[29] J. Racine, *Phèdre* (Paris: Classiques Larousse, 1971), p. 15.

[30] Assumptions of the transparency of all cultures and their ability to interpret them unproblematically are discussed in S. Greenblatt, *Marvellous Possessions* (Oxford: Clarendon Press, 1991), p. 95.

irreparably undermined in this chapter are our own assumptions regarding the universality of European art: *Phèdre* in the tropics has become a farce. Cultural miscegenation reaches a carnivalesque apotheosis towards the end of the novel, when Ti Noel, having looted *Sans Souci*, is wearing a satin and lace dresscoat that had belonged to Henri Christophe together with his own straw hat moulded into a bicorn, and is sitting on three volumes of the *Grande Encyclopédie*, playing with a doll and listening to a German Ländler repeated interminably on a music box. He is on his way to understanding his role as king and saviour of mankind.

In this study of the links that exist between magical realism and humour, I have concentrated on one work alone, *El reino de este mundo*, believing it to be not only a prototypical but also a paradigmatic magical-realist text. Admittedly, and rightly, some magical-realist authors are more immediately associated with humour than others, and García Márquez's novels, for example, are unquestionably funny in a way that Carpentier's are not. Had I been writing about García Márquez, or Donoso or Allende, though not in the case of Rulfo or Asturias, I would have used terms from the vocabulary of humour which are manifestly absent here, for example, hilarity, jest, cheerfulness, mirth, amusement, laughter. These are aspects of humour that may or may not be present in magical-realist texts, residual consequences as it were, rather than essential components of the kind of serious humour that I have been discussing, which is principally concerned with exploiting creatively and iconoclastically the hidden relations between disparate things. However, neither magical realism nor humour deals in solutions, but in a heightened awareness of perhaps unresolvable dualities, and this may be their strongest connection. Further critical study of this neglected link should bring fruitful and unexpected insights.

Magical Realism and Children's Literature: Isabel Allende's *La Ciudad de las Bestias*

Philip Swanson

The Tension of the Magical and the Real

Magical realism is an inevitably paradoxical term. Thus the most obvious question to ask about it is also the most fraught: how far does it reveal or obscure reality? In the study of Latin American literature, critics have, historically, been divided broadly between those who see the magical or fantastic dimension as underlining the essentially fictional or unknowable nature of both literature and reality, and those who see the magical or fantastic as a means of opening up imaginative new perspectives on social or political reality.

There is no doubt that political readings of Latin American literature are now in the ascendancy, but they are often far from unproblematic. For example, the famous opening of the best-known magical-realist novel, *Cien años de soledad* (*One Hundred Years of Solitude*, 1967), in which the father introduces his children to reading creatively and to the dazzling beauty of the most fabulous diamond on earth (actually the previously unknown substance, ice), could be read either as an incitement to freedom of thought or as the revelation of the unavoidable limitations of error-prone human understanding. Indeed, it has been argued that García Márquez's fantasy-laden allegorical approach to history creates a rich literary experience but a rather ineffective political commentary, whereas Isabel Allende's *La casa de los espíritus* (*The House of the Spirits*, 1982) – despite being derided as a pale imitation of the seminal Colombian novel – enjoys sharper political focus precisely because it systematically subverts the magical dimension in order to confront the reader with harsh reality.[1]

---

[1] Philip Swanson, *Latin American Fiction: A Short Introduction* (Oxford: Blackwell, 2005) gives a fuller account of the issues raised here. With regard to the critical divide mentioned, compare, for example, Donald Shaw, *Nueva narrativa hispanoamericana* (Madrid: Cátedra, 1999) and Gerald Martin, *Journeys through the Labyrinth* (London: Verso, 1989). See also Swanson, *The New Novel in Latin America: Politics and Popular Culture after the Boom* (Manchester and New York; Manchester University Press, 1995) for a commentary

Tensions in Literature for Children

Such debates about so-called magical-realist fiction are remarkably similar to critical concerns surrounding children's literature, and it is surprising that more has not been made of the links between magical realism and fiction for children. Conventional views of writing for children would draw attention to the centrality of fantasy and magic, yet equally allude to the long tradition of the instructional or even moralizing vein of such writing. Back in 1749, Sarah Fielding's Preface to *The Governess or Little Female Academy* told her young readers that once they grasp that 'the true Use of Books is to make you wiser and better, you will then have both Profit and Pleasure from what you read'.[2] The history of children's literature shows a fairly complex pattern of variations on and responses to Fielding's proposal, but the work of critics such as Nicholas Tucker has nonetheless documented 'the central tension between didacticism and imagination, the educational camp versus the literary'.[3]

There are probably three main aspects to this tension. Firstly, as with magical realism, the problem arises as to how and where the young reader is to draw the line between fantasy and reality or between reading as entertainment and reading as instruction or consciousness-raising: this is not at all clear or easily resolvable. Secondly, authors of children's literature tend, of course, to be adults and this means that there is always to some degree an imbalance in power relations between author and reader. This is a complex matter, and children's literature throughout its history has ranged from open didacticism, to the desire to shape and influence via the disguise of notions of freedom (as in, say, the fairy tale), to the celebration of the child's open-mindedness or even natural resistance to control. Either way, 'the tension between the degree of control and freedom is continually played out in children's literature throughout its history'.[4]

Thirdly, and related to the preceding point, the idea of the innocence of the child reader is deeply problematic. Romantic thought, both in England and America, posited, in opposition to the initial eighteenth-century concern with

on this division and Martin, 'Alvaro Mutis and the Ends of History', *Studies in Twentieth Century Literature*, 19 (1995), 117–31, for a response. A useful survey of critical reactions to Allende is Beth Jörgensen,' "Un puñado de críticos": Navigating the Critical Readings of Isabel Allende's Work', in *Isabel Allende Today*, eds Rosemary G. Feal and Yvette Miller (Pittsburgh: Latin American Literary Review Press, 2002), pp. 128–46.

[2] Sarah Fielding, The *Governess or Little Female Academy* (London: Oxford University Press, 1968), p. 91. Qtd. by Charles Sarland, 'The Impossibility of Innocence: Ideology, Politics and Children's Literature', in *Understanding Children's Literature*, ed. Peter Hunt (London and New York: Routledge, 1999), p. 40.

[3] Qtd. by Jean Webb, 'Text, Culture, and Postcolonial Children's Literature: A Comparative Perspective', in *Voices of the Other: Children's Literature and the Postcolonial Context*, ed. Roderick McGillis (New York and London: Garland, 1999). The original reference is Nicholas Tucker, *Suitable for Children? Controversies in Children's Literature* (Falmer: Sussex University Press, 1976), pp. 71–88 (p. 73).

[4] Deborah Cogan Thacker and Jean Webb, *Introducing Children's Literature* (London and New York: Routledge, 2002), p. 19, see also pp. 18–19.

evangelism and moral guidance, the idea of childhood as a pure and innocent state associated with the ideals of the imagination and the sublime (see Cogan Thacker and Webb, pp. 13–25). This idea has been enormously influential, though nowadays critics generally accept that 'all literature for children is, in some way, ideologically driven'.[5] Jacqueline Rose's pioneering deconstruction of the myth of Peter Pan in 1984 was a major critique of the ways in which children's literature constructs the child reader as 'innocent' (and therefore in some way outside culture and the state and representing a kind of universal experience).[6] Moreover, her critique has a strong postcolonial dimension in that it presents children as a version of the colonial subject ('colonized' by 'adults').

The Case of Latin America and Isabel Allende

The potential links between Latin American magical realism and a children's literature variation on it are obvious: the connection between the child experience and: that of native indigenous populations in particular or subcontinental identity in general, ideas of primitivism and the idealization or construction of versions of 'nature' and the New World, the shifting renderings of the foundational Latin American topos of Civilization and Barbarism. Moreover, there are two related points that are of further relevance in the case of Isabel Allende's brand of magical realism: the traditional association of children's literature with the popular and the feminine (Sarland, pp. 48–9; McGillis, p. xxi), both of which again raise issues of power, privilege, and positionality.

Isabel Allende's excursion into children's literature began in 2002 with *La Ciudad de las Bestias* (City of the Beasts), marketed as a story for 'young adults' and also readers of all ages.[7] The idea for the novel was suggested to Allende by her three grandchildren who asked her to write a tale based on a story she used to tell them about the Amazon region. The novel's protagonist, Californian teenager Alexander Cold, is probably something of an echo of her own grandson, Alejandro (Allende's daughter Paula was Paula Frías, the surname connoting 'cold' in Spanish). The fifteen-year-old Alexander stays with his tough

---

[5] Webb, 'Text, Culture, and Postcolonial Children's Literature: A Comparative Perspective', p. 71, is alluding to the position adopted by John Stephens in his *Language and Ideology in Children's Fiction* (London: Longman, 1992).

[6] Jacqueline Rose, *The Case of Peter Pan or The Impossibility of Children's Fiction* (Philadelphia: University of Pennsylvania Press, 1992).

[7] A sequel, *El Reino del Dragón de Oro* (Kingdom of the Golden Dragon), appeared in 2003 and a third in the series, *El Bosque de los Pigmeos* (Forest of the Pygmies), in 2004. Unusually in Spanish, capital letters are employed for the novels' titles. Allende was not totally unfamiliar with the world of children's writing before the twenty-first century: according to Linda Gould Levine, she directed the children's magazine *Mapato* and published two books for children around the late 1960s and early 1970s; see 'Weaving Life into Fiction', in Feal and Miller, pp. 1–25 (p. 5).

paternal grandmother, Kate, while his seriously ill mother undergoes chemotherapy treatment for cancer in a Texas hospital.

He accompanies Kate, a magazine reporter for the *International Geographic* (presumably a thinly veiled variation of the *National Geographic*), on an expedition deep into the Brazilian and Venezuelan Amazon, the mission being to identify a legendary creature (described as a kind of Yeti of the Amazon) known as the Beast. Here Alexander, along with his new friend Nadia, the twelve- or thirteen-year-old daughter of a local guide, enjoys an adventure with echoes of both Harry Potter[8] and Tin Tin or Indiana Jones, combining elements of fantasy and the juvenile thriller: the young pair have encounters with jungle or magical animals, are 'kidnapped' by a mysterious indigenous tribe known as the People of the Mist, hook up with a magical shaman, discover El Dorado[9] and the kingdom of the Beasts, and foil a fiendish plan to kill off the Indians in order to open up their land for exploitation by a particularly villainous mining entrepreneur.

North and South, First World and Third World: Cultural Relativism and Ambiguity

Alexander's journey from California via New York City to the Amazon is, it seems, a journey into the world of magic that implicitly and explicitly challenges Western logical conceptions of reality in general and First-World notions of reality in particular. For example, as they leave behind Manaus (presented as a sort of frontier town) to penetrate deeper into the jungle by sailing up the Río Negro to the Upper Orinoco, the members of the expedition 'avanzaban como en sueños por un territorio alucinante'), into 'territorio mágico' ('moved as if in a dream through a landscape of fantasy', into 'a magical land') (p. 54/pp. 63–4).[10] Later when Alexander explores the interior of the 'sacred mountain' where he will find the Water of Life that may cure his mother, he is said to be 'en medio de la región más remota del planeta, donde no funcionaban las leyes conocidas': 'ya no podia confiar sólo en la razón, había entrado al territorio incierto de los sueños, la intuición y la magia' ('in the middle of the most remote region of the planet, where the rules he was used to didn't count': 'he couldn't put his trust in reason after having experienced the hazy territory of dreams, intuition and magic') (p. 198/p. 250).

---

[8] Comparisons have been made with the Harry Potter novels, though they are probably more conservative than Allende's series. Deborah Cogan Thacker and Jean Webb, *Introducing Children's Literature*, argue that the Harry Potter books are not challenging or subversive, and 'posit a reader who requires consolation in a difficult world, rather than a reader willing to make his or her own meaning' (p. 147).

[9] In a double play on myth and reality, El Dorado is both real and false: it exists but the gold is not real (p. 207/p. 262).

[10] Isabel Allende, *La Ciudad de las Bestias* (Barcelona: Random House Mondadori, 2002); *City of the Beasts*, trans. Margaret Sayers Peden (London: Flamingo, 2002). References to the novel will give the Spanish page reference first followed by a page reference for the English translation.

In one sense, all this is problematic, especially for cultural critics. Not only does the idea of 'marvelling' at a subcontinental Other perceived as 'magical' risk encoding a neo-colonialist perspective, it might also appear to posit a universalist notion of the human condition in which 'life' or 'reality' are fundamentally ambiguous or unknowable. Even the apparent recuperation of indigenous mysticism leads to what is essentially a Borgesian intellectual existential cliché: 'todo lo que ocurre en el universo es una ilusión, puros sueños dentro de otros sueños' ('all that happens in the universe is an illusion, dreams within dreams') (p. 185/p. 233).

However, 'ambiguity' in Isabel Allende is never really a question of the reactionary scepticism sometimes associated with the New Novel of the Latin American Boom,[11] but, rather, simply an anti-hegemonic gesture, a way of indicating alternative perspectives on the world. There is, undoubtedly, since the death of her daughter in 1992 and the publication of the memoir *Paula* (1994), a stronger spiritual dimension to both her work and public comments.[12] This is probably more pronounced in the sequel to the present novel, but in *La Ciudad de las Bestias*, there is some emphasis on the mix of destiny or karma and intuition or free will (p. 198/p. 250) which seems to constitute Allende's middle-brow spirituality. But while cynics might dismiss her 'ideas' as a species of New Age mumbo-jumbo, the mystical quality to her writing does not amount to a disavowal of concrete social issues and once again actually functions as an emotional gesture of humane concern in the face of unbridled materialism and pressure to conform to a late capitalist agenda.

As with other magical-realist literature, one obvious social effect of the depiction of Alexander's journey from 'First' to 'Third' World is that it sets up a series of challenges to cultural assumptions. Vaccinations and the power of the printed word are presented to the Indians as white man's magic (e.g. p. 128/p. 156, p. 262/p. 336). Alexander's precious, complicated Swiss Army Knife is used as a personal adornment by the unimpressed shaman Walimai (p. 254/pp. 324–5).[13] Iyomi, the leader of the sparsely dressed 'gente de la neblina' or People of the Mist, comically sympathizes with the 'forasteros . . . tan perdidos', whom she sees as 'esos pobres seres vestidos de trapos hediondos' ('foreigners . . . lost in her presence', 'the poor creatures dressed in stinking cloth') (p. 297/p. 381). Climactically, the expedition leader, the arrogant anthropologist Professor Ludovic Leblanc, who has dazzled the world with his stories of wild jungle tribes

---

[11] For a fuller account of the significance of ambiguity in the Latin American New Novel, see Swanson, *Latin American Fiction: A Short Introduction*.

[12] This development can be traced by reading the interviews in John Rodden (ed.), *Conversations with Isabel Allende* (Austin: University of Texas Press, 2004).

[13] Walimai does, however, later learn to use the knife in a practical way to free the bound Alexander (pp. 291–92/p. 373). Depending on one's point of view, this complicates or reinforces the idea of cultural relativism. It may seem to hint at the superiority of Alexander's culture, or it may simply allude to the possibility of a meaningfully transculturative relationship between First and Third World.

and cannibals, is forced to the realization that 'los salvajes no eran los indios, sino ellos' ('they themselves were the savages, not the Indians') (p. 277/p. 354).

The Material World and the Natural World –
Civilization and Barbarism

The 'savagery' of the white men takes the form of commerce and science in opposition to the natural and harmonious world of the indigenous peoples. Alexander is already aware that the Amazon region, 'último paraíso del planeta, era destruida sistemáticamente por la codicia de empresarios y aventureros' and that 'llegaban en masa los colonos y salían por toneladas las maderas y los minerales' ('the last paradise on the planet, was being systematically destroyed by the greed of entrepreneurs and adventurers' and that 'settlers were coming in and tons of wood and minerals were going out') (p. 43/p. 48) – a situation exemplified for him by the evil plan of the businessman Mauro Carías to eradicate a community of natives for his own commercial ends. Carías' ally is science in the form of Dr Omayra Torres' vaccination programme (in reality a plan to inject the Indians with what would be, for them, a fatal dose of the measles virus), while Leblanc demonstrates that, for his like, nature is at the service of science, even though Kate points out that the pursuit of scientific anthropology often leads to delusion and madness (pp. 63–4/pp. 74–5).

The alliance of trade and science was traditionally at the heart of juvenile literature from its foundational English roots in Victorian times onwards. English children's literature in the imperial nineteenth century often dealt with adventure (including the hunting of exotic beasts) in far-off wildernesses, but adventure was justified by or offered a route into a collapsed notion of trade and science which allowed for the human dominance of nature and the moral training of the young (see MacKenzie, pp. 145–7). Of course, Allende, in a new place and age, seeks to invert the traditional message of colonial juvenile fiction, particularly in a specifically Latin American context. More than once, the expedition and Carías' entrepreneurialism are linked – implicitly at least – to the *conquista* or conquest and colonization of the Americas, most notably via the attempted introduction of the measles virus (the majority of Indians died during the conquest not from massacres but from the introduction to the New World of diseases for which they had no immunity).

Trade and science were also key components of Independence discourse in Latin America and at the conceptual heart of Domingo Faustino Sarmiento's hugely influential notion of Civilization and Barbarism in which the path to progress and modernization was thought to be inevitably linked to the promotion of European and North American values in the untamed interior of the newly independent subcontinent.[14] In something of an echo of Mario Vargas Llosa's

---

[14] For a fuller discussion of Civilization and Barbarism, see Swanson (ed.), *The Companion to Latin American Studies* (London: Arnold, 2003), pp. 69–85.

portrayal of the Peruvian jungle town of Iquitos in *Pantaleón y las visitadoras* (trans. Captain Pantoja and the Special Service, 1973), Manaus and even more so the remote hamlet of Santa María de la Lluvia are presented as fragile oases straddling the border between civilization and barbarism, barely resisting being overrun by the wildness of the jungle (pp. 45–6/pp. 51–2 and pp. 56–8/pp. 66–9). But, of course, as Leblanc's dramatic conclusion above demonstrates, and inverting the traditional idea in colonial juvenile stories of science and trade as a means to morality and peace (MacKenzie, p. 161), the real barbarians are the representatives of so-called 'civilización' or civilization. Indeed the People of the Mist are seen to embody an alternative yet totally valid form of 'civilization', in many ways more attractive than the greedy egocentricity of what others in the novel defend as 'progress'. Civilization and Barbarism are matters of perception and assumption, not unlike the dragon Alexander encounters in the sacred mountain of the Beasts which is not 'terrible' or 'repulsive' as in European legends but 'beautiful' and full of 'joy and vitality' as in Chinese celebrations (p. 203/pp. 256–7). Indeed Nadia, who will grow up 'sabia y salvaje en la selva' ('wild and wise in the jungle') (p. 315/p. 406), could be taken as the representation of the positive face of 'barbarism', that is the natural exuberance of Latin America that, properly channelled rather than perverted as in the case of Mauro Carías and his corrupt sidekick, can achieve positive and beneficial results.

A First-World Hero?

In this sense, Nadia is an echo not only of Allende's most famous creation, Clara from *La casa de los espíritus* (*The House of the Spirits*), but also perhaps – though much less conservatively – Marisela from one of the most famous civilization-and-barbarism novels, Rómulo Gallegos' *Doña Bárbara* (1929).[15] Marisela represents what Gallegos thought of as the *alma de la raza* or soul of the common people in a pure or uncontaminated state, her role being to teach the civilizer that his function is not to crush native barbarism but to direct the natural energy that comes from primitivism into a more meaningful direction. Such a reading would also identify Alexander with Marisela's admirer Santos Luzardo, the civilizer who comes from the outside but learns – though perhaps less whole-heartedly than Alexander – valuable lessons from his experience in the interior. Of course, the problem is that this aspect of Allende's narrative risks identifying native peoples with the primitive and liberal urban North Americans with the progressive. The way of life of the People of the Mist is ultimately to be guaranteed by the promotion of a Foundation to protect them, whose effectiveness depends on the eloquence of Kate Cold's writing and the international

---

[15] To make more of the comparisons, see, on Clara, Swanson, *The New Novel in Latin America*, pp. 153–4, and, on *Doña Bárbara*, Swanson (ed.), *The Companion to Latin American Studies*, pp. 77–8.

prestige of Ludovic Leblanc (pp. 311–12/401–2). Indigenous values may offer an important lesson to the West and North, but it seems that it is only the West and North who can save them.

While *La Ciudad de las Bestias* is a considerable advance on the adventure stories for youngsters by the likes of nineteenth-century liberal imperialists such as Mayne Reid or R.M. Ballantyne, the exotic adventure backdrop – despite the novel's contemporary eco-thriller trappings – is still a stage for the moral education of a First-World hero. A young American is very much at the heart of this Latin American tale and his story has strong individualist overtones as well the boyhood-to-manhood lesson-learning so typical of Reid and Ballantyne's books. The opening of the novel really presents Alexander as a vulnerable child, overwhelmed by the familial disintegration set in motion by his mother's cancer (p. 12/p. 5). The sight of her hair being cut in preparation for chemotherapy sends the boy into a fit of impotent rage in which he wrecks his room and curls up into what is essentially a foetal ball (p. 15/pp. 9–10). The idea may be that Alexander will now undergo a kind of rebirth and journey into adulthood and responsibility through the offices of his older guide, Kate, and through the experience of character-forming adventure.

Kate has always exposed her grandchildren to terrifying stories based on her travels around the world (p. 22/p. 19) and seems to set Alexander a test from the start by failing to pick him up on his arrival in New York City. He is thus confronted with gritty urban realities (including robbery), with the result that 'tuvo que hacer un tremendo esfuerzo por combatir las ganas de echarse a llorar como un chiquillo' ('it took all his strength not to bawl like a baby') (p. 34/p. 35). Yet his jungle adventure makes a man of him. He literally undergoes a rite of passage in the painful initiation ceremony for the male members of the Indian tribe: 'debía convertirse en hombre y recibir sus armas de guerrero'; 'supo en verdad que su infancia había quedado atrás y que a partir de esa noche podría valerse solo' ('[he] must become a man and receive his warrior's weapons'; 'he knew that, in truth, he had left his childhood behind and from that night on he would be able to look after himself') (pp. 183, 187/pp. 230, 237). He ultimately thanks Kate for severing his link with childish security (pp. 198–9/p. 250) and by the end of the novel the roles are even reversed, with Alexander offering her sage advice: 'Veo que has crecido mucho en estas semanas, Alexander', comments Kate ('I see that you have matured [literally, "grown up"] a lot in these weeks, Alexander') (p. 304/p. 391).

Indeed, Alexander becomes a real hero. His name means 'defender of men' and marks him as a warrior for noble causes (pp. 263–4/pp. 337–8); taking on the identity of his awesomely powerful totemic animal, he becomes Jaguar,[16] and

---

[16] This is an interesting variation on the anthropomorphism which is so typical of children's stories right up to the Disney phenomenon. Normally animals are given human attributes, but here the opposite happens, suggesting perhaps a more humble and harmonious relationship with nature. There may also be an echo of Rudyard Kipling's *Jungle Book*, which

his feat of extraordinary bravery in his epically-described penetration deep into the interior of the sacred mountain leads him to be potential saviour of both the Indians and his own mother. There is clearly something very individualistic about this. Despite the connection to Nature via his seeming animal metamorphosis, despite his loss of self-centredness in the communal spirit of the People of the Mist (pp. 165–6/p. 206) and despite the experience of communication with the Beasts through 'sueño colectivo' ('collective dream') (p. 221/p. 280), Alexander is still the central agent and hero of the novel. The very fact that the bird of ill omen seen in the collective dream is the same bird Alexander saw in his own personal dream about his mother, before his journey to the Amazon, may suggest the individualism behind the veneer of collectivism. However, this heroic individualism is still some way from that of conventional imperial boys' adventures. Alexander's attempt to impress the natives by imitating Tarzan fails comically (pp. 143–4/pp. 177–8): the liberal imperial fantasy is thus shown to be no more than a hopeless fiction.

If anything, Alexander becomes a gentle and sensitive 'feminized' hero, whose key role is to be negotiator between the natives and the *nahab* or white men – negotiation being an image of the dissolution of patriarchal binary logic. Moreover, he wins over the natives and the Beasts not by violence but by the beauty of his flute playing, music suggesting a 'feminine' Cixousian or Kristevan semiotic world in which non-binary emotional communication is more valuable than the Law of the Father in the Symbolic Order.[17] A North American hero he may be, but Alexander is also a projection of an ideal liberal teenage First-World hero with a more empathetic relationship with the South and the ability to prompt such feelings of empathy amongst other youngsters from the North.

Primitivism and Innocence

The other side of the equation concerns the indigenous people and their association with primitivism. A maverick local priest (who can be vaguely associated with Liberation Theology) comments of the Indians that 'habían vivido miles de años en armonía con la naturaleza, como Adán y Eva en el Paraíso' ('they had lived in harmony with nature for thousands of years, like Adam and Eve in

---

extols the law of the jungle over that of man yet does so in a way that marks the strength of imperial peoples; see John M. MacKenzie, 'Hunting and the Natural World in Juvenile Literature', in *Imperialism and Juvenile Literature*, ed. Jeffrey Richards (Manchester and New York: Manchester University Press, 1989), pp. 144–72 (pp. 169–70).

[17] For more detail on feminist theory and readings of Allende, see Swanson, *The New Novel in Latin America*, pp. 145–70. The flute is perhaps an ambiguous image, as it may also call to mind the evangelizing impulses of the Spanish conquest. The calming of the Indians through flute playing is reminiscent of Roland Joffe's film *The Mission* (1986) in which a kindly Jesuit priest uses music to communicate with the Guaraní Indians, only to find himself ultimately caught up in Spanish and Portuguese imperial politics.

Paradise') (p. 309/p. 398), while their way of life is described at one stage in terms of an idealized primitive communalism (pp. 163–4/pp. 203–5). The fantasy of native edenic primitivism is problematic because it values myth over reality and also risks projecting the Indians as passive and lacking in agency. Hence, here, they easily fall victim to the rapacious appetites of oligarchs or *cacique* figures in cahoots with the authorities (a situation embodied by Mauro Carías' alliance with the barracks commander Captain Ariosto) or can only be protected by the external agencies of an international Foundation. At the same time, though, they are self-sufficient, in many ways morally superior to the white man and ultimately able to adapt, survive and probably largely preserve their isolationist existence.

In many ways, the Indians' primitivism is not dissimilar to the ideal of childhood innocence. Leading critic of children's literature, Peter Hunt, explains the predominance of fantasy (and there are a number of instances of pure fantasy in *La Ciudad de las Bestias*[18]) in such literature in this way: 'Children can be seen as equivalent to primitives, who have (it is assumed) a simple faith in animism and an inherent understanding of certain narrative patterns; or are equivalent to the "folk" (a naïve construction) who originated the folk-tale, for whom the world outside the door of the hut was full of who-knew-what wonders and terrors.'[19] In a sense, it is the childhood innocence of Alexander and Nadia that allows them to identify and communicate with the Indians, the spirit-like shaman and the Beasts, something of which most of the adults are incapable. Yet if childhood implies innocence and openness, there is also, as has been seen, a narrative of learning and adaptation. Allende's novel does not really develop a strong theory of transculturation with regard to the indigenous peoples, but it does suggest that compromise is important and that some degree of adaptation may be necessary to ensure the survival of an essentially good and noble culture. But the real point is that the novel's focus is on the behaviour of the non-indigenous. Cynics may choose to see the natives as patronizingly presented foils for the development of an external liberal conscience, but the novel is being written precisely for young middle-class readers in the hope that they will be receptive to the text's liberal agenda and grow and develop accordingly.

North-South/First-Third Reconfigured

In fact, *La Ciudad de las Bestias* is probably about the 'First World' as much as it is about the so-called 'Third'. Allende is based in the USA and has written

---

[18] Many examples of fantasy in the novel have their roots in possible perceptions of reality. Even the dragon and the sloth-like Beasts can be explained as part of a stalled evolutionary or metabolic process brought on by separation and isolation; however, creatures such as Walimai's fluttering spirit wife seem plainly fantastic (pp. 204–5/pp. 258–9).

[19] Peter Hunt, *Children's Literature* (Oxford: Blackwell, 2001), p. 269.

about the positive as well as negative aspects of the North American experience, proposing some possible potentially meaningful compromise positions.[20] Her novels are published more or less simultaneously in Spanish and English these days, and even the Spanish versions of the sequels to *La Ciudad de las Bestias* were published by HarperCollins in New York. The young hero of the present novel emerges from the USA and is presumed to be about to return there at the end. His role, then, is not only to benefit the native peoples of the Amazon but also his peers in the USA.

In some ways, Latin America is used in the novel as a mirror to promote reflection on North American experience. Part of the inversion of the traditional Civilization-versus-Barbarism ethic is to show that in many ways the First World is just as barbaric as the Third is sometimes thought to be. In the first chapter Alexander reacts to the Amazon as the polar opposite of civilization (p. 18/p. 14), yet his experience of New York City in the following chapter is his real introduction to danger and barbarism. The girl Morgana – with her tatty clothes, nose ring, spiky dog collar, blue nails and short orange imitation-leather jacket – is just as exotic as any of the jungle dwellers Alexander will meet in the Amazon, though less trustworthy: she robs him and he feels lost in a world of down-and-outs, deceit, grime and filthy latrines. An earlier indirect reference to the 1999 Columbine High School massacre in Colorado (p. 19/p. 15) reinforces the idea of a negative North American primitivism. At the same time, the magic of the jungle reaches and is part of North America too. The mythical Rahakanariwa of indigenous lore is also the bird Alexander dreams of in relation to his mother on the novel's opening page before he even knows he is going to the Amazon. Moreover, while in the depths of the Amazon region, Alexander magically visits and offers comfort to his mother in her Texan hospital (pp. 189–91/pp. 237–9) and may even be able to save her life thanks to the magical (or natural?) Water of Life that he retrieves from the sacred mountain. Cold rationalism, unfettered capitalism and rampant individualism are not, then, the way forward for a meaningful existence in the US: give and take with the sort of humane or more spiritual communal values associated with peoples or belief systems often dismissed in the United States may make for a more productive way of and quality of life.

The Magical and Moral Instruction

In the end, then, Allende's tale does have something of the moralistic tone of earlier children's literature, even though it updates and liberalizes the moral agenda and still posits the open-mindedness of the child as a source of potential enlightenment for adults. And in its storyline about the *International Geographic* and

---

[20] For more on Allende's novels and the USA, see Swanson, 'California Dreaming: Mixture, Muddle and Meaning in Isabel Allende's North American Narratives', *Journal of Iberian and Latin American Studies*, 9 (2003), 57–68.

the dissemination of anthropological research, it does seem to address the theme of writing and moral or ethical intention. At one stage the vain anthropologist Leblanc insists on being photographed with a dead anaconda wrapped around him but in a way that makes it look alive (p. 115/p. 138), alerting us to the manipulative nature of representation, an idea developed earlier in a discussion about the way anthropologists have allegedly doctored their documentary evidence or promoted their own subjective versions of the indigenous experience (p. 107/p. 129). More comically, at the end, it becomes apparent that Leblanc's new book will be full of untruths as he keenly laps up the pack of lies being wittily fed to him by the Indian warrior Tahama, obviously more mischievously astute than the First-World intellectual is aware (p. 305/p. 391–2).

Indeed, the entire thriller plot is built around the idea of the misrepresentation of reality: the beautiful pro-indigenous doctor, Omayra Torres, is not what she seems to be and the scam of which she, Carías and Ariosto are part is to use the legitimizing function of the *International Geographic* to 'prove' that the Indians had been vaccinated when in reality they had been infected. But at the same time it is photographs taken of Carías and Ariosto in compromising circumstances by an English photographer that provide the proof that exposes the evil plan and reveals the truth to the world (p. 311/pp. 400–1). Moreover, it is Kate's writing that will protect the Beasts (by convincing the world that they do no not exist) and the People of the Mist (by generating international outrage about the attempts to exploit them and support for their protection) (p. 304/pp. 390–1). This well-travelled story-spinning grandmother and writer is probably something of an echo of Allende herself. Just as Kate initiates Alexander into a wonderful new and transforming world (p. 198/p. 250), Allende initiates her readers into a magical world that she hopes will transform their understanding of reality. This is what magical realism is all about for Allende: what she calls the 'magic of words' is the ability to communicate with one's readers in a manner that may, in some small way, help better the real external world (Swanson, *The New Novel*, pp. 146–7).

The Magical and the Popular

Moreover, Allende's version of magical realism is a specifically female or 'feminine' one (Swanson, *The New Novel*, pp. 145–70). Critics of children's literature have often noted its perceived connection with the feminine, but both can be equally associated with innocence, the primitive, nature and the popular. McGillis, for example, links women, children and (North American) Indians with powerlessness and invisibility (p. xxi),[21] while Cogan Thacker and Webb

---

[21] Interestingly, the People of the Mist have the ability to appear invisible, a sign of their opposition to the world of the *nahab*, but also perhaps an indication of the marginal status of the Indian.

argue that 'the relatively minor status of literature for children' is due to 'its close connection with mothering and the feminine' (p. 149). In *La Ciudad de las Bestias*, the young female, Nadia, is said to be equivalent to nature and also neither Indian nor foreigner, neither woman nor spirit (p. 91/p. 109): she, like the Indians and perhaps the jungle itself, is a non-binary entity beyond the rigid realm of masculine patriarchal logic.

Similarly, Allende does not pretend to be a highly rational intellectual but merely an emotional communicator, responding to a question about critical assessments of her oeuvre with: 'I don't know how to answer in an intelligent, academic, scholarly way. I can only tell you how I feel. I write [my work] with my feelings . . .' (Rodden, p. 2). Allende is above all a popular writer, writing on the whole middle-brow novels that aim to transmit some degree of emotional understanding about human beings and the social and political issues that affect them. Rather than a cynical attempt to plunder J.K. Rowling, just as she was accused of plundering García Márquez, her turn to children's literature is a natural progression as it is a way of using the 'magic' of writing to communicate in a simple yet challenging way and via a popular format what she feels to be important issues for our times. And, what is more, whether cultural critics approve or not, she is communicating as much to a young audience in North America and elsewhere as she is to one in Latin America, an audience – as the novel itself implies (p. 118/p. 143) – that needs stimulation to think about life beyond the limited arena of TV and video games. One young reader doing a web review of the English version of *La Ciudad de las Bestias* commented thus:

> The aspect of fantasy did force me to look a long way into my imagination, maybe a little further than your average sixteen year old feels comfortable with! [. . .] The book raises many thought-provoking ideas about society and different interpretations of what this word really means. It makes you question your own perception of society. A powerful writer will always make you question your own beliefs and views and Allende does this with great subtlety. It raises such points as *our civilization is just the reverse: no ceremony, only massacres*. This made me question my beliefs about what society is and what it is to be part of our society at this present time.[22]

This sounds like exactly the sort of reaction Allende would have hoped for. On her and children's terms, *La Ciudad de las Bestias* has to be judged as a successful variation on the practices of magical realism for a new generation.

---

[22] The reviewer is Meghan Ormerod, 'Review of *City of the Beasts*', *Black Star Review* (July 2004) (http://www.blackstarreview.com).

Unsavoury Representations in Laura Esquivel's
Like Water for Chocolate

Helene Price

'He maintained that magic, like cooking (. . .),
was a particularly feminine affair.'[1]

Of all the novels to come out of Latin America, Laura Esquivel's *Como agua para chocolate* (1989)[2] is surely one of the most commercially successful. The same may be said of its cinematic counterpart, which was directed by the novelist's then husband Alfonso Arau in 1992, when Arau wrote a screenplay that faithfully emulated the structure and spirit of his wife's work. The film was, to a large extent, responsible for the regeneration of the Mexican film industry, as the country's most commercially successful film of the decade of its release. The statistics are now familiar: the book was the second best-selling novel in Mexico in the year of its publication and its English translation rocketed into the New York Times best-seller list in 1993 and remained there for a significant period. It has already been translated into twenty-nine different languages. The film, clearly boosted by sales of the novel, won eighteen international awards and was the highest-grossing foreign language film in the U.S. in 1993.[3]

There were several reasons for this phenomenal success. The book contained all the right 'ingredients': a fast flowing plot, a heart-wrenching love story, an original yet familiar structure (the cookery-book 'mode') and, last, but most certainly not least, a tablespoon of magic. It is this last element that has led critics to speak of *Like Water for Chocolate* as a work of magical realism. Yet little more than a second glance at either the text or the film reveals that these works go entirely against the grain of the revolutionary ethos associated with magical realism. Esquivel's employment of elements of magic bolsters an entirely

---

[1] Esteban Trueba in Isabel Allende, *La casa de los espíritus* (Barcelona: Plaza & Janés, 1982), 10th edn, p. 148. My translation.

[2] Laura Esquivel, *Como agua para chocolate* (Mexico City: Planeta, 1989).

[3] See Deborah Shaw, 'Seducing the Public: Images of Mexico in *Like Water for Chocolate* and *Amores Perros*', in *Contemporary Cinema of Latin America: 10 Key Films* (London: Continuum, 2003), pp. 36–51.

reactionary ideology that serves to reinforce patriarchal stereotypes of femininity and condone the master-slave dialectic, whilst fetishising Mexican identity. In the absence of the transgressive and subversive impulses that Parkinson Zamora and Faris speak of,[4] the works of Laura Esquivel and Alfonso Arau reinforce the 'traditional' boundaries of gender, race and class. In fact, they reveal more about the ways in which Europeans, Americans and even urban middle-class Mexicans wish to perceive Mexican rural reality. The prevailing ideology of the text is conservative, so it follows that *Like Water for Chocolate* differs from the majority of other magical-realist narratives in that it is not intrinsically postcolonial.

1. Magical Elements in the Text

Like Water for Chocolate follows the fate of Tita, a young woman from the land-owning classes in Mexico in the early twentieth century. She meets and falls in love with Pedro, but their desire to marry and consummate their love is thwarted by an archaic family tradition that requires Tita, as the youngest daughter, to care for her mother for the rest of the latter's days, forgoing marriage and a life of her own. Tita's elder sister is offered to Pedro in her place and the couple live in the family home whilst Tita is relegated to the kitchen where she grows up under the compassionate guidance of Nacha, the family cook, who is of Amerindian origin. All Tita's emotions of frustration, anger, desire and clandestine passion are poured into the dishes that she cooks up with startling results. For the emotion with which Tita approaches each new recipe is magically transmitted to whoever consumes her dishes and all the while the tabooed love that she and Pedro share boils and bubbles beneath the surface. The novel's structure is of integral importance to the plot since each of the twelve chapters, which span approximately forty years of Mexico's revolutionary and post-revolutionary history, are preceded by a recipe, whose creation and consumption form the basis of the chapters' events.

Both book and film do emulate the magical-realist style, in that fantastic occurrences are recounted, in a matter-of-fact tone, as if they were common-place events. In other words, within the ontological parameters of the text, magical things really do happen. The narrative adopts the *mise en abyme* format, as it is Tita's grand-niece who recounts her life story via the reading of her recipe books in the present tense of the novel's narrative. The 'metaphysical dimensions . . . common in contemporary magical realism'[5] are seen in Alba's reordering of her grandmother's notebooks[6] or the parchments of Melquíades

---

[4] Lois Parkinson Zamora and Wendy B. Faris (eds), *Magical Realism: Theory, History, Community* (Durham & London: Duke University Press, 1995).

[5] Wendy B. Faris, 'Scheherazade's Children: Magical Realism and Postmodern Fiction', in Zamora and Faris, *Magical Realism: Theory, History, Community*, pp. 163–90.

[6] See Allende, *La casa de los espíritus*, pp. 453–4: 'Mi abuela escribió durante años en sus cuadernos de anotar la vida. . . Los tengo aquí, a mis pies'.

that Aureliano finds and reads.[7] As it is the reader of the notebook, in each of the three cases, who gives birth, in effect, to the telling of the tale through his own reading, the narrative is effectively set within an 'other', inter-literary dimension, placing it a step away from the intended reader of the phenomenal world. This 'world within a world' impression adds to the insular, enclosed and hence magical nature of the text, as the text appears to create itself. Furthermore, the action is set in temporal terms at a point in the past which is conducive to its romantic feel, and geographically at a frontier between two lands (the U.S. – Mexican border) with their conflicting cultural orders. Lastly, the narrative contains all those elements of 'otherness' (according to the moral and scientific laws that govern official Western discourse) conducive to the creation of a magical universe, such as taboo, apparitions and the occasional appearance of elements pertaining to a non-Western culture and worldview such as superstition and folklore.

Gender and Reinforcement of Patriarchy

The book opens with Tita's birth on the kitchen tabletop and, in a clear example of hyperbole, the infant is 'literally washed into this world on a great tide of tears that spilled over the edge of the table and flooded across the floor' (p. 10).[8] This flood of tears soon evaporates and the residue of salt is swept up and used for seasoning food, as if Tita's culinary abilities were embedded within her actual physical being. Hence we have an improbable event that is accepted by the characters as quite normal, followed by their manipulation of its outcome for practical usage – here, enters the realism, just. It is because Tita was born in the kitchen, we are told, that in later life she will have such affinity for and adopt it as her space: 'Thanks to her unnatural birth, Tita felt a deep love for the kitchen, where she spent most of her life from the day she was born' (p. 10). Hence the improbable circumstances of Tita's birth produce her love for the kitchen and its activities, leading to her willing adoption of the traditional female space and role of nourisher that reinforces conventional notions of female-hood within the text. Unlike her fellow countrywoman centuries before her, Sor Juana Inés de la Cruz, who used her relegation to the traditional female space of the kitchen for the acquisition of knowledge via a series of scientific experiments, Tita happily becomes an accomplished cook and revels in her role of feeding her family. Her magical birth, rather than liberating Tita, as one might expect, merely propels her

---

[7] See Gabriel García Márquez, *Cien años de soledad* (Madrid: Ediciones Cátedra, 1967), 8th edn, pp. 556–9. For an extensive discussion of the Archive of Melquíades, see Roberto González Echevarría, *Myth and Archive: A Theory of Latin American Narrative* (Durham, NC: Duke University Press, 1998), pp. 21–30.

[8] All translations are taken from *Like Water for Chocolate*, translated by Carol Christensen and Thomas Christensen (New York/London: Double Day/Black Swan, 1993).

into a role that reinforces negative gender stereotypes – indeed, had Tita been male, one must wonder whether the tears of a male child could conceivably have materialised into the food of life.

Tita's relegation to the kitchen is completed by her mother who, in true fairy-tale fashion,[9] forbids her to marry Pedro and banishes her to the kitchen. Whilst the battle-axe Mamá Elena is a strong and dominant woman, she cannot be considered a positive role model for women, for her cruelty and despotism imply that for a woman to be strong, she must be a ruthless, masculine and authoritarian woman who rules with an iron fist. She effectively becomes the patriarch (or matriarch) of the novel, merely perpetuating the status quo that leads to the subjugation of women and possesses none of the positive attributes typically associated with femininity such as compassion or the will to defy stereotypical gender roles; interestingly, she is unable to breast-feed her youngest daughter upon the death of her husband. This obstacle to true love would have been an opportune reason for Tita to rebel against tradition by defiance or flight. However, Tita accepts without question her mother's desires and reinforces the notion of women as passive and dependent subjects.

The first of the magical episodes begins when Tita's tears of desperation and frustration fall into the cake she is baking for Rosaura and Pedro's wedding, altering the texture of the topping and wetting the dough. On the day of the wedding, no sooner have the guests devoured their first mouthful of cake than they are filled with 'a great wave of longing' (p. 39) and begin to sob uncontrollably, remembering their lost true loves. This 'strange intoxication' (p. 39) exteriorises itself by means of 'an acute attack of melancholy and frustration – that seized the guests and scattered them across the patio' (p. 39) and terminates in a 'collective vomiting' (p. 39) that ruins Rosaura's day. The impression given is that the emotions that Tita felt upon baking have seeped into the cake and overwhelmed the guests, like a 'spell' (p. 39), and the film emphasises this point more since, as Tita walks past each guest, he/she begins to cry. This magical event leads to the supposition that the impeding of true love is a punishable offence, and the reader spares no pity for the selfish Rosaura who married the man that her younger sister loved. Magic, here, is used against the woman who prevents the realisation of Tita's conventional dreams of marrying and becoming a loving wife. The way in which Mamá Elena simply 'swaps' Rosaura over for Tita reinforces the notion that women are commodities, to be given and exchanged, without thought for their needs.

---

[9] The story is reminiscent of the Cinderella fairy-tale, with Mamá Elena as the wicked stepmother who will not let Tita meet her Prince Charming, while Nacha is the fairy godmother and Rosaura, the ugly sister. This tried and tested formula must be in part responsible for the mass appeal of the novel. For further discussion, see Janet Giannotti, *A Companion Text for 'Like Water for Chocolate'* (Ann Arbor, MI: The University of Michigan Press, 1999), pp. 117–22; and Stephen M. Hart, *Companion to Latin American Film* (London: Tamesis, 2004), pp. 174–6.

The next dish Tita prepares is quails on a bed of rose petals that she takes from a bouquet offered to her by Pedro. Tita, delighted at her gift, squeezes the roses so tightly to her chest that the thorns pierce her skin. It is the 'the fusion of Tita's blood and the roses from Pedro' (p. 48) that leads to the 'explosive' results that ensue. For, the dish 'acts as an aphrodisiac' (p. 48) upon its consumers and leaves everyone in a state of profound sexual arousal. The text makes clear that it is the desire and excitement provoked in Tita by the roses that produce this effect, rather as if Tita were subconsciously projecting her passion into the food: 'It was as if a strange alchemical process had dissolved her entire being in rose petal sauce' (p. 50). By referring to the magical 'art' of alchemy, the text reinforces the element of the fantastical present in this occurrence. Furthermore, the image of Tita influencing the ingredients in the pot on the stove before her is redolent of white magic, in that it suggests the work of a spell, albeit an unconsciously made one, as, ultimately, she seduces Pedro through her cooking, as if it were a sexual magic wand, very different from the poison of Carpentier's *The Kingdom of this World*.[10]

The recipe may have been passed to Tita by her spiritual mother Nacha, but, on a second level, it could be argued that it is Pedro who, inciting desire in Tita and influencing her behaviour, truly instigates the episode. Indeed, although the novel can be considered feminocentric in that it revolves around female characters, it is ultimately Pedro who controls their irrational behaviour and interactions, be it Tita, Rosaura or the formidable Mamá Elena. Despite the text having a female protagonist and an abundance of women characters, the action revolves around the presence of one male character (a weak one at that) and the sentiments that he stirs in them, reinforcing the notion that women are guided by emotions and that their lives revolve around men and sentiments. Magic thereby contributes to the sentimentalising of women rather than transgressing the boundaries of the conventional binary oppositions set up between male and female.[11] It is Pedro who causes the squabbles, tears and relocations which effectively distance female characters from one another and cause a household divide. In a similar vein, Tita, as she consoles herself over Pedro, knits a blanket of sublime proportions, much as Pelagia embroiders a jacket awaiting her absent lover in *Captain Corelli's Mandolin*[12] or Penelope, undoing her weaving whilst

---

[10] Alejo Carpentier, *El reino de este mundo* (Mexico City: Siglo Veintiuno, 1949).

[11] In their introduction to *Magical Realism: Theory, History, Community* (1995), Lois Parkinson Zamora and Wendy B. Faris suggest that 'magical realism is a mode suited to exploring – and transgressing – boundaries' (pp. 5–6). Amongst the list they provide of 'boundaries' appear the binary oppositions of 'self and other', 'male and female'. I would argue that a work such as *Como agua para chocolate* serves merely to maintain these boundaries. It follows then, that *Como agua para chocolate* differs from the majority of other magical-realist narratives, in that it is not intrinsically post colonial. In point of fact, the prevailing ideology of the text is conservative.

[12] See Louis de Bernières, *Captain Corelli's Mandolin* (London: Martin Secker & Warburg / Vintage, 1994).

yearning for Odysseus. This common motif advocates female passivity, fidelity and dependence on the male subject. Women in *Like Water for Chocolate* are sentimentalized, much as they were in nineteenth-century fiction and the romance novel, acting from the heart and not from the head.

The portrayal of women is also essentialist. When Rosaura is unable to breast-feed her daughter, it is from Tita's virgin breast that the child is fed. Tita herself questions this miracle: 'Tita couldn't believe it. It wasn't possible for an unmarried woman to have milk, short of a supernatural act' (p. 70). This 'supernatural' act aligns Tita with the concept of the 'eternal feminine', the naturally maternal woman whose role is to nurture and protect. She is described as 'Ceres herself, goddess of plenty, (p. 70), which elevates her maternal instincts to the realms of mythology. Tita's main strengths lie in her mother-earth-like qualities of nurturing and nourishing, the text even makes plain that: 'If there was one thing that Tita couldn't resist, it was a hungry person asking for food' (p. 70). By contrast, Rosaura, unable to feed her child, fails in her womanly duties and, in this way, women in the story are divided into categories of 'natural' and 'unnatural', based on their abilities to nurture, feed and love. When the infant is separated from Tita he starves and dies. Ultimately, a supernatural act has been used to reinforce the idea that what is positive in a woman is centred upon biological abilities that associate her with reproduction and motherhood. The film goes further in romanticising Tita's earth mother appeal by focussing on (and thus fetishising) her breasts under the idolising gaze of Pedro, who is clearly aroused by the scene of mother and child before him. The frame of Pedro gazing lovingly at Tita is redolent of the holy family. In this way, visual imagery is used in the film to reiterate and valorise the hegemonic religion of Catholicism. Furthermore, in the film Tita has a very feminine look about her. Her dresses are long, flowery and billowing, her hair falls gently over her shoulders, framing her face; Lumi Cavazos, who interprets her, has a graceful air about her and a delicate sort of beauty.

Tita and Pedro do consummate their love in what could be seen as Tita's attempt to rebel against the established order, but the novel is merely fooling us. As Deborah A. Shaw points out, temptation to rebel, 'is motivated by Tita's desire to conform to traditional notions of femininity where an ideal woman needs to be a wife, mother and nurturer if she is to be fulfilled' (Shaw, p. 117). Tita's *raison d'être* is to bear Pedro's children and serve him as a loyal wife. The novel ends with the couple, finally reunited and making love. Unfortunately, Pedro dies and Tita chooses to follow him by eating matches to set herself alight, in another supernatural act. Despite the fact that it is Tita's grand-niece who has narrated the story by way of voiceovers up to this point, as the ranch burns, it is the voice of John Brown, reciting his grandmother's theory, with which the novel ends. Hence it is a man who has the final say in this female-dominated film. Neither is there anything to suggest that attitudes have become more progressive. As Tita's niece marries John's son, it is she that seems to have succeeded, attaining her destined role, where her spinster aunt, left unmarried and alone, has failed.

Race and Class

Gertrudis, the product of her mother's clandestine affair with a mulatto, was an illegitimate child of mixed race. The actress chosen to play her in the film, inexplicably, has ginger hair and in no way resembles a woman of mixed race, which seems to be a weakness on behalf of Arau and the casting director with regards to the incorporation of representatives of ethnic groups. Her presence, however, along with that of the Indian servants Nacha and Chenca introduces the notion of Mexico as a heterogeneous nation into the work. The inclusion of members of the autochthonous culture, in the form of servant workers from poorer classes as well as those brought into the country for slavery, would have been an ideal opportunity for Esquivel to employ the magical-realist mode to examine ideologies of racism and servitude but is one that she entirely passes up. What is more, in a cynical fashion, the narrative almost promotes racial stereotypes. An example of this is seen when Gertrudis returns to the ranch with her lover and his troops and a dance is held in their honour. Her dancing abilities whip up a stir and whilst Rosaura remains puzzled as to the source of such talent, Tita, having chanced on a photo of a 'well-dressed mulatto' is acutely aware: 'she knew perfectly well who had given Gertrudis her rhythm and other qualities' (p. 162). In this instance, 'other qualities' refers to Gertrudis's insatiable sexual appetite, which requires her to work as a whore in order to satisfy her needs. Whilst this is an unusually liberating proposition in the text from the female perspective, the comment equates Gertrudis's natural feel for rhythm and her sexual prowess, common stereotypes associated with the black race,[13] with the black blood in her veins. The implication that blacks are good dancers and great lovers is not overtly negative; however, it does tend to caricaturise and naturalise the race, reiterating popular stereotypes that associate Blacks with carnal and primitive instincts.

Neither does the text adopt a liberal premise with regard to the ranch's Indian servants, as it avoids challenging their subjugated position in Mexican society. In point of fact, the servants appear to be utterly content with their lot. The way in which they are incorporated into the family, especially by Gertrudis and Tita, presents them almost as family members, proposing an idyllic acceptance of harmony between races which quite clearly did not exist in Latin America at the turn of the century. In this way the film masks the reality of the social and racial inequalities that existed at large in Mexico at that time. John Kraniauskas identifies this as one reason for the film's popularity with middle-class audiences: 'Despite all the changes brought about in Mexican society by the Revolution and its aftermath, they (audiences) can still feel comfortable with those things that

---

[13] For a discussion on the representation of black women in literature, see G.R. Coulthard, *Race and Colour in Caribbean Literature* (London: Oxford University Press, 1962), particularly chapter VII, 'The Coloured Woman in Caribbean Poetry', where the author notes that 'Negro figures, male or female, invariably appear in an atmosphere of violence, heavy sensuality, frenetic dancing' (p. 94).

have not changed: the servants in their kitchen' (pp. 42–3).[14] In this sense both book and film promote a traditional, middle-class ideology, unusual for a magical realist text, but seemingly comforting to the urban middle-class Mexican, whose position in society it reconfirms. Nacha, having dedicated her life to serving the family has abdicated her chances of having her own family but the text does not problematize this. She dies early in the text, leaving the younger Chencha as the only representative of her class and race. The film, with its wooden acting performances,[15] further promulgates the stereotype of the intellectually inferior native, with the actress who interprets the part of Chencha portraying her to all intents and purposes as a simple, grinning idiot, a caricature of the uneducated Indian. In addition her speech is broken and grammatically incorrect, as we see in the example: 'Es q'el Felipe ya'stá aquí y dice ¡que si petatió' (p. 89), contrasting to that of the white characters. Unfortunately, the English translation, 'Felipe has come back and he says he's dead' (p. 89) does not convey the discrepancy between the grammatically correct Spanish of the other characters and the colloquial and grammatically incorrect Spanish of Chencha. Ultimately, no radical position is assumed with regard to the social conditions of the lower classes; rather than denouncing servitude and the despoliation and exploitation of indigenous subjects, it actually justifies it, by its stereotypical portrayal of contented servants who do not question their place in society.

Mexico and the Revolution: Revolutionary Discourse Denied

It is the middle sister, Gertrudis, who experiences the strongest effects of the petal sauce when she becomes so consumed by sexual longing that she is forced to run to the out-house to shower and cool down. The text describes how via the food that Tita has prepared 'a new system of communication' had developed, whereby 'Tita was the transmitter, Pedro the receiver, and poor Gertrudis the medium, the conducting body through which the singular sexual message was passed' (p. 49). She sets the shower alight as the water turns to steam which rises off her trembling body. Her scent reaches a member of the Villista forces, who as if guided by 'a higher power' (p. 51), tracks her down and scoops her naked onto his horse. They ride off into the sunset together, enacting that most recognisable cliché of the Romance genre. From the above events it is clear that the narrative embraces the romantic style, which the film compounds as it is shot in hazy sepia tones, with images of sunsets and starry skies and a flowing musical score. The soldier who carries off Gertrudis has clearly inhaled the pheromones she emits, but never in the phenomenal world would they be so powerful as to utterly overwhelm him.

[14] John Kraniauskas, 'Como agua para chocolate', *Sight and Sound*, 210 (1993), 42–3.
[15] Deborah Shaw, 'Seducing the Public', refers to the 'stilted' performance of Marco Leonardi, who plays Pedro, p. 47.

The arrival of this soldier and the episode at a later point in the novel when he brings Gertrudis home with his troops are the only two instances when the narrative is aware of the presence of revolutionary forces. They dance, drink and make merry but their arrival prompts no consideration of the Mexican Revolution. All we are told of the conflict is found in the words 'the rebel forces and federal troops were engaged in a fierce battle' (p. 51), which reveal affinity to neither side, plunging the narrative into ideological ignorance. The struggle is taking place somewhere outside of the ranch but has little effect on its inhabitants' lives. Revolutionaries appear only in caricaturised form. From this we may deduce that although the text contains a heavy dose of magic, and ordinary logic is consistently disrupted, it deliberately avoids engagement with Mexican history, politics or social reality, leaving the second element of the term 'magical realism' relatively redundant. An amusing incident the shower episode may be, it, nevertheless, deliberately eludes Mexican reality. Despite the story's situation in a moment of significant historical magnitude, the time of the Mexican Revolution, the ethics, purposes and day to day realities of the cause are all but glossed over, if read in the light of other narratives set in the time by other Mexican women writers, such as *Los recuerdos del porvenir* (1963)[16] or *Hasta no verte Jesús mío* (1969).[17]

In *Como agua para chocolate* magic defines Mexican-ness. Its inclusion portrays the Mexican nation as an enchanting 'other' to the industrialised West through its links with the folkloric and exoticism. Here, magical realism is denied its subversive potential, reinforcing the image of a primitive country that has been left behind by the narratives of modernity and scientific rationality. Promotional slogans that advertised the film in the U.S. used the phrase: 'Experience the Magic' as their selling point which suggests that the film's appeal to non-Mexican audiences was dependent on magic. Harmony H. Wu believes that here magic realism has fixed a 'frozen identity of Mexican-ness' and 'becomes not a challenge to Western rationality and scientific discourse but rather reaffirms their hegemonic position of power'.[18] Mexico is hence imagined as a peripheral nation and, magical elements, rather than re-centralising Mexico as a nation with regard to the U.S., as other narratives of magical realism have done, merely serve to pigeonhole it as backward and pre-industrial. In short, the film does nothing to suggest that Mexican society has progressed and become urbanised and magic serves to marginalise Mexico from modernity, allowing the U.S. to define itself as the centre.

Similarly, natural medicinal remedies are given preference over scientifically elaborated ones in Mexico. Tita, treating Pedro's burns with egg whites and raw potatoes, turns to magical, natural remedies because 'these were the best ways she

---

[16] Elena Garro, *Los recuerdos del porvenir* (Mexico City: Joaquín Mortiz, 1963).

[17] Elena Poniatowska, *Hasta no verte Jesús mío* (Mexico City: Ediciones Era, 1969).

[18] Harmony H. Wu, 'Consuming Tacos and Enchiladas: Gender and the Nation in *Como agua para chocolate*', *Visible Nations: Latin American Cinema and Video*, ed. Chon A. Noriega (Minneapolis: University of Minnesota Press, 2000), pp. 174–92 (p. 188).

knew to deal with burns' (p. 181). It is Tita's suitor, the gringo Dr John Brown, who eventually cures her when she goes mad (or hysterical) – but she has to cross the border into Texas in order for this to happen. Dr John Brown, epitomising male scientific progress, spends his time in his laboratory and, dramatically, it is against this backdrop that he reveals his grandmother's (a Kickapoo Indian) theory of matchsticks. For several pages, John has impressed Tita with his knowledge and aptitude as he performs several scientific experiments. However, a noticeable change in tone appears when he explains (sympathetically, it must be said) her belief that a box of matches exists inside any one of us that can only be ignited by the breath of a loved one. The White American in the narrative stands for science, materialism and reason, whilst his grandmother, representing neighbouring Mexico, symbolises magic and myth, as two opposing world viewpoints are placed in juxtaposition. The backdrop of the laboratory in the film provides a dramatic contrast to the theories of Mexican magic, which will not be lost on the spectator.

Conclusion

As Tita seduces Pedro through food, magic seduces the reader and spectator. However, although magic happenings weave their way through book and film, they employ none of the 'political-consciousness-raising powers'[19] associated with the magical-realist mode. Indeed, magic in the film merely reiterates (except maybe in the case of Gertrudis's sexuality) stereotypical and outdated representations of women, ethnic groups and the Mexican nation. The white patriarchy dominates, women's strength lies in their domesticity and Mexico is charming, but in a backward way. Both book and film avoid addressing Mexico's problematic role within the narratives of modernity or as a peripheral nation in terms of the U.S., Europe and the West. The text shows no profound awareness of the political and social conditions operating during the Mexican Revolution, which becomes at best a flimsy backdrop to an essentialist and conservative love story. If we accept Alejo Carpentier's claim in his essay, 'On the Marvellous Real in America', that 'the novelists of Latin America' are the 'witnesses, historians, interpreters of our great reality',[20] then my contention is that the works of Laura Esquivel and Alfonso Arau reveal more about the way in which Europeans, Americans and even urban, middle-class Mexicans wish to perceive Mexican rural reality. *Como agua para chocolate* used the style rather than the substance of magical realism.

---

[19] Theo L. D'haen, 'Magical Realism and Postmodernism: Decentering Privileged Centers', in Parkinson Zamora and Faris (eds), *Magical Realism: Theory, History, Community*, pp. 191–208 (p. 202).

[20] This essay, entitled 'The Baroque and the Marvellous Real in America', is reproduced in the above-mentioned *Magical Realism: Theory, History, Community*, pp. 89–108. It was originally presented as a lecture in the Caracas Athenaeum on 22 May 1975 and was published in Spanish in Alejo Carpentier, *La novela latinoamericana en vísperas de un nuevo siglo* (Mexico City: Siglo XXI, 1981), 'Lo barroco y lo real maravilloso', pp. 111–32.

Not So Innocent – An Israeli Tale of Subversion: Dorit Rabinyan's *Persian Brides*

Tsila (Abramovitz) Ratner

Persian Brides, a novel by the Israeli woman writer Dorit Rabinyan, takes place in the Jewish quarter of a small Persian village ruled by cunning ghosts, devils and strong-minded women, at the turn of the twentieth century.[1] The plot revolves around the desperate journeys of two girls/women, that of the pregnant fifteen-years-old Flora who sneaks out of her mother's house at night to look for her swindler husband who has deserted her, and that of little eleven years old Nazie, Flora's orphaned cousin, who leaves the same house at dawn to seek the local mullah's permission to marry her cousin Moussa.

The geographical and temporal location of the narrative and its focus on women's stories places it outside the hegemonic Israeli discourse. It takes place in Persia in the pre-state era and thereby no critique of the Israeli narrative is apparent and its female perspective seems to avoid the national project and the male authority over it altogether.[2] The combination of women's issues and the oriental context at the heart of the narrative enhances a semblance of innocent marginality. It enables the hegemonic gaze of the western and male Israeli discourse to conceptualize it as a folkloristic tale, thus securing its marginality and attributing the novel's popularity to its colourful ethnicity.[3]

However, far from being innocent, *Persian Brides* disguises a deep subversion when under the semblance of ethnic folklore it exposes the Orientalist nature of

---

[1] Dorit Rabinyan, *Persian Brides*, trans. Yael Lotan (Edinburgh: Canongate, 1998).

[2] The exclusion of women, particularly of the non-European ones, from the national/history narrative is well documented, as in Henriette Dahan Kalev's 'Oriental Women: Identity and Herstory', in M. Shilo, R. Kark and G. Hasan-Rokem (eds), *Jewish Women in the Yishuv and Zionism* (Jerusalem: Yad Ben Zvi Press, 2001) (Hebrew).

[3] Ethnicity in the Israeli context used to employ the Orientalist discourse as it evolved around West/East issues. There is clearly a difference between the attribution of ethnicity to European communities, whose position is secured in the master narrative, and its attribution to 'oriental' communities, which are marginalized by it. Aziza Khazoom, 'Turning into a Minority, Questioning Gender: Iraqi Women in the 50s', in Hanan Hever, Yehuda Shenhav (eds), *Mizrahim in Israel: A Critical Observation into Israeli Ethnicity* (Tel-Aviv: Van Leer & Hakibbutz Hameuchad, 2002) (Hebrew).

the Israeli discourse, rather than focusing on its particular manifestations the way other Israeli writers of Eastern origins do.[4] The use of fantastic elements is instrumental to this subversive reading. Through them the narrative progresses from stereotypical categories of representation, which conceptualize the fantastic as ethnic folklore and consequently deepen the Orientalist East/West dichotomy, towards the presentation of the fantastic as magical realism, consequently creating a liminality and hybridity, rather than rigid categories of space and identity.[5]

The beginning of the novel reinforces the Orientalist view of the small Persian village as ignorant, backward, sexually uninhibited and irrational via its female protagonists, whose life is determined by their bodies and mainly by their reproductive function. Thus the Orientalist view of the feminine and its heightened sensuality is enhanced. Fantastic elements woven into the women's stories are responsible for the Orientalist representations, not only for their content but also for their narratological function as the exaggerated and hyperbolical rhetoric of the oriental discourse, contrary to the rational realism of the western one. As long as this categorization is maintained, the fantastic is contained within the space allocated to oriental ethnic folklore within the dominant western discourse. But when the same fantastic elements break away, sipping into the dominant discourse, they change their identity from ethnic to hybrid, from marginal into mainstream, and the mechanism that has contained them is destabilized.

Persian Brides constructs this shift from marginality to subversion in a dialectical process whereby the exclusive interpretation of the fantastic as ethnic folklore collapses. Instead, fantastic elements are organized so as to form a narrative of magical realism, which cannot maintain its stability either. This dialectic is constructed by splitting the plot of the novel into two parallel ones, following the journeys of its girls-protagonists: while Flora's journey builds a narrative of magical realism, Nazie's quest moves along rational and realistic lines. The two journeys reflect, interact and destabilize each other, enhancing differences and similarities that cannot be contained in two separate categories. Thus, the oriental/western, fantastic/rational dichotomies lose the presumed essentialist nature of stable categories of identity that construct ethnicities. They are presented in a constant state of shifting and changing, similar to the unstable notions of real/unreal, is/is-not, which constitute magical realism through hesitation and suspension of probabilities.[6] The liminality emerging from the construction of

---

[4] Such as Sami Michael, Shimon Balas, Dan Bnaya-Seri, Eli Amir whose writing refers to the relegated status of Jews of Arab countries. The complexities shown in their writing are discussed in Nancy Berg's *Exile from Exile: Israeli Writers from Iraq* (New York: State University of New York Press, 1996).

[5] The term 'hybridity' is used here in its generic meaning, namely, challenging clearly marked differentiations by blurring their boundaries, which enables contingent, dynamic and changeable identities to emerge.

[6] The parallel yet conflicting journeys of Nazie and Flora are concrete realization of the definition of magical realism as the antimony of a simultaneous presence of two conflicting

the fantastic as magical realism becomes therefore a site of resistance, as it exposes ambivalence in the dominant discourse. Nazie's 'western' and realistic characteristics, revealed in her journey to the mullah, shift the ethnic demarcation when her oriental otherness is shown to be inherent to the hegemonic discourse itself, while Flora's narrative of magical realism cannot be contained within any exclusive category either.[7]

From its onset, the novel locates its plot and protagonists in women's rooms, in the kitchen where Nazie sits on the cold floor, as befits her low orphaned status in her aunt's household, and Flora, weeping for her deserting husband, sits on embroidered cushions that can hardly sustain her big, pregnant body. Flora who is 'big body and little brain', epitomizes the Orient: she is capricious, sensual, irrational, spoilt and uninhibited. Nazie is presented as her opposite: her body is thin and childish, a far cry from Flora's voluptuous fertility; she is quiet and exploited, but rational and perceptive.[8] On that night, pregnant Flora fancies a watermelon and, although out of season, it has to be found otherwise evil demons will take hold of her unborn baby. Indeed, the village whore had fared much worse when amidst sand storms and frightened flights of birds she had borne monstrous twins to the king of demons. Nonetheless, something must to be done to overturn Flora's predicament. If her brother, Moussa, cannot find her a watermelon, he will have to collect the neighbours' saliva in a goblet for Flora to drink. And from what Nazie has heard in the bathhouse, Flora's agony is the consequence of conceiving her baby during the night of a lunar eclipse. Such is the power of the eclipse that all measures prescribed by the council of Flora's aunts, such as: passing water over an egg, inhaling the smoke of burning weeds, pleading with the moon to remove the curse, profuse yawning and singing love songs from the rooftop, could not outplay it.

Flora's watermelon urge is therefore connected to a complex of beliefs in supernatural forces, most of them of evil nature, that rule over human lives.

---

discursive codes. As in: Tzvetan Todorov in *The Fantastic: A Structural Approach to a Literary Genre* (New York: Cornell University Press, 1975), pp. 31–3; Eric Rabkin, *The Fantastic in Literature* (Princeton: Princeton University Press, 1976), pp. 4–8. However, the novel deconstructs the exclusive nature of each of them to form hybrid identities.

[7] This ambivalence within the hegemonic discourse destabilizes the concept of ethnicity even further as it dissolves the boundaries of demarcation, as Homi Bhabha has shown in 'Signs Taken for Wonders: Questions of Ambivalence and Authority Under a Tree Outside Delhi', *Critical Inquiry*, 12.1 (Autumn 1985), 144–65. In the case of *Persian Brides* the Israeli discourse, professedly western, is shown to contain the elements declared and marginalized as oriental ethnicity. Hence, ethnicity is shown to be culturally constructed, rather than essentialist, as in Stuart Hall, 'New Ethnicities', in D. Morley and K.H. Chen (eds), *Stuart Hall, Critical Dialogues in Cultural Studies* (London & New York: Routledge, 1996), pp. 441–9.

[8] Nazie's silence in her aunt's household becomes a site of resistance in several ways: she keeps her emotions and dreams for herself, thereby highlighting Flora's extrovert, emotional and 'oriental' nature, which in turn places Nazie at the 'western' opposite; Nazie's dreams will culminate in her successful manipulation of marriage laws. Thus her subservience hides a maturing/knowing process through which she steps out of her relegated status.

These beliefs are the domain of women in the novel, although men dare not contest them. Throughout the novel women live their lives by an intricate codex of maneuvers aimed at avoiding, overturning and surviving the decrees and malice of these evil forces. Managing evil becomes as domestic a chore as raising children, washing, feeding and surviving marriages. All these chores are carried out in full view of other women. Very little remains private in the village; women talk, examine and peep into each others' houses and bodies, evoking a strong sense of harem life, enhanced by the Orientalist gaze.[9]

Except for the narration of Flora's journey, tales of the supernatural usually refer to traditional 'folkloristic wisdom' and they are delivered through the perspectives of Nazie and other village women. The subsequent link between the traditional role of women as storytellers and stereotypical representation of women's talk/chat undermines the authority of the stories. The only man who talks and tells is Shahin, Flora's shifty husband, who cheats and blackmails the women he seduces by his tall tales and fake silk fabric. Shahin, a grotesque cross-eyed and lice-ridden Casanova, testifies to women's gullibility, diminishing the authority of their stories even further. Although a man, his somewhat feminine appearance and untrustworthy ways single him out from other men in the novel. Thus the connection between gender and narrating the fantastic is reinforced, expanding the Orientalist view of ethnicity.

The transparency of women's fantastic tales contributes to this ethnic demarcation as they lend themselves quite readily to alternative interpretations which offer plausible and rational readings, consequently showing the villagers' tales to be superstitious and ignorant. For example, there is little doubt that the babies born to the village whore are not the demon's sons but conjugal twins, or that the plague that had devastated the village at the time of Nazie's birth was not the result of the dead chewing on their shrouds, but an epidemic that can't be fought off by digging graves and painting everything red. Once the western discourse constructs such readings, the fantastic is firmly contained within the marginalized framework of ethnic folklore.

However, as the narrative unfolds, these categories lose their hold and, subsequently, transparency gives way to complexity. The story/history of Nazie's birth at the time of the plague illustrates this shift towards multi-layered readings. For the women who keep telling Nazie about her birth in the dark kitchen, the story of the communal disaster, interwoven with 'superstitious' tales, is not merely an historical account. It is rather a magnified background for the incredible and mythical fight of Nazie's mother, who fought against a husband who wished the baby-girl dead; nature which sees to it that small and ill babies, such as Nazie, die; and a community who waited impatiently for her death and her burial, so

---

[9] This sexualized vision of the East blocks off access to women's deprivation by patriarchy on the one hand and to their solidarity on the other hand. However, the novel overturns this stereotypical view when the symbiotic relationships between Flora and Nazie unfold to reveal support and empathy rather than jealousy.

that graves could be dug out to reveal those dead responsible for the plague. The story of Nazie's mother is a female history of resistance and solidarity that relies on women's telling. These tellers pass on to Nazie the complexity of the maternal in patriarchy, reflected in the mother's attempts to abort yet another baby girl; the legacy of survival against the odds, reflected in the mother's fight to keep the baby alive; and the baby's miraculous recovery. The story will enable Nazie to encode its legacy in order to subvert the life prescribed to her by the inferiority of her social status as an orphan and her physical inferiority as her childish body is not fit for marriage/reproduction. The story will empower Nazie to circumvent the law that prohibits underage marriage and to deconstruct marriage as a sexual/reproductive concept. Nazie will marry her beloved Moussa before menstruation and her love will be emotionally rather than sexually consummated.

Nazie is the carrier of subversion in more than one sense. Her relationship with her cousin Flora breaks away from the framework of social hierarchy prescribed and implemented by Flora's mother. Instead of following the Cinderella role of the neglected and abused orphaned girl, the narrative builds symbiotic relationships between the two cousins in which the shift from folkloristic ethnicity to magical realism is embedded. That night, after eating a watermelon, Flora has secretly left home. Nazie, who shared her bed, was the first one to notice it but, instead of raising the alarm, she sets out on her own secret journey to secure a marriage permit from the mullah. The actions of the two girls reflect each other although neither had premeditated nor coordinated their actions, and intimacy can only partially explain it. The girls choose different paths and different narrative modes for carrying out their quests. While Nazie's plot follows realistic patterns, Flora's journey signifies a departure towards magical realism.

Flora's journey is a lone one; no one witnesses her travels in the dark village streets crawling with lusty men and opium dens or her carriage ride to the town where she has spent her wedding night with Shahin, hoping he would be found there. Once she steps out of the village boundaries her narrative is not processed by the village women and does not depend on hearsay and rumours. The authority of the narration on which magical realism relies for its suspension of reality cannot thus be questioned. The journey Flora is taking is incredible, for who would have imagined that the 'little brain' who has never left the village on her own could find her way to the next town; even more so is its end. Flora finds Shahin living with Lily who is pregnant with his child, in a house, which transforms the fantastic folklore into magical realism. The house and its owner Lily, the Bahai woman who sells medicines made of snake venom, are shrouded in mystery. The house is covered in shells and decorated with 'stuffed fish' above its door, dry fountains with stone-fish in its garden and marble. Lily is the ultimate Foreigner for Flora: she is a pale ghost-like woman (or perhaps not a woman) whose arms 'were tattooed with blue and green snakes down to the fingertips' (Rabinyan, p. 162). A family of snakes inhabits the house alongside Lily, and a treasure is hidden in its cellar walls.

The story of the house is first told by Shahin who tries to pacify Flora, explaining his desertion by the prospect of getting hold of the hidden treasure for the sake of her baby. Lily's mother, according to his story, had discovered the snakes after moving to the house, formerly inhabited by rich merchants. Every night she left food in the cellar and by the next morning she found gold coins, left for her by the snakes as a reward. Shahin, renowned for his lies, is not reliable at the best of times; particularly in this case, facing Flora's fury and devastation. Therefore, when a different history of the house is introduced, immediately after his version, his reliability is undermined even further. The new version tells of the two rich merchants who had to leave the house in a hurry never to return, leaving their money hidden in its walls. This version provides a plausible explanation for the gold coins, thus placing Shahin's story among other folklore tales in the novel. However, the new version, authorized by the narrator, concludes: 'A Bahai family without sons settled in the two storeys of the abandoned house, and a family of snakes moved into the basement' (Rabinyan, p. 174). Into the careful construction of a realistic narrative (the history of the merchants) a hypothesis which suspends realism (the family of snakes) is introduced and the fantastic gains credibility. It is presented unequivocally as an objective/real phenomenon or, in other words, it shifts its status from fantastic Oriental folklore into magical realism.[10]

The shift towards magical realism offers a complex of readings, ranging from the psychoanalytical to the metaphysical, none of which remains exclusive in the narrative. Snakes, stuffed fish, stone dry fountains and secrets in the cellar obviously belong to psychoanalytical readings while Lily, a play on Lillith the she-devil, belongs to a 'metaphysical' arena for a battle between good (Flora) and evil (Lily).[11] The obvious symbolism of phallic snakes, stone-fish as dead fertility, and cellars as subconscious primal sexual drives are rescued from transparency, when used to ridicule Shahin's misogyny, his greediness and grotesque Oedipal relationship with his father.[12]

These same elements also construct an ironic reading of the biblical Garden of Eden narrative, where seductive snake/woman (Lily) brought about the downfall of 'innocent' man (Shahin). Re-reading the Garden of Eden story not only parodies Shahin and Lily, but introduces new notions to the narrative that transform previous conceptions, those of the reader's view of silly Flora, and those of Flora herself. Her arrival at the house is a violent moment of awakening.

---

[10] Magical realism is used extensively in Israeli literature to subvert normative defense mechanisms, not only those employed for the oriental/western agenda. Robert Alter, 'Magic Realism in the Israeli Novel', in A. Mintz (ed.), *The Boom in Contemporary Israeli Fiction* (Hanover & London: University Press of New England, 1997), pp. 17–34.

[11] Good/evil duality is prevalent in fantastic narratives as Rosemary Jackson shows in *Fantasy: The Literature of Subversion* (London & New York: Methuen, 1981), pp. 53–6.

[12] Misogyny is Shahin's main characteristic as manifested in his dismissive treatment of women and his tall tales. His father's story, killing his wife by shoving her into an oven, and warning that seduced women must not conceive, are parodies of the Oedipal complex. Shahin fails to follow his father's teaching as Lily is pregnant with his child and his plan to kill her is diverted by the smell of the bread she is baking for him.

Confused and devastated she allows Shahin and Lily to draw her into their bed, but when their lovemaking becomes too passionate, she tries to escape what she perceives as perverse. Mistaking a window for a door, she falls down to her death, an ironic realization of falling-from-grace. Flora's death is the devastating consequence of the emergence of the uncanny. Not only in the Freudian sense of the objectification of unconscious sexual desires/fears, but also as Hélène Cixous has shown it to be, the experience of death/absence that the uncanny evokes when it empties the real of its meaning.[13] Flora's fall is the fall into a void that the uncanny has disclosed. Moreover, Lily's house is described as a house of death (turning fish into stone, etc.) from the moment Flora has arrived there. Flora is expelled from paradise (Garden of Eden) because of her newly acquired knowledge of the meaning of good and evil, or rather their empty meaning, which transforms her familiar world. Her violent death magnifies the destabilizing and uncanny nature of the fantastic, as the psychological reading cannot fully contain it within a unified reality. After all, the child Lily carries remains in the house as a real phenomenon after the death of Flora and her unborn child, thus expanding the good/evil dichotomy beyond the realm of subjective consciousness.

Consciousness raising or acquisition of knowledge triggers subversion through the shift from the ethnic to magical realism. While the folkloristic interpretation, epitomized by Flora before her journey, is not-knowing, the move to magical realism is all about knowing. Acquisition of knowledge also characterizes Nazie's parallel journey to the mullah, although in her case it is knowledge of the system rather than of the self. Nazie has to get a special marriage permit because her body has not yet reached maturity. In order to persuade the local mullah she needs to look older, therefore she puts on Flora's wedding dress and makes up her face. When these measures fail, she tears off her gold fish-shaped earings and offers them to the mullah who succumbs either to the bribe and her determination or to the symbolic menstruation (the bleeding ears). The successful outcome of her journey seems to endorse the western attributes she represents (knowledge, initiative, deliberation) at the expense of the oriental ones that have lead to Flora's death. While Flora remains true to the inscription of women's body even in her death, for she responds intuitively by following her 'gut reactions', Nazie rejects this inscription. She calculates her moves out of understanding the symbolic language of the body in patriarchy, replacing the reproduction discourse with an alternative one, conceptualizing the body in a modern western way.[14] Yet, the detailed analogy between Flora's and Nazie's journeys seems to repudiate this categorization, pointing out similarities rather than differences.

---

[13] Hélène Cixous, 'Fiction and its Phantoms: A Reading of Freud's 'Das Unheimliche' ('The Uncanny')', trans. R. Denomme, *New Literary History*, 7.3 (Spring 1976), 525–48.

[14] Roni Halperin, 'The Alternative Discourse of the Body', in Yael Azmon (ed.), *Will You Listen to my Voice?: Representations of Women in Israeli Culture* (Tel-Aviv: Van Leer & Hakibbutz Hameuchad, 2001), pp. 184–98. (Hebrew).

From the Orientalist perspective, locating the acquisition of knowledge at the site of the fantastic, which at its 'folkloristic' stage was synonymous with ignorance and superstitions, is ironic. Furthermore, women's knowledge, undermined by the initial categorization of folklore tales, is elevated in the context of magical realism. Lily's mother has kept her negotiations with the snakes a secret. She revealed it only to her daughter, warning her never to tell it to a man, even to a much loved husband: 'men she said are greedy, impatient and ungrateful. Only women, who brood all their lives on the secrets of life and of the kitchen, are capable of preserving the secrets of the cellar too, and of extracting blessings and remedies from the snakes' venom' (Rabinyan, p. 169). Lily's mother rewrites the story of the Garden of Eden. In her version of the story, Woman had the knowledge of the nature and rule of Man, which knowledgeable Lily uses to her own ends, while unknowledgeable Flora falls victim to. Lily's mother elevates the status of women's stories. What was dismissed as domesticity (kitchen) and craft (remedies) is actually the secret of life, outside and inside the cellar, or consciousness and sub-consciousness. Nazie's manipulation of the system, her mother's fight, as well as Flora's mother, who shows she has learnt that women had better take care of themselves rather than of their houses, prove Lily's mother right. The shift from ethnic/folkloristic to magical realism then is the empowering shift towards self-determination that defies categorization.

The move towards magical realism fuses the two axes around which the narrative evolves, that of the Nazie/Flora relationship and that of narrating the fantastic. Against the background of the Oriental journey of Flora, Nazie's counterpart, characterized as western, is read as its partial internalization (assuming Flora's looks and her status as a married woman), thus creating hybrid categories of identity. Correlatively, the fantastic as oriental folklore is exchanged for magical realism that resists categorization. Hence the boundaries that marked West/East and realistic/fantastic become blurred. This does not mean that the fantastic assumes an all-realistic countenance. To the contrary, the reading of the house of snakes authorized by the narrator and its biblical allusion, insistently sustain the ambiguity surrounding the fantastic. It is this ambiguity that ideologically empowers the fantastic by placing it in a liminal space that negates the initial Orientalist categorization presented at the onset of the narrative. This liminality questions the assumed stability of categories of ethnicity within the hegemonic Israeli discourse, showing them to be negotiable and exchangeable. Thus, the so-called innocent narrative of women and demons in far away Persia becomes a powerful narrative of subversion and resistance.

Magical Realism as Ideology:
Narrative Evasions in the Work of Nakagami Kenji

Mark Morris

Nakagami: 'Even in Japan now lots of people read Latin American literature, and young Latin American authors are being introduced one after another. Señor Borges, as a person of the first generation [of the new Latin American writing], I wonder how you regard that?

Borges: 'There is really nothing worth reading. Please go find some other culture.' (Laughter) . . .

                – Nakagami Kenji, *America, America: Amerika, Amerika*

Magic realism now comes to be understood as a kind of narrative raw material derived essentially from peasant society, drawing in sophisticated ways on the world of village or even tribal myth. . . . Recent debates, meanwhile, have complicated all this with yet a different kind of issue: namely the problem of the political or mystificatory value, respectively, of such texts.

                – Fredric Jameson, *'On Magic Realism in Film'*

I'm haunted by one character in Mario Vargas Llosa's *The Green House*. He's known by the name Fushía – which could come from the Japanese surname Fujiya; he is often addressed by the nickname Japonito – the little Jap. (The English translation opts for Jappy – not a word I've ever heard.) He's wandered over the border from Brazil into Peru after a violent gaol-break: 'Do you know that I sent them to the hospital? The newspapers talked about Japanese cruelty, . . . Oriental vengeance'.[1] He will become a pirate, organising one group of native jungle 'indios' to prey on others and steal their hard-won rubber harvest. By the end of the novel, he is back in the jungle, ravaged by leprosy, a 'small pile of living and bloody flesh' (Vargas Llosa, p. 368).[2]

---

[1] Mario Vargas Llosa, *The Green House* [*La casa verde*, 1965] (London: Picador, 1986), p. 23.

[2] Nakagami died in1994. I think he would have been hugely, wickedly gratified if he could ever have learned that the Fushía of *The Green House* had been derived in part from legends concerning a real-enough renegade Japanese-Brazilian name of Tushía (bounced back and

Given the fact that Brazil and Peru were the two countries in South America which attracted the largest number of Japanese migrants from the late-nineteenth century to the first four decades of the twentieth,[3] there is nothing surprising about a Japanese character popping up in South American writing. Observers of the political scene in Peru might even allow themselves the mildly Borgesian fantasy – in fact, I doubt they could resist it – of seeing in 'el Japonito' a cruel prefiguring of Vargas Llosa's political nemesis, Peruvian patriot, globe-trotting born-again Japanese citizen, Alberto Fujimori.[4]

My own fantasy is more literary, if still Borgesian. My Fushía, or Fujiya, has wandered into Vargas Llosa's novelistic jungle of circa 1965 from a book by Nakagami Kenji. The latter is called *Sennen no yuraku*, 'A Thousand Years of Pleasure', and was strangely enough published in 1982. Its six chapters tell the tales of six hard men: gamblers, thieves, cocksmen, dreamers, all of them from

---

forth in Portuguese and Spanish, probably Tsuchiya – one more ordinary Japanese surname). The legends were collected by the young Vargas Llosa on his first trip into the Amazonian jungle in 1958. As he wrote back then concerning this ' "blue beard of the jungle" ':

> He could be a character taken from a macabre novel. His name is Tushía – he is of Japanese origin – and he lives on the Santiago river on an island. In that inaccessible region, Tushía rules like a feudal lord.
> He has a personal harem made up of many women.

Kristal, Efraín, *Temptation of the Word: The Novels of Mario Vargas Llosa* (Liverpool: Liverpool University Press, 1998), p. 45.

[3] According to a survey conducted by the Japanese government in 1938, there were almost 198,000 Japanese residents in Brazil. 'This was followed by Hawaii at 151,850 and the continental US with 114,685. In Latin America, the second largest community at 22,150 was in Peru'; Stewart Lone, *The Japanese Community in Brazil, 1908–1940: Between Samurai and Carnival* (Basingstoke & New York: Palgrave, 2001), p. 135. If you factor in marriages and children, then Brazil is reasoned to have had 'a Nikkei [of Japanese origin] community that by the mid-1930s was well over half a million'; see Jeffrey Lesser, 'In Search of the Hyphen: Nikkei and Struggle over Brazilian National Identity', in *New Worlds, New Lives: Globalization and People of Japanese descent in the Americas and Latin America*, eds Lane Ryo Hirabayashi *et al.* (Stanford: Stanford University Press, 2000), p. 39. One of the most compelling stories of more recent Japanese-Brazilian experience has been the 'remigration' of some younger Nikkei Brazilians to Japan. 'The number of Japanese-Brazilians returning to Japan as temporary migrant workers in the fifteen years between 1985 and 1999 surpassed one quarter of a million, and has also surpassed the total number of Japanese citizens who have migrated to Brazil since 1908'; see Edson Mori, 'The Japanese-Brazilian *Dekasegi* Phenomenon', in *New Worlds, New Lives: Globalization and People of Japanese descent in the Americas and Latin America*, p. 238. I add this historical footnote merely to indicate that beyond evasions and excursions involving Nakagami's fictional characters lies a long, continuing story of migration between Japan and Latin America. Indeed, the winner in 1935 of the very first Akutagawa Prize, the Japanese Booker or Pulitzer, was Ishikawa Tatsuzô. His story 'Sôbô', 'Common people', was based on his own brief spell as a migrant to Brazil at the peak of emigration in 1930.

[4] During the 1990 presidential election in Peru, it seems many conservative Nikkei voters supported Vargas Llosa rather than the eventual victor Fujimori. The question of race marked

a bloodline named Nakamoto, doomed to painful or violent ends. Men such as Shin'ichirô.

A Thousand Years of Pleasure

Shin'ichirô's tale is entitled 'Strange Tales of La Plata'. Nakagami was working on the story during a sojourn in New York City during the early 1980s when Jorge Luis Borges, accompanied as was usual by then by his companion María Kodama, happened to visit the city. I don't know if the latter's Japanese ancestry in any way facilitated Nakagami's arrangements for the interview with one of his literary heroes, but he does include her comments in the published version I've cited from at the beginning of this essay. Nakagami explained the story he was writing like this: 'I've written a story about Argentina called "Strange Tales of La Plata". There have been many people from my home region of Kishû [Wakayama] who migrated to Argentina, Brazil and quite a few other places. So when I wrote the story I imagined the La Plata River in Argentina – that is, a river of silver, and a scene where there was silver in all kinds of places. There was silver everywhere.'[5]

Shin'ichirô was a loner who had tried his hand at a bit of Robin Hood-esque burglary, tried raising warblers on the side – local geisha prized the droppings as skin cleanser – and had colourful sexual conjunctions with several women. One of them, a former migrant returned from South America, plants the seed of his own eventual evasion from the *roji* – literally the 'alleyways', the ghetto or barrio in which much of Nakagami's fiction is located. He finally writes back to the *roji* from somewhere that may, or may not, be Argentina:

> The first letter: Suddenly saw a wide, wide prairie, grass stretching as far as the eye can see. Everything silver. The children eat food containing lots of silver and so they shit silver and die. The second letter: They said you could

some of the nastier moments of both campaigns, despite Vargas Llosa's efforts to reign in some of his FREDEMO Party loudmouths. Fujimori gave at least as good as he got. 'Fujimori, using this ethnic attack to his favour, won many votes by repeating the slogan "Little whites on one side, and Chinitos and Cholitos [Chinese and Indians] on the other" '; Raúl Araki, 'An Approach to the Formation of Nikkei Identity in Peru', in *New Worlds, New Lives: Globalization and People of Japanese descent in the Americas and Latin America*, pp. 84–5. Apropos of the character Japonito, and the exiled ex-president for that matter, it is worth mentioning that in Latin America such ethnic/racial labelling, in either Spanish or Portuguese, lacks some of the verbal violence packed into English language equivalents when launched from white British or North American mouths. An interesting analysis of the structuring force of race within Vargas Llosa's fiction is James W. Brown, ' "El Síndrome del expatriado": Mario Vargas Llosa y el racismo peruano', in *Mario Vargas Llosa*, ed. José Miguel Oviedo (Madrid: Taurus, 1987), pp. 15–24.

[5] Nakagami Kenji, *America, America: Amerika, Amerika* (Tokyo: Kadokawa Bunko, 1992), pp. 155–6. All translations from Japanese are my own.

buy a woman there and I go and they let me tie her up and have her, and they say, 'Pay up with something that can't be converted into gold or silver.' The third letter: Destruction of the Incas. [NB. Fictional characters don't have to be good at geography or history.] The fourth letter: A drunk who changed into an eagle flew about dangling his prick.[6]

After two years away, Shin'ichirô returns to the *roji*, a broken man. At the end of his tale, he is found stretched out dead besides a half-drained cup of liquid mercury.

Or perhaps Fushía is some sort of kin with Miyoshi, one other of the dangerous young men in 'A Thousand Years of Pleasure'. Nothing so well becomes his life as the manner of his departure from it. He does so in a style that has less to do with Vargas Llosa and more with the young García Márquez (or Carpentier? or even Borges?). Certainly the title of the book registers Nakagami's debt to his favourite among all Latin American authors, even while that title ambitiously claims to multiply the time-span ten-fold and reverse the emotional valence of *One Hundred Years of Solitude*. Nakagami leaves the telling of Miyoshi's fate to Oryû, the age-less midwife, all-purpose remembrancer and narrator of the *roji*:

> About the time the sun touched the earth and the warmth mounted up and the *natsufuyô* petals began to close, Miyoshi attached a rope to the cherry tree planted way around the side of the bamboo grove, and hung himself and died. It was the 10th of August. Auntie Oryû sighed, recollecting how at that very moment the dragon tattooed into his back stirred its limbs and began to crawl upwards; it stuck its head from out of Miyoshi's back and slipped forth. How on earth could his back have contained it? It swelled up huge, climbed further, and it wrapped its body twice around Miyoshi's body dangling from the branch. It gazed about as if to gauge signs of anyone approaching. Then slowly, taking its time, displaying a fat reptilian belly covered in scales like burnished silver, it continued to slip free, and when it had discovered itself completely Miyoshi's body was concealed, covered by the reptilian belly wrapped around it from head to toe. . . . There was a noise on the wind and it lifted its face as though ready to take flight. The dragon suddenly lifted its face into the sky and all the while unravelling its coils like so many loops of rope coming undone, it rose into the sky, then in a moment it had soared into the heavens, it flew a beeline such as to sunder earth from sky, whereupon lightening flashed and, arrived up above the clouds, it made one great circle about the place, and roared – the sound echoed off the clouds and turned to thunder.
> The rain began to fall the day Miyoshi died. (Nakagami, *Sennen*, pp. 76–7)

In attempting to package together narrative evasions, the fiction of magical realism and something as portentous as ideology, I am obviously trying to look beyond the literal stuff of characters making a dash for the border or going on futile quests for rivers and prairies of silver or escaping from life itself in an

---

[6] Nakagami Kenji, *Sennen no yuraku* [1982] (Tokyo: Kawade Bunko, 1992), p. 198.

explosion of gaudy images shaped into dramatic phrasing. What fascinates me about Nakagami's particular recasting of Latin American fiction is not simply the positive, creative force it lent his project but also something 'negative', or at least some things left out, evaded.

Nakagami is not the only Japanese writer to have tapped into 'magical realism [as] an international commodity'.[7] I've written elsewhere about the special way he was able to twin his reading of writers such as Vargas Llosa and García Márquez with that of one writer who was a significant point of reference and source of imaginative connections for many Latin American writers and their contemporaries in Japan – William Faulkner.[8] Although the Japanese literary field, of which he was a part, however marginal or contrary, does not generally fit any too snugly within, say, the contours of Franco Moretti's geography of world literature[9] or Pascale Casanova's world republic of letters,[10] Nakagami's tactical application of lessons learned from 'el Viejo' Faulkner and Latin American novelists matches well Casanova's vision of marginal, peripheral writers competing in the global cultural marketplace:

> Today it is these authors from the confines of the world who, having learned
> long ago to confront the specific laws and forces inscribed within the
> unequal structure of the literary universe and being conscious that they must
> be consecrated by the centres in order to have any chance of survival as
> writers, are the most open to the most recent aesthetic 'inventions', . . . to
> new Latin American novelistic solutions.
> (Casanova, pp. 67–8 [my translation])

In generating the fictional microcosm of the *roji*, and the sub-microcosm within it – the violent, homo-social brotherhood of machismo participated in by characters such as Shin'ichirô and Miyoshi, or the Tsuyoshi and Tanaka of the work I want to look at next – Nakagami did take the blueprint of a Yoknapatawpha County, as well as elements from García Márquez' Macondo (or from the isolated homo-social tensions of *Chronicle of a Death Foretold*) and from the fictional barrios of Lima, Callao and Piura through which Vargas Llosa's young males strut (as well as from the military academy of *The Time of the Hero*) and no doubt from early stories of Borges himself such as the classic 'Man on Pink Corner' in *A Universal History of Infamy*.[11]

---

[7] Lois Parkinson Zamora and Wendy Faris, 'Introduction: Daquiri Birds and Flaubertian Parrot(ie)s', in *Magical Realism: Theory, History, Community*, eds Zamora & Faris (Durham and London: Duke University Press, 1995), p. 2.

[8] Mark Morris, 'Gossip and history: Nakagami, Faulkner, García Márquez', *Japan Forum*, 8.1 (1996), 35–50.

[9] Franco Moretti, 'Conjectures on World Literature', *New Left Review*, 1 (Jan-Feb 2000), 54–68.

[10] Pascale Casanova, *La République mondiale des lettres* (Paris: Seuil, 1999).

[11] The fictional world of Porteño *compadritos* – one source for Nakagami's violent young men – grows not only out of Borges' youthful fascination with his city's popular culture of

However, the communities he created are not just fictional ghettos or barrios, marked by magically mystified plagues of poverty and exploitation, spun out of a head full of foreign tales of exotic local colour. The *roji* is his fictional dreaming of a real community such as the *buraku* or ghetto of his hometown Shingû in Wakayama prefecture. Communities of Japanese people, known generally as *burakumin*, who inhabited *buraku* scattered about Japan, were once treated not only as non-Japanese, but as hardly human (hinin, 'non-human', was an official category applied to them in pre-modern Japan; one other abusive word, *eta*, may be the ugliest term of abuse in the language still). They were at times subject to prejudices, oppression and occasional violence as bad as that experienced by India's untouchables. This past is sometimes acknowledged in Nakagami's writings, especially in essays such as the powerful 1978 back-to-roots travelogue *Kishû: Ki no kuni, ne no kuni monogatari* ('Ki Province: Tales of the trees of the land, of the roots of the land'). It is referred to several times by Oryû within the pages of 'A Thousand Years of Pleasure'. She has, for instance, heard from others what happened when the new Meiji government tried in 1871 to abolish the old categories of *eta* or *hinin*. 'The official diktat had gone forth, claiming all four classes to be equal, high and low all the same; it was by the bamboo spears of those farmers who'd found it outrageous that they'd been pierced, their homes put to the torch.' And she surmises that 'nobody ever apologised for what they'd done in the past. They may claim all classes to be equal, but if once again there were to be the kind of material shortages of long ago, if a disastrous earthquake were to strike as it had before, it was likely they'd all be slaughtered' (Nakagami, *Sennen*, p. 181; see also pp. 65, 130–1, 138).

In narrative practice, however, Nakagami rarely places the inhabitants of the *roji* in conflict with the rest of Japanese society in Shingû or with 'mainstream' Japanese characters anywhere else. For the most part they fight and kill each other, marry and have elaborate sexual relations with one another; their dramas have meaning and life only in the eyes and memories of each other. Conflict and contradiction tend to remain in the past. This foreshortening of the social and political seems inevitably to produce narratives that risk overly primitivising, exoticising the fictional avatars of the real *burakumin* whose hyperbolic ghosts they presume to be. (Let me recast the proposition in a Márquezean shorthand: imagine a Macondo without the United Fruit Company, with no brutally suppressed strike since no railway carried no bananas to no part of the rest of Colombia and the world market.) It may be that this evasion of conflict and contradiction was one factor which has

---

milongas, tango and dangerous characters (James Woodall, *The Man in the Mirror of the Book: A Life of Jorge Luis Borges* [London: Sceptre, 1996], pp. 19–20, 76–77, 93–5), but also from his attraction to one strange book encountered not long after its first publication: Herbert Asbury's 1927 *The Gangs of New York*. See Borges' distinctly pre-Hollywood 'Monk Eastman, Purveyor of Iniquities', in Jorge Luis Borges, *Collected Fictions*, trans. Andrew Hurley (New York and London: Penguin, 1998), pp. 25–30. Taking advantage of both the Scorsese film and Borges' cultural capital, Random House's reissue of *The Gangs of New York* inserts the first few pages of Borges' tale before Asbury's old Introduction.

generally allowed Japanese critics and readers to continue to read Nakagami's fiction without feeling challenged in their ordinary middle-class *mauvaise foi*.

Wings of the Sun

Nakagami Kenji wrote *Nichirin no tsubasa* ('Wings of the Sun') after and very much in the wake of 'A Thousand Years of Pleasure'. It is a lighter work, much less ornate and more tuned to the carnavalesque potential of some of his repertory company of *roji* characters. Two of the hard lads, Tsuyoshi and a mate always referred to weirdly as 'Mr Tanaka', have liberated a refrigerated van the former used for bringing fish to Shingû from the north coast, and two more young toughs have nicked an estate wagon. They set off across Japan on an unlikely pilgrimage. This is the story of a barrio on wheels, the *roji* roadshow. The van's cargo this time is a group of seven old aunties from the *roji*. The ghetto has been demolished, its denizens scattered. The young lads spring the old women from a rest home and decide to take them to see some of Japan outside the ghetto.

They go first to Ise to visit Japan's most important Shintô shrine, then on to places associated with the women's past lives working in the spinning mills or as prostitutes, and also to places of scenic beauty. There can be no return to a *roji* which no longer exists. This is an ultimate evasion. Journey's end for the five aunties who have survived till Chapter 9 (one has died visiting a daughter, one other has disappeared) is Tokyo and the surroundings of the Imperial Palace.

There are no direct markers of a Latin connection in 'Wings of the Sun'. Yet all that exuberance of style, and many of the strengths as well as fictional evasions of the previous work, make themselves felt here as well. Indeed, while tracing connections of Latin American writing in 'A Thousand Years of Pleasure' can seem a bit reductive, like shooting symbolic fish in a narrative barrel, to me it is more intriguing to tease out connections that never quite show their hand. I would like briefly to consider two aspects of 'Wings of the Sun' which relate to a kind of ideology, to the sort of thematic foreshortening referred to above. One is the myth of origins provided for the now defunct ghetto; the second concerns a certain linking of extremes, through which Nakagami appears to try out an imperial version of magical realism.

Early in the journey as they roll on towards Ise, one of the old aunties recollects a story about the beginnings of the *roji*:

> It all began at a lotus pond, the site of a fresh water spring in the hills above the eventual *roji*. A man and woman from elsewhere came across it, decided to build a hut there taking advantage of the fresh water and using the trees for timber. A child was born. 'What they said in the *roji* was that the child was no normal child. They said it had three arms or four limbs like an animal. Yet the parents' love for this child was total, so they brought it up and had no other children. When it was five the child drowned in the pond.'[12]

---

[12] Nakagami Kenji, *Nichirin no tsubasa* [1984] (Tokyo: Bunshun Bunko, 1992), p. 22.

One other auntie chips in, 'In order to raise that child, they had drowned other children born one after another in the lotus pond!' The narration expands the anecdote:

> In order to bring up the child fated to be born as though an animal, they buried the next child born, as well as the next one after that, in the mud of the pond, cut off their breath. Every spring the lotus plants blossomed with beautiful flowers. After the [first] child died the two of them took the spring water welling up from the lotus pond and used it, as they began the task of treating the hides of dead horses. (Nakagami, *Nichirin*, p. 22)

So rather than a community formed through exclusion from and conflict with the rest of Japanese society in the town of Shingû or region of Wakayama, this *roji* generated itself almost spontaneously: ancestors appear, commit ancestral crimes, and found a tradition of leather working. The mixing of beauty and death so prominent in 'A Thousand Years of Pleasure' here takes on folkloric colouration. Yet in imagining a child marked by animal-like features, and in deploying characters with similar traits in other texts, Nakagami risks the same danger he does when spinning out an imagery of blood and pollution in his tales of the cursed Nakamoto lads. Through their historical association with dirty and defiling trades – disposal of animal and human corpses, serving as gaolers and executioners, leather working, sandal making – *burakumin* were often victims of abusive superstitions about their animality. Nakagami may have believed that having come from a *buraku* neighbourhood, he could take such risks. No non-*buraku* author would in recent decades have escaped severe censure for doing the same.[13]

Even during the early stages of the journey, the aunties sense that they are leaving ordinary reality behind. At their first halt one observes, 'It's only a little while since we started driving yet we've made it here – so, aunties, it feels like we've dashed through the heavens, come flying from mountain to mountain' (Nakagami, *Nichirin*, p. 11). Others voices agree that while they're shut up in the

---

[13] There is a lot of business about blood in 'A Thousand Years of Pleasure', as in other texts dealing with the Nakamoto lineage of doomed young men. Oryû will attribute Miyoshi's dazzling good looks to 'the undeniable Nakamoto blood flowing through flesh that made you wonder how delicious it would taste if you hacked some off, cut it up to eat' (Nakagami, *Sennen*, p. 49). She tells us that the catastrophes hovering over them are due to some ancestral curse. Generations ago some sinful Ur-Nakamoto may have slaughtered a pregnant beast, one other perhaps failed to recognise Buddha disguised as a beggar and refused him water to drink: 'Whatever one might claim, now there was actually nothing any one of the young lads could do to halt their gradual destruction due to that blood, stagnant yet for that very reason all the more pure, which flowed within them' (Nakagami, *Sennen*, p. 50). Dramatic stuff no doubt, but Nakagami is playing a dangerous game with such a primitivist exoticism. Modern pseudo-science was only too ready to reinforce older patterns of prejudice when, from the late-nineteenth to early twentieth centuries, *burakumin* might be characterised as genetically defective, bearers of tainted blood.

van as it motors along the highway, 'you lay down on the bedding, put your ear
to the floor, but it doesn't sound like we're running along the surface of the earth'
(Nakagami, *Nichirin*, p. 12). Things get more magical in proximity to the force
of the gods and a once divine Emperor.

When they arrived in front of Ise Shrine the sky was all milky white. None of
the old women seemed able to contain the excitement in her heart . . .. Auntie
San stood there, holding her bamboo-handled broom . . . and breathed in a deep
breath to quell the joy in her breast. It was as though, along with the chilly
morning air, there had entered into her breast the spirit of a god who would
purify her of the bodily poisons accumulated by her up till now . . .
   'When the sun rises up, there'll be lots of worshippers, so let's start cleaning
from way inside,' said Auntie Yoso, instructing them to get cleaning just like it
was the roji village hall. . . .
   There was morning mist flowing past like white cotton. To Auntie San,
suddenly that mist appeared like some umbilicus used by the god – it seemed
that perhaps she was now being granted a glimpse with her very eyes into the
wooden grove of the god only freshly reborn from out of the mists of the
night . . ..

Auntie San began sweeping the sacred gravel path with her broom, and more and
more she had a feeling that long ago she herself had served a noble deity who, were
one to gaze directly upon him open-eyed would annihilate you with his resplen-
dence; she had been a woman who consoled the god for the pain felt each time, day
after day, he was reborn anew; she had aided him, taking upon her own body pollution one hardly dare call pollution, produced ever so slightly each time he was
born anew; and she felt that were she to work away like this, continued to work
herself to the bone, the god might slip forth from his tabernacle, come right up to
her ear and call out, 'San – you've done well.' Auntie San gave a start, stood frozen
to the spot – were those august words a daydream? (Nakagami, *Nichirin*, pp. 82–4)

Magic and the Emperor

What seems at stake in this and other passages is both a sort of Shintoification
of magical realism, and the presentation of a different tale of origins both more
profound and more troubling than that mentioned above.

It is generally accepted that the first traceable *buraku*-like hamlets or urban
enclaves seem to have emerged not only with the increasingly complex division
of labour in and around the early capital, but also in association with an increasingly sanctified emperor supported by religious institutions devoted to numerous
rites involving purification. In a sense, Auntie San is the auntie of all *burakumin*.
The problem for me is that she enjoys the job.

Arrived in Tokyo, the old women are eager to catch a glimpse of the Imperial
Palace, or at least the palace grounds. Tsuyoshi and 'Mr Tanaka' drop the five
remaining aunties off at the broad plaza near the main entrance. They step

forward toward the tight-shut gateway, then stop to remove their shoes before
kneeling in prayer:

> The cab drivers looked at the old women in amazement. From the road a horn
> honked, as if to tease the old women. Auntie San stared at the gate where a
> fresh-faced sentry stood guard; she gazed at a shimmer of white light flashing
> in space and reflected down in the water of the moat and she sensed that there
> beyond the gate was a person more dazzling than the sun, one who would wait
> beside her and listen to her as she began to relate, in her harsh husky voice,
> what she had been through. Auntie San's heart was full. She wanted to appeal
> directly to him, say that she had long continued to embrace a feeling, just like
> those feelings when she had been young and left abandoned by some man,
> feelings that did not begrudge all the sadness savoured living thousands of
> years there in the roji behind the lowest of all the hills in Kumano, nor the
> sacrifice of – all the while longing for the warmth of the sun, for the sun, one
> could become weapons and shield – one life, two lives . . . .
>   From behind, someone called, 'Auntie!' Auntie San turned to face the voice,
> saw through squinted eyes Tsuyoshi's face dazzling, the sun behind him. She
> rose up slowly. 'Yes, how fine. It's because the Emperor lives here that the
> likes of us rubbish are able to live our own lives.' (Nakagami, *Nichirin*, p. 357)

Imperial anti-realism? Imperial magical realism? I don't know what to term the
style Nakagami has forged here. The non-real association of *burakumin* Tsuyoshi
with the radiance of the Emperor is elaborated elsewhere in 'Wings of the Sun'
(p. 355). One can suspect that writing, as he was in this work, in a lighter vein,
aiming at a more popular audience, Nakagami was in part enjoying a laugh at his
liberal friends' critical attitude towards the imperial family. He was never shy
about provoking controversy and certainly cultivated, when it suited him, an
image of himself as too rough, too wild for liberal protocols. And 'Wings of the
Sun' is no simple magical-realist hymn to the Emperors; it is often truly funny
and, when the tough lads pick up young women on their travels, inventively
obscene. Yet pronouncements made in other forums and passages in his essays
show him halfway seriously fascinated by the conjunction of emperor and
burakumin, as though the extreme opposites of the social scale might somehow
logically combine against the great middling mass of ordinary prejudice. It is
said that back at the time of the 1871 proclamation, which, in theory, freed the
excluded *burakumin* from the legal discrimination of the past, many of them had
felt a sense of gratitude towards the Emperor Meiji in whose name the proclamation had been issued. It is noticeable as well that in some of the earliest representations of *burakumin* in fiction from late that same century, any sympathy
or support *burakumin* characters were likely to receive from outside the ghetto
was conceived as coming from aristocratic rather than middle-class figures.
Perhaps Nakagami's example may simply remind us that while 'magical
realism's assault on . . . basic structures of rationalism and realism has inevitable
ideological impact', it is not necessarily the case that 'magical-realist texts are
subversive' (Zamora & Faris, pp. 67–8). I prefer to stick close to Fredric

Jameson, and the Latin American critics he draws upon, and to keep one eye fixed on the potential 'mystificatory value . . . of such texts'[14] when reading Nakagami or Latin American or any other novelists.

And so it happens that at journey's end, the remaining aunties just disappear. The two lads, Tsuyoshi and 'Mr Tanaka', return to their van and find the old women gone, as is most of their gear. They have disappeared into the megalopolis, perhaps into a vision of divine and imperial glory at the empty centre of the empire of signs. A garrulously empty centre from which a powerful anti-democratic ideology might still reach forth, some of us still persist in worrying, to console those weak enough, frightened enough or angry enough to need it.

[14] Jameson, Fredric, 'Magic Realism in Film', *Critical Inquiry*, 12 (Winter 1986), 301–25 (p. 302).

Legend, Fantasy and the Birth of the New in
Los funerales de la Mamá Grande
by Gabriel García Márquez

Robin Fiddian

Critics have for a long time acknowledged the insight and artistry of Gabriel García Márquez's fictional representations of the mindsets – political, religious, cultural, and imaginative – of Latin American societies of contemporary and recent times. In the context of a colloquium on magical realism and fantastic modes of writing, the title story of the author's first major collection of short fictions, *Los funerales de la Mamá Grande (Big Mama's Funeral)* (1962), cries out for attention, representing, as it does, a landmark in García Márquez's evolution away from a realistic style of writing that he practised with few exceptions during the mid-nineteen-fifties, towards another mode that has variously been called 'fantasy', 'magical realism', and 'a new brand of realism [. . .] expanded and enhanced by magical improbabilities [. . .]'.[1] Featured as the last story in the eponymous collection, 'Big Mama's Funeral' was also the last-written, dating, by most accounts, from the end of 1959.[2] In addition to occupying a pivotal position in the author's output, there are also grounds for considering the story symptomatic of a moment of crisis in Latin American political history of the time. With this dual perspective in mind, the model of magical realism proposed by Stephen Slemon provides a yardstick for measuring the exactness of fit between 'Big Mama's Funeral' and that narrative mode, whilst the discipline of post colonial studies brings new and complementary perspectives to

---

[1] George R. McMurray, *García Márquez* (New York: Frederick Ungar, 1977), p. 65. The story had been characterized earlier as a 'fantasy' by Judith Goetzinger, 'The Emergence of a Folk Myth in "Los funerales de la mamá grande"', *Revista de estudios hispánicos* (Alabama) VI.2 (1972), 237–48 (p. 247). James Higgins invokes the term 'magical realism', wisely surrounding it with scare quotes, in 'Gabriel García Márquez', included in Philip Swanson (ed.), *Landmarks in Latin American Fiction* (London: Routledge, 1990), pp. 141–60 (p. 144).

[2] Mario Vargas Llosa asserts that García Márquez wrote the story at the end of 1959 in Bogotá, in *García Márquez: Historia de un deicidio* (Barcelona: Barral, 1971), p. 58. This claim is corroborated by Jacques Gilard in the prologue to volume IV of his compilation, Gabriel García Márquez, *Obra periodística*, 6 vols. (Barcelona: Bruguera, 1982), pp. 71–2.

bear on a story whose ideological and technical complexities still remain to be appreciated in full.

La Marquesita de la Sierpe: A Living Legend

A review of work published on 'Big Mama's Funeral' uncovers a surprising blind spot, vis-à-vis connections with an earlier series of journalistic articles by García Márquez on a legendary figure known as La Marquesita de la Sierpe.[3] As early as 1952, García Márquez had written about 'una española bondadosa y menuda, dueña de una fabulosa riqueza [. . .] a quien se conoció con el nombre de la Marquesita' (a petite and kindly Spanish woman with fabulous wealth, who became known by the name 'la Marquesita'). According to popular belief, the woman lived on her own in La Sierpe, 'un país de leyenda dentro de la costa atlántica de Colombia' (a legendary land in the Atlantic coastal region of northern Colombia) (p. 117), where she was regarded as 'una especie de gran mamá de quienes le servían' (a kind of mother figure to all who worked for her). 'La Marquesita vivía sola en una casa, pero una vez al año hacía un largo viaje por toda la región, visitando a sus protegidos, sanando a los enfermos y resolviendo problemas económicos' (La Marquesita lived all on her own, but once a year she would journey through the length and breadth of the region and visit those who were in her care, curing them of their ills and solving any economic problems they had) (p. 119).

Equally at home within the natural and the supernatural, 'La Marquesita podía estar en diferentes lugares a la vez, caminar sobre las aguas y llamar desde su casa a una persona en cualquier lugar de La Sierpe en que ésta se encontrara' (La Marquesita could be in different places at once, she could walk on water and summon any individual to her home, no matter where in La Sierpe they might be). 'Lo único que no podía hacer era resucitar a los muertos, porque el alma de los muertos no le pertenecía. "La Marquesita tenía pacto con el diablo", explican en La Sierpe' (The only thing she could not do was bring the dead back to life, because she had no power over the souls of the dead. 'La Marquesita had a pact with the Devil', so the inhabitants of La Sierpe say). Significantly, the use of the present tense, in this last sentence ('so the inhabitants of La Sierpe say'),

---

[3] See, in particular, 'La Marquesita de la Sierpe: Malaria, hechicería y supersticiones en una región de la costa atlántica. El hombre que pisó la leyenda', included in Gabriel García Márquez, *Obra periodística*, II, pp. 117–21; page references cited in the text of the present study are to this edition, and all translations are my own. The first critic – to my knowledge – to refer to this material and the two companion pieces that are reproduced on pp. 136–40 and 145–53 of the same volume, was Robert L. Sims, 'Matriarchal and Patriarchal Patterns in Gabriel García Márquez's *Leaf Storm*, "Big Mama's Funeral" and *One Hundred Years of Solitude*: the Synergetic, Mythic and *Bricolage* Synthesis', in Bradley A. Shaw & Vera Nora-Godwin (eds), *Critical Perspectives on Gabriel García Márquez* (Lincoln, Nebraska: Society of Spanish and Spanish-American Studies, 1986), pp. 33–49 (pp. 36–7).

attests to the actual currency of the legend of La Marquesita at the time of its (fictional) recording back in 1952 – a point that is foreshadowed in the earlier assertion that the folk of La Sierpe 'creen en la Marquesita' (believe in La Marquesita) (p. 119) and confirmed shortly after in the report that 'La leyenda dice que La Marquesita vivió todo el tiempo que quiso. Y según la versión más generalizada, quiso vivir más de 200 años' (Legend has it that La Marquesita lived as long she wished. According to the most widespread belief, her wish was to live for over two hundred years) (p. 120).

To those familiar with García Márquez's story, the connections between the 1952 articles and the fictional narrative of 1959 are obvious, justifying the view of the two works as intertexts.[4]

Narrative Tone and Structure

The very first paragraph of 'Big Mama's Funeral' incorporates references to the matriarch's title and longevity in a narrative introduction that is remarkable for its directness and popular tone of address:

> Esta es, incrédulos del mundo entero, la verídica historia de la Mamá Grande, soberana absoluta del reino de Macondo, que vivió en función de dominio durante 92 años y murió en olor de santidad un martes del setiembre pasado, y a cuyos funerales vino el Sumo Pontífice.
>
> (This, oh incredulous people of the world, is the true story of Big Mama, sovereign of the kingdom of Macondo, who exercised absolute power for a period of 92 years and died a saintly death on a Tuesday of September last, and whose funeral was attended by the Pope).[5]

From the very start, we are addressed as universal readers and challenged to accept as historical truth an account delivered by a narrator whose speech is reminiscent of popular story-telling and street discourse. The opening paragraph is predicated on the assumption that we should believe two propositions: the first is the existence of Big Mama, who has just died after nearly a century of sovereign rule over a Spanish-speaking regional community; the second is the – at least imaginary – existence of the realm of Macondo. Later on, when we learn that Big Mama began to rule her kingdom at the age of twenty-two (p. 133), it will become increasingly difficult to believe in the literal truth of her existence; rather, we will be persuaded that the prevailing style of narration is fantastic and hyperbolic. Yet, the introduction, almost immediately, of references to the 'Sumo

---

[4] I use the term 'intertext' in line with Michael Riffaterre, 'Interview', *Diacritics*, XI.4 (1981), 12–16.

[5] *Los funerales de la Mamá Grande* (Buenos Aires: Sudamericana, 1969), pp. 125–47 (p. 127). All page references cited in the text are to this edition, and all translations into English are my own.

Pontífice' (The Pope) and of several place-names identified with northern Colombia, appeals to a shared sense of worldly reality that gives at least some credence to the narrator's claim that his story is a 'chronicle' (p. 144).

Certain familiar paradigms of geo-political and historical knowledge are inscribed early on in the text, allowing Caribbean, Latin American and his-panophone readers alike to recognise immediately some typical traits of the world of Macondo. 'Big Mama's Funeral' registers an opposition between the local and the national, in which it privileges 'los gaiteros de San Jacinto, los con-trabandistas de la Guajira' (the bagpipers of San Jacinto, the smugglers of la Guajira) and other local types over the figure-heads of national government ('el presidente de la república y sus ministros'; 'the President of the Republic and his Ministers', p. 127); the narrator displays a close affinity with what Ángel Rama termed appositely the 'complejo cultural' of a local or regional community,[6] in this case the *costa* region of Colombia where García Márquez was born and spent the first twelve years of his life. Onto this regional template is grafted a relation between the local and the universal, evoked through the mention of the attendance, at Big Mama's funeral, of no less a personage than his Holiness the Pope. To the amusement of this commentator at least, the head of the Universal and Apostolic Church is absorbed summarily into the local domain, where he has no option but to languish in a backwater for weeks on end, handing out sweets to children in an irreverent inversion of hierarchical assumptions about author-ity and subjects, and centres and peripheries.

With regard to temporal setting, the narrative evokes a fictional present – in the wake of Big Mama's funeral – that can be understood with reference to a past marked by Spanish colonial rule and post colonial national independence. Big Mama's centenarian priest, el padre Antonio Isabel, and her gun-toting nephew, Nicanor, appear as easily recognisable ciphers of the twin institutions of the Catholic Church and *caciquismo* (local bossism), which, along with 'militares de robusto tórax acorazado de insignias' (military officers with powerful chests armour-plated with medals) (p. 145), took charge of the affairs of most Spanish American countries at the end of the colonial phase of their history, continuing throughout the period of their independence, down, in many cases, to the pres-ent day.

Two other features that stand out at the beginning of 'Big Mama's Funeral' are an explicit concern with historiography – by which I mean the nature and con-struction of historical accounts – and an awareness of the process of narrative itself, including the moment of enunciation. The longer of the two paragraphs of exposition claims Big Mama's funeral as 'la más espléndida ocasión funeraria que registren los anales históricos' (the most splendid funeral occasion that will ever be mentioned in the annals of history), stressing the element of qualitative

---

[6] Rama characterizes the different 'complejos culturales' of the regions of Colombia in *García Márquez. Edificación de un arte nacional y popular* (Montevideo: Universidad de la República, 1987), p. 13.

judgement that determines both the inclusion and the relative place of events in the historical record. The paragraph also bears witness to the narrator's determination to register the details of what he calls 'this national commotion', before the arrival of the official historians (antes de que tengan tiempo de llegar los historiadores) (p. 127); his declaration of a pre-emptive strike raises important questions about who is speaking. On behalf of what group? And in the interests of which, and whose, truth?

After the exposition of 'Big Mama's Funeral', the narrative content of the story is organised into two roughly symmetrical parts: the first of these dwells on the final hours of the dying matriarch up until the moment when she 'emit[s] a sonorous belch' and dies (p. 137). Thereafter, the focus shifts to the preparations and eventual celebration of Big Mama's funeral, which attracts an array of national and international dignitaries to Macondo. A final paragraph expands the narrative perspective, reporting the aftermath of the funeral and gesturing ever so subtly towards the larger significance of Big Mama's death in the political and historical spheres.

Big Mama

On closer reading, the first part of García Márquez's narrative builds up a portrait of Big Mama through the medium of a narrator who displays unrivalled knowledge about her personal and family history and is far from impartial in his judgements and observations. He characterises Big Mama, first, as 'soberana absoluta del reino de Macondo' (absolute monarch of Macondo) (p. 127) and, shortly after, as 'la matrona más rica y poderosa del mundo' (the richest and most powerful matron in the world) (p. 130). The shift from 'soberana' to 'matrona' betrays a certain casualness with respect to conceptual categories, while the double superlative in 'más rica y poderosa del mundo' makes a claim that is patently hyperbolical. Subsequently, we are told that Big Mama is used to commanding droves of underlings who populate her vast estate (her 'hacienda desmedida', p. 128) like the members of a tribe ('su tribu', p. 130). Despite internal evidence locating the narrative in and around the late nineteen-fifties, the descriptions of Big Mama's personal dealings are redolent of serfdom and the feudal order of medieval Europe. With greater precision, the narrator attests to 'una hegemonía que colmaba dos siglos' (more than two centuries of hegemony) (p. 129) centred around her family name, Castañeda y Montero, which is now destined to disappear. The existence of a dynastic line corrupted by endogamy carries parodic echoes of several of the royal families of Europe fabled for their inbreeding and degeneracy, while the number of bastards wandering around Big Mama's estate evokes the stigmatised stories of family life told in numerous Spanish American novels, of which the most famous and quintessential, perhaps, is *Pedro Páramo* (1955) by Juan Rulfo (Mexico, 1918–86).

In a detailed account, the narrator of 'Big Mama's Funeral' traces her 'patrimonio físico', or material wealth, back to the Colonial period and three *encomiendas* – grants of land and Indian labourers – 'que con el transcurso del tiempo, en virtud de intrincados matrimonios de conveniencia, se habían acumulado bajo el dominio de la Mamá Grande' (which over time, as a result of ingeniously contrived marriages of convenience, had amassed under Mama Grande's control) (p. 135). Amounting to approximately one hundred hectares, the land would have remained fallow, but for the decision of Big Mama's ancestors to rent it out piecemeal to three hundred and fifty two families who would put it to productive use. This arrangement guaranteed Big Mama annual income in the form of rent and a proportion of the agricultural output, at the same time as it prevented the State from reclaiming the land. The concentration, within Big Mama's domain, of the six prosperous boroughs ('poblaciones') of the district of Macondo brought additional benefits in the form of tax revenue on buildings, and payments that the government was obliged to make 'por el uso que los ciudadanos hacían en las calles' (for the townsfolk's enjoyment of rights of way). Through these and other 'circunstancias históricas', or accidents of history (p. 135), Big Mama's economic resources and her power base appear as a distorted version of the Spanish colonial heritage in the Americas, further imaged as a stash of treasure 'enterra[do] en algún lugar de la casa durante la Guerra de Independencia' (buried somewhere in the house during the war of Independence) and never found, in spite of excavations carried out by successive generations of family members (p. 136).

The exaggeration and distortion noted above also colour the litany, pronounced by Big Mama on her deathbed, of her 'bienes morales', or moral possessions (p. 136). This 'patrimonio invisible' (invisible heritage) (p. 137) – in the narrator's alternative notation – mixes up institutional, material, political, and philosophical categories such as the nation's territorial waters and the colours of the flag, human rights, free elections, the supreme court of justice, linguistic purity, the ship of state, and republican traditions, in a sprawling list of no fewer than forty items that mimics Big Mama's indiscriminate appetite for moral and political control. The passage is not devoid of humour deriving from its incongruous juxtapositions and relentless satire – particularly of the rhetoric and ideology of a conservative class identified quintessentially, in García Márquez's mind, with the Colombian capital, Bogotá ('la Atenas sudamericana', the Athens of South America, p. 137). But the narrator also makes the serious point that the appropriation, by Big Mama and her cronies, of the ideals and catchwords of democracy along with the values and slogans of a stagnant and reactionary conservatism, gave moral legitimacy to a centuries-long monopoly on power.

The narrator's point about moral legitimacy ('la justificación moral', p. 137) opens up the question of who might be responsible for a regime of hegemony and privilege that has endured so long. Speaking in his own voice, and no longer ventriloquising as Big Mama, the narrator devotes considerable space to criticizing the national authorities in Bogotá for their historical connivance in the dynastic abuse of power. Big Mama's involvement in violent and illegal practices, including armed support for warring political factions and rampant electoral fraud, does not deter the ruling classes from regarding her as their ally. In their view, 'Ella era la prioridad del poder tradicional sobre la autoridad transitoria, el predominio de la clase sobre la plebe, la trascendencia de la sabiduría divina sobre la improvisación mortal' (She embodied the prior claim of traditional power over transitory forms of authority, the superiority of class over the common people, [and] the prevalence of divine wisdom over the improvisation of mere mortals) (p. 139). As soon as he learns of her death, the Head of State orders nine days of national mourning and solemnly ascribes Big Mama to 'la categoría de heroína muerta por la patria en el campo de batalla' (the category of heroine who has given up her life for the fatherland on the field of battle) (p. 140).

That the representatives of national institutions should side with the defenders of local tradition and inherited privilege is perhaps to be expected, along with the satirical barbs directed by the narrator against the figure of the president and that of Big Mama. A more interesting aspect of his assessment of Big Mama's anachronistic regime is his criticism of the role of the common people in its historical operations and continuity. For, whilst it cannot be denied that the people have been victims of what is de facto a feudal abuse of power, they are, he suggests, also guilty of complicity in their own repression and mystification. He makes this point early on in his narration when he says, 'Nadie conocía el origen, ni los límites ni el valor real del patrimonio, pero todo el mundo se había acostumbrado a creer que la Mamá Grande era dueña de las aguas corrientes y estancadas, llovidas y por llover, y de los caminos vecinales, los postes del telégrafo, los años bisiestos y el calor, y que tenía además un derecho heredado sobre vida y haciendas' (No one knew precisely how [Mama Grande's] estate had come into being, how far it extended, or how much it was really worth, but everybody had come to believe that Mama Grande had control over running and stagnant waters, past and future rainfall, local thoroughfares, telegraph poles, leap years and the heat, and that she also had inherited rights over their lives and property) (pp. 129–30). Custom and belief are factors in the persistence of the status quo, including belief in the most irrational and ridiculous propositions, such as Big Mama's 'ownership' – natural, and therefore incontestable – of past and future rainfall and leap-years – just two of many absurdities that are attributed to the *pueblo* by one who knows its motivations, including nostalgia for an aristocratic order, its prejudices, and most damagingly, its moral and rational deficiencies. The point is reinforced in the following paragraph: 'A nadie se le había ocurrido pensar que la Mamá Grande fuera mortal' (It hadn't occurred to anybody that Mama Grande might die one day) (p. 130).

The Narrator

The position of the narrator within this critique is complex and many-sided. Because he identifies with *costa* culture, he resists the centralizing impulses of national authority and feels proud that no less a personage than the Pope should visit 'el reino de la balsamina y de la iguana' (the realm of the balsam apple and the iguana) (p. 143) and play a cameo role in the greatest spectacle ever seen in

Macondo. Regionalist sentiment goes so far as to align him with that dimension of Big Mama's persona which makes her a symbol of *costa* worth and glory. However, he offers few apologies for the ordinary people of Macondo, and fewer still for their exploitative sovereign, Big Mama, as I shall now illustrate.

In his presentation of Big Mama, the narrator exploits a full range of carnivalesque techniques to diminish her aura and demystify the legends that help maintain her grip on power. Principally, he centres attention on her massive physique, which he subjects to some vicious, if colourful jibes. An early image represents Big Mama taking the evening air on the terrace, 'con todo el peso de sus vísceras y su autoridad aplastado en su viejo mecedor' (with the full weight of her guts and her authority squashed into her old rocking chair) (p. 130). Contempt takes on openly misogynous inflections in a later scene of Big Mama stretched out on her deathbed, with barely a sign of life detectable in the gentle movement of her matriarchal boobs ('en la tenue respiración de sus tetas matriarcales'). At this point, the narrator chooses to elaborate: 'La Mamá Grande [. . .], que fue dotada por la naturaleza para amamantar ella sola a toda su especie, agonizaba virgen y sin hijos' (Big Mama, whom Nature [had] endowed with enough milk to feed all her race, was dying a virgin and without issue) (p. 133) – a condemnation of instinctual denial and sterility that may be explained in part as relaying popular hostility toward Big Mama, but whose vulgarity and vindictiveness are none the less remarkable for that.

With the announcement of her death, Big Mama ceases to occupy the foreground of narrative attention and becomes a mere point of reference in a larger drama, which is that of her funeral. Overshadowed by national politics and the figure of the Pope, who, with delightful disregard for probability, makes the journey from the Vatican to the tropics by gondola and overnight, Big Mama is mentioned only in passing in the second half of the story. In the final paragraphs, reports of the 'grandeur', 'splendour', and 'glory' of her funeral are shown to be tongue in cheek, as they yield to an unflattering depiction of the entombment of her putrefied corpse and to the suggestion that her story contains both a lesson and a warning ('lección y escarmiento', p. 147) to future generations. Through this evocation of a topos of exemplary literature, the narrator gestures towards possibilities of interpretation which are likely to compromise Big Mama's reputation and further discredit her in the eyes of the reader.

Modes of Fiction

In the light of the foregoing analysis of the narrative design of 'Big Mama's Funeral', it is appropriate to consider two essential questions: first, what connection exists between García Márquez's narrative and the modes, as we understand them, of the fantastic and/or magical realism? And, second, what connection exists between 'Big Mama's Funeral' and the category of the post-colonial? Apropos the first matter, it is difficult to see how García Márquez's story narrates anything that might be considered fantastic in the manner of the worlds depicted by Edgar Allan Poe, Jorge Luis Borges, Carlos Fuentes (in stories such as 'Chac Mool' or 'Tlactocatzine, del jardín de Flandes'), or Julio Cortázar (in innumerable short works). I am willing to concede the mixture of the familiar and the implausible in García Márquez's imaginary town of Macondo and his story of a tropical matriarch who dies at the age of one hundred and fourteen and is granted a State funeral. But there is nothing magical in this; rather, there is a stretching of credibility, aided by generous helpings of humour. We are not yet in the realm of flying carpets or acts of levitation that will occur on an undifferentiated plane of events in *Cien años de soledad (One Hundred Years of Solitude)* (1967). Nor are we immersed in the imaginary world(s) of native American peoples, recreated with anthropological exactitude by Miguel Angel Asturias in *Hombres de maíz (Men of Maize)* (1949), for example.[7] What we are dealing with is a simulacrum of a popular mind-set, including its fantasies and its myths; but the representation keeps that mind-set at a critical distance. The narrator's oral style, so racy and hyperbolic, is only partly in tune with popular attitudes; at certain points, he removes himself from the realm of the mimesis and passes judgement on it, as he elaborates his peculiar 'chronicle' or story of a 'national commotion'.

The narrator makes much of his mission to capture that commotion before it becomes encoded in the official language of historiography. If we try to characterise his treatment of historical material, it comes close to the second aspect of representation of social relations, in the model of magical-realist narrative proposed by Stephen Slemon as long ago as 1986. In what has proved to be a seminal essay,[8] Slemon focussed on magical-realist narratives within a post colonial context and postulated as one of three key features, 'the foreshortening of history so that the time scheme of the [story] metaphorically contains the long process of colonization and its aftermath'. 'Big Mama's Funeral' offers an allegorical reading of colonial and post colonial social relations in a tropical Hispanic environment, which mirrors exactly that stratagem of representation. García Márquez's story also exemplifies the transformational realism referred to by Slemon, where 'the site of the [magical-realist] text, though described in familiar and local terms, is metonymic of the postcolonial culture as a whole' (p. 411). There is arguably less tight a fit between 'Big Mama's Funeral' and

---

[7] Amaryll Chanady remarks on the production, in *Men of Maize*, of 'a world view different from the Western one', in 'Territorialization of the Imaginary', included in Lois Parkinson Zamora and Wendy B. Faris (eds), *Magical Realism: Theory, History, Community* (Durham NC and London: Duke University Press, 1995), pp. 125–44 (p. 141). For a succinct summary of Asturias and magical realism, the reader is referred to Donald L. Shaw, *A Companion to Modern Spanish American Fiction* (London: Tamesis, 2002), pp. 90–2.

[8] Stephen Slemon, 'Magic Realism as Postcolonial Discourse'. The essay originated in a paper delivered at a conference held in 1986. It was published first in 1988 and reproduced thereafter in Lois Parkinson Zamora and Wendy B. Faris (eds), *Magical Realism: Theory, History, Community*, pp. 407-26. Page references cited in the text of the present study are to this later edition.

Slemon's third criterion or property of magical-realist narrative. That criterion is formulated as 'the thematic foregrounding of those gaps, absences, and silences produced by the colonial encounter and reflected in the text's disjunctive language of narration. On this third level', Slemon adds, 'the magical-realist texts tend to display a preoccupation with images of borders and [centres] and to work toward destabilizing their fixity' (pp. 411–12).

It is certainly true that 'Big Mama's Funeral' asserts thematically the positive value of the margin against the spurious authority of the centre; also, that the narrator's discourse offers itself as a deliberate challenge to 'el blablablá histórico' of national officialdom (p. 141). However, the gulf between his discourse and the pervasive ignorance and self-deception of the common people strikes me as being of a different order from Slemon's 'disjunctive language of narration', which is better illustrated, perhaps, in the conflicting perspectives of *One Hundred Years of Solitude*. There, García Márquez will articulate a conflict between two versions, or visions, of history and self-determination, around various members of the Buendía family (from Ursula to the last Aureliano) and other, less mystified citizens of Macondo who respond to the impositions of colonialism and neo-colonialism in quite different, and salutary ways. As interpreted by a long line of critics stretching down to Alfred J. López,[9] the differences in outlook between the Buendías and the non-Buendías work well as an illustration of Slemon's 'metaphysical clash or double vision inherent in colonial history and language' (p. 420): in fact, I suspect that Slemon derived his three-pronged model of the magical-realist narrative precisely from García Márquez's practice in *One Hundred Years of Solitude*. But for me, the narrative of 'Big Mama's Funeral' operates rather differently, not least because, in the final paragraph of that story, the perspective of the narrator wins out over that of the people and crystallises in an unambiguous, if understated, conclusion regarding the ultimate significance of Big Mama's death. Surveying, in that paragraph, the aftermath of the funeral, the narrator comments on the people's blindness to what was going on around them, so mystified were they by 'el espectáculo del poder' (the spectacle of power). Along with many other oversights, they failed to notice the haste with which Big Mama's surviving relatives dismantled the family home, in striking disregard for the old matriarch and her dynastic line. It is at this point in the narrative that the narrator comments, 'Algunos de los allí presentes dispusieron de la suficiente clarividencia para comprender que estaban asistiendo al nacimiento de una nueva época' (Some of those present were sufficiently alert to realise that they were witnessing the birth of a new era) (p. 146). Quite unambiguously, the text offers its readers a considered evaluation of Big

---

[9] Alfred J. López, *Posts and Pasts: a Theory of Postcolonialism* (Albany NY: State University Press of New York, 2001), pp. 150–65. It is unfortunate that López's book is marred by misprints, solecisms and mistranslations from Spanish sources; that said, there is much interesting material in Chapter V of his book, where he discusses Alejo Carpentier, *One Hundred Years of Solitude*, and Salman Rushdie.

Mama's passing, conveying a two-fold truth, first, about the relativity of historical understanding, which is restricted – in accordance with classic Marxist doctrine – to a few clear-sighted individuals, and second, about the momentous
reality of a historic change affecting the life of a community that has known
nothing but repression for centuries.

Political History and Post colonial Allegory

The notion of the birth of a new era responds, I believe, to a dual motivation.
First and foremost, it is a logical consequence of events within the world of the
text, where the death of Big Mama – long overdue – is more than likely to result
in the collapse of the anachronistic system of which she is the bloated embodiment. In addition to this, we cannot discount an extra-textual stimulus for change
in the community's attitude. If we extrapolate from the fictional realm of
Macondo to contemporary circumstance in northern Colombia and, more generally, throughout the Caribbean basin, then we encounter a regional context of
'incertidumbre política' (political unrest, p. 132) whose most dramatic manifestation, and the one with the widest reverberations, has to be the Cuban
Revolution, begun inauspiciously in December 1956 and rounded off with the
triumphant entry of Fidel Castro's guerrilla troops into La Habana, from which
the dictator Fulgencio Batista had already fled, in January 1959.[10]

Political history and allegorical narrative are brought into alignment crucially,
at this point. The death of feudal, colonial and neo-colonial practices in the fictional realm of Macondo coincides with the birth of a new moral and political
order on the Caribbean island that will promptly become the focus of the world's
attention and various expectations. It is here that the date of composition and
moment of enunciation of García Márquez's narrative acquire their keenest relevance. Written in 1959, 'Big Mama's Funeral' captures and translates the seis-
mic shift affecting the political order of the hispanophone and non-hispanophone
Caribbean, and that of the world beyond. Poised at the moment of schism, it is
no surprise that the narrative should be inspired by a sense of urgency about reg-
istering the details of a national and international commotion, before historians
of a different persuasion appropriate events for their own agendas. If this
extended allegorical reading is valid, then 'Big Mama's Funeral' deserves to be
recognised as occupying a prominent place within the cultural and discursive
space surrounding the historical processes of decolonisation and, eventually, the

---

[10] On the Cuban Revolution, see Hugh Thomas, *Cuba or the Pursuit of Freedom* (London:
Eyre & Spottiswoode, 1971). No less pertinent here is García Márquez's earlier experience,
first hand, of the collapse, in Venezuela at the beginning of 1958, of the dictatorship of Marcos
Pérez Jiménez. On this crucial event and García Márquez's joyful reaction to the end of a
decade of repression, see Stephen Minta, *Gabriel García Márquez: Writer of Colombia*
(London: Jonathan Cape, 1987), pp. 57–8.

tricontinentalism that will radiate out from Cuba in the mid-nineteen-sixties.[11] Whether we call the mode and the style of 'Big Mama's Funeral' magical realism or post-colonial allegory,[12] the text heralds the birth of a new political order which really did materialise, for some years at least, and to which García Márquez has remained stubbornly loyal down to the present day.

[11] For an authoritative analysis of 'tricontinentalism' and the Caribbean, see Robert J. C. Young, *Postcolonialism: an Historical Introduction* (Oxford: Blackwell, 2001), especially pp. 4–6 and 204–16. I have also explored the Latin American articulation of the tricontinental and the role played in that enterprise by the Mexican intellectual, Leopoldo Zea, in 'Latin America and Beyond: Transcontinental Dialogue in the Work of Leopoldo Zea', *interventions*, V.1 (2003), 113–24.

[12] I sound a deliberate and partial echo, here, of Fredric Jameson's once-celebrated work on 'Third World Allegory', not so much for its possible relevance to 'Big Mama's Funeral' as for the link, clearly consonant with my interpretation of García Márquez's story, that Jameson establishes between satire and the utopian impulse: 'All satire', Jameson observes, 'necessarily carries a utopian frame of reference within itself.' See 'Third-world Literature in the Era of Multinational Capitalism', in Michael Hardt & Kathi Weeks (eds), *The Jameson Reader* (Oxford: Blackwell, 2000), pp. 315–39 (p. 330).

Part IV: Empire, Nation, Magic

Introduction

Wen-chin Ouyang

> Almost every year the United Nations admits new members. And many 'old nations,' once thought fully consolidated, find themselves challenged by 'sub'-nationalisms within their borders – nationalisms which, naturally, dream of shedding this subness one happy day. The reality is quite plain: the 'end of the era of nationalism', so long prophesied, is not remotely in sight. Indeed, nation-ness is the most universally legitimate value in the political life of our time.
>
> *–Benedict Anderson*

More than two decades after the publication of these famous words, Benedict Anderson's reflection on the grip of nation-ness in contemporary imaginings of community continues to hold true even today, when observers of the dire consequences of nationalism gone awry have been cautioning against militant nationalism and advocating a move towards postnational construction of community for just as long. Nationalism informs not only political thought and action, but also the ways in which history is written, literary texts shaped and literary criticism mapped. The seemingly conflicting impulses driving political, literary or critical discourses today may be seen as differing responses to nationalism and its institutions of knowledge, and more particularly to the nation-state as a paradigm of knowledge that serves as a site of resistance to and interrogation by other forms of organization of political power and intellectual labour. Magical realism, in its combination of the fantastic and the real, has been producing political discourses that partake in imagining communities as 'limited, sovereign' nations with roots in 'time immemorial' derived from what are often termed 'local' or 'indigenous' myths, religions and cultures, while subverting realism that has been so much part of the post-Enlightenment empirical worldview that included nationalism. This nationalist impulse, often disguised as vague empire-writes-back and hybridity-accommodating type of postcolonial politics in the body of criticism surrounding magical realism of Spanish America, comes to the fore in the literary texts produced outside the immediate environment of magical realism's 'homeland'.

Jonathan Allison takes the familiar notion of magical realism as 'a narrative mode' to task in 'Magical Nationalism, Lyric Poetry and the Marvellous: W.B. Yeats and Seamus Heaney', and argues persuasively that the combination of the fantastic and the real in Irish lyrical poetry is no different from magical realism, and in fact, its politics coincides with the postcolonial impulses of the mode so prevalent in the novel. By bringing into lyrical poetry elements from Irish mythology and folklore, Yeats and Heaney effectively participate in what may be called Irish nationalism and imagine an Irish nation that has roots in a mythical past. In its imagining of nation with a distinct history, Irish lyrical poetry becomes the site on which resistance to the hegemonic master discourse of the British empire takes place. Empire, however, is not monolithic. Stefan Sperl situates the anti-imperialist impulse in Ibrāhīm al-Kawnī's quartet, *The Lunar Eclipse*, in Libyan Tuaregs' response to the waves of invasion that have historically infringed upon the sanctity of their habitat, the *Sahara* desert. Al-Kawnī's revival of Tuareg mythology and incorporation of desert magic in his stupendous narrative project 'write back' at the discourses of power belonging to what Sperl terms 'empire complex' made up of five layers of colonization (Roman, Arab, Ottoman, French and Italian), interrogating, subverting and condemning their tyranny, as well as imagining a Tuareg nation on the *Sahara* landscape. Indictment of 'empire' is, however, far from absolute. Sufi Islam, the legacy of Arab colonization, in fact comes to be the worldview internalized in the text. Not all writers of Muslim background accept Islam in such unproblematic fashion. John Erickson takes magical realism's interrogation of the colonial epistemological system a step further in 'Magical Realism and Nomadic Writing in the Maghreb'. He looks at the effects of integrating nomadic thought into magical realism on potential cultural remappings in a close reading of *The Sand Child* by Taher Ben Jelloun. The freedom, or seemingly chaotic trajectory, of nomadic thought carves out of the tight grip of the polarity driven 'Western' and 'Islamic' systems of knowledge new paths towards alternative configurations of culture that will be home to multiplicity and diversity. The longing for heterogeneity reaches a feverish pitch in Salman Rushdie's novels. Stephanie Jones argues in 'Of Numerology and Butterflies: Magical Realism in Salman Rushdie's *The Satanic Verses*' that beneath the surface antagonism towards religious imaginings of community that suppress, repress and exclude difference lurks Rushdie's nostalgia for a simpler world, perhaps a world of Islam, uncomplicated by multiplicity and diversity.

The notion of 'empire' may have taken centre stage in close interrogation of magical realism in texts produced outside the context of Spanish America, but the nation has never been far from the mind even when its workings, as an episteme, are least obvious, when the texts do not actively engage in imagining community in the form of nation or nation-state. The reluctance to embrace wholeheartedly or let go completely of a community imagined on the basis of religion or ethnicity, the tension among various 'religious' and 'ethnic' communities so palpable in the texts analyzed, and the will to harmonize among them (in al-Kawnī, Ben Jelloun and Rushdie) are, in a certain sense, impossible without the structure of the nation-state that, once established on a clearly delineated geographical lot, serves as a framework for homogenizing or accommodating difference. As an epistemological system, the nation-state is equally ambivalent towards, if not suppressive of, difference. The importance of the nation-state as a paradigm of knowledge and the insight into its paradoxical role in the formation and disintegration of community become poignantly visible in the writings on the most recent Lebanese civil war. In 'From *The Thousand and One Nights* to Magical Realism: Postnational Predicament in *The Journey of Little Ghandi* by Elias Khoury', Wen-chin Ouyang looks at the ways in which the nation-state frames a marriage between the fantastic in classical Arabic storytelling and magical realism in a contemporary Lebanese novel, arguing that narrative movements in the text follow the paths of the sectarian destruction of Lebanon. The nation-state, whether dead or alive, casts long shadows even on what may be called postnational literary texts, serving as a paradigm of narration that gives shape to the novel and drives its narrative.

Magical Nationalism, Lyric Poetry and the Marvellous: W.B. Yeats and Seamus Heaney

Jonathan Allison

If the 'literary fantastic', in Tzetvan Todorov's terms, is applicable to fictional narratives only, not to poetry, in what ways can we approach the use of marvellous and fantastic elements in poetry so as to make sense of their aesthetic and ideological functions?[1] I focus on what Todorov might call the 'marvellous' in Irish legendary narratives, with particular emphasis on how one modern poet, W.B. Yeats (1865–1939) and one contemporary poet, Seamus Heaney, have adapted traditional materials for their own lyric purposes. I will argue that lyric poems using fantastic elements, shaped from indigenous folklore narratives, have the power to convey counter-cultural values and counter-imperialist descriptions of experience. In so doing, I probe the special features that are intrinsic to the lyric form that allow it to use fantastic elements productively, and consider the effects achieved when fantastic elements are borrowed from narrative and adapted to lyric poetry.

Todorov and the Fantastic

For Todorov, the 'literary fantastic' occurs in the hesitation between deciding whether a series of apparently miraculous, supernatural events narrated in fiction are indeed supernatural or rationally explicable, and within the rules of natural law – 'Does it transcend the laws of Nature as we know them?' (Todorov, p. 28). This experience of uncertainty or hesitation defines the literary fantastic:

> Either the devil is an illusion, an imaginary being; or else he really exists, precisely like other living beings – with this reservation, that we encounter him infrequently.

---

[1] See Tzetvan Todorov, *The Fantastic* (Cleveland and London: The Press of Case Western Reserve University, 1973).

> The fantastic occupies the duration of this uncertainty. Once we choose one answer or the other, we leave the fantastic for a neighbouring genre, the uncanny or the marvellous. The fantastic is that hesitation experienced by a person who knows only the laws of nature, confronting an apparently supernatural event. (Todorov, p. 25)

That is, once a decision has been reached (by the character experiencing those events, or the reader, or both), then the events are described as 'marvellous' (supernatural), or 'uncanny' (merely a trick of the mind or of perception). Accordingly, the 'fantastic' dominates only a portion of the narrative and the reader's experience of it. It is temporary, unless the period of hesitation is pro-longed for the duration of the narrative, as in some cases discussed by Neil Cornwell, such as *The Turn of the Screw*.[2] In that case, the narrative may be described as purely 'fantastic'.

Todorov considered the fantastic in the context of fictional narratives only and critics of his work have tended to focus exclusively on fiction. Accordingly, work remains to be done on the use of fantastic elements in other genres such as drama and poetry. Might the Todorovian 'hesitation' not be observed in a lyric or nar-rative poem, since the defining feature of the 'fantastic' is indecision in the face of narrative events, and such indecision is possible in response to reading certain poems? Against this, it can be argued that poetry, more than other genres, is about language itself, rather than about plot, character or story; and that poetry is based upon a different set of aesthetic principles and achieves different sorts of aesthetic effects than prose. Cornwell, for one, argues along these lines:

> Poetry, in all its forms, seems to me to require, and normally to achieve, an attitude of mind and a degree of suspension of disbelief on the part of the reader, or listener, quite distinct from those pertaining to prose fiction. Furthermore, in cases when reader hesitation of the type here envisaged might arise – perhaps in certain narrative rather than lyric poetry – the effect is likely to derive at least as much from the incantatory quality of poetic form and language as from narrative content. (*The Literary Fantastic*, p. 4)

It is not clear, in this context, how we should discuss fantastic elements in poetry – effects of surprise, imaginative or affective shock, glimpses of other-worldly manifestation, moments of metamorphosis. It is possible, as Kathryn Hume and others have posited, to think of all imaginative writing as fantasy – understood as a kind of imaginative play, as the conception of things being oth-erwise, whether within or beyond the conventions of nature.[3] For Todorov, the marvellous (as opposed to either the fantastic or the uncanny) is the realm of

---

[2] See Neil Cornwell, *The Literary Fantastic* (London: Routledge, 1991).
[3] See Kathryn Hume, *Fantasy and Mimesis: Responses to Reality in Western Literature* (New York: Methuen, 1984).

fairy tale, in which supernatural law is assumed to be operating (there are talking animals, flying people, witches, wizards and magic):

> In the case of the marvellous, supernatural elements provoke no particular reaction in either the characters or in the implicit reader. It is not an attitude toward the events described which characterizes the marvellous, but the nature of those events . . . We generally link the genre of the marvellous to that of the fairy tale. But as a matter of fact, the fairy tale is only one of the varieties of the marvellous, and the supernatural events in fairy tales provoke no surprise: neither a hundred years sleep nor a talking wolf.
> (Todorov, p. 54)

Many poems based on legend and fable are 'marvellous' in precisely this sense, or partake of marvellous qualities. In the case of lyrics based upon incidents in Irish legend, marvellous qualities are adapted to the lyric form. There is often in this appropriation the kind of political, counter-cultural charge that critics have found in the literary fantastic, and for similar reasons.

W.B. Yeats and Magical Nationalism

The poet W.B. Yeats often used legendary narratives as imaginative material, adapting fantastic or marvellous elements for his own purposes. What he produced in doing so was a species of marvellous poetry in which supernatural events are recounted with matter-of-factness, as though they are expected. No rational explanation is offered and there is no 'hesitation' between rational and supernatural explanations. The rational is eschewed, the supernatural celebrated. This is anti-rationalist, anti-realist, and ultimately anti-imperial, a valorization of the magical, pre-modern worldview of the Irish peasant, as that was understood by Anglo-Irish writers of the Revival period. Poetry such as this constitutes, perhaps, an attempt to re-write the story of the region and of 'the nation', using different paradigms from those used in the imperial British story. The process valorizes a vigorous imaginative and spiritual life, and is the basis for a movement of national redemption. Here is a politics of the marvellous, a badge of magical power, and of national identity. The process constitutes a form of counter-hegemonic magic, and of irrational Irishness, opposed to Anglo-Saxon administrative rationality.

It would be impossible to understand the work of Yeats and certain members of his circle without recognizing their occult interests and values. A founder member of the Dublin Hermetic Society, and a member of the Order of the Golden Dawn, Yeats made it clear repeatedly in his writing and his letters that magic and the occult were central to all his thought and action. As Roy Foster and other historians have pointed out, there was an element of thinking 'hand to mouth', or as we might say, of magical thinking, in Yeats's view that the so-called 'political vacuum' of the post-Parnell period (after the political leader's death in

1891), led to a channeling of spiritual, psychic and political energy into cultural endeavours.[4] In 1899, Yeats wrote:

> The fall of Parnell and the wreck of his party and of the organizations that supported it were the symbols, if not the causes, of a sudden change . . . Those who looked for the old energies, which were the utterance of the common will and hope, were unable to see that a new kind of Ireland, as full of energy as a boiling pot, was rising up amid the wreck of the old kind, and that the national life was finding a new utterance.[5]

Yeats's belief in supernatural power in political and cultural realms – in the national imaginary, broadly speaking – renders his political philosophy very much *of its time*, and fundamentally magical. He believed in the capacity to meet the marvellous in everyday life, to transform (as in 'Easter 1916') the grey quotidian of a Dublin street, in which men go to their desks and offices, into a sublime and 'terrible beauty', a manifestation of national resurgence, at once natural and supernatural in its cause.[6]

Anglo-Irish Literary Revival

The late nineteenth-century and early twentieth-century Anglo-Irish Literary Revival was tied to the resuscitation of key Irish-language literary texts, many ancient in provenance, some of them copied and translated from eighteenth-century manuscripts in the Royal Irish Academy and Trinity College Dublin, and others from much older sources. Many of these texts were fabulous: legendary fantasy tales, in which supernatural events went unquestioned, and were encountered on a regular basis. They were less 'fantastic' than 'marvellous', in the Todorovian sense, but they expressed a fundamentally magical worldview, in which odd things happened to ordinary folk. In tales such as 'The Voyage of Bran', 'The Voyage of Mael Duin', and the 'Dream of Oengus', characters would find themselves out of their element, in another world, or trapped in a liminal space between this and that world; sometimes tales were tied to Christian meanings, enforcing a Christian telos, despite the apparently pagan nature of those encounters and peregrinations.[7] Anglo-Irish writers of the Revival period built on such mythologies, adapted and re-told them in various ways, in prose fiction, poetry and drama.

---

[4] See R.F. Foster, 'Thinking from Hand to Mouth: Anglo-Irish Literature, Gaelic Nationalism and Irish Politics in the 1890s', in *Paddy and Mr. Punch: Connections in Irish and English History* (London: Allen Lane, Penguin, 1993), pp. 262–80.

[5] W.B. Yeats, *Uncollected Prose by W.B. Yeats*, eds John P. Frayne and Colton Johnson (London: Macmillan; New York: Columbia UP, 1976), II, p. 185.

[6] W.B. Yeats, *The Poems*, 2nd edn, ed. Richard J. Finneran (New York: Scribner, 1997), pp. 182–3.

[7] P.W. Joyce (trans.), *Old Celtic Romances* (London: David Nutt, 1894).

Many of Yeats's early lyrics rely on mythology of this sort: 'The Stolen Child' feeds off popular legends of child abduction by fairies, and of the world of fairy, to which the child is beckoned in the poem, and where he apparently goes at the end: 'For he comes, the human child, / To the waters and the wild / With a faery, hand in hand . . .' (*The Poems*, p. 17). That world, characterized as transcendent of suffering and time, is a *leitmotif* of the literature, adumbrated in a poem like 'The Wanderings of Oisin' (in which the protagonist is lured away by the beautiful fairy Princess, Niamh, with whom he lives for 300 years), and 'The Hosting of the Sidhe', in which a fairy host stampedes on horseback across the countryside (*The Poems*, pp. 361–94; p. 51).

Millenarian expectations that an apocalyptic battle might be fought against Ireland's enemies near the Valley of the Black Pig are encoded in traditional materials, adapted by Yeats in his poem of that name:

> The dews drop slowly and dreams gather: unknown spears
> Suddenly hurtle before my dream-awakened eyes,
> And then the clash of fallen horsemen and the cries
> Of unknown perishing armies beat about my ears. (*The Poems*, p. 62)

This echoes the hopes and alleged premonitions of a radical spiritual revolution, attached to a political upheaval, which Yeats vaguely alluded to in prose writings of the late 1890s and after. 'Miracle' was a word he felt drawn to in February 1900, when he wrote, in criticism of meliorist views of progress: 'It is one of our illusions . . . that life moves slowly and evenly toward perfection. Progress is miracle, and it is sudden, because miracles are the work of an all-powerful energy.'[8] Here is the germ of Yeats's thinking in his poem about the 1916 rising, 'Easter 1916' (*The Poems*, pp. 182–3). The birth of 'terrible beauty' was a miraculous release and magical channeling of energy, and the birth of something beyond any individual's scope. It is at once the product of human will and of supernatural power. The conceit is an instance of magical thinking typical of the poet and others whose worldview was shaped by similarly marvellous narratives. One of these narratives was the story of Ireland itself, with its deterministic shape, and its miraculous-revolutionary telos, of which all other Irish narratives – not least the ancient tales – were seen as premonitions, types, and (as it were) echoes.[9]

'The Song of Wandering Aengus' and Nationalist Ideology

It comes as no surprise, therefore, that when P.S. O'Hegarty writes his obituary of Yeats he reads the story of Aengus (as recast in Yeats's poignant fable of

---

[8] W.B. Yeats, *Essays and Introductions* (New York: Macmillan, 1961), pp. 171–2.
[9] See R.F. Foster, 'The Story of Ireland', in *The Irish Story: Telling Tales and Making it up in Ireland* (London: Allen Lane, Penguin, 2001), pp. 1–22.

unconsummated love and deferred satisfaction, 'The Song of Wandering Aengus') as a marvellous image of the seemingly permanent longing for national self-determination.[10] 'The Song of Wandering Aengus' is based on a legend rendered in 'The Dream of Oenghus', presumed to be eighth-century in origin (P.W. Joyce, pp. 93–7) – although Yeats claimed that he took the story from 'a Greek folk song' (*The Poems*, p. 55). The poem is a modern appropriation of an ancient story, in which the magical metamorphosis of fish into girl is replicated. There is no Todorovian 'hesitation' between a rational and a supernatural explanation here: the character sees nothing peculiar in the transformation of the fish into a 'glimmering girl'. However, the intensity of his instantaneous love suggests that he may be in a trance or under a spell. Crucial to the ideological undertow of the poem is the fact it is a revival of a Gaelic legend, a poem which draws from 'marvellous' ancient materials. The supernatural qualities in the original are adapted to the lyric poem. Cultural regeneration is sought through contact with Gaelic cultural origins. I note that this lyric involves considerable strategic adaptation of the original anonymous Irish tale. In the original, Oenghus finally caught his fairy bride, who had come to him in a dream or half sleep. His catching up with her and the final consummation, when the happy couple sail off together as white birds, is not the subject of Yeats's lyric. In his personal life, longing was an important feature (Maud Gonne once said that if she had accepted his hand the world would have been deprived of poetry). For a reader of this as national allegory, such as P.S. O'Hegarty, the nation itself (and its young men awakened to national politics), is still in the longing phase. Aengus goes into the woods 'because a fire was in my head' and fishes with a hazel rod and a berry on his hook. He catches a trout, which suddenly becomes a beautiful girl, who calls his name and runs away into the wilderness. He vows to find her and kiss her:

> And walk among long, dappled grass,
> And pluck till time and times are done
> The silver apples of the moon,
> The golden apples of the sun.

For O'Hegarty, it is a coded statement, ventriloquised through adapted traditional materials, about a liminal phase of national development, with the protagonist caught (fabulously) between perception of the image of the future and fulfillment of that future:

> He has once or twice been criticized for not writing poems like the 'Aislingi' poems about beautiful maidens which were really poems about Ireland. And yet he is the only modern Irish poet who has written poems which are love poems and yet speak to the national heart as well . . . When he sang of

---

[10] P.S. O'Hegarty, 'W.B. Yeats and Revolutionary Ireland of His Time' [sic], *Dublin Magazine* (July–September 1939), pp. 22–4.

somebody who was old with wandering, searching for the 'silver apples of the moon, the golden apples of the sun', we knew what they meant, and we wandered on content toward the Dark Tower. (p. 24)

So, the fable has much to say about that magical nationalism which is inextricably tied to this story, and (according to this reading of the poem) to all other stories of Ireland. It is a re-writing of the national story, which is saturated by the ideology of perpetual longing as noble and unfailingly romantic. It suggests the nobility of defeat, if only because the golden apples of the sun are always in prospect.

Peter Kuch defined the Todorovian fantastic as 'a mode of speaking or writing which, having been obliged to admit what it considers to be the supernatural, neither explains it nor explains it away'.[11] His chief Yeatsian example of the 'fantastic' is that moment when the symbolic figure of Cathleen ni Houlihan (nonetheless embodied in naturalistic form), in Lady Gregory's and Yeats's 1902 play of that name, departs the scene, having perorated on the subject of necessary martyrdom. This scene

> anchors *Cathleen ni Houlihan* in the fantastic. Peter Gillane, who has seen his eldest son Michael fall under the spell of the Shan Van Vocht and turn his back on a strenuously bargained marriage settlement that would consolidate the family's holdings of land, asks his younger son if he saw his brother depart in thrall to an old woman. 'I did not', the twelve year old Patrick replies, 'but I saw a young girl and she had the walk of a queen.' And at that the curtain closes. *Cathleen ni Houlihan* exemplifies the fantastic because it refuses to explain the supernatural as anything other than self-evident. (Kuch, p. 14)

The crux of the play lies in the double function of the old woman as symbol of the nation and as naturalistic character in the drama, providing a reason for Michael's departure. The playgoer or reader has to see her in this double role; the greater narrative provided by Irish nationalist history allows one to see her as the mythic 'Shan Van Vocht' (Old Woman of Ireland), but the reader of fiction demands that she operate on the same level (with her weary demeanour, her shoddy shoes) as the naturalistic characters on stage. As Kuch has said, this marvellous woman 'is neither explained nor explained away'; she is certainly an old woman, but also a supernatural being:

> *Peter [to Patrick, laying a hand on his arm].* Did you see an old woman going down the path?
> *Patrick.* I did not, but I saw a young girl, and she had the walk of a queen.

---

[11] Peter Kuch, 'Writing "Easter 1916"', in Bruce Stewart (ed.), *That Other World: The Supernatural and the Fantastic in Irish Literature and its Contexts*, 2 (1998), 1–17 (p. 1).

For a 'fantastic' moment or two, the audience cannot decide who or what she is. Again, this magical figure is an icon of the master narrative of empire being rewritten in the interests of Irish nationalist ideology.

Seamus Heaney's 'Lightenings' and 'The Air Ship'

The 'marvellous' tale – such as that of wandering Aengus – begins like a fairy tale, in which supernatural events take place without question. The reader is in no doubt that natural law has been suspended and may be suspended for the duration of the tale. The entry of a natural character into that supernatural environment and his awe in the face of events is integral to the drama. The distance between natural and supernatural law is implicit in the story, but it is the operation of the latter that is being demonstrated. The distinction between reality and unreality is actually reinforced by being spectacularly blurred or undermined in the fictional narrative. In an evocative poem by Seamus Heaney, published in the volume *Seeing Things*, the distinction between the two is called into question. The poem is based upon an anonymous, early modern Irish legend, translated by Kenneth Hurlstone Jackson. The oddness of this fantasy is the way in which it is played out in that bastion of Catholic orthodoxy, rectitude and law, Clonmacnoise monastery:

> One day the monks of Clonmacnoise were holding a meeting on the floor of the church, and as they were at their deliberations there they saw a ship sailing over them in the air, going as if it were on the sea. When the crew of the ship saw the meeting and the inhabited place below them, they dropped anchor, and the anchor came right down on to the floor of the church, and the priests seized it. A man came down out of the ship after the anchor, and he was swimming as if he were in the water, till he reached the anchor; and they were dragging him down then. 'For God's sake let me go!' said he, 'for you are drowning me.' Then he left them, swimming in the air as before, taking his anchor with him.[12]

Heaney's 12-line poem comprises four three-line stanzas; it is one of a long series of 12-line lyrics called 'Lightenings', suggesting points of illumination, epiphanies, or striking moments of religious or psychic clarity.[13] This is a sequence of poems about the individual's spiritual destiny, but that does not deprive it of the power to represent more than the self. In an adjacent poem in the volume, the speaker admits it took him fifty years before he could learn to 'credit marvels', and this poem among others is an admission, aesthetically and

---

[12] Kenneth Hurlstone Jackson (translator and editor), 'The Air Ship', in *A Celtic Miscellany* (Harmondsworth: Penguin, 1971), p. 165. 'The Air Ship' is described as 'Irish; author unknown; fourteenth-fifteenth century?'

[13] Seamus Heaney, *Seeing Things* (London: Faber & Faber, 1991), p. 62.

ethically, of the marvellous or supernatural. In the fabulous ur-text, 'The Air Ship', the narrator begins by taking the point of view of the monks on the floor, but then sympathy shifts to the sailors, from the second sentence on. The monks behave very dubiously in regard to the swimming sailor: 'and they were dragging him down then'. It is only the drowning sailor's passionate protest that secures his release. In the Heaney version, the point of view is more securely that of the monks, who are gentler and kinder than those in the ur-text. The kind Abbot is Heaney's addition; his injunction to his obedient monks secures the immediate release of the drowning prisoner, and permits that wonderful closing epiphany: 'and the man climbed back / Out of the marvellous as he had known it'. The poem appropriates fabulous matter from a traditional narrative, and the sense of national history is preserved with the phrase, 'the annals say'. There is a moment of hesitation in the reader, in response to the phrase, 'A ship appeared above them in the air'. We are not quite sure how to take this. Not until the abbot speaks, admitting the existence of the ghostly sailor, authorising the reader to lend the poem supernatural valence, do we feel able to surrender to the marvellous. Prior to that, we feel the puzzling chill of the fantastic; it is therefore possible to experience a fleeting effect of hesitation within this lyric, an effect more commonly attributed to fantastic prose fiction. This particular poem is an important moment in Heaney's stylistic history and indeed his spiritual autobiography – his acceptance of 'lightening' and of 'marvels' – but it carries wider public significance.

The poem establishes a link between the magical thinking underpinning the nationalism of Yeats's revolutionary generation, paying tribute to that tradition, and hinting at its noble but altered continuance. The poem offers a re-writing of the national annals, but Heaney's recourse to traditional matter differs considerably from Yeats's recourse to similar materials, in his day. No longer tied to the decolonising imperatives of Revivalist cultural nationalism, contemporary poets may revisit traditional indigenous narratives from new perspectives, focusing on different values and aesthetic needs. Heaney's achievement is to highlight the qualities in the ur-text which question the relationship between the fantastic and the real, undermining traditional conceptions of that dichotomy by stressing that, for the sailor, the monks are themselves marvellous and otherworldly. Everybody, including marvellous creatures, has the capacity to come up against a bewildering otherness which might challenge their fundamental axioms. Therefore, in his lyric adaptation of legendary narrative, Heaney questions the conventional relationship between the 'fantastic' and the 'real', in the context of a re-writing of a national story, as recorded in 'the annals'.

Empire and Magic in a Tuareg Novel:
Ibrāhīm al-Kawnī's *al-Khusūf* (*The Lunar Eclipse*)

Stefan Sperl

Ibrāhīm al-Kawnī was born in 1948 in a remote region of the Libyan desert near the border with Algeria and Niger. According to his own testimony he grew up speaking Tamashek, the Tuareg language, and only learnt Arabic after the age of twelve when he went to school in one of the oasis towns of Southern Libya. He states that from an early age onwards he had developed the ambition of writing what he calls 'the epic of the desert', a task which, in his view, had yet to be accomplished.[1] After a long period of gestation, much of it spent in Poland and Russia where he came to know the work of his literary mentor Dostoevsky, al-Kawnī burst on to the literary stage in the late 1980s with a succession of remarkable books, some twenty by now, which brought him fame and international recognition.[2]

The chief protagonist in all his works is the Sahara desert, which he describes in one of his early short stories as 'God's regent on this earth who carries out His edicts and commands in harsh totality'.[3] In his recent interview, he went yet further, stating that 'God, man and beast are joined into one body called Sahara' (al-Kawnī, *Discours*, p. 98). This fusion of the transcendental and the real in al-Kawnī's vision of the desert resides at the core of his extensive oeuvre and is, perhaps, the principle reason why it may be placed within the remit of magical realism as has been observed by a number of critics. Hafez credits him with having provided Arabic literature 'with a dimension of magic realism similar to that

---

[1] al-Kawnī, Ibrāhīm, 'Le discours du désert (témoignage)', in *La Poétique de l'espace dans la littérature arabe moderne*, eds Boutros Hallaq, Robin Ostle and Stefan Wild (Paris: Presses Sorbonne Nouvelle, 2002), p. 96.

[2] Some his works (but not the novel discussed in this study) have been translated into several languages. The first to appear in English is *The Bleeding of the Stone*, trans. Mayy Jayyusi and Christopher Middleton (Moreton-in-Marsh: Arris, 2003). Several recent studies of his work are found in Boutros Hallaq Robin Ostle and Stefan Wild (eds), *La Poétique de l'espace dans la littérature arabe moderne*.

[3] Al-Kawnī, Ibrāhīm, *al-Khurūj al-Awwal ilā Waṭan al-Ru'ā al-Samāwiyya* (Limassol: Dār al-Tanwīr lil-Tibā'a wa 'l-Nashr, 1992), p. 24. The phrase occurs in the story *Ilā Ayna Yā Badawī ilā Ayna* which first appeared in the collection of stories entitled *Jur'a min dam* (1983).

in Latin American fiction',[4] while Eissa considers that in al-Kawnī's work magical realism has the effect of fusing man and his desert environment into a single entity by erasing 'the conventional distinction between character and space'.[5]

The objective of this paper is to examine more closely the interface between the magical and the real in Ibrāhīm al-Kawnī's first novel, a substantial work in four volumes written between 1986 and 1988 which carries the title *al-Khusūf* ('The Lunar Eclipse'). It narrates the story of Shaykh Ghūmā, a Tuareg tribal chief and warrior who faces the progressive loss of all that he holds dear: his off-spring, his friends, his beloved, his favourite animals and plants and, perhaps most painfully of all, his desert abode. Increasingly isolated in his old age he remains unbowed to the end when he wins a final, political victory for his people. Woven around the Shaykh's story are numerous subplots and flashbacks which together provide a richly layered account of the encroachment of 'civilisation' and modernity into the furthest recesses of the desert and the concomitant end of a nomadic culture of immemorial ancestry. An integral part of this culture is adherence to, and belief in, magical practices which play a major role in the development of the plot.

Imperial Invaders

Taken together, the historical flashbacks which occur throughout the novel provide the picture of an unbroken assault upon the people of the Sahara desert by a succession of Northern powers which together may be called the 'Empire complex': the Romans, the Ottomans, the French, the Italians and, finally, the authorities of the newly independent Arab Kingdom of Libya based in the coastal cities. Despotism is the quality they share to an equal extent and the prison is their hallmark. The first building erected by the Ottoman governor of Southern Libya is a dungeon, though he could not extend his grasp much beyond his oasis stronghold. Thanks to more advanced technical means the Italians are able to track down their victims in the remotest corners of the desert and imprison them at will. In their acts of repression, the authorities of the Libyan state are labelled by the local inhabitants as 'new colonialists', worse than their Italian predecessors (IV, p. 30; see also III, p. 23), and no different from the Ottomans in their use of the Southern oases as places of exile for dissidents (IV, p. 254).

If despotism is one chief characteristic of the 'empire complex', rapaciousness is the other. All exponents of imperial rule share it in equal measure, their objective being acquisition of the resources of the desert: oil, gold, water, animals,

---

[4] Sabry Hafez, 'The Novel of the Desert, Poetics of Space and Dialectics of Freedom', in *La Poétique de l'espace dans la littérature arabe moderne*, pp. 55–84 (p. 60).

[5] Ashraf Eissa, 'Poetics of the Desert in Ibrāhīm al-Kawnī's "The Maiden's Wāw", in *La Poétique de l'espace dans la littérature arabe moderne*, pp. 85–94 (p. 92).

women and men. The first Ottoman governor of the South, Sa'ādī Bey is driven and ultimately destroyed by his greed for gold (II, p. 104), while his successor Nūrī Bey exacts the *ius prima nocte* (II, p. 106), a practise which results in the savage mutilation of a man who tried to protect the honour of his daughter (II, p. 131). The French invasion aims to secure the desert's reserves in oil until it is successfully halted by a confederation of Tuareg tribes. In a revealing exchange Ghūmā and his Tuareg allies express their belief that had they not thwarted the French expedition it might have led to the discovery of the secret treasure left behind by Tānis, a legendary Tuareg queen; this would have desecrated the virginity of the desert and enslaved its people for ever (I, pp. 97–8). Ironically, the ultimate discovery in the desert of an underground treasure associated with Tānis is not brought about by a military campaign but by Mori, an Italian archaeologist working in the service of the corrupt Libyan government which thus shows itself once more as being nothing but a further manifestation of imperial rapaciousness.

Despotism and greed, the twin hallmarks of the 'empire complex', are diametrically opposed to the two principles of desert life most cherished by Shaykh Ghūmā: freedom and abstinence. When asked by the Italians, who took him prisoner during the war of independence, why he fought them with such ferocity to defend a naked and empty land, Ghūmā only answers: the desert is freedom (*al-ṣaḥrā' hiya 'l-ḥuriyya*, III, p. 91). This freedom comes, however, at a price. Opting for it means living an austere existence at risk of 'death by thirst' (IV, p. 60), or the loss of kith and kin in a flash flood. In Ghūmā's view this willingness to make do with deprivation is a source of virtue and pride: indeed 'the glory of the desert people is abstinence' (*'aẓamat ahl al-ṣaḥrā' hiya al-zuhd*, II, p. 248). The term *zuhd*, here translated as 'abstinence', carries with it significant religious overtones; it implies indifference to worldly goods in preference to the promise of the Hereafter and is a cardinal virtue among mystics and ascetics in the Islamic tradition. The implication is that desert life in its very austerity brings man closer to the fulfilment of his destiny as a spiritual being.

As such, the freedom and abstinence of the desert contrast not only with the destructive principles of the 'empire complex' but with any lifestyle involving permanent settlement and the accumulation of material well being. Agriculture, attachment to possessions, moral depravity and corrupt power politics are, in Ghūmā's view, the ingrained and inter-connected features of what others would deem to be 'civilisation', and the 'empire complex' is only the most extreme manifestation thereof. As observed by Hafez, the contrast between desert and oasis runs through al-Kawnī work as a whole[6] and is one of the fundamental axes of a worldview which the author has developed and refined in ever new ways in the progress of his work.

---

[6] See Hafez, p. 20.

The Vagaries of Magic

The theme of magic permeates the entire novel at numerous levels. Two distinct aspects may be considered, however. One relates to magical practises and beliefs which are portrayed as part of everyday life in the social environment in which the novel is set; the other, rather more important for our purposes, relates to the mysterious power of the natural forces inherent in the desert landscape.

Magic as a feature of Saharan social life is manifest in a plethora of tales and sub-plots on witchdoctors, diviners and magicians, many of them women, and some of them reputedly supernatural beings, which give the impression of having been transposed directly from folklore, and greatly enrich the plot of the novel. Magic in this form is a distinctly Southern phenomenon, most at home in the cities on the African fringes of the desert such as Timbuktu, Aghadez or Kano, and appears to be a pre-Islamic and, in some instances, positively sacrilegious craft.[7] While most people take its power to work miracles for granted and resort to it in moments of need, Shaykh Ghūmā views the antics of magicians with a degree of detachment, despite the fact that Muhammadū, the most prominent exponent of magic in the book, is also his closest friend. The limited powers of magic and magicians are certainly in evidence in their confrontation with the exponents of the 'empire complex', despite the fact that the latter represents the greatest danger faced by the desert. Neither the Ottomans, nor the Italians nor, indeed, the Libyan authorities are in any way dented by them. During his campaign against the Italians the great diviner Muhammadū has to endure the humiliation of being taken prisoner while defecating in the desert, and his magic is only sufficient to help the fighters escape alive from a crushing defeat (al-Kawnī, al-Khusūf, III, p. 95).

The second type of magic, that inherent in the desert itself, is of an altogether different and rather more powerful kind. As described by al-Kawnī and perceived through Ghūmā's eyes, the entire desert environment, its landscape, the permutations of its climate, its flora, its fauna, even down to its scorpions, ants and flies, is animated by a mysterious force, as reflected in the following paragraph:

> The silence makes the wind speak in the rustling of the trees. The language of the rustle is magical (*sāhira*) in the silence of the desert. Rustling in the palms leaves, the wind dispenses revelations (*mūhin*). What does it reveal (*yūhī*)? What does it hint at? What does it whisper? What does it wish to say with these mutterings? It is the language of eternity (*azal*) which discloses the secret of existence (*sirr al-wujūd*) and, at the last moment, recoils. (IV, p. 284)

While the secret remains shrouded in mystery, the wording of the passage underlines the transcendental nature of the 'marvellous' displayed in the magical

---

[7] On the African roots of folkloric magic also in Latin American magic realism see David Mikics, 'Derek Walcott and Alejo Carpentier: Nature, History and the Caribbean Writer', in *Magical Realism, Theory, History, Community*, eds Lois Parkinson Zamora and Wendy B. Faris (Durham & London: Duke University Press, 1995), pp. 372–404 (p. 373).

language of the wind. The latter is described as a source of revelation or, in Arabic, *waḥy*, a term also used denote the revelation of the Qur'ān. In conjunction with the notions of eternity and divine revelation, the image of the 'disclosure of a secret' also acquires distinct religious overtones, for it is habitually used by Islamic mysticism to circumscribe the contemplation of the divine essence and hence the pinnacle of the mystic quest. This passage, along with many others throughout the novel, therefore suggests that the desert environment is animate, articulate, and carries with it a message from the unseen which is not accessible to all nor perceptible at all times.

The hint at a transcendental message, though never fully grasped, in the manifestations of nature is a feature of the entire novel and is implicit also in factual, apparently 'realist' descriptions devoid of any overt reference to 'magic', 'secrets' or anything supernatural. As the novel progresses the reader becomes increasingly alert to the magical depth of natural phenomena, and an atmosphere is created in which even the soberest and most 'realist' passages evoke the existence of something inexhaustible and unknowable. It is here that the author achieves at the highest level what Luis Leal describes as the veritable aim of the magical-realist: 'capture the magic that palpitates in things'.[8]

Lucretius and Saharan Wisdom

In his essay on nature in the works of Derek Walcott and Alejo Carpentier, David Mikics discusses the manner in which Walcott confronts 'the weight of historical memory' in the Caribbean by forging 'fantastic analogies' between the Graeco-Hellenic world and the contemporary West Indies (pp. 373, 378). He points out that this is most notably the case in his major epic *Omeros* (1990) which appears to have been composed at the same time as *al-Khusūf* (1989). Here, Walcott wrests the Homeric legacy away from exclusive ownership by the dominant culture of Europe and shows its heroes to be incarnate among the ordinary folk of the Island of St. Lucia.

Like Walcott, al-Kawnī views the legacy of classical antiquity as a hallmark of the imperial cultures of the North, but he deals with the topic in a different manner which combines appropriation at one level with devaluation and rejection at another. This is most tellingly illustrated in the story of Bordello, an Italian army captain steeped in Latin literature who comes to Libya dreaming to emulate the exploits of Scipio Africanus. When his ambitions founder he lets out his frustration by ordering the savage torture of Ajjār, a humble but stubborn Tuareg shepherd. While egging on the torturers Bordello, increasingly drunk, cites verses from Lucretius' *De Rerum Natura,* the associations of which unmask the futility of his demented ambitions while confirming precepts held to be imparted by the desert.

---

[8] Cited in María-Elena Angulo, *Magical Realism: Social Context and Discourse* (New York: Garland, 1995), p. 6.

One of these citations amounts to a condemnation of the imperialist endeavour altogether: 'far better to lead a quiet life than to long for sovereign authority and lordship over kingdoms' (*al-sa'y ilā .. 'urūsh al-qayāṣira,* al-Kawnī, IV, p. 163; *regere imperio res,* Lucretius, 5:1127–8).[9] In the passage from which this quote is taken the Latin poet extols the virtue of the philosopher's contentment with little in a manner which recalls the ideal of *zuhd,* the abstemiousness which Ghūmā deems, as we have seen, to be 'the glory of the desert people'. Furthermore, the Arabic word al-Kawnī uses to render 'quiet life' (the Latin *quietum*) is *sakīna,* a term redolent with Islamic mysticism which Shaykh Ghūmā in another context declares to be the goal of his spiritual quest when he says: 'I'm only searching for *sakīna*' (*lā aṭlubu illā 'l-sakīna,* IV, p. 58). It so happens, moreover, that Ājjār, the shepherd whose life Bordello is engaged in destroying as he utters the quote, is the very embodiment of the 'quiet life' in its practical form, for Ājjār has never wished for anything other than to abide with his family and his flock in the remote corner of the desert which he loves and calls his home (see IV, pp. 139–41).

Bordello thus finds himself unwittingly attempting to subjugate a remote desert people in whom the philosophy of his favourite Latin poet is as alive as Homer is in Walcott's St. Lucia. It is he, the heir of Rome, who has betrayed its principles and, in doing so, demonstrated the ineffectiveness of the cultural baggage in which he prides himself. Ghūmā and Ājjār, on the other hand, have no need for Lucretius for they can derive the same wisdom from 'the nature of the universe' which is their own. It follows that the so-called 'primitive' nomads of the desert harbour universal insights which the adepts of so-called civilisation ignore in their relentless quest for wealth and power while, at the same time, claiming them as their own. Walcott's fusion of the Homeric world and the Caribbean aims 'to liberate history's destructive aspect into an imaginative sense of future' (Mikics, p. 382); al-Kawnī's fusion of Lucretius and Saharan wisdom, on the other hand, diagnoses 'history's destructive aspect' as a betrayal of the insights of the past. Both, however, achieve to an equal extent the rehabilitation and humanisation of the marginalized people they are writing about: the humble fishermen and former slaves of the Caribbean, and the impoverished nomads of the desert.

Another, different aspect of al-Kawnī's appropriation of antiquity concerns his ingenious use of the Platonic myth of Atlantis as a means to turn the Sahara from the outer periphery of the civilised world into its centre. As shown by Deheuvels,[10] al-Kawnī is not the first to have searched for Atlantis in the Sahara

---

[9] Titus Lucretius, *On The Nature Of The Universe,* trans. Ronald E. Latham, rev. John Godwin (London: Penguin Classics, 1994). References to Lucretius are cited according to chapter and verse number.

[10] Luc-Willy Deheuvels, 'Le "lieu" de l'utopie dans l'ouevre d'Ibrāhīm al-Kawnī', in Boutros Hallaq, Robin Ostle, Stefan Wild (eds), *La Poétique de l'espace dans la littérature arabe moderne,* pp. 25–42 (p. 35).

desert but his originality consists in amalgamating the Platonic story with the myth of Tanit / Tānis, the Phoenician goddess of fertility, and thus re-inventing, or 'rediscover[ing]' the forgotten mythological sub-stratum of the Tuareg people as discussed above. In a further recourse to antiquity al-Kawnī identifies the people of the legendary empire of Tānis with the Garamantians mentioned by Herodotus as the inhabitants of the Libyan desert, a procedure through which the lost pre-historic roots of the Saharan people become history and the magical is, once more, fused with the real. In al-Kawnī's view, the Saharan rock engravings are another piece of evidence that a rich culture once flourished there 'eleven thousand years ago', and his entire oeuvre can be understood as an attempt to recuperate and rediscover this world by recourse to the fragmented legends which have survived to this day (see al-Kawnī, *Discours*, p. 97).

The Ruin of the Land

In his attempt at confronting modernity, as manifest most starkly in the 'empire complex', through the reawakened memory of an ancient culture, al-Kawnī aligns himself with what appears to be one of the hallmarks of magical realism. It is akin to Derek Walcott's self-identification with the Caribs, the original inhabitants of his native land (Mikics, p. 393–5), and parallels the Amerindian past evoked in the works of William Goyen, Elena Garro and Juan Rulfo, as discussed in Lois Zamora's masterly study 'Magical Romance / Magical Realism: Ghosts in US and Latin American Fiction'.[11] Like these authors, al-Kawnī can be said to write 'out of a sense of cultural displacement – displacement of traditional communities, indigenous and rural, and the resulting ruin of the land' (Zamora, p. 541).[12] There are a number of instructive differences, however. The first relates to the historical circumstances of the cultural displacement involved, the second to the type of community and its relation to the land, and the third to the legacy of Islam, a central element in al-Kawnī's work which has no counterpart in the other authors.

For the American magical-realists, including Carpentier and García Márquez, the experience of displacement reflected in their works is a process which stretches back into history, down to the Spanish conquest centuries ago. In the works of Goyen, Garro and Rulfo, the Amerindian past and what it represented –

---

[11] Lois Parkinson Zamora, 'Magical Romance/Magical Realism: Ghosts in US and Latin American Fiction', in *Magical Realism, Theory, History, Community*, pp. 487–550.

[12] It is interesting to note that the desire to return to this land by melting into it through a process of 'physical integration into the earth', 'which Zamora discusses with respect to the works of William Goyen (Zamora, 'Magical Romance', p. 527), becomes a major topic of al-Kawnī's later writings such as *al-Fam* discussed by S. Hafez ('Novel of the Desert') and *Waṭan al-Ru'ā al-Samāwiyya* discussed by Rima Sleiman in her article, 'Ville, oasis, desert: la négation de la Création', in *La Poétique de l'espace dans la littérature arabe moderne*, pp. 43–54.

'the integral relation of human, natural and cosmic realms' in Nahuatl cosmology, the perception of nature as humanized, embodied and 'invested . . . with supernatural powers' (Zamora, pp. 528, 536) – can only be recalled through a descent to the ghosts of the dead. For al-Kawnī, on the other hand, the cultural displacement suffered by the Saharan nomads is a contemporary event. The loss is fresh, it is experienced here and now, in the struggles of Shaykh Ghūmā who still perceives the transcendental message immanent in nature though he is perhaps the last to do so. Thus Walcott, as noted by Mikics (p. 393), recalls the suicide of the Carib Indians of the island of Grenada which took place in 1651, while a comparable event in al-Kawnī's novel, the voluntary demise of Ghūmā's young companion and potential successor Amūd, takes place in the Libya of the 1950s or 60s. The Caribs preferred death to capture by the British; Amūd and his wife choose to die rather lose the freedom of their desert life (al-Kawnī, *al-Khusūf*, II, pp. 284–6).

This difference has implications for the role of nature, which is as prominent in the novels of the New World as it is in al-Kawnī. With respect to Walcott and Carpentier, Mikics perceives that nature functions as an escape from the travails of history (p. 396). However, the promise of this escape remains ultimately unfulfilled since it fails to engender a new sense of belonging. Indeed, 'the West Indian setting, like Carpentier's marvellous real, reveals its magic only to the stranger' (p. 388); moreover, 'there is something empty in the "nothing" that remains after the New World landscape has been denuded of its cruel and complex history' (p. 392). Al-Kawnī's work, however, is not an expression of a 'flight into nature as escape from history' (p. 385) but rather the opposite: it charts an expulsion from nature by the combined forces of history and nature itself. Ghūmā is indeed a stranger, but not because he is an outsider coming to view the marvels of the desert; rather, he is the last insider who feels himself to be an integral part of it. The wilderness, for Ghūma, is indeed empty: 'there is nothing in the desert' (*lā yūjad shay'fī 'l-sahrā'*, al-Kawnī, *al-Khusūf*, IV, p. 59). However, in its very emptiness the desert has a moral function; it imparts courage, abstemiousness and nobility, and may even guide man to his inner self. The prime means through which the desert is able to achieve these tasks – and here we come to a key difference between stranger and insider in their encounter with nature – is through the affliction of suffering. The stranger is a guest who barely leaves the protective cocoon of civilisation and merely comes to view. The insider, like Ghūmā and his tribe, is exposed to the elements with the minimum of man-made mediation and thus suffers the brunt of an environment that is, if anything, more hostile, treacherous and cruel than history itself. It gives birth to al-Kawnī's sombre ideology, palpable in all his works, whereby freedom and spiritual elevation can only be gained through bodily sacrifice and the furthest limits of physical pain.

The second major difference noted above concerns the peculiar relationship to the land among the Tuareg nomads depicted by al-Kawnī. There is undoubtedly a degree of parentage in the immanence of the forces of nature as they appear in the works of magical-realists: Aguilera Malta's Ecuadorian jungle, Ben Okri's

Nigerian forest, William Goyen's earth of 'deep East Texas', Walcott's Caribbean sea and al-Kawnī's Sahara all fit Octavio Paz's description of the Mexican landscape as depicted by Juan Rulfo. It is

> a symbol and something more than a symbol: a voice entering into the dialogue, and in the end the principle character of the story . . . (It) never refers only to itself; it points always to something else, to something beyond itself. It is a metaphysic, a religion, an idea of man and the cosmos. (cited in Zamora, p. 523)

The recapture of this ancient vision carries within itself an intense protest against the mentality of modernity which sees nature merely as a resource to be purchased, conquered and exploited, a mentality deeply implicated in the 'cultural displacement' of indigenous communities and the 'ruin of the land' identified by Zamora as a driving force of magical realism altogether (p. 541).[13]

The uniqueness of al-Kawnī's protest resides in the fact that it emanates from a community which, while displaced most recently, exhibits a lifestyle rooted in the most distant past. For Ghūmā, the 'ruin of the land' begins with the plough and the injury it brings to the surface of the earth, and the most painful tragedy for him is that first commercial transaction when, in order to survive in the oasis in which he has taken refuge, he purchases agricultural land with the proceeds from the sale of his herd. Al-Kawnī's voice of protest reflects the deep-seated division between desert and sown that has marked North Africa and the Levant since the dawn of history but it expresses more than that. It is suffused with pessimism and ontological doubt in the validity and viability of human civilisation as a whole which, in his view, is bent on destroying nature and hence itself.

The Islamic dimension marks the other significant difference between al-Kawnī and the magical realism of the New World. While the latter charts the interaction between three principal cultural layers, Amerindian, African and European, in *al-Khusūf* there are four. Africa and Europe appear in familiar roles, one bearer of magic, the other of empire; between them is the indigenous culture of the Tuareg, and, fused with it and yet distinct, Islam. Historically speaking, Islamic culture and, by extension, Arabic culture and the Arabic language, are alien imports in the Saharan world and thus figure as attributes of the empire complex, as manifest in the despotic Ottoman governors and the corrupt officials of the Libyan state; they are also the hallmarks of the no less corrupt and

---

[13] Another parallel between *al-Khusūf* and other magical-realist novels is the theme of nature's nemesis against the white intruders. In al-Kawnī's work a Greek engineer's attempt to defy the jinn and drill for water in Ādrār leads to a catastrophic flood; similarly the white man who attempts to carve a road through Ben Okri's magic forest is swallowed up by the earth (Ben Okri, *The Famished Road* [London: Jonathan Cape, 1991], pp. 285–8) while Aguilera Malta's Don Goyo is mysteriously murdered by the trees he has decided to sell out to the white man (Aguilera Malta, *Don Goyo* [Clifton: Humana Press, 1980], pp. 176–96).

ineffectual Muslim clergy of the Southern oases and as such coterminous with
the inherent flaws of sedentary life. Among the Tuareg tribesmen, however,
Islamic spirituality is not perceived as alien but engages in a peculiar symbiosis
with ancient indigenous beliefs.

In choosing to write his works in Arabic, the Tuareg al-Kawnī is comparable
to Indian authors writing in English or West African authors writing in French; to
make his voice heard, he resorts to an imperial tongue, though Tuareg words and
expressions figure in his works and are explained by footnotes. The use of Arabic
is, however, far more than a means of access to a wider audience. As illustrated
in the examples discussed above, al-Kawnī draws on the religious associations
inherent in Arabic as the language of the Qur'ān and resorts to these as a means
to sacralize nature and thus reveal the magic beneath the real. Through this procedure the desert environment as a whole is turned into a divine revelation, a kind
of Qur'ān made of matter instead of words. It could be argued that al-Kawnī thus
subverts the instrument of monotheism by using it as a means to regenerate a more
ancient, animist, even polytheist vision of the cosmos and that this approach is
nothing less than another example of the periphery confronting and undermining
the narrative of empire. However, it would be equally valid to say that his vision
is not incompatible with Islamic spirituality. Indeed, nature and revelation are
conjoined in the Arabic word *āya* which means both 'verse of the Qur'ān' and
'sign of divine power'; among the most prominent of these signs are, as emphasised throughout the sacred text, the manifestations of the natural world.

Magical Realism and Nomadic Writing in the Maghreb

John D. Erickson

In one of his poems the American poet Robert Frost speaks of coming to a fork in the road and choosing one of the diverging ways. But he wonders about the 'road not taken', which will always hold its allure for him. Magical realism, following Frost's 'road not taken', opens onto different ways, alternate paths to perceiving the world and the interrelation between empirical reality and the fantastic.

Most critics have viewed magical realism as a mode of literary and artistic expression whose view and mapping of the world depart from those of mainstream Western thought and literature, evolving from the logocentric tradition. Magical realism is often equated with the fantastic, which ushers in the unexpected intrusion of the otherworldly in the midst of the workaday world, resulting in what Roger Caillois calls 'a strange and almost unbearable irruption in the real world'.[1] Magical realism frequently if not usually takes the form of a narrative of resistance against dominant or master narratives touting so-called universal truths that reject all other narratives.

Magical Realism and the Fantastic Narrative

Some commentators of the fantastic narrative see it as turning on the eventual resolution of the otherworldly through rational explanation. This particular definition of the fantastic parts company with magical realism, for the latter is not rationally explained. On the contrary, magical realism departs from reasoned argument (logos) by putting into play magical phenomena not reducible to reasoned explanation, and introduces antipodal theories of existence that are coequal: the empirical world of reason and logic and the supernatural world of unreason. The supernatural sunders the arbitrary coherence of the empirical world ordered by logocentric thought, by revealing it to be, not a universally

---

[1] Roger Caillois, *Anthologie du fantastique* (Paris: Gallimard, 1966), I, p. 8.

valid representation of external reality, but no more than one of several possible representations. With regard to the fantastic Caillois sees 'the regularity [of] the world order so painfully established and proved by the methodical investigation of experimental science, [ceding] to the assault of irreconcilable, nocturnal, demonic forces' (p. 23). But magical realism differs from the fantastic by simultaneously presenting the 'magical' and the 'real' realms as coexisting, not the displacement of one by the other.

Magical realism, in challenging traditional discourse, has often been considered a marginal or outsider discourse. The late French philosopher Jean-François Lyotard views it differently: 'there is no such thing as a margin. What speaks of margins is the Empire that reflects its boundaries, its borders, its marches (regions to be conquered).'[2] The distinction between insider and outsider discourses is moot, for what distinguishes an insider discourse is solely the fact that it has become privileged through the process of imposing itself on a populace and propagandizing itself as containing universal truths that nullify all other discourses. Magical realism as a mode of resistance brings about a 'leveling' of narrative by depriving the master narrative of its unique positional value and its privileged character and by exposing the arbitrary nature of the philosophical precepts that legitimate it, thus revealing it, as I have said elsewhere, to be just one discourse among many.[3]

Magical Realism and Nomadic Thought

Valbuena Briones argues that magical realism, far from being confined to Latin American narratives, is 'a universal tendency [. . .] inherent in human existence'.[4] Magical realism takes different forms in various cultures. Several Arabic narratives – most notably the *1001 Nights* – exhibit the magically real. In French-speaking North Africa, magical realism is closely related to what is often spoken of as nomadic thought, that is, verbal or written expression unbound by conventional ways of writing and speaking, which recognizes no absolute boundaries but crosses frontiers of thinking and expression freely, just as desert nomads themselves have done for several millennia. Maghrebi writing has been strongly influenced by the concept of nomadic thought elaborated by Gilles Deleuze and Felix Guattari, first in *Anti-Oedipus*, then in *A Thousand Plateaus*.[5] Nomadic

---

[2] Jean-François Lyotard, 'Sur la force des faibles', *L'Arc*, 64 (1976), 4–12.

[3] See my *Islam and Postcolonial Narrative* (Cambridge: Cambridge University Press, 1998), p. 19 et passim, where I speak of the phenomenon I call 'leveling' as a discursive strategy in challenging magisterial discourses that presume to impose universal dicta.

[4] A. Valbuena Briones, 'Una cala en el realismo mágico', *Cuadernos Americanos*, 166. 5 (Sept.–Oct. 1969), 225–40 (p. 236).

[5] Gilles Deleuze & Félix Guattari, *A Thousand Plateaus: Capitalism and Schizophrenia* (Minneapolis: University of Minnesota Press, 1987); *Capitalisme et Schizophrénie: L'Anti-Œdipe* (Paris: Éditions de Minuit, 1972).

thought contests the social and religious strictures of nationalist, fundamentalist and nativist agencies, as well as the politics of globalization. In opposition to the static, totalistic, reductionist ideology and strategies of statist and theocratic institutions it valorizes becoming, movement and pluralism.[6]

Nomadic tribes such as the Tuareg reflect a structural arrangement that diminishes centralized authority, thereby putting into question any hegemonic system that seeks to domesticate pastoral groups through sedentarism.[7] The late Kateb Yacine, perhaps the foremost Maghrebi writer in French, speaks of the refusal of some postcolonial writers to become 'domesticated', that is, to submit unquestioningly to the structures of power that frame them in. Kateb says,

> In our Arabic tradition, there are some poets who have refuted even the message of the Prophet. People believe them to be proud, but it is not true. It is a matter rather of a total confidence in the word as word and the refusal to become domesticated. There is the true poet. He is someone who does not claim to make of his word something that domesticates men and that teaches them to live, but on the contrary someone who brings them a freedom, a freedom often uncomfortable moreover. I believe that the true message of the poet lies in this. It is not the fact of saying to the people that you must do this or you must do that; it is precisely to break all frames that have been placed around them so that they might bound back.[8]

The 'true poets' for Kateb are those who through their works seek to create new, alternative discourses that are neither unitary nor totalistic but achieve a freeing of difference and serve as models for the people who suffer under merciless social constraints. Michel Maffesoli speaks of the 'delusion of oneness' as being at the root of totalitarian violence in the modern world.[9] Such a delusion underlies the drive towards homogeneity, a reduction to a unitary system that seeks to domesticate the masses, to make of the many one, that opposes pluralism and multiculturalism, that delimits, contains and immobilizes. Cartesian logic and binary thinking would supplant the divergency of thought – 'a thought of the multiple – of dispersed and nomadic multiplicity that none of the constraints of the Same limit or rearrange'.[10]

---

[6] Deleuze and Guattari, *Nomadology: The War Machine* (New York: Columbia University Press, 1986).

[7] See Michael E. Meeker, *Literature and Violence in North Arabia* (Cambridge, UK: Cambridge University Press, 1979), p. 221 et passim. Also see my essay 'Nomadic Thought, Postcolonialism and Maghrebian Writing', in *Postcolonial Theory and Francophone Literary Studies*, eds H. Adlai Murdoch and Anne Donadey (Gainesville: University Press of Florida, 2005), pp. 67–86.

[8] Kateb Yacine, 'Le rôle de l'écrivain dans un état socialiste', *Anthologie des écrivains maghrébins d'expression française* (Paris: Présence Africaine, 1965), pp. 179–80.

[9] Michel Maffesoli, *Du nomadisme: Vagabondages initiatiques* (Paris: Librairie Générale Française, Le Livre de poche, 1997), p. 22.

[10] Michel Foucault, 'Theatricum philosophicum', *Dits et écrits I: 1954–1975* (Paris: Gallimard, 2001), p. 958.

What may be said of nomadic thought can be said of magical realism. These related phenomena appear in the works of several major Maghrebi writers: in the feminist narratives of Assia Djebar and Malika Mokeddem of Algeria, in the anti-Islamist or anti-*intégriste* texts of Rachid Boudjedra and Tahar Djaout (assassinated in 1963 by the Islamists), in the prison writings of the Moroccan Abdellatif Laâbi, and in the works of the novelist, critic and philosopher Abdelkebir Khatibi. But perhaps the writings of the Moroccan novelist Tahar Ben Jelloun best exemplify magical realism and its Maghrebian form of nomadic thought, particularly his writings that date from the 1980s, such as *L'Ecrivain public* (1983, *The Public Scribe*) and *L'Enfant de sable* (1985, *The Sand Child*).[11]

Tahar Ben Jelloun and Narrative Displacement

Ben Jelloun's work often evinces the intrusion of the magical and supernatural into the so-called real world: characters that mysteriously merge into one another and assume multiple personas; writing as event (created spontaneously as the narrative unfolds); a vocabulary of movement (routes, paths), closures and openings (doors, gates, thresholds onto other worlds) that eschew orthodox ways and passageways; the collapse of time and space – all of which challenge the rational. Ben Jelloun strews his work with ubiquitous references to the state of absence, related most often to the phenomenon of errancy. Absence and errancy correspond in Ben Jelloun's writing to a quest 'to inscribe open-endedness and non-presence in order to liberate the text from a repressive verisimilitude and release it to the imaginary'.[12] Mental or psychological displacement through imagination or fantasy, or through unfamiliar perception, engenders spatial displacement (nomadism, errancy, magical realism), and vice-versa.

As public letter writers, scribes, and itinerant storytellers, Ben Jelloun's protagonists represent figures of performance and inventiveness. The protagonist of *L'Ecrivain public* in a brief foreword speaks of setting out to write a story 'in the hope of defacing [*dévisager*] the confused image in the mirror' (p. 9). He proposes to tell the story of 'someone who is always elsewhere – a man in a hurry. Scarcely does he arrive than he is already off for elsewhere. [. . .] Without his masks, he is nothing. Or rather, he is a man among men, interchangeable' (p. 9). The scribe says, 'I like knowledge distant and inaccessible. As a public scribe I have often dreamt of entering into somebody's intimate life and scrambling

[11] Tahar Ben Jelloun, *L'Écrivain public* (Paris: Editions du Seuil,1983), my translation; and *L'Enfant de sable* (Paris: Editions du Seuil, 1985), for which I use the English translation of Alan Sheridan, *The Sand Child* (Baltimore and London: The Johns Hopkins University Press, 2000).

[12] As Marguerite Duras says of her own work. Qtd. in Jeanne Garane, '*Cette enfant blanche de l'Asie*: Orientalism, Colonialism, and *Métissage* in Marguerite Duras's *L'Amant*', in *French Cultural Studies: Criticism at the Crossroads*, eds Marie-Pierre Le Hir and Dana Strand (Albany: State University of New York Press, 2000), p. 237.

recollections so as to create a new memory in which no one would recognize the other' (p. 11). Ben Jelloun's scribe often invents letters that substitute for the ones illiterates dictate to him, sometimes saying the exact opposite of what the latter intended. He admits that he has the tendency to make things up, to fabulation. He concludes by telling the reader that he (the reader) is not obliged to read his (the scribe's) story from beginning to end but can page through it, read a chapter in the middle, then come back to the beginning. This unorthodox narrative sequencing he suggests calls to mind what writers like Julio Cortázar and Raymond Queneau have done to untrack the continuity and transparency of conventional writing.

One could say that all fiction makes things up. But the difference is how and to what purpose. So-called 'reality' in the novel depends of course on verisimilitude – making things seem real. The way of going about that has created the convention of the well-made narrative based on an Aristotelian model: a beginning, a well regulated action that mounts to a climax, a resolution or denouement whereby the action unravels and is resolved in a harmonious and intelligible manner. The enabling process of the conventional narrative is based on logic, which orders it in a clear and unambiguous way though the linking of events by cause and effect – all of which leads to a rationalized view of the world that attempts to imitate empirical reality in a convincing fashion. The French novelist Alain Robbe-Grillet has said that the technical elements of the conventional story function 'to impose the image of a stable, coherent, continuous, univocal, thoroughly decipherable universe' – whereas the perceptual elements of magical-realist and nomadic thought seek out variant directions.[13]

Ben Jelloun's *Sand Child* is strongly figured by magical-realist and nomadic writing, presenting a world characterized by the overlap and confusion of characters, genres, and worlds composed of contradictory predicates. The result is a grammar of movement and permutation, illimitable errancy and rebellious unorthodoxy. An example occurs near the beginning of the novel when the storyteller, speaking to his audience on the great square Djemaa el Fna (the meeting place of the dead) in Marrakech, tells them that the hero/heroine Ahmed/Zahra, a female child raised as a male, entrusted to him the book containing the secrets of his/her life. He tells them that the book has seven gates pierced in a wall at least two meters thick and as high as three stout men. He will open the gates for them as they make their way. He says, 'Our steps invent the path as we proceed; behind us they leave no trace, only the void' (pp. 7–8). They start with the Thursday Gate, the day the hero was born – 'Let us call him Ahmed' (p. 9). He tells his listeners: 'You have chosen to listen to me, so follow me to the end . . . The end of what?' he asks, adding "Circular streets have no end!"' (p. 12).

The next day they pass through the Friday Gate as he relates the childhood of Ahmed, the day following through the Saturday Gate (the gate of Ahmed's

---

[13] Alain Robbe-Grillet, 'Sur quelques notions périmées', in *Pour un nouveau roman* (Paris: Éditions de Minuit, Collection Idées, 1963), pp. 29–53.

adolescence), 'a very obscure period', the storyteller says, whose blanks are 'left for the reader to fill in as he will' (p. 27). They arrive at the Bab El Had, 'the outer gate, the wall erected to put an end to a situation'. Despite his previous assurances, the storyteller warns them it will be their last gate. From that moment on, they will no longer pass through the city gates but through forgotten openings and breaches in the wall (p. 45).

The Disintegration of the Narrative World

The way the storyteller leads us is doubtful, uncertain, invented as we proceed ('You do not know where I am leading you. Fear not, I do not know, either', p. 12). It reflects the permutations and changes that take place in the narrative itself. The supposed book of Ahmed and the journal he allegedly kept are as unstable as the narrative – they threaten to disintegrate or disappear. At the end of the novel, the instability of the narrative that has all along haunted us leaves its final mark: we are told that the book of Ahmed/Zahra, on which the storytelling has drawn, was 'emptied of its writings by the full moon' (p. 165), washed clean, like a palimpsest ready to be written over and over, endlessly. A cluster of metaphors of erasure or illegibility occurs: the great notebook rendered undecipherable by tears that have dropped onto it (p. 37); letters with unreadable signatures (p. 41); the brief notes of Ahmed and his anonymous correspondent that are unreadable or 'strange' (p. 66), replete with crossed-out words (p. 72); the insects carrying off words and images from the disintegrating manuscript, a process hastened by a stream that runs through its pages (pp. 81–2); Zahra's mirror that mists over (p. 87).

The uncertainty of the way is paralleled by the instability of the characters: not only that of the androgynous protagonist Ahmed/Zahra, but the storytellers, notably the Blind Troubadour, who is thinly disguised as the real-life Jorge Luis Borges. Elsewhere I have discussed the question of intertextuality and Ben Jelloun's parody of Borges. In addressing other raconteurs, Amar and Salem, the Blind Troubadour speaks of being in their 'tale', of traveling from afar, 'from another century, thrown into one tale by another tale', of having been 'expelled' from other tales (p. 135). He tells them he is crossing a bridge between dreams. Like dreams, places become interchangeable, exist simultaneously and within each other, like tales within tales. In speaking of their frequenting a cafe in Marrakech, he speaks of how at the same time they find themselves in the heart of Buenos Aires! During the visit of an unknown woman to his library in Buenos Aires, he relates the sensation he had of being a character in a book, even of being a book (p. 139). The woman who visits him, 'probably an Arab', hands him a letter of introduction from one Stephen Albert, a character in a short story of Borges. To confound things further, the voice recalls to him a voice he had previously heard in a book he had read – that of Tawaddud in the 1001 Nights.

The most mind-stretching instance of shifting from one narrative level to another occurs as he speaks of himself as emerging from and having lived a story, the concluding words of which he cites identify it as Borges' short story, 'The Circular Ruins'. Borges' narrative describes a magician awaiting death, who, desiring to dream into being a man, comes to understand that 'he, too, was an apparition, that someone else was dreaming him'.[14] What purpose does this interpenetration of narrative levels, which pushes illogic and contradiction to the limit, serve? Ben Jelloun refuses us any possibility of definitively understanding the narrators and characters, of making any sense ultimately out of the story itself. He pushes the phenomenon of narrative embedding or enclosure to an extreme, by enclosing stories within stories to such a degree that levels blend into each other, barriers separating characters and creators/tellers are broken through and become traversable; that narrators/characters pass freely from one narrative level to another, moving in and out of stories without impingement, just as we move in and out of dreams and in and out of the characters themselves.

A paradigm for the narrative of Ben Jelloun is the fictional model Borges introduces in 'The Garden of Forking Paths'. The character Stephen Albert explains to the narrator the solution of Ts'ui Pen, who set out to write an infinite book. It must be circular in nature, 'forking in time, not in space' (p. 26). In traditional fictional narrative, when confronted with alternatives, one chooses one and omits the others, whereas Ts'ui Pen's narrative, rather than choosing one of the paths at a fork, would choose all paths simultaneously – the image of the universe in which there exists no 'uniform, absolute time' (p. 28).

We are struck by the similarity of Ben Jelloun's narrative, with its diverse and varied endings, as a choice of all possible paths. One is also reminded of how the Blind Troubadour, reading a narrative by Al Mo'atassim discovered in the fifteenth century, finds the meaning of seven keys left to him by Ahmed/Zahra to open the seven portals of the city. He speculates that 'a storyteller from the far South tried to penetrate these gates, but destiny or malevolence prevented the poor man from succeeding' (pp. 148–9). The evident allusion to our storyteller implies that either he lived simultaneously at the time of the medieval manuscript and in the twentieth century, or that the manuscript speaks into the future, such that chronology shatters and the storyteller wanders unimpeded through any and all times and places. The motif of 'keys', moreover, that appears throughout the narrative (keys to the seven doors of the city, to the seven gardens of the soul, the key to the 'secret' that lies within the box, the keys given to the Blind Troubadour by the unknown woman), by the close of the narrative leaves the reader thoroughly disbelieving of keys. Ben Jelloun's narrative draws us in, expels us, and we are wiser for being no wiser, for realizing that 'keys' do not exist and, if they appear to exist, are not to be trusted, for they either do not open doors or open doors onto illusion or nothingness.

---

[14] *The Sand Child*, p. 136; Jorge Luis Borges, *Labyrinths: Selected Stories & Other Writings* (New York: New Directions, 1964), p. 50.

Seizing Control of the Sign

Tahar Ben Jelloun holds in common with the Maghrebi writers I have mentioned the refusal to be domesticated, as Kateb has said. They seek to create a new space for their writing, a fertile soil in which will germinate a non-totalizing, alternative discourse. They write out of 'the very experience of uprooting, disjunction and metamorphosis' described by Salman Rushdie in regard to displaced peoples.[15]

Ben Jelloun as well as the other North African authors I have mentioned do not attempt to effect a simple poetics of reversal by replacing one power frame by another. They do not counter the various dichotomies in the discourses of the Islamic faith system or of Western cultural systems by the simple act of reversal, for in such a case the binary oppositions that legitimize discourses of power – truth/falsity, male/female, for example – would merely be reaffirmed. But by playing with the aleatory nature of language, its proclivity to escape us, each in his or her own way seeks to seize control of the sign and to bring about what Abdelkebir Khatibi terms 'translation', that is, the transformation or re-vision and reworking of the foreign linguistic and cultural values of the European tongue they wield, and their reinscription into a new context of value reflecting the indivisible union of diverse tongues and diverse cultures.

These authors, who are elsewhere, as Ben Jelloun's Scribe says, with relation to the dominant discourses, inhabit 'locations' (to use Rushdie's term) that comprise not just the distanced geographical and psychological places whence they come, but the 'elsewhere' of the intertextuality that also marks their writings. Though all narratives take root in preceding works, the source material for magical realist narratives – in large part consciously derived – tells us a good deal about the types of narrative encountered.

The notion of intertextuality has much to do with the phenomenon the French call *métissage* and the Spanish *mestizaje* – the bastardized or culturally/artistically/racially mixed or diluted. It bespeaks the interpenetration of cultures, the use made of other ideas and cultural positionings. It inveighs against any notion of a literary or cultural imperialism that rules by exclusivity. Such activity as we have seen in the writers studied is magical-realist and nomadic, in the sense given to that term by Deleuze and Guattari. The nomadic and magical-realist aspect of the writing of the Maghrebi authors lies in the strategic move of spatial shifting from site to site, from other text to other text, from plateau to plateau that mediates meaning.

The breaches and forgotten openings of *The Sand Child* metaphorize the passages effected by nomadic wanderings that reflect displacement, constant shifting of *loci*. We move incessantly from one cultural, social, and literary terrain to another, from one elsewhere to another, out of reach of the delimiting action of master discourses and of a prescriptive, absolutistic master canon.

---

[15] Salman Rushdie, *Imaginary Homelands. Essays and Criticism, 1981–1991* (London: Granta Books/New York: Viking Penguin, 1991).

'Métissage' – Moving from Plateau to Plateau

Métissage introduces magical-realist elements, whose mixture of fantasy and reality expands the traditional realist narrative. Intermixing or *métissage* appears in the manner authors traverse genres and blend them in such pronounced ways in their works – prose fiction, poetry, historical and mythic narrative, proverbs, songs, religious texts, popular folk tales, classical rhetorical forms, oral speech transcriptions, dialogic and dramatic discourse.

This mixing of genres puts in mind the pervasive resemblances between post-colonial, magical-realist and nomadic writings and what is often called post-modern writing, particularly in the ways in which they expand and mongrelize the conventional narrative, in their extensive use of irony, and in the development of a new antiphonal and antinomical rhetoric (a new sophism).

Ben Jelloun's magical-realist or nomadic narrative calls into question the assumption that life is made up of a space and time continuum that is forward flowing, dominated by sight and vision.[16] It does so by breaking through the bounds of the visual world and opening up another world in which discontinu-ity and indeterminacy rule; where narratives are unending, circular, and turn back on themselves; where words cohabit with insects and give themselves up to nat-ural processes; where writing cedes to a blank page or superimposes itself on previous writing in an endless palimpsest; where blindness turns us from vision to a world of auditory, tactile, olfactory sensations.

The Sand Child draws precisely on those powers of the human mind and senses that George Steiner speaks of when he asserts that, 'Beyond the present chaos lies the possibility of "new configurations" of perception; man's dormant senses, his powers of integration, the chthonic, magic fiber of his being, will be liberated from the closed, passive system of Gutenberg literacy' (Steiner, p. 256). Magical-realist and nomadic counter-narratives offer just such liberation. While still drawing on the resources of Western and Islamic thought, in contriving alternate discourses flowing out of postcolonial and otherly sensibilities and perceptions, they nonetheless leave behind the linear, closed worlds of Western and Islamic magisterial narratives and discourses and the ideological forces subtending them.

---

[16] George Steiner, *Language and Silence* (New York: Atheneum, 1982), p. 254.

Of Numerology and Butterflies: Magical Realism in Salman Rushdie's *The Satanic Verses*

Stephanie Jones

Between Falling and Flying

The Satanic Verses begins and does not begin with a blast, a terrorist bomb in the skies above the English Channel.[1] The text actually opens with the moments after the blast: the explosion is only told on page 87. The millenarian explosion of terrorist activity is, then, itself blasted out of its own sense of place in time – denied its self-aggrandising space in history – by the text itself. This textual explosion conjures Walter Benjamin's 'materialist historiography' which 'blasts open the continuum of history'. Against 'historicism', Benjamin writes of the 'constructive principle' of historiography that crucially works from 'the notion of a present which is not a transition, but in which time stands still and has come to a stop'.[2] This is the endless ending and beginning of Rushdie's text, a moment of crisis restructuring history against the assumed discreteness of subjects in time. The text begins with its two protagonists, Saladin Chamcha and Gibreel Farishta, singing and talking as they slow-fall from the exploding aeroplane: 'Gibreelsaladin Farishtachmcha, condemned to this endless but also ending angelicdevelish fall, did not become aware of the moment at which the process of their transmutation began' (Rushdie, *Satanic*, p. 5). This still/falling/flying moment provokes an intricately spliced narrative in which time runs strangely (back and) towards the apparent collapse of subjectivity and history into a twisting deconstructive play of language.

Using Benjamin's ideas, Homi Bhabha writes against a teleological 'transcendental temporality' and 'locate[s] an aesthetic in this time of inscription whose stillness is not stasis but a shock'.[3] Bhabha defines this 'transit' aesthetic

---

[1] Salman Rushdie, *The Satanic Verses* (London: Random House, 1998 [1988]).

[2] Walter Benjamin, *Illuminations*, trans. Harry Zohn, ed. Hannah Arendt (London: Fontana Press, 1992), p. 254.

[3] Homi K. Bhabha, 'The World and the Home', *Social Text*, 10.2–3 (1992), 141–53 (p. 144).

as 'a revolutionary chance in the fight for the oppressed past'. For him, all forms
of suppression can be challenged by such temporally and linguistically
revolutionary expressions of 'transnational histories of migrants, the colonized,
or political refugees' (Bhabha, p. 146). In *The Satanic Verses*, the hectic and
broken temporality of the text disrupts the monumental histories arising out of
both the time of the nation and the pure, transcendental revolutionary agendas of
terrorism and religious (and other) fundamentalisms. The text begins in an
almost arrested moment. It floats above Britain of the early 1970s, and a ground-
swell of racism promoting a pure national space, and it floats beneath the
aeroplane hijacked by the Sikh terrorists seeking the purity of a Khalistan.
However, such moments of stasis within the text are not, significantly, always
such moments of liberating, revelatory shock.

The group whose bomb begins and does not begin the novel is re-inscribed
again and again in the text, a technique that defies, by deferring, their monu-
mentalism. They are most notably textually reincarnated in the suspended
utopian revolution of the time obsessed Kensington Imam. The Imam, 'frozen'
in 'a dream of glorious return', yearns for a homecoming beyond history
(Rushdie, *Satanic*, p. 205). Described as 'a ball hurled high into the air', his condition is notably similar to that of Saladin and Gibreel floating towards the sea.
Out of his frustrated stasis, the Imam explodes into devastating movement, flies
to his homeland, expunges the word 'clock' from the dictionaries and, in one of
the least ambiguous images in the book, is pictured 'lying in the palace forecourt
with his mouth yawning open at the gates; as the people march through the gates
he swallows them whole' (Rushdie, *Satanic*, p. 215). The suspended moments
within *The Satanic Verses* can, then, begin the 'monstrous' annihilation of history
and time in the purifying triumph of monologism. Or they can begin the claiming of a skew temporality and a multiple, leaking impurity of identity. Against
Bhabha's emphatic celebration of the deconstructive impetus, it may be that
these parallel moments of stasis hint at a hesitancy, a qualm, a recognition that
the extreme of (the) one comes too close to the extreme of (the many) other.
Against even Rushdie's own critical rhetoric of absolute 'impurity', *The Satanic
Verses* may be read to suggest that the absolving quality of fiction – of the
specific quirky element that is story – is found somewhere more prosaically
in-between the extreme significations of (religious) teleology and (secular)
multiplicity. This begins with the comically prosaic and real-to-life dialogue that
resists too expansive and absolute an interpretation of the opening semantic and
magical breakdown between falling and flying.[4]

Ascension is one of the mundane miracles that almost defines the genre of
magical-realist fiction.[5] In *The Satanic Verses*, Rushdie initiates his plethoric

---

[4] Salman Rushdie, 'In Good Faith', in *Imaginary Homelands: Essays and Criticism
1981–1991* (London: Granta, 1992 [1991]), pp. 393–414.

[5] For a discussion of the many winged creatures and flights within magical-realist modes
of writing, see Wendy B. Faris, *Ordinary Enchantments: Magical Realism and the
Remystification of Narrative* (Nashville: Vanderbilt UP, 2004), p. 56.

narrative by upsetting the difference between both the physical facts and moral valences of falling and flying in a way that connects his text to Blake and back to Milton; to a tradition of works in which the angelic quality of flight is dropped, and the devilish quality of falling is held up to be understood. Writing of the political implications of flight in the work of Milan Kundera, Wendy Faris points out that (with 'Heidegger, Nietzsche, and their existentialist successors'), Kundera 'condemns' flight, 'as it may evade issues of mortality and history' (Faris, *Ordinary*, p. 58). In *The Satanic Verses*, the questioning is more circumspect. Rather than direct condemnation, the novel allows, as it were, the binary opposition between flying and falling (angelic and devilish states) to demonstrate its own deconstruction. Saladin and Gibreel fall buoyantly; they drop, but are suspended. During their air-time, the abstract qualities of the angel and devil are distilled and distributed (evenly or unevenly? this is one of the impossible questions of the book) between the two ordinary-extraordinary men. In their immediate and discombobulating future, as they splash their way out of the English channel, their confusion of identity manifests not just the migrant condition, but becomes 'a metaphor' – in Rushdie's own word – 'for all humanity' (Rushdie, *Imaginary*, p. 394). However, while the text is opened up by this statement (as well as by the less metaphorical idea of the migrant nature of all humanity into which it easily twists), the novel itself also – in each uniquely cavorting narrative strand – resists this very mode of encompassing declaration. While there is magic in their flight/fall, Saladin and Gibreel speak not of the grand and the metaphysical, but tease, bicker and chat in small and ordinary terms.

In his seminal essay 'Magic Realism as Postcolonial Discourse', Stephen Slemon warns that 'the critical use of the concept of magical realism can . . . signify resistance to monumental theories of literary practice . . . At the same time, of course, the concept of magic realism itself threatens to become a monumentalizing category . . . upon which the massive problem of difference in literary expression can be managed into recognizable meaning in one swift pass'.[6] Turning this point around, it can be said that it is all too easy to monumentalise the infinite fact of difference as the impetus and endless end of magical realism: that the defining techniques of this (trend or tradition of) literature always already read as an absolute resistance to binary systems of thought and monologic historiographies, becoming an absolute celebration of malleable subjectivities and the infinite possibilities of narrative. Because of the fraught publication history of *The Satanic Verses* itself, Rushdie's novel has been particularly useful – or particularly vulnerable – to aggrandising abstractions of magical realism. In their important introduction to the themes and major texts emerging from literary critical work on magical realism, Lois Parkinson Zamora and Wendy Faris identify Rushdie's *The Satanic Verses* as 'The most

---

[6] Stephen Slemon, 'Magic Realism as Postcolonial Discourse', *Magical Realism: Theory, History, Community*, eds Lois Parkinson Zamora and Wendy Faris (Durham and London: Duke UP, 1995), pp. 407–26 (p. 408).

controversial magical-realist text of all'.[7] The novel, however, has often been
over-determined by the controversy of the *fatwa* – the death-sentence – declared
against Rushdie by Ayatollah Ruholla Khomeini in 1989 on the grounds that
The Satanic Verses blasphemes against Islam. The *fatwa* was lifted in 1998, but
the decade of events without the text have often obscured the controversy of
doubt enacted within the text itself. In his comment that '*The Satanic Verses* is
not, in my view, an antireligious novel', Rushdie hints at the commitment, not
just to the abstract notion of belief, but to local communities of belief with
which he is attempting to wrangle.[8] This statement points to specific narratives
of respect, loss and redemption glossed over by critical concentration on the
post-structuralist aspects of the text, and more generally within the Anglo-
western academy by the flurry of liberal outrage focused on the writer's right
to blaspheme (not to mention some of the strange half-sympathies with the
fatwa which dismissed Rushdie's plight on the grounds that he should have
known better).[9] The aim of this essay is to explore how Rushdie uses the apparently boundless mode of magical realism, not only to indicate the excitements
and discomforts of endless multiplicity, but – albeit with trepidation – to seek a
covert and careful relief in more bounded ideas of organic local and
transplanted diasporic collectivities.

Between Two and 1001

The Satanic Verses explores the more prosaic ideas of grounded community
within an insistent and playful, sometimes magical and almost overwhelming
poetic of numbers. In 'Beauty and the Beast: Dualism as Despotism in the Fiction
of Salman Rushdie', M. Keith Booker traces the motif of paired characters
through Rushdie's novels. He describes how the author sets these oppositions up
only to demonstrate 'that the apparent polar opposites are in fact interchangeable
and mutually interdependent'.[10] But as in Rushdie's work itself, Booker's analysis of the instability of binary structures quickly becomes a recognition of more

---

[7] Wendy B. Faris and Zamora, Lois Parkinson. 'Introduction', in *Magical Realism:
Theory, History, Community*, eds Lois Parkinson Zamora and Wendy Faris (Durham and
London: Duke UP, 1995), p. 9.

[8] Salman Rushdie, 'The Book Burning', *New York Review of Books*, 36.3 (2 March
1989), p. 26.

[9] For analyses of 'the Rushdie affair', see Sadik Jalal Al-Azm, 'The Importance of Being
Earnest about Salman Rushdie', in *Reading Rushdie: Perspectives on the Fiction of Salman
Rushdie*, ed. D.M. Fletcher (Amsterdam: Rodopi, 1994) pp. 254–92; and *The Rushdie Letters:
Freedom to Speak, Freedom to Write*, ed. Steve MacDonogh (Lincoln: University of Nebraska
Press, 1993).

[10] M. Keith Booker, 'Beauty and the Beast: Dualism as Despotism in the Fiction of Salman
Rushdie', in *Reading Rushdie: Perspectives on the Fiction of Salman Rushdie*, ed.
D.M. Fletcher (Amsterdam: Rodopi, 1994), pp. 237–54 (p. 238).

infinite confusions. Booker moves from a consideration of the falsity of the two to the incomprehensibility of the Sheherazadean one thousand and one that is the recurring signifier of infinite metamorphoses, exciting possibilities and the power of fiction across Rushdie's texts. In *Midnight's Children*, Saleem Sinai's identity is compromised at birth, not only because he is swapped as a newborn with his alter ego Shiva, but because he is one of 1001 children born at the moment of India's independence.[11] While Saleem is the most unreliable of narrators, the description of his unwitting telepathy – his transformation into a radio transmitter for the other 1000 children – powerfully signifies, not just his symbolic relationship to the nation, but also a more quotidian and terrifying bloating and fragmentation of identity. Similarly, where *The Satanic Verses* begins with the breakdown of identity between Saladin and Gibreel, this binary confusion gives way to the recognition of other splinterings of identity. It isn't only the magic of the slow-fall that has prompted dis- and re-integrations of identity: within the real that preceded the explosion, the idea of self was far from unitary. In Saladin Chamcha's adumbrated name (from Chamchawallah to Chamcha) Rushdie signifies the crisis and loss of his Anglophilia, further emphasised by the colloquial meaning of Chamcha as, in Rushdie's explanation, 'a person who sucks up to powerful people'.[12] But even further, in his public persona as the 'Man of a Thousand Voices and a Voice', Chamcha's identity slips in and out of the fictions of his professional work (Rushdie, *Satanic*, p. 60). However, between two and 1001, the binary and the infinite through which Rushdie's texts are most obviously structured, other numbers take on particular and spectacular significance. A less noted motif is three.

In *Shame*, the narrator has three mothers in three fiercely reclusive sisters.[13] In an exemplary incident of the magical real – the verging of the most earthly matter of birth on the miraculous – while one sister becomes pregnant (in the ordinary way), their identities are so intertwined that the other two experience sympathetic pregnancies, the pains of labour and the ability to breastfeed. Which woman is the narrator's biological mother remains unknown, and is even forgotten by the sisters themselves as they coalesce into an intimidating uber-identity. In *Fury*, the outrageous anger of the protagonist Malik Solanka is often described as a visitation by the three screeching and voracious, sexually-charged furies of classical mythology.[14] And in *The Satanic Verses*, the three Goddesses, Allah's or Shaitan's 'fiendish backing group' – Lat, Manat, Uzza – are at the heart of the text, the subjects of the satanic verse themselves (Rushdie, *Satanic*, p. 91). The verse of recognition and acceptance – 'They are the exalted

[11] Salman Rushdie, *Midnight's Children* (Book Club Associates and Jonathan Cape: London, 1982 [1981]).

[12] Quoted in Booker, p. 242. Rushdie, 'The Empire Writes Back with a Vengeance', *The Times* (London, 3 July 1982), p. 8.

[13] Salman Rushdie, *Shame* (London: Picador, 1984 [1983]).

[14] Salman Rushdie, *Fury* (London: Jonathon Cape, 2001).

birds, and their intercession is desired indeed' – is later recanted by the Prophet, who comes (after a wrestling match with Gibreel) to believe that the words came not through the archangel Gibreel, not from Allah, but from 'Shaitan' (Rushdie, *Satanic*, p. 114, p. 123). The story of the recanted verses ends with an exhausted Gibreel – modern-day movie star, archaic diabolical archangel, and anti-protagonist – in his dreams/not-dreams:

> Often now, he finds himself alone on the summit of Mount Cone, washed by the cold, falling stars, and then they fall upon him from the night sky, the three winged creatures, Lat Uzza Manat, flapping around his head, clawing at his eyes, biting, whipping him with their hair, their wings. He puts up his hands to protect himself, but their revenge is tireless. . . . He struggles against them, but they are faster, nimbler, winged. (Rushdie, *Satanic*, p. 126)

In Rushdie's texts, three is a powerful, feminine number that challenges monologism and monotheism, imploding masculine binary hierarchies. In a text that is celebrated for its celebration of multiplicity, it might be expected that such a three would be exalted. But in consonance with Faris's reading of flight as an often nihilistic motif, these winged creatures are destroyers. Throughout Rushdie's work, and most prominently in *The Satanic Verses*, the image of the three signifies threat, dissatisfaction, loss of emotional control and a too loose hold on identity and language (these women screech and cry). In this, Rushdie seems not just to be reproducing a clichéd fear of feminine sexuality, but to apprehend the dangers of the collapsing tropes of alterity. At one level his portraiture of the three reveals a residual patriarchal attitude that belies the strong and quirky women that inhabit less ambivalently real zones within his texts. But at another level, he hints at the cautious yearning for boundedness that I would argue informs some of the most moving sections of *The Satanic Verses*, and indeed Rushdie's other novels. Within Rushdie's work, religions and communities of faith are not always or simply appalling or ridiculous, but are sympathetically shot with nostalgia and a definitively human yearning. Booker summarises Rushdie's sense of religious need by pointing to the character of Adaam Aziz in *Midnight's Children* who, having lost his religious faith experiences the sensation of 'a hole at the heart of his very self'. He suggests that, bereft of religion, Rushdie offers paradoxical 'alternative myths for the modern age' in his tales of fragmenting subjectivities (Booker, p. 252). However, I would argue that his texts attempt to fill the hole, not just in this sum-total valuing of literature itself, but through a more specific doubt about the nature of doubt and collectives of faith embedded in the text. If the driving sense of Rushdie's work is derision and fear of the purities that ground – not just religious – hegemonies, then it is also wary of a pure form of impurity (an hegemony of impurity) and the devolution of story into a secular allegorical reification of hybridity. Where purity is made puerile and/or revealed as dangerous, a coherence is nevertheless sought. In *The Satanic Verses*, this is drawn out most poignantly in the chapters on the Ayesha Haj, a story that is unwittingly and unwillingly dreamed, hallucinated, willed or prophesied by Gibreel.

Between the Abstraction of Numbers and the Texture of Butterflies

In *The Satanic Verses*, our narrator (Satan himself, apologist and usurper?) often tells us that '*it was and it was not so*, as the old stories used to say, *it happened and it never did*' (Rushdie, *Satanic*, p. 35). One of the defining characteristics listed by Faris in her influential enumeration of the elements of magical realism is hesitancy 'between two contradictory understandings of events'.[15] In her more extensive survey of the form, Faris develops this notion of hesitancy into the concept of 'defocalisation' and the idea of the 'ineffable in-between' (Faris, *Ordinary*, p. 43, p. 45). These terms comprehend wily and unreliable narrators, but more crucially attempt to understand the fuller generic sense of indeterminacy, mystery and 'irreducible strangeness' that is conjured beyond the particularities of any one narrator's identity (Faris, *Ordinary*, p. 68). In *The Satanic Verses*, this sense is most acute in Gibreel's dream-sequences, in which the omniscient narrator follows (or conducts?) Gibreel's movement between three discrete but parallel narratives: of the exiled Imam, the Prophet, and the Ayesha Haj. The tenor of these sequences is disorienting, oscillating between irony, bemusement, awe and an agony of empathy, occasionally interrupted by expressions of Gibreel's sleepy frustration. He like the reader doesn't know the status of the events, their place in time, in his head, beyond or within this world's history. But most crucially, he is both controlled and controlling, inadvertently but powerfully prompting events with words passively or unhappily spoken to the Prophet, the Imam and Ayesha, apparently (?) in Allah's name. This confusion of will is a radically defocalising move by the author that stymies the reader's attempts to fix on a moral perspective. The ineffable atmosphere of these scenes between their possible dream-status and quotidian detail divert the temptation to read them as allegory, trapping the reader in perplexity even when the point of the narrative seems terribly real and horribly clear, as it does in the incident of the stoning of the baby within the Ayesha Haj sequences.

The narrative of Ayesha describes a beautiful, epileptic orphan girl who convinces a group of villagers to follow her on a pilgrimage to the sea, which she claims will part and allow them to walk to Mecca. One of the more briefly described episodes on the pilgrims' way involves a foundling, left on the steps of a mosque at which the pilgrims have stopped for Friday prayers. The Imam exclaims to his congregation that the child 'was born in devilment'. Asked for her opinion on the child, Ayesha makes the cryptic pronouncement: 'Everything will be asked of us', she replied. 'The crowd, needing no clearer invitation, stoned the baby to death' (Rushdie, *Satanic*, p. 497).

While the scene reveals the devastating power of the mob, it is also part of the larger narrative on the nature of language. The suspended, deadly, ridiculous

---

[15] Wendy B. Faris, 'Scheherazade's Children: Magical Realism and Postmodern Fiction', in *Magical Realism: Theory, History, Community*, eds Lois Parkinson Zamora and Wendy Faris (Durham and London: Duke UP, 1995), pp. 163–90 (p. 171).

phrase repeats (with slight variation) the words apparently given to Ayesha by Gibreel, through which she has convinced and often rallies the villagers: 'Everything is required of us, and everything will be given' (Rushdie, *Satanic*, p. 235). The variation in her phrase links the scene to the story of the playfully named scribe Salman, who tests the Prophet through very slight but deliberate mistranscriptions of the word of God. This story, however, may be read as less about the fallibility of the Prophet than about the moral need to interpret and discuss, to commune at a more mundane level. Ayesha holds tightly but passively to her hyperbole of prophecy as though it expresses clarity. Her inability or refusal to do no more than recite is at extreme odds with the tripping, spilling, adjectival language of Rushdie himself 'what Faris refers to as the 'carnivalesque spirit' of magic realism in which '[l]anguage is used extravagantly, expending its resources beyond its referential needs'. She describes a language of excess, suited to the 'grand and extravagant' passions that are so wild they burst the bounds of realism. In Rushdie's work, this 'Baroque mode of overextension' does all this and more (Faris, 'Sheherazade', p. 184). In every sentence, the author inscribes an anti-dogmatic, super-Bahktinian aesthetic of debate and qualification over command and recitation. It is intensely consistent with this aesthetic that the concentrated descriptions of the magical-real elements within the Ayesha Haj narrative work into a crucially poignant imagining of community and the power of belief.

The story of Ayesha and her pilgrims is based on an actual historical event in which thirty-eight Shia Muslims walked into the Arabian Sea in the expectation that the waters would part, allowing them to walk to Karbala. They were moved to this act of conviction by a young woman who claimed to be in contact with the twelfth Imam. Most of the pilgrims drowned, but those who survived were arrested for attempting to leave Pakistan without visas. In Sara Suleri's view, 'such fictive material renders magic realism obsolete'.[16] The clouds of butterflies that swarm thickly around the girl and texture the story – and to which Rushdie devotes an extravagant proportion of the narrative – are reduced in Suleri's reading to a sign of Ayesha's chastity, an analysis that ignores their almost sentient behaviour and magical charge (Suleri, p. 233). For Pierre François, Ayesha is unambiguously a 'destroyer'. In understanding her as a 'death instinct' and 'chaotic womb', he denies her parallel with the human agonies of the Prophet and implies she is bound only to the three furious Goddesses.[17] Sadik Jalal Al-Azm deals similarly shortly with the creaturely phenomena. In a reading that only picks out the 'mock-heroic tone that turns into a biting satire of the stupidity of the whole affair', the butterflies emphatically symbolise 'the religious

---

[16] Sara Suleri, 'Contraband Histories: Salman Rushdie and the Embodiment of Blasphemy', in *Reading Rushdie: Perspectives on the Fiction of Salman Rushdie*, ed. D.M. Fletcher (Amsterdam: Rodopi, 1994), pp. 221–35 (p. 232).

[17] Pierre François, 'Salman Rushdie's Philosophical Materialism in *The Satanic Verses*', in *Reading Rushdie: Perspectives on the Fiction of Salman Rushdie*, ed. D.M. Fletcher (Amsterdam: Rodopi, 1994), pp. 305–19 (p. 314).

illusions and false hopes that Ayesha lives on and then feeds to the simple and poor' (Al-Azim, p. 258). Such decisively dismissive readings seem at odds with the lush ponderings the author devotes to the butterflies. Abstracting the butterflies to a single static metaphor, these critical approaches ignore their very real, powdery, physical presence in the village and amongst the pilgrims, as well as their magical attachments and select detachments. Conversely, within the lineaments of a tragic-comic narrative infused with a sense of sympathy and yearning, it is difficult to accept the butterflies' odd physical presence and behaviour as in itself their point. Faris writes that 'in contrast to the magical images constructed by surrealism out of ordinary objects, which aim to appear virtually unmotivated and thus programmatically resist interpretation, magical-real images, while projecting a similar initial aura of surprising craziness, tend to reveal their motivations – psychological, social, emotional, political – after some scrutiny' (Faris, 'Sheherazade', p. 171). In the abundance of Rushdie's writing, the butterflies appear to bear meaning on all these planes.

Between Placed and Displaced Communities

Within the economy of the novel, flight – beginning with the protagonists, and linked both to the fundamentalist Imam and to the winged Goddesses – can signify the ahistoricism of both too hard a monotheism and too rampant a multiplicity. In their fantastic numbers, the butterflies seem to more fully perplex the binary worldview. At some moments in the narrative they appear to be a manifestation of Allah, at others of Satan, suspending the meaning of the story between the two. In a text that at every turn disrupts the association of God and Satan with fixed moral categories, it is difficult to know to whom the butterfly moments of grace are owed. Having left the pilgrims during an almost supernaturally violent storm (which saved them from being attacked, and was itself interpreted as Allah's work), the butterflies reappear to gather and lead the pilgrims back together. 'Every single member of the pilgrimage' is found, healed by the soft touch of wings (or so claims are made) and led back to the road by 'long lines of the little creatures'. The members of the Ayesha Haj return to their journey 'coated from neck to ankles in golden butterflies' (Rushdie, Satanic, pp. 494–5). However, it is directly after this miraculous event that the baby is stoned to death by the local congregation, leading both reader and the pilgrims to doubt Ayesha's status. Further, the butterflies hover and land around the outside of the mosque, but won't enter it, which could signify their devilish nature, or God's disquiet at the killing of the baby. As Faris comments, 'an irreducible element, like a good fetish, keeps incompatible ideas alive' (Faris, 'Ordinary', p. 61).

In using the anthropology of fetish to explore the elusive nature of magical-real objects, Faris recognises it as an aesthetic grounded in the archaic and most often brought about 'through proximity to ancient culture or nature' (Faris, 'Ordinary', p. 62). In the Ayesha Haj narrative, the butterflies signify an older story: 'They had been the familiar spirits, or so the legend ran, of a local saint, the holy woman known only as Bibiji' (Rushdie, *Satanic*, p. 217). The village's name of 'Titlipur' (butterfly home) positions the story of Bibiji (suggesting a generic grandmotherly goddess, the name heightens the sense of fable) as the founding-myth of the community. Further, the village is described as having 'grown up in the shade of an immense banyan-tree . . . By now the growth of tree into village and village into tree had become so intricate that it was impossible to differentiate between the two' (Rushdie, *Satanic*, p. 222). Within this narrative, the butterflies become less important as markers of metaphysical and religious angst, but rather signify an organically bound idea of community. While Rushdie's texts abound with examples of damaging communalisms, he is also crucially interested in the power and redemptive qualities of community. The butterflies, leading the villages into a deathly, life-affirming belief beyond themselves, also ('like a good fetish') signify their belief in themselves as an organic, multiple entity. The story of the Ayesha Haj ends with the village-tree burning and, within the fire, the image of the waters parting and opening the way to Mecca as a man's heart breaks (Rushdie, *Satanic*, p. 507). While the final scene is of a fantastic erotic destruction (in line with François's reading) – as the man splits from his Adam's apple to his groin and Ayesha reaches inside him – the fuller emotional resonance leading up to the end of the story focuses nostalgically on the death of the community: butterflies have been replaced by moths and the village has 'crumbled to dust' (Rushdie, *Satanic*, pp. 505–6).

The story of Titlipur explored above is unusual in that Rushdie is primarily a writer of cities. One of his major talents is to conjure the sense of multiple, archaic-modern, diasporic communities that exist within and make up a metropolis. Encompassing the story of Titlipur, the longer and larger story of Saladin Chamcha's involvements with the migrants of London moves towards a similarly intense sensibility of community. Rushdie's novel is arguably saved from the ahistoricising potential of the deconstructive spread of the text by the particularity of Chamcha's bewildered angst between the holding networks of diasporic communities and a despairing-hope in exile. Chamcha may be read as centrally and uncomfortably located between his defensive Anglophilic statement – 'we're not Indian like you' – and its turn, later in the text, into a defiance of this connective 'we'. Chamcha is offered refuge in a London home at the heart of the city's South Asian community: ' "Best place for you is here. . . . Where else but here, with us, among your own people, your own kind?" When he is alone, Chamcha answers the rhetorical question: "I'm not your kind," he said distinctly into the night. "You're not my people. I've spent half my life trying to get away from you" ' (Rushdie, *Satanic*, p. 253). But in stating that he has spent 'half' his life trying to ensure this removal, he implicitly admits to the other half of his life as part, involved, as connected – as 'we'. Chamcha speaks pompously to himself:

> I am by nature an inward man, he said silently. . . . I have struggled, in my fashion, to find my way towards an appreciation of the high things, toward a small

> measure of fineness . . . But it eluded me. I have become embroiled, in things, in the world and its messes, and I cannot resist. (Rushdie, *Satanic*, p. 260)

Against his determination to keep out of the world and its messes, Chamcha becomes, in a desperately ironic twist, a cult community figure. He literally grows into a symbol of solidarity and community empowerment. Rubber imitations of his all-too-real, magically emerging devil's horns – the very physical signs of his ambivalence and will to disconnection – are appropriated for but against him (Rushdie, *Satanic*, p. 286). Without realising they mock him, his supporters disarm him of the paradoxical security of his will to exile. They draw him into the local community, not just despite himself, but almost despite the impetus of the carnivalesque narrative itself. As with the butterflies of Titlipur, the boundless potential of Chamcha's horny 'fetish' is – if not fully resolved into – nonetheless a sign of redemption through community affiliation.

In defence of *The Satanic Verses*, Rushdie states that he was 'attempt[ing] to do what the word novel seems to insist upon: to see the world anew' (Rushdie, *Imaginary*, p. 393). Returning to the larger effect of the novel as elucidated through Benjamin's ideas as engaged by Bhabha, it may be that the secular hegemonies potential in narratives of nations and the religious hegemonies potential in narratives of faith are challenged by the collapsing and multiplying shape of Rushdie's stories. But while he relishes the boundless newness of language – the pure–impure revelry of words that takes him both into the grain of life and sweeps the narrative into the 'ineffable' – this insistence is bounded by a modern-archaic sense of the emotional and homely realities of organic and transplanted communities. It is possible to understand the more intricate negotiations between the real and the magical as pointed towards creating newly-old myths around these smaller collectivities of people; and that in his very oscillation between frustrated condemnation and yearning affection Rushdie is seeking a renewal of community that is itself a fuller and more real challenge to destructive monologisms than the abstractions of a pure multiplicity.

From *The Thousand and One Nights* to Magical Realism: Postnational Predicament in *The Journey of Little Ghandi* by Elias Khoury

Wen-chin Ouyang

> I recall Alice's words and try to imagine what happened, but I keep finding holes in the story. All stories are full of holes. We no longer know how to tell stories, we don't know anything anymore. The story of Little Ghandi ended. This journey ended, and life ended.
>
> –Elias Khoury
> *(The Journey of Little Ghandi, p. 7)*

This refrain, repeated at the beginning of all the middle five chapters in Elias Khoury's novel, *The Journey of Little Ghandi*,[1] anticipates the type of story and storytelling that will follow, and encapsulates the kind of intellectual crises Lebanese writers have had to grapple with during and subsequent to the Lebanese civil war (1975–91). Written and published towards the end of the war, 1989, the novel tells the stories of an array of characters who die or disappear in a random fashion during and immediately after the Israeli invasion of Lebanon and occupation of Beirut (1982–84). The stories may be structured around the central theme of the Israeli invasion, but the scope of the novel goes beyond this particular historical event. It interrogates the sense, or nonsense, of a civil war driven by sectarian passions and leading to the destruction of a community. The word journey in the title may be taken to mean at one level the journey through the time of the civil war and the war-torn landscape of Lebanon, a landscape now littered with memories of death. The explicit link between story and death evokes immediately the *Thousand and One Nights*, in which stories are told to postpone death, to keep it at bay. When the story ends, life ends too.

---

[1] The original Arabic version, *Riḥlat Ghāndī al-Ṣaghīr*, was published by the Lebanese avant-garde Dār al-Ādāb in 1989. The English translation by Paula Haydar appeared in 1994 as part of University of Minnesota Press's (Minneapolis and London) *Emergent Literatures Series*. All quotations are from the English translation.

Paradoxically, death, or the desire to keep it at bay, generates story, as the civil war has done for Lebanese writing at the time.

That story equals life, as Sabah Ghandour points out in her 'Foreword' to the English translation,[2] draws attention not only to the existential resonance of the *Nights* in the novel, but also a number of similarities between the two works. The novel mimics the frame-within-frame structure of the *Nights*. *The Journey of Little Ghandi*, in seven chapters, is made up of three main interwoven narratives. The first and final short chapters, which frame the novel, tell the story of the narrator, or textualized novelist's search for story. The middle chapters, which are of varying length, recount the stories Alice, a waitress turned prostitute then maid, tells the novelist of herself and of Little Ghandi, a waiter turned restaurant owner, garbage collector then shoe shiner. Within these three overlapping frames, one story grows out of another, each triggered by the mention of the name of a character. There is, above all, the combination of the fantastic and the real that is very much part of the textual landscape of the *Nights*. The combination of the fantastic and the real in Khoury's novel, however, is more in line with magical realism in that the stories are grounded in this world rather than another created from the past or imagination, and speaks of a reality that, in the context of the civil war, is more fantastic than fantasy. That there can be no explanation why the protagonist of the novel, Abd al-Karim, is given the name Little Ghandi, is symbolic and symptomatic of the incomprehensibility of reality.

The Fantastic, the Real and Magical Realism

In chapter five, the longest and perhaps most central chapter of the novel, the story explodes into myriad fragments as the names dropped into the narrative grow out of control. Amidst this narrative chaos, a central theme emerges: the nonsense of sectarianism. The history of sects in Lebanon is a checkered one; the genealogy of each is impossible to construct because inter-faith mobility has been constant albeit unpredictable. Here the fantastic and the real converge to give expression to the extra-reasonable grounds for war. Reverend Amin, married to the daughter of a Greek Orthodox priest and spends the last days of his life in a nursing home run by a Greek Orthodox church, begins his career as an Evangelical priest and ends it as a Protestant pastor with a church of his own. More significantly, his maternal grandmother, Um Tanios, becomes a Muslim saint towards the end of her life. Diagnosed with senility, she has been bedridden for years when she suddenly begins screaming that she sees the Prophet Muhammad in her dream. Her Muslim neighbors hear her and force their way into her house, making Amin's mother bathe and change her in order to prepare her for receiving guests. Her Muslim guests come into her room, listen to her dream, then help her get up and walk. A miracle is declared and her house is

---

[2] Sabah Ghandour, 'Foreword', *The Journey of Little Ghandi*, pp. xi-xx.

turned into a Muslim shrine. When she finally dies, her Muslim neighbors fight with her family over the right to bury her in a Muslim cemetery (pp. 100–4).

The borders separating sects are at best fuzzy and at worst nonsensical. Father John al-Mazraani, the priest of the Greek Orthodox Church of Beirut, comes to be convinced that 'it was all the same in the end' (p. 110) because death, the certain outcome of life, equalizes, and because sectarian belonging does not make a difference in life. In a conversation with Alice, '[h]e asked her why she didn't come to church on Sundays'. This exchange follows:

> "How can I, Father, I'm a Muslim."
> "A Muslim? I can't believe it. You look like you could've studied at the nuns' school."
> "I was a student of the whorehouse. It's all the same, Father." (p. 110)

The encounters of Alice, clearly a symbol, albeit misogynous, of Lebanon, rival the stories of Reverend Amin in their amazing qualities. As she bounces from the bed of one sectarian militia leader to that of another, she lives through one 'strange' experience after another. One militia leader, for example, makes love to her while both are fully clothed.

Little Ghandi is arguably a magical-realist text in that it exhibits the signs of magical realism summed up by Wendy B. Faris in 'Scheherazade's Children: Magical Realism and Postmodern Fiction'[3] as the mode of expression that 'combines realism and the fantastic in such a way that magical elements grow organically out of the reality portrayed' (p. 163). There too is no antinomy between the fantastic and the real in Khoury's novel and the intrusion of the fantastic does not lead to the creation of two different worlds.[4] Faris speaks of magical-realist texts as Scheherazade's children 'because they might be imagined as "replenished" postmodern narrators, born of the death-charged atmosphere of high modernist fiction, but able somehow to pass beyond it' (p. 163), 'herald[ing], perhaps, a new youth of narrative' (p. 163). She sees the *Nights*' 'generativity' operating at all levels of fictions she identifies as Scheherazade's children: 'on the structural plane with stories that grow out of other stories; on the mimetic front with characters who duplicate themselves in miraculous feats of doubling; in the metaphorical register with images that take on lives of their own and engender others beyond themselves, independent of their referential worlds' (p. 164). She also identifies 'European realism' as the precursor that Latin American magical realism must overcome (pp. 164–5). It is not difficult to trace in Khoury's novel the *Nights*' generative narrative strategies Faris articulates, and to incorporate this work into the category of postmodernist fiction

---

[3] Published in *Magical Realism: Theory, History, Community*, eds Lois Parkinson Zamora and Wendy B. Faris (Durham and London: Duke University Press, 1995), pp. 163–90.

[4] For a discussion of this quality of magical realism, see Amaryll Beatrice Chanady, *Magical Realism and the Fantastic: Resolved Versus Unresolved Antinomy* (New York & London: Garland Publishing, Inc., 1985).

that, like Faris's magical realism, tries to overcome European realism. Khoury's text is indeed haunted by the realist agenda even as it problematizes the effectiveness of realism. The ultimate goal of the novel, as in other realist and magical-realist works, is to convey reality, however incomprehensible it may be, and to write history on the basis of this reality.

The feel of this text is, however, distinct from other magical-realist works written in Arabic or other languages, perhaps because the precursors it establishes as its interlocutors fall outside the mainstream magical-realist texts; in fact, they go beyond postcolonial magical engagement with realism. For one thing, apocalypse does not herald an alternative world, and, for another, there is no recovery of local history from the grand narrative of empire. It rather struggles to write, not re-write, history. It is a text stubbornly grounded in here and now, looking at the past without nostalgia, or desire to recuperate it. It is not the type of hybrid text interested in harmonizing diversity, for the secular suppression of sectarian differences is precisely the problem. In this configuration of the politics of aesthetics, the novel understandably allies itself with texts that do not purport to do so. Its intertextuality with the *Nights* is filtered through Borges,[5] who was under the spell of the *Nights*, and of Cortázar, who was in a way a student of Borges.[6] Borges and Cortázar are two Argentine authors whose place in magical realism is ambivalent, perhaps because of the absence in their works of the kind of postcolonial impulse found in writers such as García Márquez and Allende. There is, however, little doubt that the *Nights*, as a literary text, is a precursor to all their works. The techniques of the fantastic Borges articulates and implements in his works, which find echoes in Cortázar's works, summed up by James E. Irby as 'the work within the work, contamination of reality by the dream, the voyage in time and the double' (*Labyrinths*, p. xviii),[7] are inspired by storytelling in the *Nights*. Khoury's narrative strategies follow the Borgesian principles more closely than, let us say, other Arabic texts that identify the *Nights* as their precursor and construct their genealogy around this text, authenticating the Arabic novel and legitimating storytelling.[8] Instead of re-writing *Nights'* stories, as a majority of Arab authors do, Khoury makes use of the Borgesian fantastic techniques to create a narrative labyrinth the ways in and out of which are infinite and indefinite.

---

[5] For a recent discussion of the *Nights's* influence on Borges, see Evelyn Fishburn, 'Traces of the *Thousand and One Nights* in Borges,' *Middle Eastern Literatures*, 7.2 (July 2004), 213–22.

[6] Elias Khoury is an admirer of Alain Robbe-Grillet, one of the French novelists who spearhead the *nouveau roman*. The influence of Robbe-Grillet on Khoury, tangible in *The Journey of Little Ghandi*, is another story that will need to be addressed in a separate paper.

[7] James E. Irby, 'Introduction,' Jorge Luis Borges, *Labyrinths: Selected Stories and Other Writings*, ed. Donald A. Yates and Jame E. Irby (New York: New Directions Books, 1964), pp. xv-xxiii.

[8] For the pervasiveness of intertextuality within the *Nights* in Arabic writing, see, for example, Muṣṭafā 'Abd al-Ghanī, *Shahrazād fī l-fikr al-'arabī al-ḥadīth* (cairo: Dār al-Shurūq, 1985 [1995]); Muhsin J. al-Mūsawī's *Tharāt Shahrazād: fann al-sard al-'arabī-ḥadīth* (Beirut:

The work within work principle is expanded into an elaborate web of framing. At one level the Lebanese civil war frames the Israeli invasion, which in turn frames the stories of the novelist, Alice and Little Ghandi, which too frame other stories. At another level, the narrative of the textualized novelist frames that of Alice, which in turn frames that of Little Ghandi, with the three narrative voices overlapping in such a way that it is impossible to discern for certain who is telling the story. Contamination of reality by the dream works visibly in stories of inter-faith mobility (as in the story of Um Tanios) and subtly in the novelist's journey into memories of war. Are the stories of Alice and Little Ghandi real? Has he met them? Has he spoken to them? Or are they figments of his imagination? Here is where doubling wreaks havoc with perception. Alice and Little Ghandi are in a way each other's double. Husn, Little Ghandi's son, splinters into three personae. And Little Ghandi's family line seems a series of duplication as their names suggest, from Abd al-Karim of Little Ghandi, to Husn of his father, Abd al-Karim of his grandfather; names that repeat themselves in an alternate fashion all the way back to time immemorial. Above all, the same story repeats itself five times and the varying versions can be read in the fashion of Cortázar's hopscotch, whereby any point in the novel can be the beginning or the end of the story.

To speak of *The Journey of Little Ghandi* in terms of postmodernism or magical realism is unsatisfying because they explain only partially the politics and the shape of the text. While postmodernism resists definition and escapes specificity, magical realism locates the politics of the text in the particular context of postcolonial resistance to European grand narrative in general and European realism in particular. More important, they vexingly obfuscate the singularity of each text and the unique politics, grounded in history and geography, of its engagement with the world, literary trends as well as other texts. The Arabic novel's intertextuality with the *Nights*, divergent from that of European, North American and Spanish American responses,[9] provides a glimpse of the differing ontological and epistemological priorities at work in each text. At the outset, death may be literary in postmodern fiction but it is literal

---

Dār al-Ādāb, 1993); and Mohammad Shaheen, *The Modern Arabic Short Story: Shahrazad Returns* (Houndsmills: Palgrave Macmillan, 1989 [2002]). For discussions of the role of intertextuality with the Nights in authenticating the Arabic novel, see, for example, Wen-chin Ouyang, 'Whose Story Is It? Sindbad the Sailor in Literature and Film,' *Middle Eastern Literatures*, 7.2 (July 2004), 133–47; and 'Metamorphoses of Scheherazade in Literature and Film', *Bulletin of SOAS*, 66.3 (October 2003), 402–18.

[9] See, for example, Peter L. Carracciolo, ed. *The Arabian Nights in English Literature* (New York: St. Martin's Press, 1988); and Muhsin Jassim al-Musawi (aka Ali), *Scheherazade in England: A Study of Nineteenth-Century English Criticism of the Arabian Nights* (Washington, D.C.; Three Continents Press, 1981) and *Anglo-Orient: Easterners in Textual Camps* (Tunis: Centre de Publication Universitaire, 2000). See also *Ideological Variations and Narrative Horizons: New Perspectives on the Arabian Nights*, special issue of *Middle Eastern Literatures*, 7.2 (July 2004), guest editor, Wen-chin Ouyang; and the special issue on the *Nights* of *Fabula*, 45.3/4 (2004), guest editor, Ulrich Marzolph.

in Khoury's text. 'We write, we resist and we die', Khoury declares as he sur-
veys the death and chaos surrounding him (*Zaman al-iḥtilāl*, p. 251). Writing is
both resistance to and acceptance of death, death being the price a writer must
be prepared to pay for voicing an opinion now that assassination has become the
norm and the law of the jungle has pervaded. The Arabic novel may have allied
itself with the postcolonial politics of the Spanish American brand of magical
realism, striving to rescue its history from the grand narrative of empire, but it
has also mapped its own trajectory of engagement with empire and its discourses
of power on the basis of its own 'national longing for form'.[10] What shapes
Khoury's novel is not only the postcolonial impulse informing magical realism,
but also its engagement with Arab nationalism, a project that is responsive to
colonialism and generative of its own paradigm of knowledge articulated in the
form of the imagined community that is the nation-state. The Lebanese civil war
has underscored the centrality of the nation-state in shaping literary texts and
triggering the kind of ontological and epistemological crisis I alluded to earlier,
when it becomes the source of trouble.

Postcoloniality, Nationalism and Realism

The long years of the civil war saw the destruction of Lebanon, the nation-state
that emerged in 1943 out of the ashes of European territorial contests in the
Middle East and French colonization of what is now known as Lebanon. They
more particularly witnessed the rapid disintegration of Beirut, the once model
'modern' capital of the Arab world, 'transforming from the Switzerland of the
East to Hong Kong, Saigon, to Calcutta, to Sri Lanka' (p. 5). The Utopian dream
pinned on the nation-state that was Lebanon turned into apocalyptic nightmare,
and Camelot into City of Brass. The melting pot of different cultures, faiths and
races imploded, a victim of its own diversity. Secularity, another attendant principle of nationalism, twin to modernity and democracy, beat the drum of defeat
in the face of escalating sectarian violence epitomized by the assassination in
1982 of president elect, a young charismatic Maronite Bashir al-Jumayyil who,
it was hoped, would bring an end to the civil war. The final blow to the Lebanese
'state of fantasy', to borrow Jacqueline Rose's term,[11] came in the form of an
Israeli invasion in 1982 that would mark the beginning of a short but memorable
foreign occupation reminiscent of the earlier Crusades and the more recent
French colonization. Nationalism, the grand postcolonial project intended to
restore the colonies to their former civilizational glory shorn of theocracy and
autocracy in the postindependent era was now completely devastated. The
nation-state, the nationalist paradigm of knowledge, has proven inadequate to

---

[10] Both term and concept are borrowed from Timothy Brennan, 'The national longing for
form', *Nation and Narration*, ed. Homi Bhabha (London and New York: Routledge, 1990),
44–70.
[11] See Jacqueline Rose, *States of Fantasy* (Oxford: Clarendon Press, 1996).

replace empire or religion as a way of imagining community and the individual's place in it. It has not been able to fill the metaphysical emptiness vacated by empire and religion, leaving a troubling, palpable absence that will haunt contemporary literary texts, whether modern or postmodern, postcolonial, national or postnational.

The fall of the nation-state, as both reality and utopian fantasy, is necessarily accompanied by an intellectual crisis of ontological and epistemological kind that is, paradoxically, determined by the degree in which nationalism, as an ideology, has taken hold of both thought and imagination. Khoury is today one of the leading Arab public intellectuals, journalists and novelists working in Beirut. He is what Timothy Brennan would call a 'cosmopolitan' writer,[12] who is equally at home in Arabic, French and English, or Beirut, Paris and New York. His cosmopolitan lifestyle notwithstanding (he frequently makes short sojourns in Paris and New York to write, teach and give public lectures) he remains an Arab at heart, deeply committed to the liberation not only of Lebanon but the entire Arab world. Liberation, in this case synonymous with decolonization in its broadest sense, is understandably on top of his political, intellectual and literary agenda. His writings, be they in the form of cultural critique,[13] literary criticism[14] or fiction,[15] are highly politicized, often centered around the unsettling and debilitating effects of colonization on Arab political and intellectual life even in the post-independent Arab world today. The legacy of colonialism crystallizes for him in the 'Question of Palestine', which has become symbolic of the multi-layered failure of nationalism; it has not been able to bring its grand projects of decolonization, modernization, secularization, democratization and Arab unity to successful completion. The continuing existence of the State of Israel and its ability to invade and occupy a neighboring Arab country at will serve as an instant, bitter reminder of this failure.

The Journey of Little Ghandi is, seen in this light, necessarily focused on the Israeli invasion. It tells the stories of a number of persons whose destinies are inexorably connected with this invasion. Little Ghandi, the male protagonist of the novel, dies on the day the Israelis enter Beirut (15 September 1982), and Alice, his female counterpart, disappears on their withdrawal (1984). The Israeli

---

[12] See Timothy Brennan, *At Home in the World: Cosmopolitanism Now* (Cambridge: Harvard University Press, 1997).

[13] Originally written as articles published in *Al-safīr* and later collected in two volumes: *Al-dhākira-mafqūda: dirāsāt naqdiyya* (Lost Memory: Critical Studies [Beirut: Mu'assasat al-Abhāth al-'Arabiyya, 1982]); and *Zaman al-ihtilāl* (The Time of Occupation [Beirut: Mu'assasat al-Abhāth al-'Arabiyya, 1985]). English translation of quotations from these two titles is my own.

[14] See *Tajribat al-bahth 'an ufuq* (In Search of Horizon [Beirut: Markaz al-Abhāth al-Filastīnī, 1974]); and *Dirāsāt fī naqd al-shi'r* (Critical Studies of Poetry [Beirut: Dār Ibn Rushd, 1979]).

[15] His novels include: *'An 'alāqāt al-dā'ira* (Beirut: Dār al-Adāb, 1975); *Al-jabal al-saghīr* (Beirut: Mu'assasat al-Abhāth al-'Arabiyya, 1977), translated into English by Maia Tabet as *Little Mountain* (Manchester: Carcanet, 1989); *Abwāb al-madīna* (Beirut: Dār Ibn Rushd,

invasion and occupation of Beirut are, however, only the catalyst of a much larger problem pervading the cultural and political climate that produced this senseless war. It crowns the achievements of the aimless violence that has consumed Lebanon. 'The war continues with no goal' (p. 182), the narrative brings the story to its close, giving a quick account of the death or disappearance in the aftermath of the Israeli withdrawal of the characters featured in the novel. The threat is in the final analysis less Israel or the colonial 'Orientalism' it partially represents but more the sectarian mentality among the Arabs. Sectarianism, a form of nationalism gone awry, has made it possible for the creation and survival of the State of Israel, the continued success of the strategy of 'divide and conquer' of previously European and now American imperialism, and more importantly, the demise of the Lebanese nation-state.

In a series of articles written between 18 January 1983 and 6 November 1984 for *Al-safīr*, a Beiruti daily newspaper of which he is the editor of the literary supplement, Khoury takes stock of the situation and tries to think ahead. Rejecting the idea of 'cultural imperialism',[16] he contradicts his contemporaries by asserting that the term is an oxymoron in that cultures do not invade but interact. 'Orientalism', as articulated by Edward Said,[17] is an imperial discourse that subordinates institutions of knowledge to capitalist hegemony and should not be mistaken for 'Western' culture. Resistance to imperialism should not take the form of anti-'Orientalist' discourse that imprisons 'Oriental' thinking in 'Orientalist' epistemology; rather, it ought to adumbrate a process of self-examination. Is the fragmentation of the Lebanese nation-state and Arab nation the cause or effect of the Israeli invasion? In fact, how does the Arab 'reality' tailor itself to the imperial capitalist agenda? These, according to Khoury, are the questions the Arabs ought to ask themselves. Self-'orientalization', the prevalent kind of antithetical engagement with 'Orientalism', which reproduces and is in imprisoned in the institutions of knowledge and discourse of power set up by the 'West', is an ineffective and undesirable strategy of resistance. The way forward demands a radical transformation of the operative Arab epistemological system, including rethinking the current make-up – both form and content – of memory (*dhākira*), the foundation of history, culture and community (*Zaman al-ihtilāl*, pp. 175–83). European colonization, American neo-colonization, the Israeli invasion and the Lebanese civil war, seen from this perspective, are memory wars; contests over how memory should be mapped then used.

1981), translated into English by Paula Haydar as *Gates of the City* (Minneapolis: University of Minnesota Press, 1993); *Al-wujūh al-baydā' (White Faces)* (Beirut: Dār Ibn Rushd, 1981); *Mamlakat al-ghurabā'* (Beirut: Dār al-Ādāb, 1993), translated into English by Paula Haydar as *The Kingdom of Strangers* (Fayettevile, University of Arkansas Press, 1996); *Tuqūs al-manfā* (Rituals of Exile [Amman: Dar al-Karmal, 1994]); *Bāb al-shams (The Sun Gate)* (Beirut: Dār al-Ādāb, 1998); and *Yālū* (Beirut: Dār al-Ādāb, 2002). His short stories include: *Al-mubtada' wa l-khabar* (Beirut: Mu'assasat al-Abhāth al-'Arabiyya, 1984).

[16] Khoury uses the terms 'ghazw al-thaqāfī' which literally means 'cultural invasion'.

[17] See Edward Said, *Orientalism* (New York: Pantheon Books, 1978).

The Lebanese civil war underscores the importance of memory in the formation and disintegration of community, culture and literature. The implosion of the Lebanese society is explicable as, Khoury argues, the triumph of mythical memory, the foundation of sectarian identity, over historical memory, the basis of modern nation-states (*Zaman al-'iḥtilāl*, p. 183). The ultimate purpose and effect of war is erasure of a certain part of memory, allowing for the creation of another that legitimates one episteme over another. 'They want us to forget', he bemoans, 'so that we drown in illusion and kill one another, while [our] land becomes occupied, [our] words lose their meaning, and death harvests us' (p. 183). For one of the unfortunate consequences of war is that it plunges the community into collective amnesia whereby history comes to a standstill and life ceases. The Lebanese civil war shot the memory of Arab modernization to smithereens, not only destroying in the process all the institutions of knowledge that emerged out of this project but also putting memory itself on trial. It is no wonder that this war stands in the way of any writing project (*Al-dhākira-mafqūda*, p. 26); modern Arabic writing, including the novel, is one of those atomized institutions of knowledge. 'The Lebanese writer', he writes in 1983, '[is no longer] able to write about the conditions in which he lives: to see, to discover, to record and give testimony' (*Zaman al-iḥtilāl*, pp. 116–17).

That the novel is implicated in the process of memory making and history writing paradoxically marks its lineage to realism, which defined its role as supportive of, or committed to, Arab nationalism especially in the first half of the twentieth century. The kind of Arabic novel that found critical legitimation followed in general the blueprint of its own brand of realism, imagining the nation, detailing its rise, and cautioning against its pitfalls. Reality was subject to mastery in two ways: it could be transformed and represented. The novel was perceived as an agent of both transformation of society and representation of reality. It necessarily cast itself in the form of this ideology and constructed itself around a plot that reigned in seemingly disparate narrative threads, giving order to chaos, educating ignorance into knowledge, and initiating political innocence into awareness, if not activism. The fate of its characters and the nation it imagined were twinned, taking part in parallel journeys of transformation. The realist Arabic novel saw itself as an historical record of the successes and failures of the nation-state and a vehicle for telling the truth about the contributions and abuses of its members. This nationalist optimism, however, began to fade in the second half of the twentieth century, more particularly after the 1967 war with Israel, when it became apparent that nationalism did not lead to modernity, unity or, more importantly, real independence.

If realism, the literary expression of post-Enlightenment optimism and scientific positivism, advanced itself as a vehicle for telling the Truth of reality during the heydays of Arab 'modernizing' nationalism, it is by now subject to concomitantly 'postmodern' and 'postnational' interrogation, subversion and makeover. The inadequacies of mimesis, the operative structure of realism, may be explicable in the loss of faith in the ability of language and narrative to represent reality and tell the Truth. Story in a literary text, symbolic of history in the broader national/ist context, comes to be 'full of holes' because it is no longer possible to 'imagine what happened' through 'words'. The empire of signs, the semiotic world of signification collapses and 'words', as signifiers, come to inhabit a realm where signifiers do not correspond to signs and signs do not connote meanings; meaning can no longer cohere. With the discrediting of language, knowledge becomes impossible, and life necessarily comes to an end. That the first chapter of the novel begins with 'But they're talking' (p. 1) and the second with 'Alice said he died' (p. 7), two short, simple sentences betraying an unrelenting obsession with language and death, is indicative of the existential and intellectual quandary in which Elias Khoury finds himself. His novel inevitably defines its mission as a quest for form. The narrator's summation of the story as 'a long journey, because it's short' (p. 194) signals that the journey is not simply that of Little Ghandi. It is rather the narrator's search for new ways to write about reality when language and narrative, as we know them, can no longer perform the task expected of them, to represent reality, once the paradigm of knowledge giving shape to the novel falls apart.

History, Story and Form

In the 'fall' of the nation-state, the novel that is the vehicle conveying its paradigm of knowledge became open to negotiation, reconsideration and reconfiguration. The search for form in Khoury's novel is, in one way, a statement of the ontological and epistemological crisis that comes with the collapse of the nation-state as a paradigm of knowledge and narration. It is, in another way, an expression of the need for a workable alternative. The twofold ontological and epistemological crisis finds expression in the Arabic novel, paradoxically driving its narrative, defining its discourse, and giving form to its text. Here, 'the form shaping ideology', to use Bakhtin's term,[18] that is the product of the postnational predicament peculiar to Lebanon inevitably collides and colludes with another form shaping ideology that has been part and parcel of the nationalist vision. The novel maps a new narrative trajectory in the shadow of the nation-state. In the absence of an alternative paradigm of knowledge, the Arabic novel, however, loses its uni-form, so to speak, and its textual space is suddenly opened up, once more, to infinite possible mappings. Therein lies the challenge: where does one begin and what narrative trajectory does one pursue? And, more important, how should reality be conveyed and history written?

> And the story is a game of names. 'And he taught Adam all the names.' When we knew the names, the story began, and when the names were extinguished, the story began. (*Little Ghandi*, p. 194)

---

[18] See M.M. Bakhtin, *Speech Genres and Other Essays*, trans. Vern W. McGee (Austin: University of Texas Press, 1986).

This last paragraph of Khoury's novel, echoing the two sentences that set up the trajectory of its narrative on the first page, 'And the story is nothing but names. When I found out their names, I found out the story' (p. 1), sums up his writerly response to the ontological and epistemological crisis brought on by the collapse of the nation-state and the accompanying suspicion surrounding realism. A name is an episteme and the story it triggers depends on the knowledge it summons. The trajectory of the various stories of Little Ghandi's son is determined by the name he uses. As Husn, he is Little Ghandi's son, as Ralph, he is a murder suspect, and as Ghassan he is a hairdresser. The structure of the novel reflects reality as epistemological fragments that do not necessarily cohere into a whole, or, as some critics would argue, the 'postmodern' move away from the universal Truth to local truths. Narrative voices are necessarily subjective, imbued with uncertainty, and narrative movements relatively free of paradigmatic restraints. The stories appear in no particular order; each is prompted by the mention of a name attached to a character that happens to touch the life of the two protagonists. The sum of their life stories is the total of the vignettes summoned by the names recalled by Alice or Little Ghandi. Alice's life is composed of her friendship with Little Ghandi and association with a variety of characters, including militia leaders, who are all her clients at one time or another. Little Ghandi's life, by the same token, is an amalgamation of stories about his father, his marriage to cousin Fawziyya, his son, his schizophrenic daughter Suad, and his friendships with Alice, Professor Davis and Reverend Amin. More important, the novel does not have a transformative plot. Contrary to realist heroes, Alice and Little Ghandi gain no insight into themselves or the world in which they live through their experience of the civil war.

Here, narrative mimics memory in that it disregards chronological structure of time and organization of events around place. History is not chains of cause and effect, and geography plays no part in the structure of history. Little Ghandi's life story, for example, is not organized around his biography, from birth to death, or his career, from waiter to shoe shiner, nor is it structured around his movements from Mashta Hasan, his birthplace, to Tripoli then Beirut and its various neighborhoods. This is even truer of Alice, whose origin remains obscure and development unremarkable. The text is littered with anecdotes, each telling a story seemingly unrelated to the others if read through the realist lens. They do, however, conjure up a sense of chaos that comes with the collapse of familiar structures propping up community and its history. History that was the grand narrative in the past is now impossible when reality makes no sense. Reality and the past, both matters of narration, cannot be coherently conveyed in the absence of a viable paradigm of knowledge. What is possible is the preservation of individual stories that may contribute to the illumination, if only partially, of reality, and to the construction of history. The opacity of reality and inaccessibility of history are reflected in Khoury's language and narrative.

'The different languages employed in the novel', Ghandour writes, 'go beyond the classical distinction between modern standard and colloquial Arabic.' They mirror dialogically the different speech genres – 'the written memory, the forgotten memory, the church, the orientalist, the macho and other languages, which go along with the "tricks" of narration'[19] – as well as the various registers that bespeak 'the social status of the speaker and the related topic' (p. xiv). Perhaps precisely because of the diversity of speech genres and registers distributed among the characters of the novel, language becomes opaque, is unable to convey concrete meanings and becomes an obstacle in inter-faith communication. No wonder the narrator exhibits signs of anxiety in his report of incidents. His language comes to be filled with questionings and ambiguities:

> I met Abd al-Karim by coincidence, but her, I don't know how I met her. Abd al-Karim, nicknamed Little Ghandi, was a shoe shiner. He never shined my shoes, but everyone had told me about him. I ran into him once and we talked for a long time. But her, I don't know, maybe another coincidence. (p. 3)

This kind of uncertainty associated with language's capacity, or lack thereof, to convey meaning, to represent inner or outer reality, and to enable communication spills over into narrative. What is the story told here? Is it the story of Alice, Little Ghandi or the novelist? And, what is their story? In fact, their stories may easily be summed up in a few sentences. This is how the novelist-narrator renders Little Ghandi's life and death in the last chapter of the novel:

> Little Ghandi was, a man who lived and died, like millions of men, on the face of this spinning earth.
> He was born in Mashta Hasan, ran away from his father, who took him to his grandfather's cave, worked in the 'Key's' Bakery in Tripoli, moved to Beirut, where he worked at Abu Ayoun's restaurant, and then worked as a shoe shiner. He got married and had two children, Husn and Suad. Husn was a barber and Suad was sick. He loved life and loved the flavor of it. Alice told him, and the Reverend Amin befriended him, and Davis turned him into a restaurant owner, and the dog died, and Ghandi grieved over the dog more than he grieved over his own father. (pp. 193–4)

However, this is only one way of writing about Little Ghandi. The central chapters are five versions of the life of Little Ghandi, all short or long expansions of the condensed biographical notice embedded in the last chapter. Many names, details and stories recur, never following the same order but are always combined with new ones. The result is at one level the unequal chapters, growing from 12 pages in chapter two (pp. 7–18) to 102 in chapter five (pp. 83–184) then dropping to 7 in chapter six (pp. 185–91), and at another the arbitrary sequence of these chapters. Each chapter is self-sufficient and can be read out of the order of their appearance. The meaning or meaninglessness of Little Ghandi's life does not depend on paradigmatic plotting, characterization or transformation; his life

---

[19] Cited from Muḥammad Barrāda, 'Al-taʿaddud al-lughawī fī l-riwāya l-ʿarabiyya', *Mawakif,* 69 (Autumn 1992), 173.

story is in effect a matter of narration. Each chapter is a demonstration of this narrative driving insight. This insight into language and narrative is, paradoxically, an affect of a new reality: the nation-state in ruins. The ruins of the nation-state resembles more a City of Brass,[20] a labyrinthine city that contains nothing but memento of a once glorious world ravaged by death, than a Camelot that will emerge in the aftermath of an apocalypse.

The nation-state cast long shadows on intellectual and literary landscapes, perhaps even in the case of Spanish America as Nicola Miller argues in *In the Shadow of the State*.[21] The postnational Arabic novel, as it negotiates the ontological and epistemological changes underlying both the postcolonial will to power and the transition from national to postnational mode of existence, engages dialogically with both the history of representation of reality – from European realism to its postmodern and postcolonial reincarnations – and the history of realism in the Arab world. The kind of interrogation of realism informing Khoury's text goes beyond the type of transgression that may be described as manifestation of what Harold Bloom terms 'anxiety of influence';[22] of a belated writer's attempt to surpass earlier authors, or of magical realism's rebellion against European realism. It grapples additionally with the various kinds of realism imported or generated within the nationalist context of the earlier postcolonial Arab world, each text producing its own politics and aesthetics. In the most recent wave of writing, the Arabic novel goes beyond the postcolonial national agenda and the trajectory of earlier postindependence texts to locate the nation-state, or the collapse thereof, as the site, not of national longing for form, but of disintegration of form. Despite the lingering skepticism surrounding the ability of language and narrative to convey reality, however, the function of the novel as history has held fast. Whether in the form of conventional realism, nationalist realism, postcolonial magical realism, postmodern anti-realism, or postnational counter-realism, story is history.

---

[20] For literary interpretation of the 'Story of the City of Brass' in the *Nights*, see Andras Hamori, 'An Allegory from the *Arabian Nights*: the City of Brass,' *Bulletin of SOAS*, 34 (1971), 9–19; and *On the Art of Medieval Arabic Literature* (Princeton: Princeton University Press, 1974), pp. 145–63; and David Pinault, 'The City of Brass,' *Story-Telling Techniques in the Arabian Nights* (Leiden: E.J. Brill, 1992), pp. 148–239.

[21] See Nicola Miller, *In the Shadow of the State: Intellectuals and the Quest for National Identity in Twentieth-Century Spanish America* (London and New York: Verso, 1999).

[22] See Harold Bloom, *The Anxiety of Influence: A Theory of Poetry* (New York: Oxford University Press, 1973).

Guide to Further Reading

Stephen M. Hart and Kenneth Reeds

The wealth of critical studies on magical realism is daunting. A search based on the key terms magic realism using the MLA database, for example, produced no less than 399 items (consulted on 21 December 2004). This brief survey can do no more than offer a few guidelines to those readers who wish to investigate the theory of magical realism in greater depth. Crucial to an understanding of the roots of the movement are the essays by Franz Roh, 'Nach Expressionismus (Magischer Realismus)' (1925), Alejo Carpentier, 'Sobre lo real maravilloso en América' (1949), Ángel Flores, 'Magical Realism in Spanish American Fiction' (1955), and Luis Leal, 'El realismo mágico en la literatura hispanoamericana' (1967). Fortunately these basic texts now appear in English translation in Lois Parkinson Zamora and Wendy Faris's excellent collection of essays, *Magical Realism: Theory, History, Community* (Durham, NC: Duke University Press, 1995), pp. 15–31, 75–88, 109–24. It is clear even from a brief re-read of this first cluster of articles and essays that it was going to prove difficult to settle on a single definition of the movement. Roh is an art historian who has little interest in literature, while Carpentier argues that 'lo real maravilloso' exists because there is something intrinsically magical about Latin America. Flores and Leal, for their part, draw up lists of magical-realist writers which do not match. Even in those early days, magical realism was difficult to pin down geographically. Despite Carpentier's wish to keep magical realism (or 'the marvellous real' which was his preferred term) exclusively for the Americas, other critics were arguing that it could be detected in Cervantes (Arturo Serrano Plaja, *Realismo 'mágico' en Cervantes: 'Don Quijote' visto desde 'Tom Sawyer' y 'El idiota'* [Madrid: Gredos, S.A., 1967], although at this early juncture the connections are tangential at best), and even in Quevedo, García Lorca and Cortázar (Ángel Valbuena Briones, 'Una cala en el realismo mágico', *Cuadernos Americanos*, 166.5 [1969], 233–41).

An extremely important study for the theorization of magical realism was Tzvetan Todorov's *Introduction à la littérature fantastique* (Paris: Seuil, 1970; English translation by Richard Howard [Cleveland and London: The Press of Case Western Reserve University, 1973]). Though it was strictly speaking a study of the genre of the fantastic – and therefore did not mention magical realism *per se* – its development of a theory of reader's 'hesitation' when confronted by a supernatural event offered rich potential for the subsequent analysis of the new genre. Lucila-Inés Mena, for example, in 'Hacia una formulación teórica del realismo mágico', *Bulletin Hispanique*, 77. 3–4 (July–December 1975), 517–24, used Todorov's theories to argue that magical realism differs from the fantastic and is more akin to the marvellous. Indeed, subsequent critics such as Amaryll Beatrice Chanady in *Magical Realism and the Fantastic: Resolved Versus Unresolved Antinomy* (New York: Garland, 1985), and Wendy Faris in her recent study, *Ordinary Enchantments: Magical Realism and the Remystification of Narrative* (Nashville: Vanderbilt University Press, 2004), have had recourse to Todorov's theories in order to draw pertinent distinctions between the fantastic and magical realism.

But it would be naive to see the discourse around magical realism gradually coming, like a Medieval scholastic debate, to a more precise definition of the term. A conference held in the early 1970s drew stark attention to the problem. In the published proceedings, Emir Rodríguez Monegal memorably alluded to the debate about magical realism as 'a dialogue between deaf people' ('Realismo mágico versus literatura fantástica: un diálogo de sordos', *Otros mundos, otros fuegos: fantasía y realismo mágico en Iberoamérica: memoria del XVI Congreso Internacional de Literatura Iberoamericana*, ed. Donald A. Yates [East Lansing, MI: Michigan State University, Latin American Studies Center, 1975], pp. 25–37). Rodríguez Monegal's view was that there were clear differences between, for example, Borges's use of the fantasic and magical realism, but that these differences were being overlooked, as suggested by an important essay he published two years later ('Surrealism, Magical Realism, Magical Fiction: A Study in Confusion', in *Surrealism/Surrealismos: Latinoamérica y España*, eds Peter G. Earle and Germán Gullón [Philadelphia, PA: Department of Romance Languages, University of Pennsylvania, 1977], pp. 25–32). The work of some critics took a page out of Rodríguez Monegal's book, contrasting magical realism with adjacent terms or concepts. Juan Barroso, for example, argued in *'Realismo mágico' y 'lo real maravilloso' en El reino de este mundo y El siglo de las luces* (Miami: Ediciones Universal, 1977) that magical realism and 'lo real maravilloso' connote different things and ought to be kept apart. Other critics, however, were keen to stress the similarities. Irlemar Chiampi's *El realismo maravilloso: forma e ideología en la novela hispanoamerica*, Spanish trans. by Agustín Martínez and Márgara Russotto (Caracas: Monte Avila Editores, C.A., 1983), combined Carpentier's term ('lo real maravilloso') and Roh's term (magical realism) to produce a new term, 'realismo maravilloso' (marvellous realism). José Antonio Bravo, *Lo real maravilloso en la narrativa latinoameri-cana actual* (Lima: Ediciones Unifé, 1984), arguing against such an idea, used Carpentier's term 'lo real maravilloso' as an overarching term which might unlock the secrets of not only *El reino de este mundo* but also Rulfo's *Pedro Páramo* and García Márquez's *Cien años de soledad*.

One of the problems was that, just as critics were trying to define magic realism, the genre was spreading to other parts of the world and producing new forms as a result of a creative mix with new cultural landscapes. Robert Young and Keith Hollaman's anthology, *Magical Realist Fiction: An Anthology* (New York: Longman, 1984) brought a number of new writers into the fold. Amaryll Beatrice Chanady's study, *Magical Realism and the Fantastic: Resolved Versus Unresolved Antinomy*, which has already been mentioned, alluded to European as well as Latin American texts in order to shore up its argument. The issue of nomenclature refused to go away. Graciela N. Ricci della Grisa, in her study, *Realismo mágico y conciencia mítica en América Latina* (Buenos Aires: Cambeiro, 1985), coined a new term, 'realismo mágico maravilloso' (magic-marvellous realism). Jean Weisberger's *Le Réalisme magique: Roman, peinture et cinéma* (Paris: Éditions l'Âge d'Homme, 1987) brought together some interdisciplinary work on fiction, the visual arts and cinema. The notion that magical realism could be restricted to one geographical area was delivered its final death-blow with the publication of Peter Hinchliffe and Ed Jewinski's *Magical Realism and Canadian Literature: Essays and Stories* (Waterloo: Waterloo Press, 1986). Canadian literature, indeed, became one of the first to explore its relationship with a style emanating from a so-called Third-World continent, as suggested by Stephen Slemon's important article, 'Magic realism as Postcolonial Discourse', which focused on Canadian literature (now collected in Parkinson Zamora and Faris's collection of essays, pp. 407–26).

In the 1990s a number of studies appeared which focused more on the social thrust of magical-realist texts. Epitomising this trend was María-Elena Angulo's *Magical Realism: Social Context and Discourse* (New York and London: Garland, 1995) which saw magical realism as 'a new way of writing which transcends the limits of the Fantastic by entering the social realm' (p. xii). The most important book of the decade was Parkinson Zamora and Faris's *Magical Realism: Theory, History, Community*. It not only offered new English transla-tions of a set of crucial texts, it also demonstrated that magical realism was now an international literary phenomenon which could not be restricted to Latin America. Two essays included in the volume, for example, Theo D'haen's 'Magical Realism and Postmodernism: Decentering Privileged Centers' (pp. 191–208) and Wendy Faris's 'Scheherazade's Children: Magical Realism and Postmodern Fiction' (pp. 163–90) are built on such a premise. Clearly by the mid-1990s Salman Rushdie and Milan Kundera were coming to be seen as just as magical-realist as Alejo Carpentier and Gabriel García Márquez. Pointing in a similar direction, Brenda Cooper, in *Magical Realism in West African Fiction: Seeing With a Third Eye* (London and New York: Routledge, 1998), used the lens of magical realism to focus on the work of three West African writers, Ben Okri, Syl Cheney-Coker, and B. Kojo Laing. Susan J. Napier, *The Fantastic in Modern Japanese Literature* (London: Routledge, 1996) traces the connections between fantasy, magical realism and Japanese writing. Pascale Casanova, *La République mondiale des lettres* (Paris: Seuil, 1999) situates magical realism within a hypothetical world literary system. Seymour Menton, *Historia verdadera del realismo mágico* (Mexico City: Fondo de Cultura Económica, 1998), uses Roh's theories as a lynch pin with which to construct a theory of magical realism as a way of seeing which unites visual artists and novelists, while Erik Camayd-Freixas, *Realismo mágico y primitivismo* (Lanham, New York and Oxford: University Press of America, 1998), relates magical realism almost exclusively to the magico-mythical outlook of the indigenous peoples of Latin America.

More recently there have been some important re-readings of the genre of magical realism via postcolonial theory. Jean-Pierre Durix's study, *Mimesis, Genres and Post-Colonial Discourse: Deconstructing Magical Realism* (London: Macmillan, 1998), for instance, shows how a number of magical-realist writers have been creating a 'counter-discourse' which subverts the hegemony of western, metropolitan discourse; particularly valuable is the essay which compares Rushdie and García Márquez (pp. 115–43). Elsa Linguanti, Francesco Casotti, and Carmen Concilio, in *Coterminous Worlds: Magical Realism and Contemporary Post-Colonial Literature in English* (Amsterdam and Atlanta: Rodopi, 1999), bring together a number of studies on writers as diverse as Ben Okri, Kojo Laing, Mia Couto, Robert Kroetsch, Joe Rosenblatt, and Salman Rushdie. Stephen M. Hart, in *Reading Magic Realism from Latin America* (London: Bloomsbury, 2001: Internet: ISBN:0747556202) offers an overview of the fiction of Carpentier, Rulfo, Arguedas and García Márquez, and in 'Magical Realism in the Americas: Politicised Ghosts in *One Hundred Years of Solitude*, *The House of the Spirits*, and *Beloved*', *Journal of Iberian and Latin American Studies*, 9.2 (2003), compares the portrayal of the supernatural in two Latin American texts and one American novel.

Wendy Faris, *Ordinary Enchantments: Magical Realism and the Remystification of Narrative* (Nashville: Vanderbilt University Press, 2004), is a major new study which analyses the traits and techniques of a number of magical-realist writers ranging from the more obvious such as García Márquez's *One Hundred Years of Solitude* (1967) and Rushdie's *Midnight's Children* (1981) to the less obvious such as D.M. Thomas's *The White Hotel* (1981), William Kennedy's *Ironweed* (1983), and Patrick Süskind's *Perfume* (1985). Of particular interest is Chapter 4 of this study which focuses on the postcolonial question (pp. 133–69). Maggie Ann Bowers's study, *Magic(al) Realism* (London: Routledge, 2004), helpfully contrasts Latin American magical realism with magical-realist novels published in the English-speaking world; the blurb interestingly enough re-ranks the magical-realists since it describes the study as illustrated with 'fresh readings of the work of eminent writers such as Salman Rushdie, Toni Morrison, Isabel Allende, Gabriel García Márquez and Angela Carter'. The book lays down some helpful criteria for distinguishing between the different types of magical realism, ranging from the postmodern (pp. 76–82), the ontological (pp. 90–5), the postcolonial (pp. 95–102), and the variant inspired by children's literature (pp. 104–9). There are also sections on magical realism in film (pp. 109–15) and in painting (pp. 115–20). The glossary, which distinguishes between 'magic realism', 'magical realism' and 'magic(al) realism' (p. 131), though, is likely to produce more problems than it solves.

Selected Bibliography

Aldama, Fredrick Luis, 'Oscar "Zeta" Acosta: Magicorealism and Chicano Auto-bio-graphe', *Literature, Interpretation, Theory*, 11.2 (2000), 199–218.

Alter, Robert, 'Magic Realism in the Israeli Novel', *Prooftexts*, 16.2 (1996), 151–68.

Angulo, María-Elena, *Magical Realism: Social Context and Discourse* (New York and London: Garland, 1995).

Barroso, Juan, *'Realismo mágico' y 'lo real maravilloso' en 'El reino de este mundo' y 'El siglo de las luces'* (Miami: Ediciones Universal, 1977).

Benyei, Tama, 'Rereading Magic Realism', *Hungarian Journal of English and American Studies*, 3.1 (1997), 149–79.

Bowers, Maggie Ann, *Magic(al) Realism* (London: Routledge, 2004).

Bravo, José Antonio, *Lo real maravilloso en la narrativa latinoamericana actual* (Lima: Ediciones Unifé, 1984).

Breinig, Helmbrecht, 'Inter-American Internationality: Updike's *Brazil*, Curley's *Mummy*, and the Question of Magic Realism', in Armin Paul Frank (ed.), *The Internationality of National Literatures in Either America: Transfer and Transformation* (Gottingen: Wallstein, 1999), pp. 245–60.

Brennan, Timothy, *Salman Rushdie and the Third World* (New York: St Martins, 1989).

Calin, William, 'Du réalisme magique dans le roman occitan: Lecture subversive de *La Santa Estela del centenario* de J. Boudou', in Jacques Gourc (ed.), *Toulouse à la croisée des cultures: Actes du Vè Congrès International de l'Association Internationale d'Études Occitanes, Toulouse, 19–24 août 1996* (Pau: Association Internationale d'Études Occitanes, 1998), pp. 477–80.

Camayd-Freixas, Erik, *Realismo mágico y primitivismo* (Lanham, New York and Oxford: University Press of America, 1998).

Carpentier, Alejo, *Tientos y diferencias* (Montevideo: Arca, 1967).

Casanova, Pascale, *La République mondiale des lettres* (Paris: Seuil, 1999).

Chanady, Amaryll Beatrice, *Magical Realism and the Fantastic: Resolved Versus Unresolved Antinomy* (New York: Garland, 1985).

Chiampi, Irlemar, *El realismo maravilloso: forma e ideología en la novela hispanoamerica*, Spanish trans. by Agustín Martínez and Márgara Russotto (Caracas: Monte Ávila Editores, C.A., 1983).

Christian, Karen, 'Performing Magical Realism: The "Boom" in Latina/o Fiction', *Americas Review*, 24.3–4 (1996), 166–78.

Campa, Román de la, 'Magical Realism and World Literature: A Genre for the Times?', *Revista Canadiense de Estudios Hispánicos*, 23.2 (1999), 205–19.

Cobo Borda, Juan Gustavo, 'Arturo Uslar Pietri: pionero del realismo mágico', *Alba de América*, 20 (2001), 51–2.

Cooper, Brenda, *Magical Realism in West African Fiction: Seeing With a Third Eye* (London and New York: Routledge, 1998).

Connell, Liam, 'Discarding Magic Realism: Modernism, Anthropology, and Critical Practice', *ARIEL*, 29.2 (1998), 95–110.

Dash, Michael, 'Marvellous Realism: The Way out of "Négritude"', in *The Post-Colonial Studies Reader*, eds Bill Ashcroft, Gareth Griffiths, and Helen Tiffin (London: Routledge, 1995), pp. 199–201.

Durix, Jean-Pierre, *Mimesis, Genres and Post-Colonial Discourse: Deconstructing Magical Realism* (London: Macmillan, 1998).

Faris, Wendy, *Ordinary Enchantments: Magical Realism and the Remystification of Narrative* (Nashville: Vanderbilt University Press, 2004).

Fiddian, Robin, 'Two Aspects of Technique in *El coronel no tiene quien le escriba*', *Neophilologus*, 69.3 (1985), 386–93.

Fiddian, Robin, 'A Prospective Post-Script: Apropos of *Love in the Times of Cholera*', in *Gabriel García Márquez: New Readings*, eds Bernard McGuirk and Richard Cardwell (Cambridge: Cambridge University Press, 1987), pp. 191–205.

Fiddian, Robin, 'The Naked and the Dead: Bodies and Their Meanings in *La hojarasca* by Gabriel García Márquez', *Romance Studies*, 19 (1991), 79–89.

Flores, Ángel, 'Magical Realism in Spanish American Fiction', *Hispania*, XXXVIII.2 (1955), 187–92.

Gaylard, Gerald, 'Meditations on Magical Realism', *Current Writing: Text and Reception in Southern Africa*, 11.2 (1999), 92–109.

Gómez Vega, Ibis, 'Subverting the "Mainstream" Paradigm through Magical Realism in Thomas King's *Green Grass, Running Water*', *Journal of the Midwest Modern Language Association*, 33.1 (2000), 1–19.

González-Rodríguez, María Luz, 'Magic Realism: Its Origins, Nature and Subsequent Influence on Canadian Literature', in Juan Ignacio Oliva (ed.), *Ensayos literarios anglocanadienses* (La Laguna: Universidad de la Laguna, 2002), pp. 87–102.

Grobler, G.M.M., 'Extraordinary Events and Primeval Images: Magic Realism in the Works of Northern Sotho Novelist O.K. Matsepe', *Literator: Journal of Literary Comparative Linguistics and Literary Studies*, 14.1 (1993), 89–97.

Guerrero, Gustavo, 'Uslar Pietri, cronista del realismo mestizo', *Cuadernos Hispanoamericanos*, 605 (November 2000), 53–62.

Hantke, Steffan, 'Disorientating Encounters: Magical Realism and American Literature on the Vietnam War', *Journal of the Fantastic in the Arts*, 12.3 (2001), 268–86.

Hart, Stephen, 'Magical Realism in Gabriel García Márquez's *Cien años de soledad*', *Inti*, 16–17 (1982–83), 37–52.

Hart, Stephen, *Reading Magic Realism from Latin America* (London: Bloomsbury, 2001: Internet: ISBN:0747556202).

Hart, Stephen, 'Magical Realism in the Americas: Politicised Ghosts in *One Hundred Years of Solitude*, *The House of the Spirits*, and *Beloved*', *Journal of Iberian and Latin American Studies*, 9.2 (2003), 115–23.

Hart, Stephen, 'Cultural Hybridity, Magical Realism, and the Language of Magic in Paulo Coelho's *The Alchemist*', *Romance Quarterly*, 51.4 (2004), 304–12.

Hartje, Mary-Ellen, 'Magic Realism: Humour Across Cultures', in Graeme Harper (ed.), *Comedy, Fantasy and Colonialism* (London: Continuum, 2002), pp. 104–16.

Hinchliffe, Peter, and Ed Jewinski (eds), *Magical Realism and Canadian Literature: Essays and Stories* (Waterloo: Waterloo Press, 1986).

Jameson, Fredric, 'On Magic Realism in Film', *Critical Enquiry*, 12 (1986), 301–25.

Jones, Stephanie, 'A Novel Genre: Polylingualism and Magical Realism in Amitav Ghosh's *The Circle of Reason*', *Bulletin of the School of Oriental and African Studies*, 66.3 (2003), 431–41.

Joseph-Vilain, Melanie, 'Writing Women Back into History: Magic Realism in André Brink's *Imaginings of Sand*', *Commonwealth Essays and Studies*, 26.1 (2003), 61–9.

Kannamal, S., 'Magical Realism and Arundhati Roy: India's Response to Emerging Literary Theories', in T.S. Anand (ed.), *Response to American Literature* (New Delhi, India: Creative, 2003), pp. 133–8.

Kofman, Andrei, 'El problema del realismo mágico en la literatura latinoamericana', *Cuadernos Americanos*, 14.4 (2000), 63–72.

Kristal, Efraín, *Invisible Work: Borges and Translation* (Nashville: Vanderbilt University Press, 2002).

Kristal, Efraín (ed.), *The Cambridge Companion to the Latin American Novel* (Cambridge: Cambridge University Press, 2005).

Leal, Luis, 'El realismo mágico en la literatura hispanoamericana', *Cuadernos Americanos*, CLIII.4 (1967), 230–5.

Linguanti, Elsa, Francesco Casotti, and Carmen Concilio (eds), *Coterminous Worlds: Magical Realism and Contemporary Post-Colonial Literature in English* (Amsterdam and Atlanta: Rodopi, 1999).

Littlewood, Derek, 'Epic and Novel in Magic Realism: From Bakhtin to *Midnight's Children*', in Jorgen Bruhn (ed.), *The Novelness of Bakhtin: Perspectives and Possibilities* (Copenhagen: University of Copenhagen, 2001), pp. 187–205.

Martinez, Thomas E., 'Magic Realism in Film and Fiction', *Anuario de Cine y Literatura en Español*, 1 (1995), 65–76.

Martínez-Gil, Víctor, 'Txekhov i Carner: Del realisme al realisme màgic', *Marges*, 56 (October 1996), 115–21.

Maufort, Marc, '"A Rustle of Wind Blowing Across Two Continents": August Wilson's Magic Realism as Expression of Empowerment', in Marc Maufort (ed.), *Voices of Power: Co-operation and Conflict in English Language and Literatures* (Liege: Belgian Association of Anglists in Higher Education, 1997), pp. 173–81.

Mena, Lucila-Inés, 'Hacia una formulación teórica del realismo mágico', *Bulletin Hispanique*, 77. 3–4 (July-December 1975), 517–24.

Menton, Seymour, *Magic Realism Rediscovered, 1918–1981* (Philadelphia: The Art Alliance Press, 1983).

Menton, Seymour, 'Magic Realism: An Annotated International Chronology of the Term', in Kirsten Nigro and Sandra Cypess (eds), *Essays in Honor of Frank Dauster* (Newark, DE: Cuesta, 1995), pp. 125–53.

Menton, Seymour, *Historia verdadera del realismo mágico* (Mexico City: Fondo de Cultura Económica, 1998).

Mishkin, Tracy, 'Magical Realism in the Short Fiction of Isaac Bashevis Singer', *Studies in American-Jewish Literature*, 22 (2003), 1–10.

Monet-Viera, Molly, 'Post-Boom Magical Realism: Appropriations and Transformation of a Genre', *Revista de Estudios Hispánicos*, 38.1 (2004), 95–117.

Moses, Michael Valdez, 'Magical Realism at World's End', *Literary Imagination: The Review of the Association of Literary Scholars and Critics*, 3.1 (2001), 105–33.

Napier, Susan J., *The Fantastic in Modern Japanese Literature* (London: Routledge, 1996).

Omerold, Beverley, 'Magical Realism in Contemporary French Caribbean Literature: Ideology or Literary Diversion?', *Australian Journal of French Studies*, 34.2 (1997), 216–26.

Palaversich, Diana, 'Rebeldes sin causa: realismo mágico vs. realismo virtual', *Hispamérica*, 29 (2000), 55–70.

Patai, Daphne, *Myth and Ideologies in Contemporary Brazilian Fiction* (Cranbury, NJ: Associated University Presses, 1983).

Pereira, Tania Maria Pantoja, 'Aspectos do realismo maravilhoso em "O Balsamo" de Fernando Canto', *Itinerarios: Revista de Literatura*, 19 (2002), 43–54.

Podgorniak, Alexandra, 'Magical Realism, Indian-Style; or, the Case of Multiple Submission: *The God of Small Things* by Arundhti Roy', in Gerhard Stilz (ed.), *Missions of Interdependence: A Literary Directory* (Amsterdam: Rodopi, 2002), pp. 255–63.

Rajan, Gita, 'Chitra Divakuruni's *The Mistress of Spices*: Deploying Mystical Realism', *Meridians: Feminism, Race, Transnationalism*, 2.2 (2002), 215–36.

Ricci della Grisa, Graciela N., *Realismo mágico y conciencia mítica en América Latina* (Buenos Aires: Cambeiro, 1985).

Rincón, Carlos, 'Postmodernismo, poscolonialismo y los nexos cartográficos del realismo mágico', *Neue Romania*, 16 (1995), 193–210.

Roberts, Sheila, 'Inheritance in Question: The Magical-Realist Mode in Afrikaans Fiction', in Rowland Smith (ed.), *Postcolonizing the Commonwealth: Studies in Literature and Culture* (Walterloo: Wilfrid Laurier University Press, 2000), pp. 87–97.

Roh, Franz, *Realismo mágico/postexpresionismo: problemas de la pintura europea más reciente*, trans. Fernando Vela (Madrid: Revista de Occidente, 1927).

Rosenberg, Teya, 'The Influence of the Second World War on Magic Realism in British Children's Literature', *Canadian Children's Liteature*, 111–12 (2003), 78–89.

Ross, Mary Ellen, 'Que le diable l'emporte: réalisme merveilleux et religion dans *La Chaise du Maréchal Ferrant*', *Canadian Literature*, 142–3 (1994), 142–56.

Rowe, William, 'Magical Realism', *Encyclopedia of Latin American Literature*, ed. Verity Smith (Chicago: Dearbourn, 1997), pp. 506–7.

Schroeder, Shannin, 'Who'll Buy These Magic Beans? The North American Magical Realist Experience', *Publications of the Arkansas Philological Association*, 26.2 (2000), 45–60.

Shaw, Donald L., *The Post-Boom in Spanish-American Fiction* (Albany, NY: State University of New York Press, 1998).

Shaw, Donald L., *A Companion to Modern Spanish American Fiction* (London: Tamesis, 2002).

Sio-Castaneira, Begona, '*The Jewbird*: Bernard Malamud's Experiment with Magical Realism', *Short Story*, 6.1 (1998), 55–64.

Slemon, Stephen, 'Magic Realism as Postcolonial Discourse', in Lois Parkinson Zamora, and Wendy Faris (eds), *Magical Realism: Theory, History, Community* (Durham, NC: Duke University Press, 1995), pp. 407–26.

Swanson, Philip, *The New Novel in Latin America: Politics and Popular Culture after the Boom* (Manchester: Manchester University Press, 1995).

Swanson, Philip, *Latin American Fiction: A Short Introduction* (Oxford: Blackwell, 2005).

Todorov, Tzvetan, *Introduction à la littérature fantastique* (Paris: Seuil, 1970; English translation by Richard Howard [Cleveland and London: The Press of Case Western Reserve University, 1973]).

Uslar Pietri, Arturo, 'Realismo mágico', *Godos, insurgentes y visionarios* (Barcelona: Seix Barral, 1985), pp. 133–40.

Valbuena Briones, Ángel, 'Una cala en el realismo mágico', *Cuadernos Americanos*, 166.5 (1969), 233–41.

Yates, Donald A. (ed.), *Otros mundos, otros fuegos: fantasía y realismo mágico en Iberoamérica: memoria del XVI Congreso Internacional de Literatura Iberoamericana* (East Lansing, MI: Michigan State University, Latin American Studies Center, 1975).

Young, Robert, and Keith Hollaman (eds), *Magical Realist Fiction: An Anthology* (New York: Longman, 1984).

Weisberger, Jean (ed.), *Le Réalisme magique: Roman, peinture et cinéma* (Paris: Éditions l'Âge d'Homme, 1987).

Wenzel, Marita, 'The Latin American Connection: History, Memory and Stories in Novels by Isabel Allende and André Brink', in *Storyscapes: South African Perspectives on Literature, Space and Identity*, ed. Hein Viljoen (New York: Peter Lang, 2004), pp. 71–88.

Whyte, Philip, 'West African Literature at the Crossroads: The Magical Realism of Ben Okri', *Commonwealth Essays and Studies*, 5 (2003), 69–79.

Wilson, Jason, *Traveller's Literary Companion to South and Central America* (London: In Print, 1993).

Wright, Derek, 'Postmodernism as Realism: Magic History in Recent West African Fiction', in Derek Wright (ed.), *Contemporary African Fiction* (Barreuth: Breitlinger, 1997), pp. 181–207.

Zamora, Lois Parkinson, *Writing the Apocalypse: Historical Vision in Contemporary U.S. and Latin American Fiction* (Cambridge: Cambridge University Press, 1995).

Zamora, Lois Parkinson, and Wendy Faris (eds), *Magical Realism: Theory, History, Community* (Durham, NC: Duke University Press, 1995).

Index